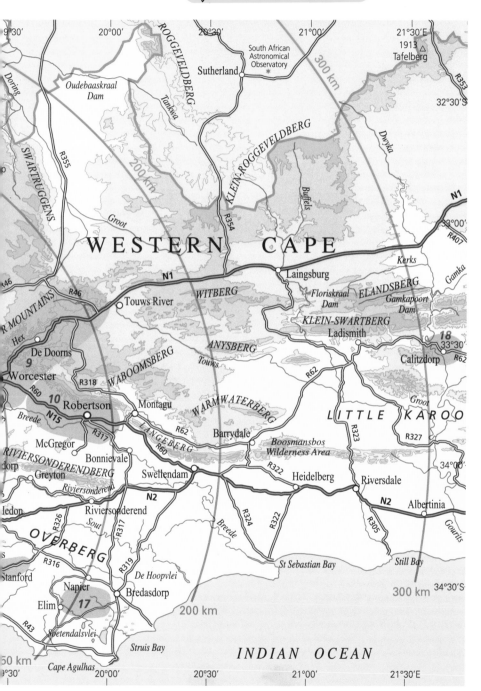

3

The
Essential Guide
to South African
Wines

The
Essential Guide
to South African
Wines

Cheviot Publishing

www.cheviot-publishing.com

PUBLISHER Cheviot Publishing cc
EDITOR Dr. Harry Stephan
DESIGNER Catherine Coetzer
PHOTOGRAPHER Jaap Scholten

Reproduction by Color / Fuzion, Greenpoint, Cape Town
Printed and bound in Singapore by Star Standard Industries Pte
Print production: Les Martens, SA Media Services

First edition published in 2006 by Cheviot Publishing cc
Second edition 2009

The Essential Guide to South African Wines, second edition
2009 © 2009 Cheviot Publishing cc

Cheviot Publishing cc
P.O. Box 5, Green Point 8051, South Africa
www.cheviot-publishing.com
Reg. No. 2005/010348/23
ISBN(13) 978-0-9802742-3-3

Contents

Anatidae – The golden duck
symbol of Steenberg

Slow – Enjoy the journey as much
as the destination

Squirrels – Frequent visitors to the
oak-lined gardens

CHAPTER 4: PROFIT AND PLEASURE

CHAPTER 5: LOCAL KNOWLEDGE

CHAPTER 3: TASTING AND UNDERSTANDING WINES AND STYLES

Vineyard musketeers – Natural pest control cleaning the vines at Jordan Estate

Freedom to play – Children and cats make the most of the outdoors at Knorhoek

Winemaker's best friend – Many wineries have a 'cellar dog' to welcome visitors

Foreword

The concept of *terroir* is often regarded with suspicion and accused of being vaguely defined, even considered window-dressing in order to enhance wine's mystery to promote sales, an Achilles heel to students of *terroir* effects and its importance on wine character.

Terroir can be defined as the relationship between the natural factors of climate, topography and soil, with human intervention as the fourth element that brings *terroir* to full expression by the correct choice of grape variety(s), cultural practices and wine-making techniques. No fixed universal recipe for this exists, confusing many devoted and aspiring wine enthusiasts and adding fuel to the arguments of non-believers. To complicate matters further, there is a persisting argument about which of the natural factors are most important. This is irrelevant as climate and soil must have a happy marriage in order to ensure unique growing conditions that culminate in a *terroir*-driven wine. The sought-after temperature conditions of an area like Darling are worthless without the support of its unique, deep, yellow- to reddish-brown granitic soils that can adequately conserve and regulate the sparse rainfall to ensure stable growing conditions.

On the other hand, the thousands of hectares of wonderful reddish-brown soils of the Plooysburg region (Northern Cape), with all the physical and chemical properties a wine producer could hope for, are worthless due to adverse climatic conditions. Market forces can also play a determining role. In an area like the Napa Valley, compared to Chardonnay, Sauvignon Blanc fruit does not fetch prices to encourage its planting on a large scale.

The complexity of and confusion around *terroir* also stems from the lack of fixed or constant relationships between natural factors. For example, in Bordeaux, what works in terms of soil and plant water regulation in Graves, is totally different from what happens in Pommerol and especially at Château Pétrus, soils that would have been rejected for viticulture without the empirically acquired present-day knowledge. There is also seldom a constant wine quality result. A soil performing well during a wet season may fail dismally during a dry season without irrigation, and vise versa. This highlights the important relationship between soil, climate and the vintage that is so prominent in marginal climates.

While most New World countries appear reluctant to acknowledge the importance of *terroir*, apparently to allow more freedom to source grapes from anywhere to produce large volumes of brand-driven wines (Andrew Jefford's 'wines of effect'), there seems to be a growing tendency towards recognising and defining areas of repute. In this regard, South Africa is the exception.

Here the effects of *terroir* are scientifically proven and are incorporated into a scientifically based demarcation system. Especially the coastal regions of South Africa are quite unique in terms of their extremely old geological formations and varied topography and thus the resultant soils on which, over millions of years, developed a much diversified and unique flora. This implies that the vine can also respond in a unique manner to these conditions.

The Essential Guide to South African Wines uses a new concept of Wine Pockets to define wine regions, which include existing demarcations, as well as regions with the potential to be officially demarcated. It firmly supports the realities of *terroir* and is a valuable contribution to a better understanding of this concept. In a very practical and useful manner, it contributes greatly to our knowledge of the diversity of wine production areas and their diverse wines. It can rightly be regarded as 'Essential' to both aspiring as well as experienced wine enthusiasts and tourists.

Dawid Saayman

A soil scientist and terroir advocate for four decades, Dawid Saayman is internationally regarded as a subject expert. Working at the cutting edge of terroir analysis, Saayman is creating a comprehensive record of South African viticultural soils and their terroir potential.

Foreword

Every good bottle of wine has one thing in common: specific origin is stated on its label. It is *Appellation d'origine contrôlée* (AOC) in France, its *Denominazione di Origine Controllata e Garantita* (D.O.C.G.) in Italy, its Wine of Origin in South Africa.

The reason why wine bottles state the 'obvious' is nothing other than the very concept of place; the human understanding of and interaction with the given parameters of that place, defined in the contents of that specific bottle. When a bottle of wine stands on a table, the space it occupies should be nothing other than a testimony to its history, culture, tradition and the preservation thereof.

European wine regions have had the luxury of changing parameters during the development of their *terroir*; even more: the luxury of time. Through natural selection, the essential varieties 'survived' from the myriad planted. In time, they became the great communicators of the place and its *terroir*. The New World wine regions, in strong contrast, took much of their form on marketing and strategy sketchpads.

The mere fact that most of the New World wine regions have planted Cabernet Sauvignon, Merlot, Chardonnay, Sauvignon Blanc, Shiraz and little else, proves that we are not searching for the specific grape to communicate the place best. If 'little' Portugal has 85 official grape varieties and numerous unofficial ones to communicate its *terroir*, then we must ask how it could be possible to maximise the New World *terroirs* with a 'Big Five' thinking pattern. The Cape is now starting to remove itself from international trends – or possibly we never really engaged – and the discovery of new regions and planting possibilities makes the South African wine scene very exciting.

The current general consumer index or relation to wine is in terms of single varieties; the 'familiar' factor. Resultingly, marketing and wine list structures (even in specialised retail) are based on varieties. These historical factors seem set to maintain the varietal fragmentation for a while longer. Yet, as our understanding of *terroir* improves, focus will shift to blending and the greater complexities possible. New varieties will allow the innovative grape grower to have a greater canvas to unleaseh the true biodiversity of the Cape. When the New World starts to think 'place', the importance of labelling grapes will fade and it will mark the birth of a new era. The freedom to plant varieties outside constructed and often restricting expectations, will allow us to choose grapes for their ability to best express the *terroir*.

It is impossible to combine fragmented thinking in terms of expected grape flavours as well as soil expression in the bottle simultaneously. Flavours are the result of climactic conditions in the grape's ripening process and that of fermentation; whereas taste, texture, minerality and mouthfeel result from the soil and are often the more consistent. The concept of *terroir* includes both, but as long as we focus only on the flavour profile, the more stereotype wines become and the more incomplete *terroir* will be.

The Cape recently saw the development of blends focused on the identity of the specific origin, without specifying grape varieties on its label. These wines mark the summit of Cape wine quality and consistency. A basic wine rule is that if you plant the perfect grape on the perfect site, and vinify it properly, consistency comes to the forefront. And consistency is what marks all great wine regions.

The Essential Guide to South African Wines, with its new concept of Wine Pockets to define wine regions, makes a significant contribution in the understanding and communication of the *terroir* concept, and in particular South African *terroir*. It is a must-read for everyone who wants to learn to appreciate the origin of great wines.

Eben Sadie

South Africa's maverick winemaker, Eben Sadie, is a thought-leader on terroir *and wine blending. This passionate oenological pioneer travels extensively, investigating the best* terroirs *and crafting his own wines.*

How to use this Guide

Whether you are a wine connoisseur using crystal drinking instruments or simple enjoying a glass of wine on occasion, this book will provide you with detailed information and vital local knowledge on South African wines.

The introductory chapter places South African wine in an historical and cultural context, and highlights a vision of our future. It summarises the industry today, including Wine Producers, Grape Varieties, Wine Styles as well as Sales, Export and Marketing. New development, Investment and significant Industry Programs are discussed. Organic and Biodynamic Viticulture, Biodiveristy and the Carbon Footprint look at our natural environment. Wine Packaging and Closures give valuable insights into these often overlooked aspect of wine. The *terroir* concept is explained in broader terms, and within the South African context. A useful guide to principle soils as well as key grape varieties is included. A Timeline takes the reader on an unforgettable 12 month journey through the vineyards and the cellar.

The bulk of the book is divided into 36 winemaking units, using the Wine Pocket system. This system provides insight into the major winegrowing areas, focusing on individual *terroir* Pockets, selected top producers and their flagship wines. Detailed maps and suggested day-driving routes include wine and local interests. All maps include significant *terroir* features, such as mountains and hills (with countours indicating height above sea level in metres), and bodies of water (riviers, oceans, lakes and estuaries). Specially commissioned photographs illustrate key viticultural areas, while text boxes highlight significant facts.

Chapter 3 on wine tasting gives insights on serving and enjoying wine and recognising wine faults. The main wine styles are defined and illustrated per varietal for easy reference within the local market.

Chapter 4 describes the financial landscape of investing in wine for profit and for pleasure. Global Positioning System (GPS) waypoints are provided for use in your own GPS unit to locate places of interest.

The last chapter provides vital local knowledge on everything from visiting South Africa and the Winelands in particular; to guidelines on transport and storage of wine, and an essential wine dictionary.

As you explore the world of South African wines, this book will prove a useful guide both at home and on your travels through the vineyards and wineries of South Africa. Enjoy wine responsibly, do not drink and drive!

TITLING OF MOUNTAINS

According to the latest *Oxford Dictionary*, "Berg" is now accepted as South African English for geographical features – mountain and hill. The majority of mountains in South Africa were named the Afrikaans, therefore the Afrikaans name is used in this book alongside the word "Berg", e.g. "Simonsberg" instead of "Simons Mountain". Where the name is from another language and has a translation into English, the English translation has been used, e.g. Obiqua Mountain, which is from Khoisan origin.

KEY TO SYMBOLS

Flagship	Email and Website
Cultivar	Aging Potential
Opening hours	Best Vintages
Telephone	Tourist Information

ABBREVIATIONS FOR GRAPE VARIETIES

Cabernet Franc (Cab F); Cabernet Sauvignon (Cab S); Chardonnay (Chard); Chenin Blanc (Chenin Bl); Gamay (Gam); Gewürztraminer (Gewürz); Grenache (Gren); Malbec (Malb); Merlot (M); Mourvèdre (Mourv); Nebbiolo (Nebb); Petit Verdot (PV); Pinot Noir (PN); Pinotage (P); Riesling (Riesl); Sauvignon Blanc (Sauv Bl); Sémillon (Sém); Shiraz (Shz); Tinta Barocca (Tinta B); Tinta Roriz (Tinta R); Tempranillo (Temp); Touriga Naçional (Tour N); Viognier (Viog); Zinfandel (Zin); Nouvelle (Nouv); Sangiovese (Sang); Barbera (Bar); Cinsaut (Cin); Roobernet (Roob); Rhine Riesling (RRies); Pinot Grigio (Pinot G); Tempranillo (Temp)

TERROIR: THE WINE-GROWING AREAS

Wine Pocket name

Colour photographs
A wealth of information
is presented in full-colour
photographs, providing a
visual feast.

Description of the Pocket
A detailed description gives
an overview of climate,
topography and other factors
relating to the *terroir* of a
Pocket.

Key facts box
Here you will find
information on the soil,
climate and main grape
varieties.

**Wine styles and top
producers**
The significant grape
varieties cultivated are
highlighted along with
individual wine styles,
the top producers and
their flagship wines.

TRAVEL: THE DRIVING ROUTES

Description of route
This section gives step-by-
step instructions to find the
featured wineries.

Travelling Tips
A selection of restaurants,
accommodation and local
tourist attractions with
contact details. Where
bookings are required or
telephone numbers differ to
the winery profile, this has
been included.

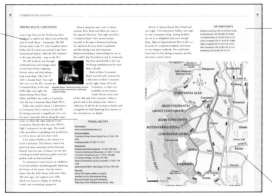

GPS waypoints
Here you will find a
complete list of global
positioning waypoints
for use with your own
GPS system.
Visit www.cheviot-
publishing.com to
download the suggested
driving routes for your
Garmin™ GPS.

Touring map
This is a suggested
route for touring the
Pocket.

TASTING: THE INDIVIDUAL WINERIES

Name of winery
This is the name of the
winery or producer.

Flagship wine
Recognise the flagship wine
with this full-colour pack shot.

Information box
This box provides further
information on the winery.

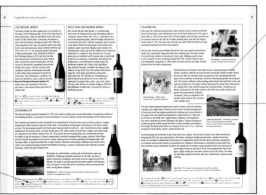

Grape cultivation
This section focuses on
the grape cultivation in
the light of the specific
terroir.

Winemaking
This section explains
winemaking techniques
and their importance to
the wine style, focusing
on the winery's flagship
wine.

Chapter 1

A recent overview of the South African wine industry

Liquid assests – The wine maturing in these barrels at Vergelegen will fetch high prices

A recent overview of the South African wine industry

Fortified – Cape Town Castle, dating back to 1666, is the oldest building in South Africa

The breathtakingly beautiful Cape Winelands are spread over a relatively small area. Approximately 102 000 hectares are planted to wine grape varieties over an area covering approximately 800 kilometres. Ranking ninth in production, South African trails the three largest producers, Spain (1,1 million ha), France (0,8 million ha) and Italy (0,8 million ha) in total vineyard hectarage.

However, the biodiversity of South Africa's winegrowing sites ensures that the area can produce an extensive range of wines to excite wine lovers the world over. The constant interplay between ancient soils and the folding landscape offers a myriad of mountain slopes, foothills, valley floors and undulating hills, making specific site selection possible. The changing aspects, with variations in sun exposure and altitude, greatly influence temperature. Coupled to this are significant climate changes

Jan van Riebeeck – Pioneer at the Cape settlement in 1652

due to prevailing winds, mountain shadows and rainfall fluctuations. All these factors combine to create some of the most intricate *terroir* sites ever discovered.

SHAPING THE INDUSTRY

South Africa is labelled as a 'New World' wine-producing country; ironically, winemaking is anything but 'new' at the tip of Africa. Vines were originally planted in the Cape of Good Hope after the first wine cultivars were imported by the Dutch East India Company (VOC). In fact, South Africa is unique in knowing the exact date on which its wine industry began, thanks to Jan van Riebeeck's diary entry of 2 February 1659. In 2009, South Africa celebrated its 350th anniversary of winemaking history. Although the Dutch were responsible for the birth of the local wine industry, their limited wine knowledge proved a definite constraint. Most of these early wines were made from unripe grapes and, together with the lack of hygiene and cellar technology, wines were over-sulphured. The situation improved after Simon van der Stel was appointed governor in 1679. Van der Stel, an enthusiastic organiser with a depth of knowledge about viticulture and winemaking, planted a vineyard on his Constantia farm. His emphasis on cellar hygiene ensured good wine from the outset. His Vin de Constance, a dessert wine from the Constantia Pocket, became world famous fuelling European demand for South African wines. Although Van der Stel's early work laid the foundation for South African wines, further improvement was an unintended consequence of King Louis XIV's revocation of the Edict of Nantes in 1688. The King's action drove Protestant Huguenots out of France, and many were granted land in the secluded Franschhoek Valley where their wine knowledge supported local grape cultivation.

KWV – The headquarters of the winemaking co-operative in Paarl

The local industry suffered many setbacks despite quality improvements and new-found markets. The dreaded root disease, *Phylloxera*, killed many vines during the 1880s. Then overproduction in the early 20th century led to a chronic decline in prices after farmers geared towards mass production. A ruling co-operative cellar, the Koöperatiewe Wijnbouwers Vereniging (KWV), was formed as a consequence with full government backing in order to control sales and stabilise pricing. A quota system, introduced in 1957, limited vine plantings in new areas and the KWV quarantine system strictly dictated which new plant material could be imported. These regulations limited producers' options and, as payments from the KWV were based on quantity, farmers failed to take into account quality aspects of their grapes and wines. A further blow came in the form of international trade sanctions during the 1980s as widespread protest against the apartheid regime became a reality.

THE TURNING POINT: NELSON MANDELA

Restrictions on international trade forced producers to turn to the local market. Unsophisticated when compared to international markets, this restriction did nothing but limit the winemaker's scope for creativity. Only after Nelson Mandela's release from political imprisonment and the subsequent democratic elections in 1994 did serious international focus fall on the South African wine industry. Mandela's support for South African wines formed a necessary political stepping stone for the true emergence of Cape wine. Mandela toasted his 1993 Nobel Peace Prize with Cape wine.

THE OLD WORLD AND THE NEW WORLD

There is an obvious geographical distinction between Europe (Old World) and the Americas, Australia and South Africa (New World), but this distinction takes on a broader meaning in wine language. It differentiates between two philosophies of winemaking. Old World winemaking is defined by tradition; wine is made in the same place, in the same way and style as in the past. Nature is the key factor. Climate variations are expected, and wine is viewed primarily as an expression of *terroir* rather than individual varieties. Characterised by elegance, complexity and tightness, Old World wines tend to have lower alcohol levels (Alc. 11–12% by Vol.). Fruit flavours relating to each variety are less pronounced, and Old World wines have a greater maturation potential that can even run into decades.

New World wines, on the other hand, are defined by progress. New technology, innovative cultivation and exploration of uncharted areas are the order of the day. Wines are created to be consistent in quality, and the role of the vintage has somewhat diminished. The wines are defined by varietal characteristics and the expression of a wine's fruit characteristics. *Terroir* as a concept is only now being explored. New World wines are more powerful, with higher alcohol levels (as much as Alc. 16% by Vol.) and tend to have a more pronounced upfront fruitiness. Made for earlier consumption, these wines certainly do have maturation potential, but not as much as the Old World wines.

South African wines are often described as lying somewhere between these two worlds, with the structure and restraint of the Old World and the fruit intensity of the New. Set to become a fully competitive world player, South Africa is one of the few New World wine countries which may have the ability to exhibit the fine qualities, elegance, balance and restraint comparable to truly great Old World wines. As the many new *terroir*-focused vineyards mature and winemakers gain an understanding of their interpretation, the sense of place in their wines will certainly deepen.

THE INDUSTRY TODAY

Following the political rebirth, international markets opened up and exports grew significantly, accounting for up to 45 per cent of local production. Inexperience and over-excitement resulted in some poor quality wines being exported, which did little to build the South African quality brand. Nor were there any true iconic wines to compete with the best

international offerings. Thus South African wines were focused on price competitiveness. Today the South African wine industry comprises more than 102 000 hectares (2007) planted to wine grape varieties over an area approximately 800 kilometres in length. It produces in excess of 800 million litres of wine (2007: 730 million, 2008: 840 million litres), about three per cent of the world's production, and ranks as number nine in overall volume production. The total annual harvest is 1 043,5 million litres (2007), of which 70 per cent is allocated to the making of wine, with the balance for brandy, distilling wine and grape juice.

Once consisting of only a few producers and co-operative cellars, the wine industry has grown from just on 200 producers (1998) to more than 550 producers (2008). During the last three years, however, there has been a decline in grape growers from 4 185 (2006) to 3 999 (2007), as well as in wine cellars crushing grapes (576 compared to 560). Currently there are 481 private cellars, 59 co-operatives and 20 producing wholesalers crushing grapes – producing more than 6 000 wines annually, an increase of 10 000 per cent on the 1960 figure. Around 80 per cent of producers are privately owned, which indicates a definite trend towards greater hands-on involvement, increased quality and a definitive development in style. The number of cellars vinifying less than 100 tons remains high at 47 per cent, evidence of the significance of micro-wineries. South Africa now competes at the highest level, both at international wine shows and for the wallets of wine enthusiasts.

Wine producers

Traditionally, **estate wineries** are the producers consumers think of when they think of a 'winery'. Estates could, under original legislation, produce wine only from grapes grown on their own land. In 2004, a new dispensation terminated the traditional 'estate' to focus on 'estate wine', which must be produced in neighbouring vineyards farmed as single units. All previously registered estates are now recognised as Units for the Production of Estate Wine. With the new system, their names may be used to brand their total wine production (i.e. estate as well as non-estate), but only certified estate wine may be labelled and marketed as such.

Flying winemakers made a significant contribution in shifting the international wine industry's focus from 'wine is made in the vineyard' (true but too simplistic), to a comprehensive system integrating *terroir*, viticulture, cellar technology and grape processing. These trained winemakers travel the world and make wine for established as well as up-and-coming cellars in various countries, gathering and exchanging a wealth of knowledge and international winemaking experience.

Another type of winemaker has emerged from the industry – the **garagiste** or artisan winemaker. These are small-scale producers, who buy grapes from growers and vinify them themselves. **Garagiste** wines are made in very limited volumes and illustrate the individuals' passion and dedication to wine as an art form, while most of them have day jobs. The wine is usually of outstanding quality with only the best grapes and wood barrels being used. See Garagiste section on page 186-189.

In South Africa, as in most other wine-producing areas, **wine merchants** buy grapes or wines from selected areas to blend and bottle wines under their own labels. Some merchants are involved in the actual winemaking process, while others buy finished wine, which they then mature, blend and bottle. Some outsource their winemaking operations to particular cellars, where they have the wine made according to their prescriptions, dictating viticulture and vinification practices. In many instances these wines still represent *terroir* characteristics and styles. Examples are Stellenbosch Bottling, Douglas Green Bellingham (DGB) and Jean Daneel.

There are 59 **co-operative wineries** in South Africa, which produce dessert and distilled wines in addition to varietal and blended wines. Most co-operatives source wines from the vineyards in their immediate proximity. Various co-operatives have adopted a company structure, aligning themselves with current trends. A number have amalgamated, with Distell, Rooiberg Cellars and Darling Cellars as good examples. As interest in South African wineries has grown, so too have international ties. For example, E & J Gallo (USA) selected Swartland Winery to produce the wine brand Sebeka. Six varieties of Sebeka wines are cultivated and vinified in South Africa and Sebeka Sauvignon Blanc won the Best Newcomer award in the United States in 2008. The wine was named after an orphaned cheetah and a portion of the sale of every bottle goes to the cheetah sanctuary in Mpumalanga. Swartland also produces Tesco's house brand for its British, European and Polish markets.

Changing grape varieties and wine styles

South Africa does not adhere to the strict regulations that govern most Old World wine areas, especially with regard to permissible varieties for certain blends, for example the Bordeaux blend. Since abolishing the quota system in 1992, the search for cooler, quality vineyards has taken winemakers to the tip of Africa and to higher elevations at the snowline.

Distell – South Africa's largest producer and marketer of wines

Today, white wine varietals comprise 55 per cent and red varietals account for 45 per cent of the national crop. In recent years, the planted area of five classic varieties (Cabernet Sauvignon, Shiraz, Merlot, Chardonnay and Sauvignon Blanc) has increased from 30 per cent to 46 per cent of total plantings, largely at the expense of Chenin Blanc. Although more Chenin Blanc is uprooted than newly planted, this variety is still the most widely cultivated in South Africa with 19 per cent planted to the total vineyard area (compared to 32 per cent in 1990). The most widely planted red varietals are Cabernet Sauvignon (13%), Shiraz (10%), Merlot (7%) and Pinotage (6%).

The local wine industry continues to align its varietal offerings in accordance with international trends. During the 1990s, there was a 10-year trend towards planting red varieties. This has led to a shortage of white wine over the past four years (WOSA, 2009). As a result, white varietals are now dominating the planting mix (2 212 ha vs 504 ha). Although more old Chenin Blanc vines are uprooted or grafted (to more popular varieties) than newly planted vines, the plantings that do occur are still higher (850 ha added) than Sauvignon Blanc and Chardonnay (471 ha and 224 ha respectively added annually). Shiraz (86 ha planted annually), previously a red-vine nurseries' favourite, now trails both Cabernet Sauvignon (118 ha) and steeply rising Pinotage (94 ha of new plantings). Pinot Noir plantings are also increasing as

new cool areas are being explored (54 ha). As vineyards mature, the proportion of very young vines versus the total plantings continues to decline: approximately 10,4 per cent are younger than four years old, while roughly 42 per cent are four to ten years of age, and 16,8 per cent are older than 20 years. This is significant, as older vines are prized for balanced growth and low yields, resulting in wines with fruit concentration and exceptional maturation potential.

In recent years, some have advocated that South Africa should produce a classified 'Cape Blend', similar to a Bordeaux blend. In defining this 'Cape Blend' some are arguing for 'origin' indicating a blend made within a particular Cape area, while others are pushing for a blend that has to incorporate at least 30 per cent Pinotage, a unique South African variety, as a blending partner. To date, no legal requirements have been set and many fine blended examples exist which exclude Pinotage.

Exchanges between local and foreign winemakers have influenced styles and varietal selections. French, Portuguese, Spanish and Italian grape varieties are now also being planted and they have attracted serious attention from blenders. This diversification of styles has presented a diverse spectrum from sparkling to fortified wines, from big, powerful, alcoholic wines to more elegant and delicate wines.

Sales, exports and marketing

Wine consumption in South Africa is much lower than in most other wine-producing nations – less than eight litres per capita per annum. In France and Italy consumers imbibe more than 50 litres per capita per annum. Whereas population figures for France and Italy are at 62 and 60 million respectively, South Africa stands at approximately 48 million. It is estimated that less than 20 per cent of South Africans regularly consume wine. Thus there is great scope for home-market growth as non-traditional

Beaded bus – Local beaders create vivid memories for visitors to the Winelands at Spier

consumers develop an interest in wine with rising living standards.

The African or black community represents about 80 per cent of the population. They were historically part of the lower income group and traditionally consumed beer as a beverage of choice. According to a 2007 report released by the University of Cape Town's Unilever Institute, however, the number of 'Black Diamonds' – the emerging black middle class – grew by 30 per cent in 2005 to 2,6 million (nearly six per cent of the total). This group constitutes almost one-third of the middle class and is worth about R180 billion, representing 28 per cent of the total South African spend. Furthermore, an estimated 52 per cent (approximately 25,2 million) of the population is female. These figures have forced new trends in marketing, targeting all races as well as women, as this group makes the bulk of wine-buying decisions as part of grocery purchases. Nearly one-third (32 per cent) of the population is younger than 15 years and there is a real incentive for education towards responsible wine consumption.

The wine industry annually contributes R16,3 billion to South Africa's GDP of which 70 per cent directly benefits the Western Cape economy. An additional R4,2 billion is generated indirectly through wine tourism activities in the Winelands. Domestic sales, in fact, increased steadily from the early 1990s to around 2000, peaking at 390 million litres per annum. Sales

Wine shop – Sales and exports are managed through various wineshops

have now declined and steadied at around 355 million litres per annum. Of the local sales, half is packaged in glass, with 60 per cent packaged in the traditional 750 ml bottle.

Exports have increased considerably from 220 million (1992) to 400 million litres (2008) (WOSA). Exports of natural (i.e. not fortified) packaged wines for 2007 reached 190,7 million litres, an increase of eight per cent on the previous year. Red wine exports grew to account for 59 per cent of all natural wines exported (2007). South Africa's current market share in the UK is nine per cent by volume and it is the fifth-largest export country to the UK market. The industry employs 257 000 people directly (cultivation, winemaking, etc.) and indirectly (packaging, retailing and tourism). Of this figure, over 100 000 people are from historically disadvantaged groups. Furthermore, as wine tourism continues to grow, its financial impact has become even more significant as the tourism industry employs over 59 000 people.

DEVELOPMENT AND TECHNOLOGY

Development of vinification techniques has also transformed winemaking: cold fermentation and the use of specialised yeasts together with selection of tiny vineyard parcels has led to a broader diversification of styles while micro-oxygenation and finishing in small oak barrels has improved complexity and refined red wines in particular. Three main styles of Sauvignon Blanc have developed: the first, labelled 'green' but not unripe with asparagus, grass and herbaceous aromas; the second, with more tropical, rich fruits, and the third, more steely and mineral, reminiscent of the Loire Valley. Chenin Blanc is a particularly versatile grape and can be used to make dry white wines, sparkling wines, dessert wines and brandy. During the 1960s a semi-sweet Chenin Blanc was the largest-selling bottled wine in the world, but poor quality tarnished its profile. Today Chenin Blanc is re-establishing its rightful place as a classic single variety wine, made from old vines (often dry-land bush vines), fermented and aged in oak. Chardonnay, once over-oaked, is returning to a more balanced form with clean primary fruit characters supported by fermentation flavours, lees contact and gentle oaking.

In recent years more cellars are using modern technology, but most winemakers are still confident of traditional methods. For example, grapes are still fermented in large, open, wooden vats. Wine is also made without adding cultured yeasts (natural fermentation) and many more wines are bottled without fining or filtration, processes which may cause a loss in flavour. Planting a variety of clones adds complexity to red wines. While most reds are aged in French oak, more American and East-European woods are being used, and wineries tend to match barrels from specific coopers to specific wine batches. Organic and biodynamic farming and wines are gaining popularity. Architecture within the winery has also developed, with the Cape now boasting some of the most impressive production facilities in the world.

BUSINESS AND FOREIGN INVESTMENT

The multi-million Rand wine industry – a great tourism magnet in the Western Cape – is one of South Africa's most dynamic and exciting business sectors. In 2000, Stellenbosch Farmers' Winery and Distillers Corporation merged to create Distell Group Limited, South Africa's largest producer and marketer of wines, spirits and ready to drinks (RTDs). The group is listed on the Johannesburg Stock Exchange, employs over 4 200 people and has an annual turnover in excess of R7,9 billion (±€0,7 billion). South African Brewers (SAB) acquired Millers Brewing Company (the second largest brewery by volume in the USA) during 2002 and thus became the second largest brewer (by volume) in the world. With interests in Europe, Africa and the

Americas, these companies resemble Fosters in Australia or Mondavi in the United States.

Since the 1990s, many international wine enthusiasts have also become involved in the South African wine industry. Some have set up joint ventures such as the husband-and-wife team of Zelma Long and Phil Freese (Vilafonté) and the French viticulturist, Michel Rolland (Remhoogte). Others have bought wineries, like Anne Cointreau-Huchon, a member of the Cointreau family, who now owns Morgenhof. The Swiss Bührer family has revitalised Saxenburg, while Paul Boutinot (United Kingdom) heads the new Waterkloof development. Anwilka Vineyard is a joint venture between Bruno Prats, former owner of Château Cos-d'Estournel, Hubert de Boüard de Laforest, co-proprietor of Château Angélus in Bordeaux, and Lowell Jooste of Klein Constantia Estate. These investors infuse the industry with new ideas and increase exports through their ties with their native countries.

INDUSTRY PROGRAMS AND SOCIAL RESPONSIBILITY

Real success is being achieved within the South African wine industry as open minds and racial equality have come to the fore. The new democracy has brought about a restructuring of traditional ownership patterns. Significant black-empowered ownership is developing, further instilling a culture of wine among a wider black population in South Africa. While several associations are working towards this objective, the South African wine industry drafted a Wine BEE (Black Economic Empowerment) charter in 2003. Under this charter, economic equity, enterprise procurement, skills and social development, as well as funding mechanisms have been put into place. A scorecard was developed to rate companies on their efforts to empower black and female workers.

A second industry document, 'South African

Wine Industry Strategy Plan', is now accepted as the strategic framework for co-operation and action with specified goals on global competitiveness and profitability, equitable access, sustainable production and responsible consumption of alcoholic products. The plan aligns the visions and goals of the wine industry to grass-root action plans managed by several supporting bodies. In 2002 the Wine Industry Ethical Trading Association (WIETA) was launched by stakeholders in the wine and agriculture industry. It aims to address socio-economic issues affecting the industry to ensure a sustainable and flourishing industry as a source of employment. Fairtrade South Africa was established (2005) to promote social and economic development; provide producer support; liaise with industry partners and develop the market for certified products in South Africa.

The South African wine industry promotes responsible alcohol consumption and education on various levels, from wine appreciation to the hospitality trade. Various programs have been established to assist in education, rehabilitation and support for those whose lives have been affected negatively by alcohol, such as the Association for Responsible Alcohol Use (ARA) fund. The Pebbles Project provides upliftment of farm worker communities and education of workers' children. A new wine brand, Fundi, was created in 2006. Proceeds from wine sales are being used to train more than 2 010 previously

Socially responsible – *Children at a Pebbles care centre show off their art work*

disadvantaged people as wine stewards by 2010, when South Africa hosts the FIFA World Cup.

The historical Boschendal estate changed hands in 2003 in a black empowerment deal valued at R323 million (€30 million), putting it at the forefront of BEE initiatives. A black empowerment consortium, Phetogo, acquired a 25,1 per cent stake in KWV in 2004 and Distell sold a 15 per cent stake in its subsidiary, South African Distilleries and Wines (SADW), to an empowerment consortium. Individuals are also making a difference: wine farmers such as Charles Back of Fairview, Beyers Truter of Beyerskloof and Paul Cluver in Elgin have assisted farm workers to buy their own houses and set up their own winemaking operations.

The private sector offers scholarships to young aspirant black winemakers to study viticulture and oenology at university and college while a vineyard academy trains vineyard workers. Programs such as the Burgundy exchange assist farm workers to complete a winemaking course in France and the Cape Winemakers Guild Protégé course nurtures promising winemakers from previously disadvantaged groups.

ORGANIC AND BIODYNAMIC AGRICULTURE

Organic farming is a form of agriculture that relies on natural enhancement and mechanical cultivation to maintain soil productivity. While it advocates crop rotation, green manure, compost and biological pest control, it excludes, or strictly limits, the use of synthetic fertilizers and pesticides, plant growth regulators, and genetically modified organisms. The movement started in the 1930s, but since the early 1990s, the market for organic products has grown rapidly. Approximately 306 000 square kilometres (30,6 million ha) worldwide are now farmed organically, representing approximately two per cent of total world farmland. Organic farming is labour and knowledge-intensive, whereas conventional farming is capital-intensive, requiring more energy and manufactured inputs.

Organic vineyard certification should confirm that no synthetic products (pesticides, herbicides, etc.) are used and vine diseases are restricted through good hygiene practices, quarantine and cultivation practices. Certain treatments, such as copper and sulphur, are approved. In the cellar, 'organic' suggests minimal processing and no use of chemical additives or synthetic additives. Winemakers pay particular attention to three aspects: the extensive (but not exclusive) use of naturally occurring yeasts; using minimum filtration/fining, and minimising the use of sulphur dioxide. Currently, South Africa has 20 registered organic producers.

Biodynamic agriculture is a method of organic farming with a basis in a spiritual worldview (anthroposophy, first propounded by Rudolf Steiner around 1924 in Germany) and conceives of the farm as a unified and individual organism. Emphasis is placed on the holistic development and interrelationship of the soil, plants and animals as a closed, self-nourishing system. Regarded by proponents as the first modern ecological farming system, the biodynamic approach incorporates organic agriculture's emphasis on manures and composts to ensure the recycling of nutrients, maintenance of soil, and the health and wellbeing of crops and animals. It does, however, exclude all artificial chemicals. Instead it advocates the use of fermented herbal and mineral preparations as compost additives and field sprays as well as an astronomical sowing and planting calendar. Therefore the term 'biodynamic' is not interchangeable with 'organic' agriculture. There are currently more than 450 biodynamic wine producers worldwide.

BIODIVERSITY

The Cape Floral Kingdom (CFK) is internationally recognised as a global biodiversity hotspot and World Heritage Site, one of the richest and most threatened reservoirs of animal and plant life on earth, containing more than 10 000 plant species. A partnership between the wine industry and the conservation sector aims to minimise the loss of threatened natural habitat and contribute to sustainable wine production through the adoption of biodiversity guidelines.

In 2004, faced with just four per cent of the CFK's unique *renosterveld* remaining and much of the fynbos ecosystems under threat, the wine industry developed a conservation partnership with the Botanical Society of South Africa, Conservation International and The Green Trust, which led to the establishment of the Biodiversity and Wine Industry Initiative. By promoting cultivation practices that enhance biodiversity in vineyards and increasing the area set aside in contractual protected areas, the

Blue Cranes – South Africa's national bird among the vineyards

Ladybird – The symbol of organic winemaking and a much welcomed pest control in the vineyard

initiative is creating a unique selling point for Brand South Africa. In only four years the wine industry has made conservation history by setting aside more ground for long-term conservation (103 000 ha) than is currently planted under vineyard, thereby making South Africa a world leader with a conservation footprint which matches the total vineyard area. In another world first, the Green Mountain Eco-Route, a biodiversity wine route, was established in 2005. It includes the Elgin, Bot River and Walker Bay Pockets and features a five-day hiking trail in the mountain fynbos and vineyards.

CONSERVATION
IN ACTION
www.bwi.co.za

Biodiversity & Wine Initiative – Pioneering partnership between the local wine industry and the conservation sector

CARBON FOOTPRINT AND CLIMATE CHANGE

Carbon footprint is a measure of the impact that human activities have on the environment in terms of the amount of greenhouse gases produced, measured in units of carbon dioxide. These gases are produced by the burning of fossil fuels for daily living. Travel needs and electricity demands are arguably the biggest contributors, but all actions have a direct or indirect impact.

Global warming is the increase in the average temperature of the Earth's near-surface air and oceans since the mid-20th century and its projected continuation. Global surface temperature has increased by $0.74 \pm 0.18°C$ $(1.33 \pm 0.32°F)$ during the 100 years ending in 2005. The Intergovernmental Panel on Climate Change (IPCC) concludes that most of the temperature increases since the mid-20th century are very likely due to the increase in greenhouse gas concentrations. The greenhouse effect is the process by which absorption and emission of infrared radiation by atmospheric gases warms a planet's lower atmosphere and surface. Global warming has seen a rise in average

global temperatures of more than half a degree Celsius over the past 30 years and could raise the Earth's temperatures by 1.4 to 5.8°C by the end of the century. Carbon dioxide is the single biggest contributor to global warming. Most wineries are implementing carbon offsets in response, mitigating their carbon emissions through the development of alternative projects such as solar or wind energy or reforestation. Optimisation of energy efficiency and recycling are also put in place to reduce the footprint.

Backsberg was South Africa's first carbon-neutral winery, the third in the world. Leading by example, the cellar has introduced many energy-efficient strategies, including a greening program close to Klapmuts and have switched to lighter vehicles to reduce emissions. The cellar boasts a methane digester which produces gas from waste fumes which supplies electricity for the entire farm. A 2 000 litre reservoir of water cools the winery by day.

WINE PACKAGING

First and foremost, packaging serves to transport wine safely and cost-effectively. The first option is bulk transport, where large volumes of wine are shipped in recyclable plastic containers and transferred to the retail containers on the receiving end. This is cost-effective due to the significantly reduced amount of packaging required and is generally used for branded and low to mid-range wines. The second option sees wine shipped retail-ready, packaged and labelled, ready for consumption. This is used mainly for top-end wines as transport costs are increased due to additional packaging material. On a more intellectual level, packaging plays a vital role in marketing, by communicating the wine's intrinsic properties.

Glass has been the mainstay of the wine packaging industry for most of its existence, however, environmental concerns and inconsistent bottle supply could dramatically change its dominant role. The inert quality of glass makes it an ideal vessel – it is transparent, strong and, together with cork, allows for continued maturation in the presence of miniscule volumes of oxygen. This 'bottle maturation' is vital for all premium wines. The colour of the glass is also key, with clear bottles mostly used for white wines, rosé and dessert wines; and green or dark bottles used for red and fortified wines. The 750 ml (75 cl) bottle is the most widely used size, but by no means the only one. Smaller bottles (375 ml, 500 ml) are popular with airlines, and larger sizes are prized by collectors because of their novelty value and tendency to promote slower wine aging.

Futuristic packaging – The innovative Wine Pouch offers a convenient carry-bag-styled package

Currently, bottle weight is a contentious issue, in some extreme cases, glass bottles tipping the scale at over two kilograms (4,4 lb). Most 750 ml bottles however weigh 450 to 650 g, with bottles for sparkling wines around 950 g, as they need to withstand greater pressure. A new trend sees wineries using light glass bottles with a recycled content. Most top wineries, however, continue to use heavier bottles and elaborate labelling to distinguish their flagship wines. Consumers are increasingly accepting alternative packaging, as these options offer reduced weight per container, recycling as well as a myriad of design and printing options. Alternative packaging, like Tetra Bricks, is available in 200 ml single-serving packs to one-litre family packs.

The **Tetra Pak** is essentially a multi-layered carton consisting of polyethylene, paperboard and aluminium foil. Tetra Pak's innovation is the aseptic processing and packaging which, when combined with ultra-heat-treated processing (UHT), allows liquid and food to be packaged and stored under room temperature conditions. Thus perishable goods can be saved and distributed over greater distances without a cold chain. Also, the packages save space because they stack together like building blocks, saving energy during distribution. The package has a twist-off cap, collapsible design and can be printed in virtually any colour, even with a metallic effect.

Polyethylene terephthalate (**PET**) is a thermoplastic polymer resin derived from oil. Due to its chemical inertness and appealing physical properties, it is used as beverage, food and liquid containers. PET is strong, impact-resistant and very lightweight. It makes a good gas and fair moisture barrier, as well as a good barrier to alcohol but requires additional layers to further reduce its oxygen permeability. It is naturally

Unusual bottling – *Large size bottles offer Kanonkop wine for special occasions*

LARGER BOTTLE SIZES			
Capacity		Bordeaux	Champagne/Burgundy
Litres	No. of bottles		
1,5	2	Magnum	Magnum
3	4	Double magnum	Jéroboam
4,5	6	Jéroboam	Rehoboam
6	8	Impériale	Methuselah
9	12	—	Salmanazar
12	16	—	Balthazar
15	20	—	Nebuchadnezzar

colourless with a high transparency. Recycling is very practical as the bottles are almost exclusively PET. As with other alternative packaging, PET is versatile in design and labelling

The innovative **Wine Pouch** (pioneered in South Africa by The Company of Wine People) offers a convenient carry-bag-styled package. It has handles for portability and on-the-go consumption, a leak-proof tap, is light and easy to squeeze into a bag or picnic hamper. It also allows the contents to be cooled more rapidly than in traditional glass. The pouch is made from three multiple protective layers of polyethylene / aluminium / polyethylene or polyethylene / polyethylene with different molecular weight. Once empty, the pouch flattens to minimise space wastage. It weighs one-twentieth of a glass bottle and takes up far less space when transported. Sadly, the wine pouch is not recyclable.

Experiments with other materials such as aluminium cans and bottles are also underway. Aluminium is easy to recycle and light to transport. A major problem, however, is lack of transparency, partly because not all consumers necessarily know that, for example, Merlot is a red wine. Designers therefore tend to make the packaging correspond to the colour of the wine to ensure correct selection.

Entry level and mid-range wines have already started shifting to PET or pouches, but top-end wines are most likely to remain in the traditional glass bottles for many years to come. The final decision by producers will depend on numerous variables including what the supply chain requires, product storage and shelf life requirements, recyclability and consumer preferences.

Wine labels are important sources of information as well as branding. The label is often the only resource a buyer has to evaluate the wine before purchasing it. The style of a label is no quality guarantee; instead, the information it contains can provide a guideline as to its quality. Information generally included on the main (front) label is: country of origin; type of wine; year of production (when the grapes were harvested); alcoholic content; the bottle size; producer; bottler and importer. Knowing the vintage is especially important when buying fine wines since the quality can vary from year to year due to climatic differences. (See Vintage Reference on page 218 .) Certain fortified and sparkling wines are made by blending wine from several vintages. Most New World producers also include the varietal(s) and geographic origin, whereas Old World producers tend to use official demarcation naming.

Wineries place varying levels of importance on the label design. Some change it annually, others hardly ever. There is also a definite divide in style preference with some preferring traditional labels, often with an image of the 'château' or winery or even a coat of arms, while others favour playful and inviting designs using bold colours and shapes. A label which does not indicate the name of the winery or the winemaker, or a wine sold without a label, is referred to as 'cleanskin' wine. Neck or back labels may appear on a bottle. The neck label may include the vintage date and certification information while the back label usually gives additional (and usually optional) information about the wine. The latter may include government required warnings (health and allergen warnings, e.g. sulphites), suggested food pairings and serving temperature.

PACKAGING FACTS			
Type of packaging	Volume of liquid	No. of glasses	Weight of container
Standard wine bottle	750 ml	6	450–650 g
Sparkling wine bottle	750 ml	6	950 g
Tetra Pak	500 ml	4	30 g
PET	500 ml	4	28 g

WINE CLOSURES

Wine closures keep the liquid inside the bottle and inhibit excessive contact with oxygen and spoilage. Amphoras were used by ancient Romans and Greeks to inhibit the oxidation of wine completely. However, glass manufacturing in the 17th century required the development of a new sealing system and cork became the primary closure.

Natural cork closures date back to the 6th century B.C. and are made from the bark of oak trees (*Quercus suber*). The bark is harvested, processed and punched in cork shapes. During processing, corks are treated to minimise growth of micro-organisms, primarily moulds and yeasts, and ultimately TCA contamination. The chemical 2,4,6- trichloroanisole (TCA) causes 'cork taint' and renders wine undrinkable. It is produced in the cork itself by micro-organism growth metabolites or by chemicals installed during cork processing. The economic losses, believed to be around six per cent of all wine, increased demand for new closure types. Natural cork allows small amounts of oxygen to permeate the wine, which in turn allows wine to age gradually. Too much or too little oxygen exposure can cause aging wines to oxidise or reduce, respectively. Natural cork remains one of the most popular closure types and generally, higher priced wines are most likely bottled with cork closures as these wines tend to be aged longer and will benefit from the oxygen. Technical corks are also derived from *Quercus suber*, but are conglomerates of leftover cork pieces. Cork is ground into small disks or pieces and glued together through a moulding or extruding process.

Synthetic corks are made from plastic materials either by a co-extrusion process where an inner core fills a second outer, smooth surface, or by polymer injection. The largest problem with synthetic corks is the greater

MCC cork – The sparkling wine bottle shapes a cylindrial cork into a mushroom shape

transfer of oxygen into the bottle, which oxidises the wine. Synthetics also tend to get stuck in the bottleneck and some corkscrews do not work with them at all. **Vino-seal** (or Vino-Lok) is a glass closure which sits on a synthetic O-ring and is held in place by a removable aluminum cap. **Screw caps** or 'Stelvin caps' are closures made only from aluminium that threads onto the bottleneck. Historically, a screw cap was 'only for low quality wines'. However, the majority of Australia's industry today is bottling wines with screw caps. These closures require specially made bottles but, the main problem is the possibility of wine reduction. Reduction involves the development of sulphur aromas due to the lack of oxygen transmission in the wine bottle. Screw caps are considered to be inexpensive, easy to open, easy to reseal, prevent 'cork taint' effect and allow bottles to be stored upright. The **Zork** was initially produced and released in Australia in 2004. It consists of three parts: a cap for protection; a foil lining that acts as an oxygen barrier, and a plunger application that creates the 'pop' when the wine is opened as well as the ability to reseal the bottle.

Traditional closures – Muselet, champagne cork, constituted cork, natural cork, natural cork with wax cover

Alternative closures – Glass stopper, screw cap, Zork, plastic cork, capsule

VISION FOR THE FUTURE

South Africa is still refining its identity and drawing closer to a system where individual regions may better suit specific grape varieties within that area than the marketing department. In new, cool areas like Elgin, Pinot Noir plantings are expanding. Sauvignon Blanc is becoming the grape of choice along the West Coast. In the Stellenbosch area, the Helderberg and Bottelary Pockets are redefining Cabernet Franc and Pinotage production respectively. Many new plantings of Shiraz in Paarl and the Swartland show great promise, and the true potential of old-vine Chenin Blanc as a classic wine is gaining recognition. Winemakers are taking a more hands-off approach, allowing wines to express their specific vineyard origins.

Recognising the importance of *terroir*, cultivation and winemaking, a blend in Constantia might consist of Sauvignon Blanc / Sémillon / Viognier, whereas the Swartland blends Syrah, Mouvèrdre and Grenache. The Helderberg producers are finding their rhythm with Cabernet Franc / Merlot / Cabernet Sauvignon / Petit Verdot blends and Robertson is producing great single varietal Chardonnays. Areas showing great potential are Wellington and Tulbagh. Further afield, Napier and the southern coastal areas look promising with well-known producers developing virgin land. Stylish packaging, innovative and contemporary label design, together with new non-cork and screw-cap closures reflect South Africa's coming of age in the global wine village.

In the past decade, South African winemakers have turned to blending white wine varietals. The two main varietals are Chardonnay and Chenin Blanc, although more complex tri-varietal blends use Viognier as well as Sauvignon Blanc. No one specific area stands out as optimum, although cooler climate regions produce the highest quality. The top blends are: Vergelegen white (Sém / Sauv Bl); Palladius

(Sadie Family Wines) based on Grenache Blanc, Viognier and Chardonnay, Magna Carta (Sauv Bl, Sém) by Steenberg and the OV (Sauv Bl, Sem) from Oak Valley. For red blends, Cabernet Sauvignon remains a cornerstone, while small volumes of Italian and Spanish varieties spice up the blends. Examples of first-rate red blends are: The Jem (Cab S, Shz, Cab F, Mal, M, Mouv, Sang, Barb) from Waterford; Hannibal (Sang, Pinot, Neb, Barb, Shz) by Bouchard Finlayson; Elevation 393 (Cab S, M, Shz) by De Trafford and Paul Sauer (Cab S, M, Cab F) from Kanonkop.

Although South Africa is currently the ninth biggest producer of wines worldwide, it occupies fifth position in the United Kingdom's retail market, currently the world's largest wine market in value terms. The UK is expected to remain the single largest export destination for the immediate future as South Africa aims for fourth position in value share of the retail sector, with value exceeding volume share. North America assumes increasing importance for local producers and new markets in Asia are extending opportunities for exports. Established European markets, notably in Scandinavia, the Benelux countries (notably the Netherlands) and Germany are also being exploited. South Africa is currently the largest New World wine exporter to the Netherlands, the second-largest exporter to Sweden and the fastest-growing New World wine category in most Canadian markets.

Visions of the future – New developments see the use of aspects as terroir definitives at Constantia Glen

South Africa:
A unique *terroir*

The South African Winelands provide a constant interplay between ancient soils, valley slopes, soaring mountains and coastal breezes, resulting in an extraordinary biodiversity which is reflected in the indigenous flora of the area. With more than 9 600 plant species, of which 70 per cent is endemic, the Western Cape is recognised as the smallest yet richest of the world's six great floral kingdoms.

Most of the Cape's wine-growing regions are influenced by either the cold Atlantic or warmer Indian Ocean, which meet at the southernmost tip of Africa. The maritime influences (regular fog and cooling sea breezes), the Mediterranean climate, the varied topography and diverse soils all combine to afford ideal conditions to create fine wines of unique character and complexity. Coupled with this is a 300-year-old winemaking tradition and history that blends Old World restrained elegance with New World accessible fruit-driven styles. The result is wines that eloquently express the unique *terroir* of the Cape. No wonder this extraordinary wealth of natural assets and tradition instils South African wines with a unique sense of place.

DEVELOPMENT OF *TERROIR* IN A SOUTH AFRICAN CONTEXT

Terroir refers to the natural features of a body of land, which interact to create a unique set of conditions. These in turn confer specific characteristics on vineyards and wines. Although literally meaning 'soil', *terroir* actually includes much more than that. The word refers to a combination of topography, climate, geology and soil variations. It also includes a human element, as biodynamic convert Michel Chapoutier has said: 'Without winemakers, the notion of *terroir* is meaningless; without mankind,

there can be no *terroir*, but we may also be the cause of its ruin.' Identification of viticultural *terroir* now receives worldwide attention, and is backed by an increasing consumer demand for understanding of the origin of each wine.

Falling in a warmer wine-growing zone, South Africa produces wines of pronounced diversity. The mesoclimatic conditions are considered an enormous asset, which makes zonation of high importance to the industry. As a result, South Africa has become a world leader in *terroir* research, using a multi-disciplinary program to identify what constitutes *terroir* and its effect on grape quality as well as wine style. This information has significantly impacted on site selection for individual varietals as well as viticultural practices including canopy management and trellising. It is now unlocking the potential of new wine-growing areas.

Geology – Geology forms the basis of *terroir*, as this describes the chemical composition and shape of the land, how it changes over time and how soils are formed. Although viticulture

Calcerous soil – Vines flourishing in the Hemel-en-Aarde Pocket

Sandy soil – Ridging increases soil volume for greater water and nutrient efficiency

in South Africa is relatively young, the geology is not, resulting in some of the most ancient viticultural soils in the world. (Some soils are traceable back to the first super-continent some 1 000 million years ago.) Massive pressures and upheavals over millions of years resulted in majestic mountain ranges with soaring peaks, steep slopes and deep valleys, creating a remarkable variety of mesoclimates and soil types. This geological inheritance goes way back in time: The late Precambrian shale and schists deposited in a marine basin some 570 to 1 000 million years ago, presently occur at 20 to 200 metre altitudes. This deposit was folded and lifted due to tectonic movement of the Pan African event, which ended 550 million years ago and eroded into rolling hills. Subsequently, intrusions of granite plutons occurred (600 million years ago), before the separation of Gondwanaland into present-day Africa, the Americas, India, Australia and Antarctica. A period of erosion and covering followed; intensive folding and lifting created the distinctive folded sandstone mountain ranges and valleys of the Cape.

Topography – Topography describes the land

PLUTONS

Plutons are dome-like intrusion of igneous magma into the earth's crust, which occurred at great depths and consequently cooled slowly. These plutons have been exposed by erosion, resulting in dome-like mountains, such as the Paarl and Paardeberg and Darling Hills, or flat-topped erosion covered by sandstone deposits like Table Mountain and Simonsberg.

NATURAL *TERROIR* UNIT

A natural *terroir* unit (NTU) is a unit of the earth's surface characterised by relatively homogenous patterns of topography, climate, geology and soil. It has a scientific agriculture potential which is reflected in the characteristics of its products, resulting finally in the concept of *terroir*.

ZONATION

Demarcating an area into units on a certain basis, for example, *terroir* or climate.

surface features, its physical shape and has a strong interaction with soil and climate. Altitude, aspect (direction in which the slope faces) and inclination of a slope are three very important factors influencing viticulture. As the southern hemisphere seasons are directly opposite to those of the northern hemisphere, known influences will be exactly the opposite as well.

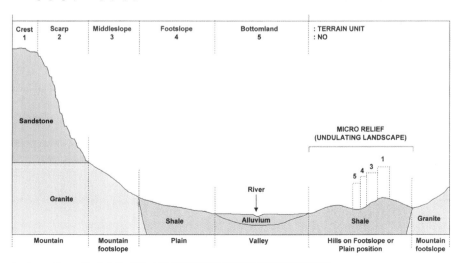

Landscape – Cross section illustrating topography of South Africa's cultivated landscape (D. Saayman)

In the southern hemisphere, north- and west-facing slopes are generally warmer than south- and east-facing slopes due to the higher inception of sunlight. Eastern slopes will, however, warm up faster than western slopes and cool earlier. During the summer months (December – March), the sun rises late and sets early behind the mountain peaks, casting deep shadows over the vineyards on the mountain slopes in the early morning and late afternoons, thus restricting the amount of sunlight hours. Certain vineyards only see the sun rising as late as 10:00 and vineyards seldom receive a maximum of 10 hours of sunlight (WOSA, 2009).

Due to these locational conditions, preference is given to the cooler southern and eastern slopes, especially for the more delicate varieties like Sauvignon Blanc and Pinot Noir. The shape of the land results in varying altitudes and multi-directional aspects, with consequential changes in solar radiation interception, temperature and wind exposure.

Climate – Viticulture originated at latitudes of 27° to 34° South, in areas with a Mediterranean climate. The Western Cape is cooler than its geographical position suggests, partly due to the cold Benguela current along the West Coast, with vine-growing areas along the coastal zone seldom stretching more than 50 kilometres from the ocean. The coastal zone has warm summers and wet, cold winters, with frost rarely a problem. Rain falls mainly between May and August, and diminishes in a northerly and northeasterly direction, the latter the result of prominent mountain ranges. Temperature is a vitally important factor, influencing every aspect of the vine's functioning. The average summer daytime temperature follows an inverse pattern to the rainfall, increasing in a northerly direction and with distance from the ocean. The combination of warm days and cool nights favours vines, as the low temperature slows grape ripening, resulting in a concentration of colour pigments and

flavour compounds in grape skins, while the long growing season yields riper fruit. (See also Carbon Footprint and Climate Change, page 21.)

Soils – Soils are highly varied and often several different types occur within a single vineyard. Soil texture and structure depends on the clay content, which binds particles together and determines how water is retained or drained. Excess water will cause vines to drown, whereas too little water will cause the vines to die of thirst. Too much clay causes the soil to compact when it experiences pressure – vine roots only develop in non-compacted soil areas. In very sandy soils, roots may develop only where they find water (e.g. drip irrigation) and not make use of the entire soil volume available. An evenly spread root system, both horizontally and vertically, is required for optimum plant health. The organic and mineral content of the soil feeds the vine; however, rich soils can cause excessive growth and mediocre fruit. Low-fertility soils with a good structure and drainage are thus preferred. The three most important soil types are sandstone-derived, granite-derived or shale-derived.

In the coastal regions, the pattern sees sandstone mountains resting on granite intrusions, surrounded by shale at lower altitudes. Further inland, shale and river deposits usually dominate, providing richer, more fertile soils. The highly regarded reddish and yellowish-brown soils are usually associated with granitic hills (e.g. Bottelary Hill) and the granitic foothills of sandstone mountains, like Table Mountain and Stellenbosch Mountain. These coloured soils, found on steep slopes at altitudes of 150 to 400 metres, are relics of a past, high rainfall, tropical era. Other soils that formed on granite occur on gently undulating hills between the mountains and the sea, 20 to 150 metres above sea level, an area invaded several times by the sea due to land recession and uplifting (WOSA, 2009).

PRINCIPLE SOILS OF SOUTH AFRICA

SANDSTONE

Lightly coloured, sandy with low nutrient and adequate water-retention properties. Contains calcium and quartz.

CLAY

Acidic. Retains water and is cool – benefit in warm conditions. In high quantities, prone to compaction and poor root development.

GRANITE

Red or yellow-coloured, acidic and found on mountain foothill slopes and ranges of hills; good physical and water-retention properties. Quartz-rich, hard and acidic, easy-draining, low-fertile soil. Some of the best soils for viticulture.

LIMESTONE

Alkaline, easy-draining, calcium-rich soil. Best suited to white cultivars (Chardonnay).

SHALE

Brown in colour, strongly structured, with good nutrient reserves and water retention.

LOAM

Equal parts of clay, silt and sand; potentially too fertile for grape cultivation.

GRAVEL

Free-draining (benefit in wet conditions), low-fertility, pebbly soil, retains heat of the sun and extends ripening beyond sunlight hours. Also retains moisture to cool soils.

SAND

Low fertility. Drains very well, prone to dryness, no storing of nutrients. Advantage of deterring *Phylloxera* beetle.

ALLUVIAL

Found on river banks and in flat land previously linked to a river. Potentially very fertile, yet sandy and silty. Not suitable for vigorous growers such as Shiraz.

BEST VINEYARD SOILS

Gravelly or rocky soils are potentially good vineyard soil as gravel acts like natural mulch, shading the vine roots from the sun. The gravel and clay combination acts like a sponge, storing water during the rainy season and redistributing it back to the roots in the dry season. This ensures constant feeding for the vines, giving them a more balanced water source, as opposed to simple irrigation.

Maritime climate

Close proximity to a large body of water such as an ocean defines a maritime climate. Key climatic factors associated with a maritime climate and their impact on vineyards are illustrated below. In the Western Cape viticultural regions, the summer warmth is moderated by the constant interaction between the rugged mountain peaks and multi-directional valley slopes, as well as the proximity of two great oceans – the Atlantic and the Indian. Cooling moisture-laden breezes blow in from the sea during the afternoon and seasonal fog is prevalent.

THE CAPE DOCTOR

Like the Mistral in France, the legendary and sometimes ferocious southeasterly wind blows across the south-western Cape during the spring and summer months.

Living up to its name, the Cape Doctor inhibits the development of diseases in the vineyards by drying grapes and dispersing air pollution, dust and pollen. It has a moderating effect on temperature, lowering it by several degrees, but rarely brings moisture to vineyards.

Aspect Vines on northern and western slopes experience warmer conditions due to higher interception of sunlight and, as a result, grapes ripen more easily than those grown on flat land. Cabernet Sauvignon, Cabernet Franc and Pinotage, which require more heat, ripen later in the season.

Cooler southern and eastern slopes (the latter warming faster and cooling earlier) host the more delicate varieties such as Sauvignon Blanc and Pinot Noir. Flat terrain often experiences difficult drainage and ridges are made on shallow soils to increase soil volume.

Hill / Mountain Mountains and hills can offer protective rain shadows. They also provide shelter against damaging winds and reduce sun exposure. Small valleys in the folds of mountains provide sheltered land, but with the added benefit of run-off water.

Canopy The leaf area of the vines; not only ripen the grapes but also act as protection against harsh sunlight.

Sun Long hours of sunlight are adequate to ripen grapes fully.

Rain A maritime climate is subject to higher annual rainfall.

Wind Wind is an important factor as it influences the water requirements of the vines and reduces humidity and subsequent fungal diseases. Very strong winds may damage vines.

LEVELS OF CLIMATE

Macro: climate of a region, what is generally referred to as 'climate'.

Meso: differs from macro due to altitude, slope inclination, aspect or distance from the sea or large bodies of water, usually describes the climate of a vineyard.

Micro: climate immediately within and surrounding a plant canopy, can differ within location and time; a few centimetres and minutes can make a difference.

Ocean Close proximity of a large body of water moderates climate by providing cool air during the day and reducing the cold of night. The air movement it generates assists in reducing disease by drying the surface of the grape bunches and leaves.

Altitude Maritime sites are often located at low altitudes

Vineyard Humidity in the canopy may cause fungal diseases. Vertical shoot positioning on a trellis system promotes air circulation and minimises rot.

Row direction is used to maximise air flow between the rows and influences sun exposure.

Trellis system The height of vines is managed on a trellis system. Bringing the cordon arms closer to the soil increases radiant heat and hastens ripening.

It is also used to spread and open the canopy to sun exposure while protecting shoots against prevailing winds.

Microclimatic control within the canopy is of great importance. In areas with relatively high humidity, leaf removal increases air movement to dry grapes; in sheltered areas, sun exposure is increased to ensure proper ripening.

Continental climate

A continental climate lacks the presence of
large bodies of water which makes it drier and
often sunnier. Continental areas experience
wider temperature variations than Maritime
areas, both from day to night and between
seasons. These variations can be beneficial as
cooler nights slow grape ripening and the long
growing season yields riper fruit; however, frost
can be a problem.

   The aspect or orientation of a slope
influences its *terroir*. In the southern
hemisphere, north-facing slopes receive more
sun and are warmer than south-facing slopes.
The reverse is true for the northern hemisphere.

Shoot positioning A thicker canopy protects grapes
from sunburn in drier and sunnier conditions.

Soil A good soil structure is more important than its
chemical composition, as the structure influences the
water, air and nutrient content.

Steep slopes Slopes provide excellent drainage. In certain areas excessive sun exposure and heat restrict vine cultivation to cooler southern aspects. Slopes promote air circulation as warm air rises and cold air descends along the hillside. This air movement helps to reduce frost.

Altitude Vines are cultivated from a mere 50 metres above sea level to an altitude of 650 metres in the mountains. Increased altitude reduces average daytime temperatures and creates cooler conditions.

Rivers Bodies of water play a less important role in continental climates.

Grape varieties

The cultivar, or grape variety, is the heart of a wine and determines the basis of flavours.

Although South Africa has no regulations regarding the selection of varieties, where they may be planted or what production yield per hectare of vines may be achieved (as is the case in France), the accepted standard for quality grape production is between five and 10 tons per hectare. A requirement for high-quality grapes is a balance between its vegetal growth (trunk, shoots and leaves) above ground and the root system of a vine. This balance will naturally be influenced by soil types, climate, topography and sun exposure. Reducing yields does not always increase quality.

The noble varieties of France have been very popular in South Africa. Cabernet Sauvignon, Merlot, Chardonnay, Sauvignon Blanc and Chenin Blanc are firm favourites with many producers. Shiraz, under the guidance of mainly Australian winemakers, is rapidly increasing its popularity among South African wine drinkers and producers. Fierce competition between producers has resulted in new varieties gaining in popularity. Viognier, Malbec, Grenache and Mourvèdre are increasingly used in high-quality blends based on French styles and are also vinified to single variety wines.

South Africa's sunny climate seldom fails to ripen grapes fully. As sugar levels increase during ripening, the natural acid decreases. Simultaneously other chemical components (flavour, aromas and colour) are formed. Historically grapes were harvested on required sugar levels alone. Today, however, most producers harvest at a point referred to as 'optimum ripeness'. Difficult to define in terms of values, this is a combination of sugar, acid, tannin, colour and other chemical levels. These parameters (within a specified range) give an indication of grapes reaching optimal ripeness and are used to determine the moment of harvest. Although chemical changes continue inside the grape, its chemical makeup at the

THE DOG ANALOGY

The easiest way to explain the difference between, for example, a 'red wine' and a 'Cabernet Sauvignon' is with the dog analogy. Imagine that each of the grape varieties is similar to a breed of dogs. As one finds Chardonnay, Viognier, Pinot Noir and Shiraz, so too we have Sheepdogs, Ridgebacks and Labradors. The wine styles (dry or sweet, red or white, still or sparkling) are akin to the tricks we teach our dogs.

Certain dogs are brilliant as guide dogs, while others are better watchdogs; some can learn tricks and others perform daring rescue missions. Not all breeds can perform all tasks equally well. Similarly, certain grape varieties are better suited to certain wine styles, such as Cabernet Sauvignon for dry red wine or red blends, rather than a sparkling wine and Tinta Barocca for Port-style wines.

THE GRAPE

The skin is the source of colour, tannins and flavour compounds, giving the wine its distinctive character.

The stalks contain bitter tannins and are rarely used in winemaking.

The bloom or wax coat on the outside of the skin contains natural yeasts, which are used for spontaneous or natural fermentation. The wax also protects the grape from disease and pests.

The pips contain bitter tannins and are generally removed during the winemaking process.

The pulp is the heart of the grape and makes up the bulk of the volume. It comprises water, sugar, acids and flavour compounds.

moment of harvest will determine the ultimate quality of a resultant wine, therefore the decision of when to harvest is critical.

As wines easily attain sufficient alcohol levels (generally above Alc. 12,5% by Vol.), South African law does not allow sugar additions in winemaking. Addition of acid (those naturally occurring in grapes: tartaric, malic), however,

Liquid sunshine – Grapes capture the sunny climate of South Africa

is allowed to balance high sugar levels. Too little acid makes wine taste bland and lifeless; excessive acid stings the palate and makes wine undrinkable. Acid gives a wine structure and balance, and remains one of the most important chemical components. Many aromas and flavours need a certain acid level to bring them to the fore.

LEADING VARIETIES

Chenin Blanc Earlier regarded as relatively ordinary, it was historically grown with high yields and poor fruit concentration. **Wine:** Examples with high acid, pleasant citrus nose and wood are popular. **Area:** In most vine-growing areas

Chardonnay Flourishes in poor, rocky soils, expressing typical butter, spicy and even nut flavours. In warm areas, rich and full bodied with softer acid. In cool conditions shows high, crisp acidity and strong mineral and flinty characters on limestone (Chablis style) (see Robertson). **Wine:** Many over-oaked. Best maturation potential among whites, three to four years. **Area:** Stellenbosch Kloof, Robertson, Franschhoek

Riesling Few examples in German style, not popular in youth but dense and oily if matured (8 y+). **Area:** Constantia

Sauvignon Blanc Prefers cooler growing conditions with a refreshing acidity. **Wine:** Typically two styles: very tropical with citrus, guava and pineapple, or more green with grass cuttings, asparagus and tinned peas. **Area:** Durbanville, Constantia, Elgin, Cape Point, Helderberg

Sémillon Often a blending partner, does well in cool areas. **Wine:** Peachy and citrus aromas and dense if aged well. **Area:** Franschhoek, Helderberg

Viognier Gloriously perfumed grape. Newly planted, used as blending partner for Shiraz (Rhône style) or with whites, very few single cultivar examples. **Area:** Swartland, Stellenbosch

Merlot Less tannin and more fruit-driven, toffee and plummy characters. Good as single variety wine with softer mouthfeel and early drinkability, or used to soften blends. **Area:** Polkadraai, Annandale

Cabernet Franc Grassy cousin of Cabernet Sauvignon, does very well as a blending partner. Is becoming popular as a single variety wine. **Area:** Helderberg

Cabernet Sauvignon Most abundant red. Ripens late, enjoys sites with long sun hours. High ratio of skin to juice, very good maturation potential due to high tannin content. Cool coastal Pockets see medium-bodied, fruit-driven styles, wines turning more tannic and dark in warmer areas. **Area:** Stellenbosch-Simonsberg, Helshoogte, Paarl

Malbec Spicy red grape, not as tannic as Cabernet Sauvignon. Good blending partner for red blend.

Mourvèdre Favourite blending partner of Shiraz. Typical blackberry flavour.

Pinotage A unique style, Cape Blend, incorporates Pinotage with various red blending partners. **Wine:** Red fruits (cherry, raspberry, strawberry and ripe plums), some hints of violets. **Area:** Bottelary, Robertson, Wellington, Tulbagh

Pinot Noir Requires meticulous handling. Prefers cool conditions, no direct sun and is sensitive to wind damage. **Wine:** Less intense with less tannin, but tends to elegantly restrained wines. Typical raspberry and strawberry flavours. **Area:** Walker Bay, Elgin

Shiraz Dark-skinned grape, making very powerful wines. **Wine:** Smoky, leathery and spicy with some red berries, can be very peppery. Does well with some American oak, giving vanilla, toasty aromas. **Area:** Simondium-Klapmuts, Paarl, Swartland

Port Fortified red wines, typically from warm areas. Uses mainly Portuguese cultivars, Tinta Barocca, Tinta Roriz and Touriga Naçional. **Area:** Klein Karoo

Wine and health

Recent studies confirm an age-old understanding – that wine can be beneficial to general health. Mounting evidence highlights the link between wine and a healthy lifestyle: regular wine drinkers tend to eat balanced diets, smoke less and exercise more. Furthermore, wine can be a powerful means of preventing certain diseases, due to its chemical composition of water, alcohol, polyphenols (resveratrol, quercetin, etc.) and other antioxidants.

The greatest benefit is associated with the regular and moderate consumption of red wine. For women, it is accepted as one glass (140 g or 5 oz) per day and for men one to two glasses. Greater amounts significantly increase certain risks. In the 1990s a gene, which seems to control aging, was identified. It is activated by polyphenols. As many diseases are associated with cellular aging, this discovery could significantly increased lifespan expectancy.

All references below denote regular and moderate wine consumption.

Arthritis – Wine increases bone density and lowers the risk of osteoporosis and rheumatoid arthritis.

Brain – Red wine lowers the risk of a stroke and delays the onset of Alzheimer's disease and other forms of dementia by neutralising toxic protein clumps that kill brain cells.

Cancer – Wine drinkers have a lower risk of contracting both oesophageal and lung cancer.

Diabetes – Red wine helps to regulate insulin sensitivity and blood glucose levels, thereby preventing type 2 diabetes.

Digestive system – Wine assists in removing potentially harmful substances found in red meats, supports digestion and lowers the risk of atherosclerosis and colon cancer.

Eyes – Wine drinkers run a lower risk of developing cataracts and contracting age-related macular degeneration.

Headaches – Assumed culprits are histamines or sulphites. However, these occur in higher concentrations in other frequently consumed foodstuffs (e.g. a serving of dried apricots contain almost 10 times the sulphites of a serving of wine).

Heart – Wine reduces the risk of atherosclerosis, heart attacks and hypertension. It activates an enzyme which processes alcohol and eliminates toxic by-products of fat breakdown in cells during a heart attack to prevent further damage to the heart.

Influenza – Quercetin, a known anti-inflammatory, may block the replication of the influenza virus and thus prevent flu.

Legs – Wine lowers the risk of peripheral artery disease, which restricts blood supply to the legs.

Liver – Alcohol and resveratrol reduce fat production and assist the liver in breaking down existing fat, thereby reducing the risk of non-alcoholic fatty liver disease.

Nutritional value – An average glass of red wine contains 3,8 grams of carbohydrates, a serving of beer twice that amount and a sweetened soft drink up to 10 times that amount. Fibre in wine reduces blood pressure and cholesterol far better than other sources of dietary fibre. The body cannot manufacture omega-3 fatty acids, but alcohol assists it to synthesize omega 3, which lowers the risk of heart disease. Wine grapes are rich in melatonin which acts as a powerful antioxidant and detoxifies cells.

Women – Alcohol may increase the risk of cancer, but recently it was found that resveratrol protects cells from becoming cancerous. Wine also reduces the risk of ovarian cancer. Doctors advise that the safest policy is to avoid alcohol during pregnancy, as its abuse is linked to cognitive and developmental disorders in children. New research indicates that, not only is it safe for pregnant women to consume a glass or two of wine per week, but that their children may perform better. Demographic advantages may also play a role.

Timeline

| JANUARY | FEBRUARY | MARCH | APRIL |

◀TICULTURE

Preparation for harvest

Harvesting equipment is prepared. Grapes are analysed chemically and with taste tests for ripeness and flavour development. The prescribed withholding period for chemical sprays is observed before harvesting.

Veraison

The grape berries increase in size and start to change colour as the first signs of ripening. Concentration of sugar and flavour components increase.

Vineyard management

Once fruitset is successful, growers may remove the underdeveloped bunches (green harvesting) to create an optimum yield and flavour concentration.

Harvest

Harvest is the busiest time of the year at the winery. Vineyards are dotted with the colours of pickers, as they harvest grapes as rapidly and gently as possible. Picking of grapes also serves as a first step in the selection of the best fruit for fermentation. Machine harvesting is not very common in South Africa.

White grapes are first to ripen, during February. Harvesting of first (mainly) white grapes for sparkling and white wine production starts in February. Red varieties ripen during March and April, with harvesting in the coolest areas commencing in April.

◀INEMAKING

Preparation of cellar

Prepare cellar for grapes; check machinery, order barrels, buy chemicals.

Sorting, crushing and destemming

On arrival, grapes are sorted, removing MOG (material other than grapes) as well as rotten, underdeveloped and damaged grapes. Grapes are transported via a receiving hopper which feeds into a destemmer / crusher where stems are removed and berries are crushed between rollers to render sugar-rich juice. White grapes and rosé grapes are pressed to remove skins, and pips and juice are cleared for fermentation.

Harvest

Grapes are harvested and delivered to the cellar for processing.

Early harvest of first (mainly) white grapes for bubbly and white wines, to obtain a more herbaceous flavour.

Harvesting of white grapes to obtain a more tropical fruit flavour. Harvesting of red varieties, and in cooler areas. Fermentation of grapes, pressing and maturation / stabilisation / bottling.

Fermentation (alcoholic)

Yeast may be added (or natural without yeast addition) to convert sugar to alcohol and carbon dioxide. Fermentation generates a large amount of heat and the temperature is carefully controlled to prevent loss of flavour. Red wine completes warm fermentation (25°–30°C) in four to seven days. Juice and skins are mixed by punching down the skins into the juice, drawing juice from the bottom of the vessel and pumping it over skins floating on top. White wines are fermented cold (16°–20°C) and may take three weeks. If grapes lack acidity, acid may be added.

Timeline

| MAY | JUNE | JULY | AUGUST |

VITICULTURE

Leaf fall

Leaves fall naturally from the vine after grapes have ripened. This marks the end of the reproductive cycle. Vineyard maintenance: After harvest, vines are given time to rest. Trellis systems are mended, dead wood is cut from vines and unproductive plants are removed. Soils are ploughed to break up any compaction.

Resting

After leaf fall, the vines go into a period of dormancy where they can survive extreme cold. Without sufficiently cold conditions, the next growing season will be poor. Vineyards in shallow soils are ridged to provide sufficient soil volume for roots.

Pruning and vine shaping

Vines are pruned to position correctly and shape the plant as well as to ensure good future yields. Although pruning can be done by machine, most growers use skilled workers.

Budbreak

Vineyards start to bud and the first green growth is visible. Soil is ploughed to aerate it.

Hazards, diseases and pests

A number of potential dangers face the vines during the course of the year. Hazardous weather conditions such as spring frost damage young growth, a hail storm can rapidly destroy a vineyard and very humid conditions may cause fungal infections. *Phylloxera*, the insect that nearly destroyed the European wine industry in the 19th century, attacks vine roots, but today most vines are grafted on resistant American rootstocks. Various insects can damage the vine and birds, deer and small rodents feed on the ripe grapes.

WINEMAKING

Pressing

Once sufficient alcohol, tannins and colour is extracted, the liquid (free-run) is run into a different container. The remaining solid matter is pressed to produce a dark liquid (press wine). Press and free-run juice may be blended to achieve a full, rich wine. Following alcoholic fermentation, some white wines are stirred on the yeast lees to increase development of flavours.

Maturation

Maturation mainly applies to barrel aging, although some wines are matured in bottle by the winery. Oak maturation is reserved for high-quality red and white wines, which may take up to two years. The porous wood allows slow oxidation, softening tannins and increasing the flavour complexity. As wine matures, it produces sediment, which may result in undesirable flavours. Using racking, the wine is drained or pumped away into a clean vessel to continue aging. Certain white wines may mature in stainless steel tanks before bottling.

Malolactic fermentation

A second fermentation done by bacteria, which may be added or done naturally. Mainly for red wine and certain dense whites (Chardonnay). Malic acid is converted to lactic acid, reducing the acidity of the wine and increasing a soft mouthfeel. This is done in barrel or tank.

SEPTEMBER   OCTOBER   NOVEMBER   DECEMBER

Planting new vines

Young vines are removed from the nurseries and are planted. Vines are planted wider apart on steep slopes as well as in areas where mechanical harvesting is done. Row direction allows strong winds to flow through the rows and reduce damage to vines.

Flowering

Small green vine flowers bloom and over the next two weeks pollination and fertilisation occur. Vines are sprayed, where necessary, against insects and fungal diseases. Vineyards in warm, dry areas are less prone to disease.

Fruit set

The fertilised flowers now develop into berries; the others fail to grow and fall off. Vine training: Following flowering, shoots are placed in the wires (trellised vines) and tied together (bush vines).

Vineyard management

New vineyards are developed. Soils are chemically balanced with additions. Soil structure is improved with ripping to prevent compaction and ensure even vine root development horizontally as well as vertically. Drainge and irrigation systems are put into place. Vine trellising is maintained.

Canopy management

Excessive canopy shade causes a decrease in bud fertility, sugar concentration, colour density, flavour and tartaric acid while it increases potassium concentration, pH and malic acid.

Fining and filtering

Fining removes tiny proteins using a carrier such as bentonite or egg white to bind with the suspended particles and cause them to sink to the bottom of the vessel. Filtration removes solids from a liquid. These clarification techniques assist in producing a clear wine, which is stable in the bottle.

Blending and bottling

In most cases, a number of barrels or tanks are blended to create a singular wine, then allowed to settle in a tank. Mobile bottling plants assist smaller producers to bottle their wine, while larger producers use automated bottling equipment. The aim is to transfer the wine safely to the bottle and preserve its character using a slow, careful fill protected from oxygen.

Bottling and release of wine

Red wines are generally bottled after maturation of a few months and aged in bottle before release to the market. Wine release dates are related as much to the market conditions as to when the wine is bottled.

Celebration of the vintage

Many wineries celebrate a sucessful harvest with special occasions. Wine tasting, wine and food pairings and meet-the-winemaker events abound. The wine industry has many fascinating traditions, for example at pressing,

the first wine from the press is thrown into the air as an offering of thanks to the wine god Bacchus.

Chapter 2

Geographical areas and pockets

Simonsberg – Breathtaking Banghoek Valley with Simonsberg (1 319 m) as seen from Rainbow's End Estate

Geographical Areas and Pockets

The Mother City – A view over Cape Town and Table Mountain from the Durbanville Pocket

Most vineyards are found in the southwestern areas of South Africa, hosting a wide range of *terroir* units that suit a large range of wine styles. Wine-producing areas are not restricted by regulations that specify the planting of varieties in specific areas; therefore varieties that were not previously known to be suited to certain areas were planted by pioneering winemakers with great success.

Although the first wine was made in 1659, a recent renaissance in winemaking practices has lifted South African wines to new heights. A flood of innovation started in the late 1960s with the arrival of German winemakers, and surged again after 1992 when South Africa became more exposed to the international wine arena. The concept of *terroir* has taken root and, together with a better understanding of viticultural practices, has boosted wine quality to a point where

A ride back into history – An old tractor reminds visitiors of Backsberg's colourful history (circa 1916)

South Africa now offers wine that equals and often exceeds international standards.

Cape Town, capital of the Western Cape Province, is South Africa's second largest city, with a population of approximately 3,5 million. It is the southern-most metropolis on the African continent, and enjoys a pleasant Mediterranean climate. The Western Cape's major wine-growing areas stretch from the heart of Namaqualand, north of the majestic Cedar Berg, to the Klein Karoo, well east of Cape Town.

However, most of the 36 wine-growing Pockets are within easy reach of Cape Town, ranging from a 20-minute drive (Constantia) to a two-hour journey (Robertson). Wine culture is well developed in the Western Cape, as the region has been producing wine for more than three-and-a-half centuries. Jan van Riebeeck, who arrived in Table Bay in 1652 to establish a refreshment station for

TEMPERATURE AND RAINFALL CONVERSION TABLE (METRIC / IMPERIAL)	
Metric	Imperial
Rainfall	
200 mm	7,9 in.
400 mm	15,8 in.
600 mm	23,6 in.
800 mm	31,5 in.
1 000 mm	39,4 in.
Temperature	
10°C	50°F
15°C	59°F
20°C	68°F
25°C	77°F
30°C	86°F
35°C	95°F

TERROIR

Topography: Mountains dominate, vineyards planted on slopes and valley floors

Soil: Varies dramatically, mostly acidic and clay based

Climate: Mediterranean – long, hot summers and wet, cold winters

Temperature: February average 24°C

Rainfall: Annual average range from 730 mm (Stellenbosch) to over 1 000 mm (Constantia)

Wind: Southeast in summer, also known as the Cape Doctor

Varieties: Cabernet Sauvignon, Cabernet Franc, Merlot, Shiraz, Pinotage, Sauvignon Blanc, Chenin Blanc, Chardonnay, Sémillon, Viognier, Muscat, Riesling

the Dutch East India Company, saw his first vintage pressed on 2 February 1659.

Most of the Western Cape's wine-growing areas enjoy a Mediterranean climate, with winter rainfall and warm, dry summers. Both climate and soil variations ensure that a wide range of wine styles and types are produced. High quality red and white wines are made, along with a rapidly increasing number of sparkling wines. The fortified wines – including Sherry, Port and Muskcadel – are renowned for both good quality and affordable prices. Gracious estates with distinctive Cape Dutch architecture, surrounded by verdant vineyards and a backdrop of mauve mountains, are as quintessentially Cape as Table Mountain. There are, however, several equally impressive cellars that are as modern as any in the world, some sunk into hillsides, taking design inspiration from works of art, others state-of-the-art steel-and-glass structures that soar skyward.

Autumn personified – A brightly coloured leaf contrasts the fallen trunk on which it rests

Cape Point Pocket

Coastal proximity – Cape Point Vineyards' vines enjoy low daytime temperatures near the Atlantic Ocean

Cape Point is the exception to vine plantings and cultivation in the Cape Winelands and represents the new face of South African wine. This Pocket is situated behind the southwestern slopes of the Constantia amphitheatre of mountains. Vineyards are a maximum of three kilometres from the cold Atlantic Ocean, dominated by the cold upwelling Benguela current. The climate is Mediterranean, but the Pocket experiences strong maritime and mountain-shelter influences. The annual rainfall exceeds 1 000 millimetres (40 in.).

Panthera leo – An African lion guards the entrance to Cape Point Vineyards

Apart from the southwestern and west slopes facing the sea, the topography of the area resembles that of the neighbouring Constantia basin. The Cape Point area is markedly cooler, however, due to the proximity of sea breezes and synoptic winds, often combined with mountainous cloud cover. The low daytime temperatures, mountain clouds and sea mists, which often cover the vineyards, produce near-perfect growing conditions for heat-sensitive grapes, such as Sauvignon Blanc and Sémillon. Sunlight hours during the growing season are sufficient to ripen varieties such as Cabernet Sauvignon.

The Pocket's granite outcrops are highly weathered and stripped of their reddish-brown soil mantle, presenting more white-coloured soils. The hills and outcrops are extensively used as a source of kaolin, a good indication of the alkalinity of the soil. Due to varying soil fertility, marked differences in vine vigour occur between vineyards, and cultivation practices vary accordingly.

Viticulture is focused on using the cool sea breezes to create slow, even ripening of grapes and continuous air movement to control humidity and combat fungal diseases.

Vine row direction is orientated so that summer winds flow down the rows (changing with the changing slope direction), while canopies are opened by removal of leaves and side shoots to allow sufficient sunlight penetration. The Pocket is still relatively young and, although it is suited to both red and white noble varieties, not all of them are planted here. The Cape Point Pocket is currently recognised for its Sauvignon Blanc, Chardonnay and Sémillon.

Cape Point Vineyards excel in this category with the wines showing herbaceous flavours mixed with tropical fruit, tight acidities and a wonderful mineral backbone. Recently, limited quantities of a second label red comprising Cabernet Sauvignon and Shiraz has been added to the range, produced from young vines on the Scarborough estate.

TERROIR

Soil: Sandstone on bleached granite

Climate: Cool, windy, high rainfall

White varieties: Sauvignon Blanc, Sémillon, Chardonnay

Red varieties: Cabernet Sauvignon, Shiraz

Wine styles: Red, white

Natural air conditioning – Mists roll in from the sea during the afternoon

Southwest-facing slopes – View over Cape Point Vineyards in the afternoon sun

The entrance – Making a statement to welcome visitors

CAPE POINT VINEYARDS

The vines are laid out on two sites near Cape Point, the southernmost tip of the Cape Peninsula, with the Noordhoek farm 1,5 kilometres from the Atlantic Ocean. Thirty-three hectares of low-yielding vineyards are cultivated, the soil and strong winds naturally limiting vigour and producing smaller grape berries. This relates to greater fruit concentration and more intense wines. White varieties are planted on sandstone- and granite-derived soils with a high percentage of clay. All wines follow the mineral structure, typical of the *terroir*. Red varieties are found on the gravelly slopes of the Scarborough estate. Three distinct styles demonstrate Sauvignon Blanc's potential: • Stonehaven – an elegant, citrusy wine from grapes grown at a low attitude. • Sauvignon Blanc – a complex wine grown on granite and clay-rich elevated slopes. Blended with a portion of Sémillon and barrel-fermented Sauvignon Blanc and aged on the lees. • Isliedh Sauvignon Blanc/Semillon (pronounced ai-lay) – a barrel-fermented wine grown on clay-rich soils, aged in wood for 10 months.

ℹ️ Isliedh 2007, Sauvignon Blanc 2007 🍷 Sauv Bl, Sém, Chard, Shz, Cab S ◉ Contact cellar for tasting times
☎ +27 (0)21 789 0900 ✉ info@cape-point.com, www. capepointvineyards.co.za ⧗ Sauv Bl 5 y, Sém & Isliedh 5–10 y 🍾 Sauv 00, 01, 04, 06; Sém 03, 05, 08 ⓘ Southern-most vineyards on the Cape Peninsula

Constantia Pocket

Vineyard haven – An early morning view of Constantia's vineyards, an oasis of green amidst Cape Town's residential areas

Historic Constantia is the site of Simon van der Stel's (one of the first governors of the Cape of Good Hope) 17th-century wine farm and the source of the world-famous 19th-century Constantia sweet dessert wines. Due to urbanisation, this small vine-growing Pocket is logded between the residential area of Constantia and Table Mountain, a World Heritage Site.

The Constantia Pocket nestles in a shallow mountain amphitheatre formed by the south jutting 'tail' of Table Mountain (1 000 m) extending into the Vlakkenberg (570 m), Constantiaberg (900 m) and Kalkbaaiberg ranges. Constantia is considered a cool cultivation area, as the mean February temperature at harvest time is only 20,6°C. Facing southeast and opening directly onto False Bay (10 km), this area receives the full benefit of its cool and moisture-laden breezes.

Healing the wound – A pruning wound is covered with a preparation to prevent infections

While the breezes moderate the daytime temperature, cloud cover and overnight condensation increase the relative humidity which often leads to the development of *Botrytis*. Strict viticultural management is required to avoid fungal infection or proper management for the production of sweet wines. An important feature of the Constantia Pocket is early morning sun which dries the vineyards from dew, aiding the prevention of vine diseases. An additional advantage is the afternoon mountain shadow which relieves the heat of day. Annual rainfall is relatively high (1 050 mm) making irrigation unnecessary.

The mountain ramparts are remnants of a solidified sandy alluvial plain, called Table Mountain Sandstone. This formation rests non-conformably on a granite intrusion that was eroded flat before the deposition of the sandstone material. On the red granite base foothills, at altitudes of 100 to 300 metres, deeply weathered reddish-brown, acidic soils have developed with excellent water-retention and drainage properties.

This acidity is easily neutralised with the first soil preparation before planting and occasional lime additions. The high-lying vineyards cling to southeastern and northeastern aspects which are moderately cool, with some warm solar radiation from the north ensuring ripening. Vineyards located lower down on the foothills enjoy slightly longer sunlight hours. This allows red varieties such as Cabernet Sauvignon to ripen fully. However, these reds reflect definite cool climate characteristics with moderate (for South Africa) alcohol levels of 13 to 14 per cent.

Due to large topographical variations, long-term viticultural practices vary over short distances between farms and even between vineyards. Vine rows planted on the contours of steep slopes are wider, sometimes even forming terraces, while the vines on flat terrain have narrow rows.In many cases, these extremes are located very close or even right next to each other.

Living water– Water filters through the moutain rock, pooling into clear streams

To combat the high humidity, row direction allows the prevailing summer southeasterly winds to flow through the rows and canopies are more open to facilitate airflow and to control fungal diseases. With a few exceptions, all vines are cordon trained and shoots are vertically positioned in trellises to provide protection from the strong prevailing winds.

Although considered a cool climate, the Pocket's *terroir* is suited to both red and white varieties due to specific locational advantages such as sunlight exposure and slightly extended

> ### TERROIR
> **Soil:** Red-brown sandstone on granite
> **Climate:** Cool, windy, high rainfall, sunlight
> **White varieties:** Sauvignon Blanc, Chardonnay, Riesling, Sémillon
> **Red varieties:** Cabernet Sauvignon, Merlot, Shiraz
> **Wine styles:** Red, white, sparkling

ripening conditions. Heat-sensitive Sauvignon Blanc and Chardonnay excel in this particular cool climate, showing distinct varietal fruit and impressive concentration, while a naturally high acidity gives the wines longevity.

Steenberg's Sauvignon Blanc shows complex herbaceous mixed with tropical fruit flavours. Constantia Uitsig is doing particularly well with a wooded Sémillon. Klein Constantia's Vin de Constance, historical favourite of Napoleon, is still an exceptional sweet wine, made from Muscat de Fontignan. White blended wines are also very popular with the Constantia producers such as Steenberg's flagship white, Magna Carta, a blend of Sauvignon Blanc from a reserve block (60%) and barrel-fermented Sémillon (40%) and arguably South Africa's most expensive white blend.

Merlot and Cabernet Sauvignon-based blends are also popular. Groot Constantia and Buitenverwachting focus on these styles and their wines show great finesse. Small parcels of other red varieties show great potential. Red wines show fine berry fruit and tight tannins, reflecting the cool climate structure and elegance.

Recently, the Constantia Pocket wineries decided to use a unique crested bottle for their flagship wines, promoting the collective range of their wines in premium glassware. An exclusive collection, including each winery's flagship wine, is also planned.

DRIVING ROUTE: CONSTANTIA

Leave Cape Town on the N2 freeway, drive southeast to explore the oldest wine-producing area in South Africa – Constantia. The M3 freeway links to the N2; a few hundred metres further the N2 turns east towards Cape Town International Airport, while the M3 continues in the same direction – stay on the M3.

The M3 winds its way through residential areas and changes name several times before regaining freeway status and descending a long, steep slope. Take Exit 15 (left) to Kendal Road. Turn right and cross over the M3, towards the Constantiaberg. At the next traffic light, turn right into Spaanschemat River Road (M42) and follow the road to a T-junction. Turn left into Constantia Main Road (M41).

Beautiful history – Buitenverwachting's old horse stables have been transformed to a welcoming reception building

Follow this road for about 3,2 kilometres to Constantia Glen's entrance on the left. Its tasting room has a magnificent view over the area's vineyards. Return along the same route, to where the signs indicate Groot Constantia. Shortly after the turn (500 m), High Constantia is on the right. This small cellar specialises in sparkling wine production, as well as dense red and white wines.

A few metres further is the entrance to Groot Constantia. This historical winery has preserved many reminders of the luxurious lifestyle from the time of Simon van der Stel, including beautiful pediment gables and lush gardens with an historical bath.

An orientation centre houses an exhibition of several artefacts and photographs depicting the history of the estate. Visit the manor house (Van der Stel's home, built more than 300 years ago) and original wine cellar, which now houses a display of drinking vessels and winemaking equipment.

Return along the same route to Spaanschemat River Road and follow the road in the opposite direction. Turn right into Klein Constantia Road. A few metres further, turn left at the sign to Buitenverwachting. An oak-lined driveway leads to paddocks and the tasting room and restaurant. Buitenverwachting is acknowledged as one of the world's Top 50 producers and its restaurant has been rated locally in the Top 10 dining establishments for more than a decade.

Return along the route to Klein Constantia Road, turn left and continue for a kilometre to Klein Constantia on the right, home of Vin de Constance, a noble wine modelled on the famous South African sweet wine of the 18th and 19th centuries. Follow a gravel road to the tasting room, where a collection of old Vin de Constance bottles and a magnificent batik depicting four seasons in the vineyards are on display.

TRAVELLING TIPS

Information:
www.constantiawineroute.co.za

Accommodation:
Constantia Uitsig Country Hotel & Spa
    +27 (0)21 794 6500
Steenberg Hotel +27 (0)21 713 2211

Restaurants:
Buitenverwachting Restaurant +27 (0)21 794 3522
Catharina's Restaurant (Steenberg) +27 (0)21 713 2222
Constantia Uitsig Restaurant +27 (0)21 794 4480
La Colombe (Uitsig) +27 (0)21 794 2390
Simon & Jonkershuis (Groot Constantia)
    +27 (0)21 794 5128
Spaanschemat River Café (Uitsig) +27 (0)21 794 1810

Interests:
African Fish Eagles (Klein Constantia)
Jewellery, picnics (Buitenverwachting)
Restaurant, hotel, spa, golf (Steenberg)
Teddy Bear Festival (Buitenverwachting) 1 May

49

Return to Spaanschemat River Road and turn right. A few kilometres further, turn right to visit Constantia Uitsig. Tasting facilities are set in its delightful pink wine and gift shop. Adjacent Spaanschemat River Café is a favourite for weekend breakfasts and boasts its own elegant cookbook. The world-class hotel and two fine-dining restauants provide luxurious country charm.

GPS WAYPOINTS

Buitenverwachting S34° 02.470 E18° 24.962
Constantia Glen S34° 00.699 E18° 24.402
Constantia Uitsig S34° 02.857 E18° 25.513
Groot Constantia S34° 01.425 E18° 25.806
High Constantia S34° 01.543 E18° 25.625
Klein Constantia S34° 02.283 E18° 25.133
Steenberg S34° 04.504 E18° 25.779

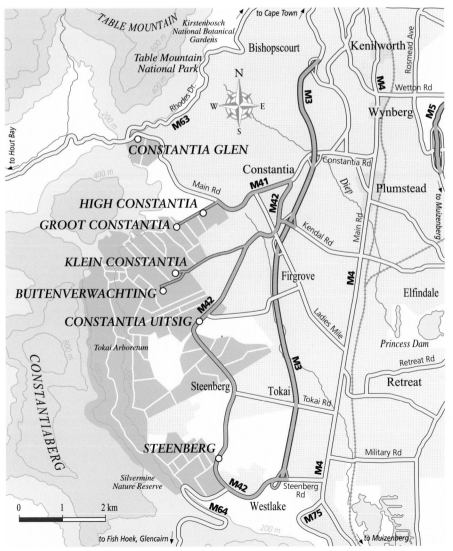

Continue along the Spaanschemat River Road, which becomes Steenberg Road as it nears the mountain. Turn right at the entrance to Steenberg. Its winemaking facilities were recently upgraded to world-class standards and the property includes a championship golf course and a five-star boutique hotel celebrating 17th-century elegance and traditions.

Vineyard perfection – Constantia Uitsig's vineyards offer low-yielding, highly concentrated wines

BUITENVERWACHTING

Buitenverwachting, first established in 1796, is a grand winery with an impressive façade. One hundred hectares of vines are cultivated on the slopes of the Constantiaberg, where the early afternoon shade and prevailing ocean breezes cool the vineyards. The planting density is high on the steep slopes due to fertile granite soils with good water retention. White varieties are planted on the coolest south- and east-facing sites with reds on the warmer northeast-facing slopes. Extended skin contact on Sauvignon Blanc concentrates its delicate flavours to an intensely aromatic wine, showing typical cool-climate minerality and naturally crisp acidity. These factors together with extended lees maturation allows for full and complex wines. Extended skin contact during fermentation is applied on all the red cultivars promoting colour and flavour extraction. All red cultivars undergo a three-year barrel (French) maturation period, with the flagship wines receiving only 100 per cent new French oak.

ℹ Christine (Bdx blend: M / Cab S / Cab F) 🍇 Sauv Bl, Cab S / F, Merlot, Malbec 🕐 Mon–Fri 09:00–17:00, Sat 09:00–13:00. Closed publ hols 📞 +27 (0)21 794 5190 ✉ info@ buitenverwachting.com, www.buitenverwachting.com 🍷 Sauv Bl 3–5 y; Bdx Blend 8–15 y 🍷 Red 03, white 06 ℹ Older vintages available, tours by appt, restaurant (rated in Top 10 in SA), picnics, teddy bear fair 1 May

CONSTANTIA GLEN

Constantia Glen is located in the saddle of the Constantiaberg. This location offers an additional two hours of afternoon sunlight during the ripening period – allowing red varieties to ripen at high elevations. Decomposed granite with a high clay content allows dry-land cultivation. Vines are trellised due to strong southeasterly winds and particular attention is paid to ensuring virus-free vineyards. Sauvignon Blanc is cultivated on south-facing slopes, taking full advantage of the cooling effects of the nearby ocean. Bunches are harvested in the early morning and then cooled to protect delicate flavours. Three-months aging on the lees adds subtle weight to the fresh, tropical, mineral notes of this elegantly balanced wine. Red varieties are naturally fermented as whole berries before the wine is gently drained into barrels to complete malolactic fermentation. Each block or batch is crushed separately, presenting the winemaker with nearly 80 batches for blending after 12 months in oak. A further six months aging as a blend, results in a dense yet balanced wine with great finesse and strong mineral notes.

ℹ Constantia Glen (M, Cab S, Cab F, PV, Malb) 🍇 Sauv Bl, Cab S, Cab F, M, PV, Malb 🕐 By appt only 📞 +27 (0)21 795 6100 ✉ wine@constantiaglen.com, www.constantiaglen.com 🍷 White 5 y+, red 8 y+ 🍷 NA ℹ Spectacular views over False Bay, new plantings of fynbos and proteas

CONSTANTIA UITSIG

Vineyards have flourished at Constantia Uitsig since the 17th century, but the 1993 maiden vintage was the first to carry the Uitsig name. Grapes are harvested in the early hours of the morning (02:30–11:00) to preserve the delicate fruit flavours, while extended skin contact increases fruit extraction on Sauvignon Blanc. Sémillon receives seven months of wood maturation in second and third-fill, 225 litre French oak barrels, resulting in a fresh, well-balanced, structured wine. The unwooded Chardonnay, made oxidatively, shows varietal aromas and flavours. Constantia White Bordeaux (70% Sém, 30% Sauv Bl) is barrel fermented for seven months in old French oak, showing an intensity of flavours. The Constantia Red blend is oak matured for 15 months (70% new wood) to give lush, ripe fruit and soft, silky tannins and bottle matured (18 months) before release. In 2005, the first vinification of a *Méthode Cap Classique* (100% Chard) was fermented in 40 per cent old French oak. The wine is matured in bottle for 24 months before it is manually disgorged.

ℹ Constantia White (Sém/Sauv Bl) 🍇 Sauv Bl, Chard (unwooded); Sém, MCC, Red (M, Cab S, Cab F) 🕐 Mon–Fri 09:00–17:00, Sat & Sun 10:00–17:00. Closed Easter Fri, Dec 25, 26; Jan 1 📞 +27 (0)21 794 1810 ✉ thewineshop@uitsig.co.za, www.constantia-uitsig.com 🍷 White 3 y, red 6–7 y 🍷 White 01, 03 ℹ Three restaurants (Top 10 of SA), luxury hotel & spa, wine & gift shop, conference facilities, cookbook

GROOT CONSTANTIA

Simon van der Stel established Groot Constantia in the late 1600s. Today the granite soils and steep slopes of the Constantiaberg provide the setting for its 100 hectares of vines. White varieties are planted on high, south-facing slopes while reds, which are planted on the lower slopes, enjoy more sunlight exposure, developing intense colour and fruit flavours. With its close proximity to the Atlantic Ocean and the vineyards planted at high elevations (240 m), the vineyards are relatively cool, ensuring slow, even ripening. Red wines are fermented at high temperatures to maximise tannin extraction. The Bordeaux-style blend (Cabernet Sauvignon / Merlot / Cabernet Franc / Malbec) matures totally in new oak for 18 months, resulting in a powerful wine with a fine tannin structure. Chardonnay is barrel fermented to add complexity and richness to the wine. Due to the cool conditions, wines have great density, elegant dry tannins and a long finish.

Gouverneurs Range – Reserve (Bdx Blend: Cab S / Merlot / Malb), Shiraz & Chardonnay Cab S, Merlot, Shz, Chard, Cab S, Pinotage, Sauvignon Blanc Daily 09:00–18:00 (Dec–Apr); 09:00–17:00 (May–Nov). Closed Easter Fri, Dec 25, Jan 1 +27 (0)21 794 5128 cellar@grootconstantia.co.za, www.grootconstantia.co.za Red 5–12 y, white 2–3 y 05, 06 Tours on the hour, restaurant, picnics from restaurants, gift shop, conference venue, walks, museum

HIGH CONSTANTIA

An 1816 record reports High Constantia's first owner, Sebastiaan van Renen, as 'preparing to make vineyards.' Today 14,5 hectares are cultivated using a low planting density (3 333/ha) due to the steep slopes. Grapes for the MCC are hand picked during several visits to each vineyard. The whole bunches are cooled before pressing in a small bag press. Once settled, the clear juice completes alcoholic and malolactic fermentation. The base wine is bottled for secondary fermentation and matures for two to four years, and riddling is done by hand. The MCC shows brioche and anise aromas and a rich, concentrated character of yeast and mineral flavours with lively bubbles. Grapes for the red flagship are all hand harvested with Cabernet Sauvignon and Cabernet Franc each harvested from single vineyards. All parcels are processed separately: cool fermentation (22–26°C) retains the cassis and earthy aromas and wines are matured in French oak (100%) for up to 30 months. Prior to bottling the best barrels are blended, rendering a cool-climate earthy wine with vanilla, coffee and leather notes.

Clos Andre MCC (vintage), Sebastiaan (Bdx Blend) MCC, Rosé, Sauv Bl, Bdx Blend, Cab F, M, Cab S, Mal, PV By appt Mon–Fri 08:00–17:00. Closed Sat, Sun; publ hols +27 (0)21 794 7171 david@highconstantia.co.za, www.highconstantia.co.za Red 8–11 y, MCC 3 y 03, 06, 04 MCC tasting by appt

KLEIN CONSTANTIA

Klein Constantia has been lovingly restored to its former glory and is now home to Vin de Constance, South Africa's iconic sweet wine that has thrilled wine lovers for many years. Historically the vineyards form part of what was once Governor van der Stel's famous Constantia property, renowned in the courts of Europe for producing sweet and luscious wines in the mid-18th and early 19th century. Positioned on the Cape Peninsula, the vineyard is blessed with a maritime climate. Its southerly aspect, combined with altitude and proximity to the cold Atlantic Ocean, makes this an ideal *terroir* for the production of aromatic white grape varieties. Vin de Constance is made using Muscat de Frontignan harvested in raisin form towards the end of March each year. The raisins are macerated on their skins for several days to extract the rich fruit and honeyed aromas as well as to facilitate pressing. Fermentation and maturation takes place in 500 litre barrels.

Vin de Constance (sweet) Muscat F, Cab S / F, PV, Malb, Chard, Sauv Bl, R Riesl, Sém Mon–Fri 08:00–17:00, Sat 09:00–13:00. Closed publ hols +27 (0)21 794 5188 info@kleinconstantia.com, www.kleinconstantia.com Vin de Constance 10 y, Red 8 y, Riesling 10 y Sauv 95, 96, 04, 05; Riesl 95; Reds 01 Historic artefacts, magnificent wall hanging in tasting room

STEENBERG

Steenberg's 62 hectares of vines are spread along the eastern slopes of the Steenberg. The lower, clay-rich slopes (60–180 m) are exposed to early morning sun, which dries the grapes and prevents fungal diseases. Afternoon mountain shadows along with the ocean breezes create cool ripening conditions. Low vigour on decomposed granite soils results in naturally low yields. The upper granite slopes are planted to white varieties while the lower-lying areas are mainly red. Sauvignon Blanc is made through a reductive process with a 90-day lees contact. This aromatic wine shows typical cool-climate herbaceous and mineral flavours. The unconventional Catharina blend reflects Steenberg's signature Nebbiolo with minty, berry flavours. The aromatic barrel-fermented Sémillon benefits from wood fermentation, adding smoky notes to its rich citrus fruit. A small component of the Chardonnay for the 1682 Brut MCC is barrel fermented, enriching its mineral and biscuit flavours.

Magna Carta (Sém, Sauv Bl), Sauv Bl Reserve (sgl vineyard); Catharina (Cab S / F / M / Shz / Neb) Various Mon–Fri 09:00–16:30, Sat, Sun & Pub hols 10:00–16:00. Closed Easter Sun, Mon; Dec 25, Jan 1 +27 (0)21 713 2211 info@steenbrg.co.za, www.steenberg-vineyards.co.za White 4 y+, red 8 y+ Sauv 03, 04; Catharina 01, 02 Restaurant, hotel, cellar tours, bistro

Durbanville Pocket

Rolling hills – The vineyards of Durbanville enjoy varying sun epxoures

The Durbanville Pocket is made up of two open-ended tunnels between prominent, stand-alone north-south running hills known as Tygerberg (Eng. Tiger Mountain) and Kanonkop (Eng. Canon Head). The hilltops are elevated about 400 metres above sea level; however, the vineyards are concentrated mainly on lower east-facing slopes at altitudes of 100 to 350 metres, which enjoy long sunlight hours, assisting in the ripening of the grapes.

Historical reminder – A perfectly preserved slave bell from the late 1700s at Altydgedacht

Although its macroclimate is comparable to that of Stellenbosch, the Durbanville Pocket has a markedly cooler mesoclimate than neighbouring Pockets such as Paarl and Stellenbosch. The reason for this is unobstructed exposure to two oceans, the Atlantic (10 km) and False Bay (28 km), as well as the general high altitude of the vineyards (up to 350 m). Even though the mean February temperature is 22,4°C, the duration of this high temperature during the day is relatively short due to the dramatic cooling effect of prevailing summer breezes, taking effect from midday. This cooling effect may cause a decrease in temperature of as much as 5°C in vineyards exposed to the breezes compared to those sheltered between the hills.

The relatively cool mesoclimate permits the cultivation of all the noble varieties, but site selection is of great importance due to large variations in slope direction. In this way, cooler and warmer sites are created with the potential to ripen both heat-sensitive white varieties as well as hardy red varieties.

The annual rainfall is a mere 400 to 500 mm (15,7–19,7 in.) and due to the isolated nature of this range of hills, there are limited water catchment areas and restricted water storage potential. Due to the lack of irrigation water, special emphasis is placed on rootstock choice, selecting drought-resistant rootstocks. Most vineyards are cultivated dry-land with supplementary irrigation given in extremely hot conditions to prevent permanent damage to vines. Subsequently deep root development (to access underground water) is a major feature of vineyards in this area.

Geologically, Durbanville differs from all other high-lying coastal-zone vineyard areas as the parent soil material found here is phyllite and greywacke formations (see text box, this page). The dominant soils derived from these formations are highly weathered, reddish-brown and well drained with good water- and nutrient-retention properties. However, unlike typical Western Cape weathered soils, these are not acidic. Vineyards are cultivated without irrigation in an attempt to reduce excessive growth vigour on the fertile soils. With only a few exceptions, vines are spur pruned with emphasis on spacing of the shoots to ensure an open canopy.

The maritime moderating influences are reflected in the pronounced cool-climate characteristics of all the varieties, but in particular the sought-after Sauvignon Blanc grapes and wines. It has also been noted that wines from the Durbanville Pocket have a distinctive 'dustiness' on the nose. Sauvignon Blanc wines show expressive fruity, cool nettle and green fig flavours. Other white wines are very food friendly with a rich melon and citrus character, with

ROCK TYPES

Phyllite: Rocks which do not respond evenly to pressure and often have a distinctly wavy appearance

Greywacke: Sandstone generally characterised by hardness, dark colour and angular grains of quartz and small rock fragments

TERROIR

Soil: Shale, red granite, schist

Climate: Warm with ocean influence, sheltered sites, moderate rainfall

White varieties: Sauvignon Blanc, Chardonnay, Chenin Blanc

Red varieties: Cabernet Sauvignon, Merlot, Shiraz, Pinotage

Wine styles: Red, white

a Chardonnay offering from Diemersdal and aromatic Sémillon from Nitida. Reds (Merlot and Cabernet Sauvignon in particular) are finely textured and accessible, even from an early age. Durbanville Hills and Hillcrest are good examples. Altydgedacht's ripe Pinotage illustrates the heat collection to ripen this late variety in wind-sheltered sites.

The Philadelphia Pocket, just north of Durbanville, is drier and viticulture practices are aimed at water conservation as well as increased water efficiency. The ocean influence is still very prominent and textured reds as well as ripe, juicy whites are produced by Capaia and Havana Hills. Soil preparation before planting and soil surface maintenance are of utmost importance in this Pocket as well, to allow water into the soil and reduce run-off waste. Yields are naturally low (less than 10 tons/ha) due to the cultivation conditions and preference is given to red varieties.

Heart of gold – Vineyards share Durbanville with wheatfields

DRIVING ROUTE: DURBANVILLE

The Durbanville Pocket starts some distance (30 km) to the east of Cape Town. The N1 northbound takes you out of the city, curving eastward towards the winelands town of Paarl.

Take Exit 23 to the R302 Bellville/Durbanville. At the intersection, turn left to Willie van Schoor Road until it joins Durban Road, just past the Tyger Valley shopping centre. Turn left down Old Oak Road (M31) and right at the next traffic light onto Tygerbergvallei Road, driving in a northerly direction. As you leave the residential area, you pass through an archway of giant oak trees – a spectacular sight in late autumn when the leaves change colour.

Gentle aspects – A view from Tygerbergvallei Road towards the Durbanville Pocket

The first winery visit is Altydgedacht on the left. This beautiful traditional winery is a combination of old and modern, with a tranquil charm. A pond at the entrance to the tasting room hosts local bird life, many of which nest in the surrounding thickets. Remember your binoculars and bird book to note your sightings. Continuing northwards from Altydgedacht, you reach the T-junction of the R302 and the M13. This intersection is effectively in the middle of Altydgedacht's grounds, and owner Oliver Parker commented that if God would kindly perform one more miracle, it would be good if Altydgedacht could be removed from this urban jungle far out to the north ...

D'Aria – An old slave bell has been transformed into a peaceful pond at D'Aria

Large barrels – Large vats store wine but have little impact on the wood flavour (Altydgedacht)

Turn right at the traffic light and drive in an easterly direction. At the next set of traffic lights, turn left (north) on St John's Road (M48), past the local polo club and race course on the right. At the first traffic circle (roundabout), take the first exit and continue driving north on Vissershok Road to visit Meerendal. This historic property has been handsomely restored to its former glory by a group of wine enthusiasts. It now hosts not only a state-of-the-art winery, but also a tasting facility, restaurant, functions venue, deli and children's play area. The hill behind the winery has been set aside for conservation of the indigenous renosterveld.

Return to the traffic circle; take the first exit to the east on Vissershok Road. At the following traffic circle take the first exit, heading north on Koeberg Road (M58). This road runs more or less parallel to Vissershok Road. The next winery to visit is Diemersdal, the most northerly of the Durbanville wineries. The impressive white-washed entrance adorned by red irises bids visitors welcome.

Return along the same road to the T-junction close to Altydgedacht and continue westwards on the M13, towards the Atlantic Ocean. Only about 600 metres further is D'Aria on the left. The winery also boasts a lovely restaurant, Poplars, which specialises in matching this Pocket's wine with exquisite cuisine. Be sure to order their 'chocolate surprise' with your coffee.

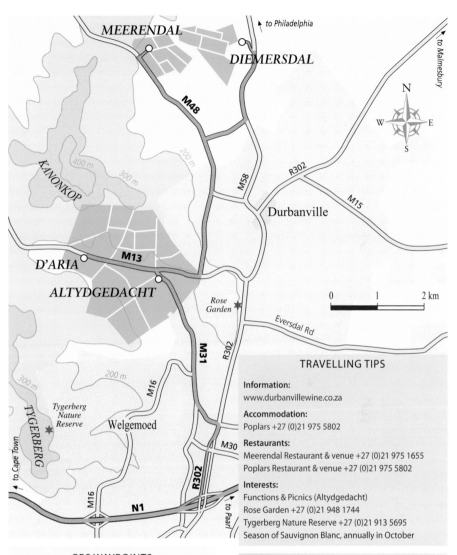

to Philadelphia

MEERENDAL

DIEMERSDAL

to Malmesbury

N

W E

S

M48

200 m

400 m

300 m

KANONKOP

M58

R302

M15

Durbanville

D'ARIA

M13

ALTYDGEDACHT

Rose
Garden

Eversdal Rd

0 1 2 km

M31

R302

300 m

200 m

M16

Tygerberg
Nature
Reserve

Welgemoed

M30

TYGERBERG

to Cape Town

M16

N1

R302

to Paarl

TRAVELLING TIPS

Information:
www.durbanvillewine.co.za

Accommodation:
Poplars +27 (0)21 975 5802

Restaurants:
Meerendal Restaurant & venue +27 (0)21 975 1655
Poplars Restaurant & venue +27 (0)21 975 5802

Interests:
Functions & Picnics (Altydgedacht)
Rose Garden +27 (0)21 948 1744
Tygerberg Nature Reserve +27 (0)21 913 5695
Season of Sauvignon Blanc, annually in October

GPS WAYPOINTS

Altydgedacht S33° 50.691 E18° 37.536
D'Aria S33° 50.433 E18° 36.555
Diemersdal S33° 48.055 E18° 38.399
Meerendal S33° 48.169 E18° 37.173

The restaurant's tranquil garden is set
amongst grandiose poplar trees and even has
a boule (petanque) court. The cottages are
also very popular.

Sun exposure – *Vineyards are planted on various aspects of the
Durbanville hills to ensure optimum ripeness*

ALTYDGEDACHT

The Parker family has farmed Altydgedacht since 1852 – an astounding six generations – with an unbroken 157-year winemaking tradition. Altydgedacht was one of the early wheat, wine and stock farms established in the late 1600s to supply ships sailing to the East. One hundred and seventy hectares of vines are cultivated on heavy clay and gravel soils on the gently sloping hills. Late summer mist and close proximity to the Atlantic Ocean contribute to cooler ripening conditions and cultivars are sited according to their heat preference. Intensive canopy management, including leaf removal and a vertical extended canopy, increase sunlight exposure, promoting flavour and colour development. The cool ripening conditions allow the grapes to hang longer than the norm, leading to more fruit-driven wine. The flagship Pinotage is from a single vineyard, made in a New World style with upfront fruit and ripe, juicy tannins. Altydgedacht is also known for Sauvignon Blanc, Barbera and a dry Alsace-style Gewürztraminer.

ℹ️ Pinotage, Gewürz 🍇 Pin, Barb, Sauv Bl, Gewürz 🕐 Mon–Fri 09:00–17:00, Sat 09:00–15:00. Closed Easter, Dec 25, 26; Jan 1 ☎ +27 (0)21 976 1295 ✉ altydgedacht@mweb.co.za, www. altydgedacht.co.za 📧 8+ y 💰 99, 01, 02 ℹ️ hands-on winery, rustic atmosphere, daytime restaurant & picnic (booking req.)

DIEMERSDAL

Diemersdal's beautifully preserved Cape Dutch architecture, built in the early 1800s, reflects the meticulous care taken by six generations of the Louw family winemakers. A special feature is the cultivation of northern, southern and eastern slopes on the gentle hills of the Dorstberg. With the cooling effect from the Atlantic Ocean and early evening mist, vines are trellised closer to the soil surface to maximise radiant heat for full ripeness. The high rainfall (700 mm) combined with the good water retention of decomposed granite soils makes dry-land cultivation possible. These favourable conditions increase growth vigour in the vine, allowing a higher grape yield of eight tons per hectare to be harvested while grapes ripen uniformly and develop concentrated varietal flavours. The approach of minimum intervention conserves the prominent varietal character of white wines, with extended lees contact adding a rich mouthfeel to the lingering fresh natural acidity. Traditional open fermenters are used for the red wines, enhancing the natural flavours and softening grape tannins.

ℹ️ Private Collection (Cab S / M, Cab F), Sauvignon Bl (sgl vineyard) 🍇 Shz, Cab S, P, Sauv Bl, Chard, M, PV, Mal, Mouv, Gren 🕐 Mon–Fri 09:00–17:00, Sat 09:00–15:00. Closed Easter, Dec 25, Jan 1 ☎ +27 (0)21 976 3361 ✉ wines@diemersdal. co.za, www.diemersdal.co.za 📧 8 y ℹ️ Traditional architecture, BYO picnics, walks

Wall of memories – The historical wall surrounding the Altydgedacht property, with a 300-year winemaking history

Cape Dutch architecture – The lovingly maintained manor house at Diemersdal

Chocolate box – The ever-popular coffee accompaniment at D'Aria's restaurant

Aerial view – Paragliding over the pristine Meerendal vineyards illustrates the importance of row direction and sun exposure

D'ARIA

First established in 1698, D'Aria was born from the 1998/99 merger of Springfield and Doordekraal farms. Today it stands as a proud member of the Durbanville Wine Valley. Owned by a consortium of BEE companies, the farm has become a wine-tourist destination, incorporating viticulture, winery, restaurant, tasting room and cottages.

Of the 80 hectares, approximately 60 have been planted to vines, exploiting a variety of slopes as well as valley positions that the area offers. Aspects vary with the slopes, but are mostly east-facing (less sun exposure) and north-facing (warmer due to more sun exposure), and row directions follow the contours. The sandy clay soils have a high growth potential and vineyards are cultivated dry-land (without any irrigation). Sauvignon Blanc for the flagship is planted on a pocket containing more limestone, giving a fresh minerality to the resulting wine. Although the onshore wind from the nearby Atlantic Ocean has a cooling effect, it can potentially damage the vines and a combination of trellised vines and bush vines is cultivated.

Grapes are hand harvest and sorted before crushing into small stainless steel fermenters. White wines are fermented cold (16°C) to preserve the delicate grassy and gooseberry notes. The red blend (Merlot/Cab S) is matured in  a combination of French and American oak for up to 18 months. The components are aged separately and return to barrel after the final blend is made to ensure a well-integrated wine. It offers red berry fruit with smoky tannins and a minty undertone. The Shiraz shows distinctive cool climate white pepper and fine tannins. The Sauvignon Blanc is made in a more grassy style with fresh acidity and citrus notes

Poplars – Local produce offers seasonally inspired dining at D'Aria restaurant

Songbird Sauvignon Blanc Blend (M / Cab S), Sauv Bl, Shz Mon–Fri 10:00–18:00, Sat & Sun 10:00–16:00 +27 (0)21 801 6772 tasting@daria.co.za, www.daria.co.za Sauv Bl 1 y Restaurant, cottages, venue (functions)

MEERENDAL

Meerendal was first granted to Jan Meerland in 1702 and by 1712 his widow Christina Stans had established 60 000 vines on the farm. The 1969 vintage carried the Meerendal name on the label for the first time. Today, 100 hectares of vines are cultivated on surrounding hills with various aspects providing interesting mesoclimatic nuances. The shale soils have a high clay content as well as a layer of underlying small rocks, ensuring very good water retention that facilitates dry-land viticulture even with the relatively low annual rainfall. The rock layer further serves to keep the soil cool during the ripening season. The nearby cold Atlantic Ocean, only 10 kilometres away, ensures slow, even ripening conditions. However, it is the age of the vines that provides the greatest influence on the elegant style and concentration of flavours.

The Prestige Range consists of five wines: grapes from selected rows of Sauvignon Blanc are barrel fermented giving a rich white wine with crisp acidity and lime characteristics; a Heritage Block Pinotage produced from one of the oldest existing bush vines Pinotage vineyards (planted in 1955) in South Africa; and a single vineyard Shiraz. In addition, there is a natural sweet Chenin Blanc and an MCC sparkling wine. The nearby hills are newly planted to Sauvignon Blanc, Pinot Noir and Chardonnay, taking full advantage of the cool location.

Grapes are all hand harvested. Strict reductive techniques protect the young wine from oxidation and extended lees maturation (4 months) yields a deeply rich and aromatic white wine. Red wines are made in traditional open fermenters and matured for 12 to 15 months in new and second-fill French barrels. Silky tannins support the bitter chocolate and cherry fruit of the Merlot, while the Shiraz is typified by juicy tannins and black pepper notes.

Renosterveld – Meerendal's conservation area includes the highly sensitive natural fynbos Renosterveld, seen here covering most of the hill

Sauvignon Blanc, Shiraz, Heritage Block Pinotage, Nat Sweet, MCC Sauv Bl, Chard, Chenin B, M, P, Shz, Cab S, Cab/M Mon–Sun 08:00–17:00. Closed Easter Fri, Dec 25 +27 (0)21 975 1655 info@meerendal.co.za, www.meerendal.co.za Sauv 4 y, Reds 7 y, Prestige reds 10–15 y 84, 94, 98, 00, 03, 05 Wine and food destination, restaurant, bistro, deli, functions venue, children's facilities

Stellenbosch Area

Oldest town – Founded in 1679, Stellenbosch is South Africa's oldest town, after Cape Town (seen from Remhoogte)

Stellenbosch could well be regarded as the wine capital of South Africa. Hosting more private cellars than any other Cape wine area, Stellenbosch is also home to the country's largest wine and spirit producer, Distell, and the centre of viticultural and oenological research and training.

Located on 34° South latitude, the town is about 40 kilometres from Cape Town and 10 kilometres from the coast, with an elevation of approximately 300 metres above sea level. Founded in 1679 by Simon van der Stel, Stellenbosch is the second oldest town in South Africa (after Cape Town) and has become a premier tourist destination. Its colourful history is reflected in the neo-Dutch, Georgian and modern Victorian architecture, encompassing simple lines, fine detail and elegant proportions. The fertile valley was diversely cultivated to supply fresh produce to the visiting ships for their long voyages to the East. Stellenbosch is also the oldest wine route in South Africa, drawing wine lovers and tourists from around the world. More than 100 wineries are open to the public, all within easy reach of the town centre. Almost all classic varietals are represented here except, to a lesser degree, some sweeter wines, where areas like the Orange River, the West Coast, the Klein Karoo as well as Worcester and Robertson, are better known.

Following closely behind Worcester and Paarl in terms of area under vine, the Stellenbosch area includes various mesoclimates, aspects, elevations and soil types. It also has the advantage of frontage onto False Bay. The Cape Doctor (prevailing southeasterly wind) works its magic here, keeping vines cool and helping to control diseases by reducing relative humidity in the vine canopy. These factors allow wine production across the stylistic range, accounting for approximately 6,5 per cent of South Africa's total wine production.

Although many vines stretch up the

mountain slopes, the lower, undulating hills are a carpet of vineyards. Even though land here is among the most expensive in the Cape Winelands, it does not deter winemakers from innovation and cutting-edge experimentation. The holy grail of *terroir* is chased by all. Specific attributes characterising the wines, the reds especially, are already discernible in many *terroir* Pockets.

Although many of the farms have been handed down through generations, foreign investors are boosting local development. Many wineries offer tours and wine tasting to visitors and settings range from the old-world charm of historic estates to large high-tech wineries, small family-owned boutique cellars and garagiste producers. With rolling hills and towering mountains as a backdrop and the ever-changing colour of the vineyards, the landscapes are constantly transformed. Harvesting is from late January to early April, when the smell of ripe grapes laces the air, creating an atmosphere of excitement. A drive around Stellenbosch and its Wine Pockets offers some of the best views of South Africa's stunning Winelands as well as festive gastronomical trips.

The town

The best way to explore the town is on foot as the narrow streets offer little parking space. Wandering around, you will find meticulously

Aspect – Bush vines on the lower slopes of Simonsberg

restored buildings. The giant oak trees lining the streets gave Stellenbosch the affectionate name of 'Eikestad' – town of oaks. The historical architecture, parks and gardens contribute to its tranquil beauty. Stellenbosch has a small-town aura with a rich lifestyle in which music and the arts thrive. The Information Bureau supplies maps, contact details and opening times of most attractions. Many attractions are centred on Dorp, Andringa and Ryneveld Streets with various arts and crafts stalls, coffee shops and fine restaurants.

Dining out in Stellenbosch is a special experience, whether alfresco under the oaks or the stars, or indoors in cosy, yet luxurious surroundings. From traditional Cape fare and European cuisine to the more exotic, there is something to tantalise the taste buds of even the most discerning diner. Restaurants and other eateries range from elegant Cape Dutch manors and country cottages to sidewalk cafés and fine dining establishments.

Local interests

The mountains and hills surrounding the town offer unequalled opportunities for hiking, cycling, mountaineering and other adventure activities. For the wildlife enthusiast, there are several opportunities for encounters with animals, with parks, sanctuaries and reserves. Many wineries offer lunch, picnic baskets or dinner. Staying in one of the many Wine Pockets is an experience in its own right – see individual Pockets and Winery Profiles for more details. Township experiences in the areas of Kayamandi, Jamestown and Cloetesville are arranged at the tourist information centre.

Educational

The University of Stellenbosch was founded in 1918 as a premier educational institution.

A century-long tradition of quality education and research has ensured the university a place among the finest academic institutions. The Department of Viticulture and Oenology, alongside the Institute for Wine Biotechnology, is the home of world-class wine research and cutting-edge technological development. Other institutions include the Cape Institute for Agricultural Training at Elsenburg and the Cape Wine Academy offering wine appreciation courses.

Stellenbosch *terroir*

The Stellenbosch landscape is generally characterised by remnant rugged sandstone overlaying granite plutons (forming the sloped foothills), exposed granite outcrops (giving rise to ranges of fairly high hills up to 400 m) as well as occasional shale. The close proximity of the ocean (about 25 km), with the cooling effect of summer sea breezes, ensures a macroclimate that is appreciably cooler than normally associated with latitudes of 33°55" to 34°10". The average summer daytime temperature is around 20°C. The pronounced topographic and altitude variation further modifies the macroclimate, resulting in very different meso- or topoclimates for different Pockets in the area, all benefiting to some degree from sea breeze effects.

The most dominant soils of the Stellenbosch area are derived from granite and are usually situated on the higher hills

> ### TERROIR
>
> **Soils:** Granitic foothills, exposed granite outcrops, shale
>
> **Climate:** Warm with ocean influence, sheltered sites, moderate rainfall
>
> **White varieties:** Chenin Blanc, Sauvignon Blanc, Chardonnay, Sémillon
>
> **Red varieties:** Cabernet Sauvignon, Merlot, Shiraz, Pinotage, Cabernet Franc
>
> **Wine styles:** Red, white, sparkling, dessert, fortified

> ### TRAVELLING TIPS
>
> **Information:**
> www.wineroute.co.za
>
> **Events:**
> Stellenbosch Wine Festival – annually in August
>
> **Natural environment:**
> The best panoramic view of the mountains surrounding Stellenbosch is seen from the lower end of Merriman Street (near the train station). To the south is first the Helderberg and then Stellenboschberg (1 175 m) with the narrow Jonkershoek Valley. To the north of this valley are the clearly discernible Pieke (twin peaks 1 494 m). The mighty Simonsberg (1 390 m) is connected to Botmanskop and the Jonkershoekberg at the saddle of Helshoogte, leading to Franschhoek.

and mountain foothills. As a result of climatic conditions during their historical formation (rapid weathering, high leaching conditions) and age (c. 50 Ma), these soils are a relic of the geological past and unique in the sense that they are acidic, acidity increasing with depth. These granite soils are yellowish to reddish-brown, with medium to high clay content. The good physical properties of the soil, as well as water drainage and holding capacity, makes dry-land (without irrigation) viticulture possible.

Pockets predominantly characterised by these granite soils are Stellenbosch Kloof, Devon Valley, Klapmuts-Simondium and those located on the Simonsberg (Helshoogte, Stellenbosch-Simonsberg, etc.). More strongly structured and duplex soils derived from granite and shale are features of Pockets like Polkadraai, Stellenbosch West, Helderberg Annandale, Helderberg Blaauwklippen and Bottelary. The Pockets of Jonkershoek, Helderberg and Schapenberg have, in addition to granitic soils, a fair amount of well-weathered yellow or reddish-brown soils and some residual soils derived from shale, with remnants of the parent rock material often still very evident.

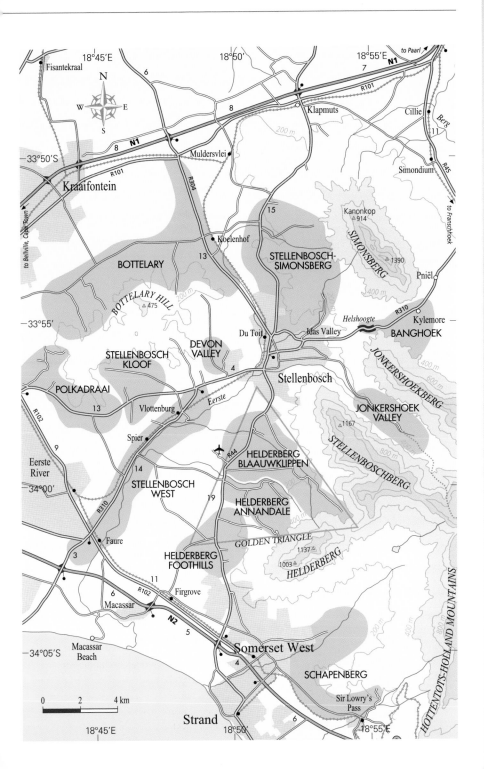

Polkadraai Pocket

Polkadraai – Follow the gentle, winding roads through the vineyards of Polkadraai

Polkadraai is situated directly west of Stellenbosch and borders the suburb of Kuils River. The Pocket lies close to False Bay (12–15 km) and benefits greatly from cooling summer sea breezes and early morning mist, which create a considerably cooler mesoclimate than the general macroclimate would indicate.

Family welcome – A sign outside Raats Family Wines

The Pocket's *terroir* is characterised by hilly topography and subsequently varying elevations, providing sites on elevations of 60 to 400 metres. Slopes face predominantly south and southwest, favourably exposing vineyards to the cooling effect of the ocean. Some well-protected north-facing slopes are slightly warmer and are planted with red varieties.

Guinea fowl – The 'official bird' of Saxenburg

The layered soils vary from granite-based on the higher elevated positions (150–400 m), to shallow, sandy soils in lower-lying areas. Lime additions are required to neutralise the acidity of these medium-potential soils. Particular effort is made to ensure deep preparation on virgin soils, in order to improve the physical and chemical properties before planting new vines. Polkadraai's changing cultivation conditions necessitate variation in viticultural practices: from low, untrellised bush vine- to upright vertical trellises. Best known for its solidly structured red wines, Polkadraai hosts many of the classic French varieties. The wines have a moderate alcohol (Alc. 13% by Vol.+) and a distinct spiciness, often combined with scents of herbs. Shiraz is very popular with spicy and powerful wines from Saxenburg, Zevenwacht as well as biodynamic producer Reyneke. This spiciness also shows strongly in the Cape Blend (Shz / Cab S) from Nico van der Merwe. The Bein Merlot is inspired by the famous Château Petrus, in the classic restrained style with a more powerful mid-palate than generally found in South Africa. De Toren's Fusion V is a blend of the classic five Bordeaux varieties, showing scents of herbs. Amani, situated on an isolated sandy patch, produces fruity Chardonnay and Merlot.

DRIVING ROUTE: POLKADRAAI

From the intersection of the R44 and Dorp Street, drive west and join the R310 (Adam Tas Road), leaving the town in a westerly direction. About four kilometres out of town, the R310 turns left (south) towards the N2 freeway, and from there, the M12 continues in a westerly direction. When you reach the Polkadraai farm stall on the right (11 km from town), turn left onto Vlaeberg Road. A few metres down the road, on the left-hand side,

is the boutique winery, Raats Family Wines. Bruwer Raats is nurturing Chenin Blanc and Cabernet Franc vines as he believes that, since no New World country has yet taken 'ownership' of these varieties, South Africa may well be the one to specialise in them.

Rejoin the M12, turn left and head west for a kilometre as the road rises again. On the crest, turn right at the sign indicating Bein Private Cellar. Just off the M12, take the first right turn. The second building (on the right) hosts the quaint boutique winery of Bein, exclusively producing Pomerol-style Merlot.

GPS WAYPOINTS

Bein Private Cellar S33° 57.729 E18° 44.061
Jacobsdal S33° 58.101 E18 43.569
Nico van der Merwe Wines S33° 56.827 E18° 43.149
Raats Family Wines S33° 58.252 E18° 44.845
Saxenburg S33° 56.827 E18° 43.149
Zevenwacht S33° 55.756 E18° 43.755

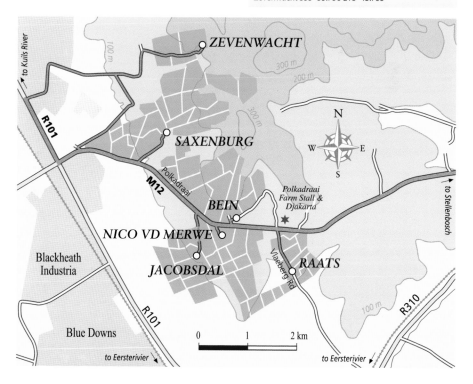

Return to the M12 to continue to tour. On the M12, Saxenburg's winemaker, Nico van der Merwe produces his own label, Nico van der Merwe Wines. A new tasting centre welcomes visitors to savour wines at their leisure. The M12 rises over the last hill to a spectacular view of Somerset West, False Bay and the suburbs of Cape Town. Turn left to visit Jacobsdal. Here only traditional methods are used and you are likely to taste with owner / winemaker Cornelius Dumas.

At the bottom of the hill is the entrance of Saxenburg on the right. A miniature game reserve flanks the driveway with small antelope roaming in camps. Premium wine producer, Saxenburg focuses on single varietal wines and its range includes a sparkling and a sweet dessert wine. It also boasts a lovely restaurant, Guinea Fowl, famous for its fish dishes and its own cookbook.

TRAVELLING TIPS

Information:
www.polkadraaihills.co.za

Accommodation:
Bein Guest Cottage +27 (0)21 881 3025
Zevenwacht Country Inn and Cottages
+27 (0)21 903 5123, reservations@zevenwacht.co.za

Restaurants:
Guinea Fowl Restaurant (Saxenburg)
+27 (0)21 906 5232
Djakarta Restaurant +27 (0)21 881 3243
Zevenwacht Restaurant +27 (0)21 903 5257,
restaurant@zevenwacht.co.za

Interests:
Cheese: Zevenwacht tasting room
Chef school: Zevenwacht + 27 (0)21 906 1033,
chefschool@zevenwacht.co.za
Djakarta: Antiques, pottery, palms, roses
Scenic donkey walks with wine tasting and snacks
Book 2 days in advance @ Bein Wine
Polkadraai farm stall +27 (0)21 881 3303
Fresh, seasonal produce
Pick your own strawberries.

BEIN PRIVATE CELLAR

Bein Private Cellar, located on the hills overlooking False Bay, produces wine from a tiny Merlot vineyard (2,2 ha). According to the Beins, it is the 'smallest professional winery in South Africa'. Soils of highly weathered granite on a gentle south-facing hill combine with ocean influences, providing a *terroir* suited to Merlot. The early morning mist and cool air ensures a slower, extended ripening period (of fruit flavours and tannins) without excessive alcohol. Ripening status is determined by infrared photography, and is harvested accordingly. Flagship Merlot is made from a single block and blended with a small percentage of Cabernet Sauvignon. The wine, made in the classic Pomerol style, has tremendous fruit concentration and elegance. Crushed grapes are cold soaked and fermented at a higher temperature (30°C) to concentrate flavours. A twelve-month maturation in a combination of new (40%), second and third-fill French barrels gives a well-rounded tannin structure to this elegant wine.

ℹ️ Bein Merlot 🏔️ M 🅾️ By appt only 🔗 +27 (0)21 881 3025
📧 lib@beinwine.com, www.beinwine.com 🍷 5–8 y
🍾 03, 05, 08 ℹ️ One of the smallest production cellars, great views, scenic donkey walks with wine tasting and snacks on mountain top (booking req), environmentally friendly

RAATS FAMILY WINES

Raats Family Wine crafts world-class wines from Chenin Blanc and Cabernet Franc. While their own vineyards develop, grapes are sourced from selected soil-specific sites. Chenin Blanc on sandstone soils offers mid-palate weight and structure with white and yellow fruit, whereas decomposed granite soils give the wine more lime, citrus, minerality and high acidity with freshness. Grapes for the Raats Chenin are sourced from three sites in Stellenbosch with an unusual sandstone-over-granite soil and very old vines (40 y+). Raats Original Chenin is harvested from individual sandstone and granite locations, fermented separately and then blended. The Cabernet Franc is grown only on granite soils, all in the Bottelary and Polkadraai Pockets. To achieve dense colour and overcome uneven ripening, the Cabernet Franc is allowed only one bunch per shoot. The grapes are given cold maceration (7 days) and fermented dry with regular pump-overs to extract maximum colour. Eighteen months maturation, using only 20 per cent new wood, results in a full, structured palate of red and black berry fruit, a typical five spice (cinnamon, clove) with a velvety, soft finish.

ℹ️ Chenin Blanc, Cabernet Franc 🏔️ Chenin Bl, Cab F 🅾️ By appt 🔗 +27 (0)21 881 3078 📧 braats@mweb.co.za, www. raats.co.za 🍷 White 4–6 y, red 6–10 y 🍾 Cab F 01, 04, 07; Chenin 04, 06

Chenin Blanc

According to local advocates, Chenin Blanc is South Africa's only shot at a world-class white wine as South African Chenin Blanc can rival such greats as white Burgundy, Sauvignon Blanc from the Loire and New Zealand. The two quality factors counting in its favour are the existence of very old vines (50 y+) as well as the inherent quality potential of bush (goblet) vines.

Compared to the Loire Valley, which frequently does not have sufficient warmth to ripen Chenin properly, South Africa has adequate sun exposure, a variation of sites (soil types), elevation and rainfall, as well as close proximity to the ocean. Prime locations are the Helderberg foothills (ocean proximity), Paardeberg (elevation and coolness) and the Malmesbury area (potential coolness for extended ripeness). Although more Chenin Blanc is uprooted than newly planted, this variety is still the most widely cultivated in South Africa with 19 per cent planted to the total vineyard area. The largest plantings are found in the Klein Karoo (32%), Paarl (16,6%) Malmesbury (22,7%), Orange River (16,9%) and Worcester (14,5%).

Chenin Blanc grows easily and bears well under most circumstances; however, due to its thin skin, humid conditions during ripening can cause rot. This versatile grape produces white wines (sweet to bone dry), still and sparkling wines as well as brandy and spirits. South Africa has determined four main style groups: (1) fresh and fruity; (2) rich and ripe, often with some oak maturation; (3) oaked, and (4) sweet.

Research on Chenin Blanc (ARC Infruitec-Nietvoorbij 2000 – 2005) found that ester levels (flavour compounds) and wine quality increase in wines made from riper grapes (24°B). Also, Chenin achieves optimal ripeness at between 21°B and 24°B (210 – 240 g/l sugar), possibly closer to the higher degree of sugar. Berry size is often reduced by pruning or restricting irrigation, since smaller berries produce higher quality wines. Furthermore direct sunlight on grapes is avoided, as grapes which ripen under indirect sunlight conditions produce higher quality wines. Choice of yeast strains as well as enzyme treatment (clarification of juice) are vital and it seems that the combination of the two produces more intense characters, better body and better overall wine quality. Examination of shelf life found that oxygen management after fermentation, up to and during bottling, is essential. To retain its fruitiness and limit the formation of bottle-aged characters, Chenin wines should be stored at temperatures below 10°C.

Internationally, there is admiration for the best South African Chenins, but also dismay at fine grapes lost by inclusion in mediocre, multi-variety blends. A significant development is the formation of the Chenin Blanc Association, an endeavour by producers devoted to enhancing both the quality and image of the variety. It is widely recognised that restricting yields and picking at a later, riper stage assures fuller flavour development. In the cellar, winemakers experiment with oak, including both new and older wood for fermentation, for aging.

South Africa is excited to have its Chenin Blanc returned to its rightful place among the world's best and most widely admired wines.

JACOBSDAL WINES

The Dumas family has been making wine on Jacobsdal, on the slopes of the Polkadraai Hills (10 km from False Bay), for three generations. Today the Old-World charm of this exclusively red wine producer still entices visitors. Of the 260 hectares, 92 hectares are planted to vines, with most being cultivated as bush vines. With the close proximity of the ocean, the granite-based soils allow for dry-land cultivation and, when combined with the age of the vines (35 y+), the vineyards produce low yields of high quality grapes. Since Jacobsdal crushed its first Pinotage vintage in 1974, the farm has used only natural yeasts and ferments in open cement tanks. Towards the end of fermentation, the free-run juice is drained off, completing fermentation without skin contact. The free-run juice then completes malolactic fermentation naturally as well, before being transferred to barrels for maturation. Once maturation is complete, the barrels are blended to create a silky yet densely flavoured Pinotage with gentle tannins. To ensure wines are consumed at their best, each wine is only released three years after its vintage date.

[i] P, Cab S ◯ Not open to public, tasting by appt only. No sales on farm, Bergkelder & liquor stores ☎ +27 (0)21 881 3336 ✉ info@jacobsdal.co.za, www. jacobsdal.co.za ▬ 10 y ▬ 94, 95, 01, 04

NICO VAN DER MERWE WINES

Nico van der Merwe's Mas Nicolas is a smoulderingly dense wine of Polkadraai Shiraz and Simonsberg Cabernet Sauvignon. Mature Shiraz vines (30 y+), cultivated on dry-land in decomposed granite, yield the deeply coloured and concentrated spicy fruit. Cabernet Sauvignon gives structure to the blend. Hand-harvested grapes are fermented *sans* sulphur in open-top vessels. Regular punch-downs and extended skin contact (up to three weeks) ensure maximum extraction for complexity. After pressing, free-run and press juice are combined and the young wine is transferred to barrels for maturation. Components are blended and bottled after a coarse filtration and light fining. Van der Merwe believes Cab / Shiraz is the Cape Blend and, without Pinotage, can deliver the elegance and richness of Cape *terroir* fruit. The seamless white blend (Sauv Bl / Sém) shows gooseberries and peaches with subtle oak. The Sémillon (ex-Schapenberg) is oak fermented and matured on its lees, while the unwooded Sauvignon Blanc adds a crisp, fresh acidity. The new cellar will host its maiden vintage in 2010 and the 2008 Blanc de Blanc MCC is also due for release in the World Cup year.

[i] Mas Nicolas (Cab S / Shz) ▦ Cab S, M, Shz, Sauv Bl, Sém ◯ By appt only ☎ +27 (0)21 881 3063 ✉ wilhelmshof@xsinet. co.za ▬ 10 y ▬ 00 [i] New cellar and tasting facilities

ZEVENWACHT

Harold and Denise Johnson acquired Zevenwacht in 1992 and created a leading wine-tourism destination, incorporating conference and wedding facilities, a restaurant and accommodation. Fine wine, however, remains the heartbeat of this historical farm.

One-hundred-and-twenty hectares are planted in an amphitheatre facing False Bay, which provides moderate summer temperatures. White varieties enjoy the cooler south- and southwest-facing slopes on elevations to 350 metres above sea level. The decomposed granite soil ensures good moisture retention and east – west row directions protect against midday heat. The warmer north- and west-facing areas (150–200 m above sea level) have a higher sand content and are cultivated to red varieties. Mature vines (10–20 y) ensure that the resulting wines are concentrated and have the ability to age for many years. A dense canopy protects sensitive Sauvignon Blanc grapes, whereas Chenin Blanc and red varieties are pruned for a less dense canopy, requiring more sun during ripening. The flagship white, 360° Sauvignon Blanc, is hand harvested from a single vineyard. Reductive winemaking is follwed by six months of lees contact and a small percentage of barrel fermentation resulting in a greener, herbaceous wine with hints of white asparagus, rocket and green tropical fruits.

Red grapes are cooled before crushing and are fermented in open-top fermenters. Following extended maceration on the skins, the wine is aged in oak barrels, providing a soft tannin structure supporting the fruit flavours. The Syrah is partially naturally fermented together with Viognier skins and aged in French oak barrels, resulting in a dense, perfumed wine with a strong Rhône influence.

Amphitheatre – Early morning mist from False Bay enfolds Zevenwacht, nestled in an amphitheatre of hills

[i] Syrah, 360° Sauvignon Blanc ▦ Sauv Bl, Chenin, Gewürz, Sém, P, M, Shz, Cab S ◯ Mon – Fri 08:30–17:00, Sat & Sun 09:30–17:00. Closed Dec 25 ☎ +27 (0)21 903 5123 ✉ info@zevenwacht.co.za, www.zevewacht.co.za ▬ Red 5–10 y, white 18 months ▬ Red 06, white 07 [i] Cheesery, conference facilities, picnics (booking rec.), accommodation, hotel, weddings (booking req.), restaurant, gift shop, Mangwanani African Day Spa

SAXENBURG

Africa was still a wild and untamed place when Joachim Sax first settled on the hills above the Kuils River, some 30 kilometres east of the Dutch settlement at the Cape of Good Hope. In 1693 Sax was one of only 350 free burghers (free farmers) granted land by Governor Simon van der Stel. He set about planting vines, and built the original manor house in 1701. Four years later, the farm was sold to Olaff and Albertus Bergh. Saxenburg developed from these early pioneers.

Almost three centuries passed before this historic farm was acquired by the Bührer family from Switzerland. Along with their close working team, they have revived the proud family tradition of Saxenburg's historic past. Fulfilling a wish to have a sister vineyard in France, the family acquired the 16th-century Château Capion near Montpellier (Languedoc) in 1996, where the same passion and single-minded dedication see fine wines being grown.

Fine dining – Caramelised almond purvey at Guinea Fowl restaurant

Colour therapy – Bright yellow contrasts the crisp white table linen

Situated between the Atlantic and Indian Oceans, Saxenburg enjoys moderate climatic conditions aided by cool ocean breezes during the summer months. Ninety hectares (of 200) are cultivated. Vines are planted on the surrounding hills with aspects from southwest to northwest, on fertile, decomposed granite and red gravel soils. The maritime influence and prevailing winds (south and southwest) create cool ripening conditions for the grapes without damaging the young shoots. Maximising this cooling effect, heat-sensitive grapes like Sauvignon Blanc, Chardonnay and Merlot are planted on the cooler southern side of the farm, while varieties with greater heat requirements (Cabernet Sauvignon, Shiraz) are planted on the warmer southwestern side, receiving more sunlight hours.

The lower relative daytime temperatures result in slower, more even ripening of grapes and a higher level of natural acid at harvest. Vineyard management is focused on restricting vigorous growth and achieving more concentration in the grapes. Vines are trellised and planted to a higher density of 3 600 vines per hectare on the fertile soils. Supplementary irrigation is only applied in very warm conditions to prevent damage to the plants. Summer pruning and suckering improve airflow around the vines to reduce humidity and disease in the canopy. The dense wines reflect the maturity of the vines (12 y+), with the exception of Chenin Blanc, which is almost 30 years old.

Capturing the wind – Saxenburg's vineyards have an uninterrupted view over the Atlantic Ocean while the rolling hills catch the afternoon breeze

Harvested grapes are fermented in open-top vessels *sans* sulphur. Selected yeast cultures and a high fermentation temperature (30°C) are used, particularly on the Shiraz, resulting in deeply coloured wines. Another two to four weeks of maceration is allowed after fermentation is completed to ensure that the colour and flavour components are stabilised and excessive tannins are precipitated out. Malolactic fermentation is completed in barrel (only from selected blocks) and in tank before the wines are matured for 18 months, using only about 40 per cent new wood. A percentage of American oak (up to 40 per cent) alongside the French oak gives a slight vanilla note and sweet tannins only for the Shiraz. The wines are generally powerful and dense with riper alcohol levels, requiring some cellaring.

Rare find – The Guinea Fowl restaurant serves fresh seafood, game and a variety of guinea fowl dishes rarely found elsewhere

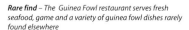

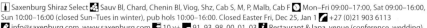
Saxenburg Shiraz Select Sauv Bl, Chard, Chenin Bl, Viog, Shz, Cab S, M, P, Malb, Cab F Mon–Fri 09:00–17:00, Sat 09:00–16:00, Sun 10:00–16:00 (closed Sun–Tues in winter), pub hols 10:00–16:00. Closed Easter Fri, Dec 25, Jan 1 +27 (0)21 903 6113 info@saxenburg.com, www.saxenburg.com 10 y+ 91, 93, 98, 00, 01, 03 Restaurant & lapa, venue (conference, wedding), olive oil, small game park, French sister-chateau wines available

Stellenbosch Kloof Pocket

Vantage point – From Jordan, you can see the picturesque Stellenbosch Kloof, nestled between the folds of the Bottelary Hills

The Stellenbosch Kloof Pocket is nestled in a valley on the south-facing side of the prominent Bottelary Hills. The climate is similar to that of neighbouring Polkadraai Pocket, but the valley floor (at 200 m above sea level) is bordered by two parallel ranges of hills, with each range reaching an elevation of 400 metres above sea level.

The Pocket thus has aspects which vary considerably. South-facing aspects are directly exposed to False Bay and its summer sea breezes, cooling the vineyards significantly. Northern aspects and the floor are sheltered and consequently warmer.

Brand image – Kanu's imposing entrance is guarded by the mythical bird of promise

Terroir in this Pocket is characterised by varying elevations, with vines located on altitudes from as little as 60 to as high as 400 metres above sea level. The soils are predominantly yellow to reddish-brown and well drained with high potential. As a granite derivative, these soils have a favourable physical structure and good water and nutrient-retention properties. More humid conditions exist on lower slopes, planted to drought-sensitive varieties (such as Merlot) and heat-sensitive white varieties (such as Sauvignon Blanc). These varying conditions necessitate variation in viticultural practices: from low, untrellised bush vines on the well-protected valley floor to vertical trellises on the exposed south-facing slopes.

White wines from Stellenbosch Kloof show white fruit and floral aromas and have great finesse, whereas the reds are more robust. Jordan Winery's range of aspects delivers an elegant Chardonnay and a drier style, *Botrytised* Noble Late Harvest, Mellifera. Although Kanu is known for its superb Chenin Blanc and *Botrytised* Noble Late, its red blend (Cab S / Merlot) also follows this tannic trend. De Morgenzon's Chenin from old bush vines boasts a rich mouthfeel with dense, layered flavours.

Cabernet Sauvignon dominates the powerful red blends from this valley. Merlot, Shiraz and even a combination of these two are used as blending partners, adding spicy and fruity notes as well as softening the tannic structure of Cabernet Sauvignon. DeWaal (Cab S / Shz / Merlot), Jordan Estate (Cab S / Merlot), Overgaauw (Cab S / F / Merlot) and Boschkloof (Cab S / Merlot) all produce red blends with an abundance of fruit, structured tannins and longevity. Boschkloof also produces a single varietal Shiraz, with powerful upfront fruit and black pepper. Overgaauw's Port from the traditional Portuguese varieties offers great intensity and promises long development.

Noble rot – The fungus Botrytis cinerea causes grapes to lose water, therefore concentrating the sugar and flavours

DRIVING ROUTE: STELLENBOSCH KLOOF

Leave Stellenbosch on the R310, driving west. About four kilometres out of town, the R310 turns left (south) towards the N2 freeway. From there the M12 continues in a westerly direction. About three kilometres further, passing Neethlingshof's fountain on the right, the road reaches a nadir and Stellenbosch Kloof Road turns off directly to the right. Exercise caution as pedestrians frequently cross the road and speed limits are enforced by roadside cameras.

Make your way along the secluded valley's winding road. Driving along Stellenbosch Kloof Road, you will see neatly laid-out vineyard blocks arranged along the north-south-facing slopes that characterise this Pocket. White-washed walls announce the entrance to the first winery on

Precision winemaking – Kathy Jordan measuring the sugar in white grape juice

the route, Overgaauw. An historical building houses the tasting room with wrought-iron lace work on the veranda. Behind the cellar, you can see the gentle south-facing slope where Overgaauw's red varieties are cultivated. Overgaauw was the first South African producer to bottle a single varietal Merlot wine in 1982. Only a few hundred metres further, the road forks. Take the left fork.

A little further along the road, to the right-hand side, is the turn-off for De Morgenzon. Characterised by outstanding quality and conscientious cultivation, De Morgenzon's vineyards is lined with fields of flowers, not only a delight to the eye but also curbing erosion and improving biodiversity in the soil. They also play classic music to the vines.

The road leads deeper into the valley, surrounded by trellised vineyards facing north, south and east, making the most of sun exposure in this cool valley. Jordan Estate's single vineyards that produce the Nine Yards Chardonnay, as well as the Mellifera NLH, are visible high on the ridge behind the cellar.

Their new Chameleon Restaurant and Deli, opened in 2009 with a Mediterranean style, emphasises locally grown fresh produce. Jordan has also recently opened a fine-dining restaurant on the Thames in London, near the Tate Modern Museum. This is a first for a South African winery. While enjoying wines and platters under the trees, observe the vineyards towards the town of Stellenbosch.

To the far left, vineyards cling to steep hills in the Jonkershoek Valley and the equally steep Helderberg to the far right. Sadly, these mountain areas are, on occasion, damaged by wild fires which spread through the indigenous fynbos and wood plantations. Fortunately, the fynbos recovers speedily and many varieties actually need fire for germination of their seeds.

Return along the same route to the M12, turn right and continue in a westerly direction. The road rises over a hill and, just short of the crest, signs indicate a turn-

TRAVELLING TIPS

Restaurants & Accommodation:
Sandrift B&B +27 (0)21 881 3075
Skilpadvlei Restaurant & accommodation
+27 (0)21 881 3237

GPS WAYPOINTS

Boschkloof S33° 57.623 E18° 46.178
De Morgenzon S33°56.459 E18°46.396
Jordan S33° 56.557 E18° 44.693
Kanu S33° 56.948 E18° 46.005
Overgaauw S33° 56.935 E18° 47.562

off to Boschkloof. A few hundred metres along the gravel road, the cellar is on the left. Boschkloof specialises in red varieties and the compact cellar gives visitors a good understanding of the winemaking process.

Kanu's imposing entrance on the M12 is guarded by the mythical bird of promise. It is said that all who fall under his shadow would be blessed with a bountiful harvest in the coming year. Follow the road downhill to the cellar and tasting room. Kanu has long been an integral part of South Africa's Chenin Blanc revolution.

Previously an over-produced, under-valued variety, Chenin Blanc was mainly used for natural white wines, juice and grape concentrate production or distillation, but a few dedicated producers have nurtured Chenin Blanc from relative obscurity to recognition as a noble wine (See page 65).

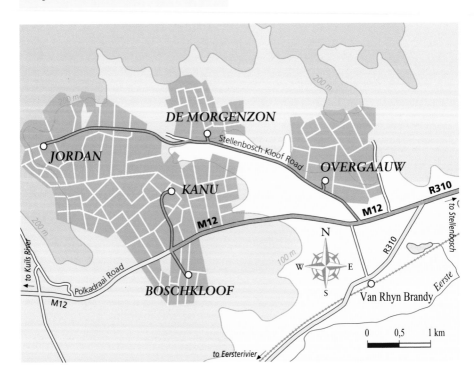

Floral delight – *The abundant flowers of De Morgenzon curbs erosion, improves soil health and delights photographers*

Machine harvesting – *Not very common, machines harvest grapes at Jordan*

Mellifera – *Cape Honey Bees happily share the vineyards with winemakers at Jordan*

Symmetry – *Overgaauw's fermentation cellar (circa 1909) is adorned by young vines*

BOSCHKLOOF

In their search to produce great red wines, Boschkloof's owners, Reenen Furter and Jacques Borman, found 30 hectares south of Stellenbosch, ideally suited to their beloved red varieties. Seventeen hectares have been planted to Chardonnay, Shiraz, Cabernet Sauvignon, Merlot and Cabernet Franc in deep red soil with decomposed granite, ensuring concentration and a tannin structure for extended aging potential. In order to give the vines sufficient sun exposure without excessive summer heat, the Cabernet Sauvignon is planted on an eastern slope while the Shiraz lies on a southern slope. Row directions (east – west) offer the grape bunches further protection from sunburn. Most of the wines are fermented naturally, if grapes are very ripe and vines were under stress selected yeast is used. Fermentation temperature is from 25 to 27°C and the total skin contact, including fermentation, can take up to 35 days. The flagship red blend is matured in new French oak barrels for 27 months, offering a classically styled wine with density and longevity.

ⓘ Conclusion (Cab S, M, Cab F, PV, Shz) 🍽 Chard, Cab S, M, Shz, Cab F ⭕ By appt if the owner is available. 📞 +27 (0)21 881 3268 ✉ jborman@adept.co.za 🍷 10 y+ 💼 03, 07

KANU

Chenin Blanc pioneer, Kanu, cultivates, fifty hectares on east- and south-facing slopes on decomposed shale soils. The elevation (100–200 m) and prevailing southeasterly winds moderate daytime temperatures. Trellising spreads the canopy and offers protection against strong winds. Very old Chenin Blanc bush vines (ex-Bottelary 28 y, Koelenhof 48 y) are cultivated on dry-land to produce low yields of highly aromatic grapes. Free-run juice of white grapes is fermented cold (12–14°C) to retain the varietal flavours and natural acidity while oak maturation adds to the weight of the wines. Red varietals are matured (18 months) in oak and are then blended to ensure that only the best barrels go into the final blend. The barrel-fermented white wines as well as the red wines undergo natural fermentation. Grapes for the Noble Late Harvest receive overnight skin contact to develop varietal character and fermentation is stopped at the desired sugar level. Oak maturation gives structure to this luxuriously textured wine, which shows tropical fruit with a *Botrytis* overlay and an invigorating acidity (9,4 g/l).

ⓘ Kanu KCB Chenin Blanc, Kia-Ora NHL, Shiraz 🍽 Cab S / F, Shz, M, PV, Viog, Sauv Bl ⭕ Mon–Fri 09:30–16:30, Sat 10:00–15:00 (Oct–May); Mon–Fri 09:30–16:30, Sat 10:00–13:00 (Jun–Sept). Publ hols 10:00–15:00 📞 +27 (0)21 881 8140 ✉ info@kanu.co.za, www.kanu.co.za 🍷 5–10 y 💼 01, 03 ⓘ Gift shop, venue (functions)

DE MORGENZON

De Morgenzon enjoys both coastal mists and cool breezes on high elevations at the end of the Stellenbosch Kloof. Rising from 145 to 360 metres above sea level, with panoramic views of both Table Bay and False Bay, De Morgenzon averages 3°C cooler than Stellenbosch. While not yet fully organic, De Morgenzon farms naturally and maintains a viable ecosystem. Wild flowers are used as cover crops and music is perpetually piped through the vineyards. Chenin Blanc and Chardonnay are grown on the higher slopes at around 300 metres above sea level, offering the greatest exposure to cooling air movement. The predominantly weathered granite soil allows dry-land cultivation and the vines are trellised to protect them against the prevailing winds. White wines are barrel fermented and aged on the lees for eight months, adding weight and complexity to these crisp and fruity wines. The Shiraz is cold soaked to ensure sufficient colour and tannin extraction, before the wine is naturally fermented. Maturation is completed over 18 months in French oak barrels, lending rich wood notes to this luxuriously fruitful wine.

Old Vine Chenin Blanc Shz, Chard, Chenin Bl, Sauv Bl Mon – Fri 09:00 – 17:00. Sat, Sun 10:00 – 14:00. Closed Easter, Dec 25, 26, Jan 1 +27 (0)21 881 3030 info@ demorgenzon.co.za, www.demorgenzon.co.za White 20 y 05, 06, 07 Music played to vines, flowers as cover crops

OVERGAAUW

Over a hundred years ago, Abraham van Velden bought a piece of land from his grandfather and named it Overgaauw. The estate's 60 hectares of vineyards are planted on south-facing slopes on decomposed granite soils. The cooling influence of the ocean results in the slow, even ripening of the grapes. Fourth-generation winemaker David van Velden's philosophy sees meticulous vineyard management, supporting the natural soil balance and producing the best fruit. In the cellar the focus is on retaining as much of the varietal's unique 'Overgaauw' character, with minimal cellar manipulation and the judicious use of wood. The Overgaauw family tradition produces red wines in the Cape European style, classic, elegant wines, rich in varietal extract. Overgaauw produced South Africa's first single varietal Merlot in 1982. Flagship Tria Corda is only released in exceptional years. Chardonnay is lightly wooded while Sauvignon Blanc reveals an interesting combination of green and rich tropical fruits.

Tria Corda (Cab S / M /Cab F) Cab S / F, M, Shz, Chard, Sauv Bl, Rosé, Sylvaner, Chenin Bl, Sém Mon – Fri 09:00– 17:00. Sat, publ hols 10:00–12:30 Closed Easter, Dec 25, 26, Jan 1 +27 (0)21 881 3815 info@overgaauw.co.za, www. overgaauw.co.za Reds 5 – 8 y, Port 8 y+ 74, 76, 82, 89, 95, 01, 03 Charming Victorian-style tasting room

JORDAN WINE ESTATE

The family-owned Jordan Estate is situated at the upper end of the Stellenbosch Kloof where it joins the Bottelary Ridge at 400 metres above sea level. One-hundred-and-five hectares of trellised vines are cultivated on wind-protected slopes with views of Table Mountain, False Bay and Stellenbosch. The judicious use of drip irrigation in dry seasons aids in extending ripening periods and naturally controls potential alcohol levels.

A western slope is home to the Cobblers Hill vineyard, planted to Cabernet Sauvignon, Merlot and Cabernet Franc. Additional Cabernet Sauvignon is planted on sun-exposed northern slopes in deep gravel soil, and Merlot on eastern slopes in deep clay-loam. The white varieties are planted on cooler south- and east-facing slopes. Natural farming practices include the use of organic mulches to reduce soil water loss and cover crops to ensure a healthy soil structure.

Fruit for the flagship range is harvested from mature vines and red varieties are fermented in overhead cone-shaped stainless steel tanks, draining directly into the press. The wines undergo spontaneous malolactic fermentation in small French oak barrels, where they mature for up to two years. Barrel-fermented white wines receive a shorter time in wood, with barrel-rolling to create a less oxidative *bâttonage* effect.

The Nine Yards Chardonnay (18 y, sgl vineyard) matures in French oak for 12 months, resulting in a full-bodied, rich wine. Named after the Cape Honey Bee inhabiting the hives on the farm, Mellifera (NLH) is made in a drier style with aromas of dried apricots and peaches and a well-structured acidity adding to the elegance.

Secluded valley - An early morning view over the Stellenbosch Kloof from Jordan Wine Estate

Cobblers Hill (Cab S / Merlot / Cab F), Nine Yards Chardonnay, Mellifera NLH Cab S, M, Cab F, Shz, Chard, Sauv Bl, Chenin Bl, Riesl Mon–Sun 09:30–16:30. Closed Easter, Dec 25, Jan 1 +27 (0)21 881 3441 info@jordanwines.com, www.jordanwines.com White 2–8 y, red 5–15 y 95, 98, 99, 01, 03, 04, 05 Annual Jordan summer festival, cellar tours by appt, proteas, natural fynbos, Jordan Restaurant (on estate) & High Timber Restaurant (on the Thames in London)

Stellenbosch West Pocket

Picture perfect – Sunset over Vergenoegd Estate with the prominent peaks of the Helderberg in the background

The topography of the Stellenbosch West Pocket constitutes soft, undulating hills of 60 to 300 metres above sea level (on the back of Bottelary Hill), flattening out to less than 20 metres close to False Bay.

Aspects here are not very prominent, except at Neethlingshof and Asara, which have higher-lying vineyards (over 300 m) on south- to southeast-facing slopes. The strong locational advantage is the ocean's close proximity (10 km), ensuring a relatively cool and temperate mesoclimate, conducive to slow and even ripening of grapes.

In the geological past, this area was inundated by the sea several times, resulting

Steeped in history – Meerlust Estate circa 1968

in viticulturally problematic soils. These are generally sandy or gravelly material on clay, derived from granite and shale and thus prone to extremes of wet and dryness. The difficult soil conditions result in moderate vine growth and production, offering similar wine character over seasons. Rootstocks adapted to shallow and wet soil conditions are used in the lower-lying areas, while vineyards on elevated sites are relieved of this problem. Vineyards vary from small, untrellised bush vines to trained vines on high trellises.

Vineyard block layout uses the cool south-westerly sea breeze that occurs in summer afternoons using mainly southwest – northeast row directions. This allows the airflow to move down the rows, cooling the vines and reducing the relative humidity around the canopy to control fungal diseases. Stellenbosch West produces fruity white wines, whereas the reds are diverse in weight, ranging from the big, serious wines to more sleek examples. Neethlingshof and Spier produce larger ranges with structured reds as well as Noble Late Harvest wines with dense richness. Vergenoegd and Asara both produce powerful Cabernet-Merlot blends with a fine tannin structure requiring maturation.

The Cabernet-based blend from Meerlust shows somewhat more restraint and elegance, as does its aromatic Pinot Noir. The Foundry makes a spicy and dense Shiraz and silky, perfumed Viognier to add to the focused diversity of the Pocket's wines.

TRAVELLING TIPS

Accommodation:
Spier Hotel +27 (0)21 809 1100,
 reservations@spier.co.za

Restaurant:
Moyo (Spier) +27 (0)21 809 1133
Pomegranate (Vergenoegd) +27 (0)21 843 3248

Attractions:
Birds of prey (Spier) +27 (0)21 858 1826,
 www.eagle-encounters.co.za
Boullé Petanque (Vergenoegd)
Cheetah Outreach (Spier) +27 (0)21 881 3242
Historical walk-about (Vergenoegd)
Outdoor theatre, picnic & deli (Spier)
 +27 (0)21 809 1100, info@spier.co.za

DRIVING ROUTE: STELLENBOSCH WEST

Take the R310 (Adam Tas Road) leading west from Stellenbosch in the direction of Cape Town. About four kilometres out of town, the R310 turns left (south) towards the N2 freeway. From here, the M12 continues in a westerly direction. The Stellenbosch West Pocket includes the first part of the M12 and continues south along the R310.

The soft, undulating hills, similar to those of the Bottelary Pocket, are very noticeable. Light-coloured soils are indicative of high proportions of sand. Due to the underlying layer of clay, the Pocket's vineyards require

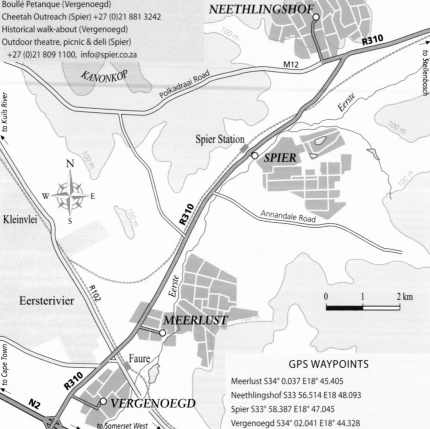

GPS WAYPOINTS
Meerlust S34° 0.037 E18° 45.405
Neethlingshof S33 56.514 E18 48.093
Spier S33° 58.387 E18° 47.045
Vergenoegd S34° 02.041 E18° 44.328

rootstocks adapted to shallow soils. At the R310 / M12 intersection, continue along the M12. Abut 400 metres further, a local Jet D'Eau fountain announces Neethlingshof. Building on its illustrious past, the farm continues to be 'History in the making' with a splendid range. A unique kilometre-long pine avenue leads to the tasting room.

Drive back towards Stellenbosch. At the R310 / M12 intersection, turn right and continue on the R310 in a southwesterly direction. Small game camps on either side of the road are home to zebra, antelope, wildebeest and ostrich. The imposing entrance to Spier Wines is on the left. A wine-tourism haven, Spier boasts luxury accommodation, restaurants, an open-air theatre, a cheetah and birds-of-prey outreach program alongside its fine wines. The manicured lawns around the dam offer the perfect picnic spot.

As the R310 descends a small hill, two dams (one on either side of the road) are visible. Meerlust's entrance on the left is masked by a lane of oak trees. A history of more than 300 years is visible in the detailed architecture of the historical buildings. The team is refining the distinctly European influence from previous winemaker, Giorgio Dalla Cia, using high-tech analysis and infrared mapping to better exploit the *terroir*.

Drive the last three kilometres of the route, crossing the bridge over the R102, to Vergenoegd. A low white wall on the left indicates the entrance. A gravel road leads to Vergenoegd's Cape Dutch homestead and tasting room. The relaxed, unpretentious atmosphere is a perfect way to end a day spent touring the Winelands. The restaurant offers a combination of local and international cuisine using fresh produce.

NEETHLINGSHOF

Neethlingshof's history spans more than 300 years. Planting started in 1692, followed by a wine cellar (circa 1802) and manor house (circa 1814). The diverse terrain, including 13 different soil types, requires dedicated vineyard management of the 220 hectares. Vertical trellising and dense panting (4 000 vines/Ha) controls growth in fertile decomposed granite soil. South facing slopes, exposed to the nearby ocean, (100 – 300 m above sea level), create cool ripening conditions, while frequent mists assist in *Botrytis* formation for Noble Late Harvest production. Red grapes are macerated and fermented in rototanks (mixing skins and juice) for improved colour extraction. Laurentius is matured for 12 months with 60 per cent new oak adding spice and toasted flavours to the fragrant black fruit nose. The wood-fermented Chardonnay matures on the lees and in bottle before release, producing a fleshy, luxurious wine. The flagship varietal wines are all from single vineyards.

[i] Laurentius (Cab S/M/Mal), NLH [icon] Various [icon] Mon –Fri 09:00–16:30 (Mar 1 – Nov 30 closes at 17:00), Closed Easter Fri, Dec 25 [icon] +27 (0)21 883 8988 [icon] info@neethlingshof.co.za www.neethlingshof.co.za [icon] Red 5 - 8 y, Laurentius 10y [icon] 96, 99, 01, 03 [i] Cellar & farm tours by appt, 2 restaurants, venue: tour groups, play area for children, open tractor tours

VERGENOEGD

Vergenoegd (Dutch: Satisfaction achieved) has been farmed by the Faure family for six generations. It was one of the first estates to bottle its own wine in 1972. The Cape Dutch homestead (circa 1773) is an historical monument. Eighty hectares of vines are cultivated only three kilometres from the ocean and receive the full cooling benefit of the prevailing winds off False Bay. The soils vary from alluvial loam to sand on a clay base with calcareous rock. Drainage systems improve the aeration of vine roots on these extremely low aspects (9 m). Attentive vineyard management opens canopies to increase airflow and thereby reduces the humidity and subsequent disease incidence. Red grapes are macerated and fermented in rototanks to ensure proper mixing of skins and juice. Extended maturation (20+ months) in 300 litre French oak barrels gives the flagship blend a rich and powerful tannin structure which benefits from maturing. These elegant wines are only released after three years.

[i] Vergenoegd (Cab S / M / Cab F) [icon] Red blend, Shz, M, PV, Malb, Tinta B, Touriga N [icon] Mon–Fri 08:00–17:00, Sat 09:30–16:00, Sun 11:00–16:00. Closed Easter Sun, Dec 25, Jan 1 [icon] +27 (0)21 843 3248 [icon] enquiries@vergenoegd.co.za, www. vergenoegd.co.za [icon] 10 y+ [icon] 72, 74, 82, 84, 95, 99, 00, 03 [i] Older vintages, cellar and vineyard tours by appt, restaurant, ducks and boule courts

SPIER

The magnificent Spier property was first established in 1692 by a German soldier named Arnoud Jansz. A long and captivating history followed. An historical building on Spier bears the date 1767: this celebrated building was constructed as a wine cellar by Albertus Myburgh, who owned the property between 1765 and 1781. Beautifully preserved, the building still stands, along with many others on Spier, as one of the finest examples of Cape Dutch architecture in the Cape Winelands.

During the late 1960s restoration work was undertaken and again after the current owners, the Enthoven family, bought the property in 1993. The winery was significantly upgraded in 2000. Today, Spier reflects the art in wine through a twofold philosophy: first, the award-winning wines reflect the art of the winemaker's craft; and second, the deep and long-term association Spier has with South African art.

Producing a wide variety of wines, some 700 hectares are currently under vineyards. Of this, 170 hectares are owned by Spier, 300 hectares are under long-term contract, and the remaining 230 hectares are under medium- to long-term lease.

Golden era – A collection of statues welcomes visitors to Spier

Moyo restaurant – A culinary experience eating under (or even in) the trees

Vineyards on the Spier farm are located at altitudes of 80 to 360 metres above sea level, on the foothills of the Helderberg. Deep, weathered granite soils provide both good drainage and water-holding capacity for the wet winters and dry, hot summers. The gentle undulating landscape is cooled by southwesterly summer breezes from False Bay, 15 km to the south, as well as westerly winds from the Atlantic Ocean, 30 kilometres to the west. Vineyards located on the Helderberg face north-west and thus receive increased sunlight exposure. The high altitude (360 m), however, ensures cool ripening conditions.

The deep soils of the Darling vineyards have an extraordinary water-retention capacity, allowing for dry-land cultivation (without any irrigation). Although low-lying at 150 to 200 metres above sea level, the temperatures are moderated by sea breezes from the nearby Atlantic Ocean.

Vineyards are also planted in Paarl on a hill between the Paardeberg and Paarlberg. The rich, red soil in this location requires little irrigation and, combined with long sunlight hours, produces deeply coloured, intensely flavoured grapes. The fruit from these sites produces a densely layered midpalate, characterised by luscious fruit and velvety tannins in the wines.

Cheetah Outreach – Cheetah ambassadors offer personal encounters with this threatened species

Eagle encounter – The Raptor Outreach offers visitors an opportunity to interact with indigenous birds of prey

Strict vineyard management ensures that only the highest quality grapes are produced while maintaining a balance with the natural surroundings. Cover crops are used extensively to prevent soil compaction and to increase aeration and drainage of excess water in the rainy winter season. Vines are trellised to spread the canopy for optimum sunlight exposure and to offer protection from prevailing winds. Underdeveloped shoots are removed (suckering) to promote air circulation and to prevent humidity-related fungal diseases.

Cabernet Sauvignon for the flagship wines is cultivated on deep, rich granite soils producing muscular wines with chalky tannins. The flagship Merlot is planted on dark, rich 'koffieklip' (Eng: coffee rock) soils with a gravelly texture resembling coffee beans. Fertile and water-retaining, these soils are naturally cool and require no irrigation. They are particularly well suited to cultivars needing even ripening.

Rich, fertile soils planted to Chardonnay give rise to flavours of white fruit and abundant lime characters. The flagship Sauvignon Blanc is planted on mineral-rich soils with good water drainage, very slightly

Captivating innovation – The Spier wine cellar is fully equipped for gentle handling of prime vineyard produce

stressing the vines as they extend their roots in search of water. This intensifies the dusty minerality and fig leaf flavours in the wine.

Outdoor picnic – Guests can spend a lazy afternoon picnicking at the dam, while kids can play in a safe and picturesque environment

Spier's Private Collection incorporates seven single cultivar wines. The pre-eminent wine, Frans K Smit is a Bordeaux-style red blend that is only produced in superlative vintages. All grapes used in the flagship wines are grown in the Stellenbosch and Helderberg vineyards.

Red grapes for the Frans K Smit are destemmed and hand sorted before being crushed. The must is cooled to approximately 12°C for a period of cold maceration and colour extraction, before fermentation commences. The cellar boasts a range of fermenters; stainless steel tanks, French oak barrels and open-top fermenters, the latter being used exclusively for the premium wines. White wines are fermented cold at 12 to 15°C, preserving their elegant fruit aromas. Red wines are fermented warm (± 24°C) to extract colour and fine tannins for structure.

The flagship blend completes malolactic fermentation in barrel to integrate wood flavours and is then matured for 27 months. Premium red wines and Chardonnay mature in oak for 6 to 12 months. A combination of French and American oak is used, incorporating both new and older barrels. This ensures a solid oak base, while retaining the fruit flavours for an elegant finish. Once the final red blend is made, the wine matures further in barrel as well as in bottle before being released.

As a conscious corporate citizen, Spier is a proud inaugural member of the Wine Industry Ethical Trade Association and one of the first members of the Biodiversity and Wine Initiative. All solid waste is measured and stored, and recycled or sold, resulting in a recycling rate of 100 per cent; while wastewater is sent to the water recycling plant. Energy- and water use is reduced at a rate of 5 per cent per year. Employment, training and business opportunities are given to members of the local community.

ℹ️ Frans K Smit (Bdx Blend), Private Collection Range: Cab S, M, P, Shz, Chenin Bl, Sauv Bl, Chard 🍽️ Chard, Chenin Bl, Sauv Bl, Viog, Cab F, Cab S, Malb, M, Mourv, PV, PN, P, Shz 🕐 Mon–Sun 09:00–17:00 incl pub hols 📞 +27 (0)21 809 1100 📧 info@spier.co.za, www. spierwines.co.za 🍷 White 3–4 y, red 7–12 y, FKS 9–12 y 🍴 FKS 04, 05, 06 🍽️ Food: 3 gourmet restaurants, picnic @ Deli. Art: ethnic arts, crafts, contemporary art. Activities: horse riding, Raptor & Cheetah Outreach, mountain biking, hiking trails, children's clubhouse. Accommodation: luxury hotel. Concerts: Amphitheatre

MEERLUST

Meerlust, one of South Africa's grand dames, dates back to 1693 when the Governor of the Cape, Simon van der Stel, granted the land to Henning Hüsing. In 1757, Johannes Albertus Myburgh purchased Meerlust and marked the foundation of the Myburgh dynasty. From the manor house to the old slave bell, from the 17th-century barn to the cellar with its beautifully moulded staircase, Meerlust is one of the Cape Winelands' architectural jewels.

Meerlust manor House – A history of wine and architecture at the hisotric estate

Today, 110 hectares of vineyards are cultivated on a range of soils diverse both in structure and texture, which allows very specific site selection for each variety on the farm. Southeasterly aspects ensure that vineyards enjoy long, sunny days without the grapes risking sunburn. Prevailing southeasterly breezes from False Bay cool down the vineyards and keep the canopy dry, minimising fungal diseases. This cooling effect, reducing the average daytime temperature by as much as 5°C in summer, creates slow, even ripening conditions, with grapes retaining naturally high acidity and achieving phenolic ripeness at slightly reduced sugar levels.

'Holbol' – An architectural detail on the cellar's staircase

Apart from a small section of alluvial soil along the Eerste River, the soils of Meerlust are predominantly clay subsoil with granitic gravel topsoil. The clay retains moisture and also naturally reduces the vines' crop and allows for higher flavour concentration in the fruit. This prevents water stress from occurring, especially in sensitive varieties like Merlot. The gravel component allows excess water to drain and promotes root development. Soil types change over a very short distance on this farm and the range of growing conditions requires very careful canopy management in order to achieve a balance between vegetative growth and crop yield.

A key viticultural element is controlling crop levels with multiple green harvests as this practice ensures uniform ripening and fruit concentration. Young vines are given very light crop loads to favour the development of a deep root system. Vineyards are picked several times to ensure that only phenolicly ripe grapes are harvested. Although blocks are replanted with the

Continuum – The fine decor details are continued in the outbuildings on the farm

best material, older 20-year-old blocks still dominate production. Grape bunches are hand harvested into small crates to prevent damage and transported to the cellar for vinification. Chardonnay is whole bunch pressed and the cleared juice is barrel fermented in heavy toasted barrels. The wine is matured on its lees for 12 months, giving a fresh creamy and minerally nose and a full-bodied, stony and chalky palate.

Hand harvesting – The delicate Pinot Noir grapes are harvested by hand at Meerlust

Destalked and crushed red grapes are cold macerated for three days to initiate extraction of colour and primary fruit flavours. The must is then inoculated with a selected yeast culture and fermented with regular punch-downs and pump-overs to ensure proper mixing of skins and juice. All blocks are vinified separately and once pressed, the free-run and pressed wines are matured separately. Malolactic fermentation is completed in French oak barrels and a combination of new and older oak allows extended maturation, and ensures wines are well integrated and balanced.

A fuller style Pinot Noir shows savoury notes with dense, rich tannins, while the Merlot has concentrated dark berry and chocolate flavours which promise evolution over a decade. The classic Rubicon flagship is rich and powerful with dark fruits, mocha notes and condensed, linear tannins, yet retains a traditional modest alcohol for understated elegance. The wine has great aging potential and will develop in the bottle for up to twenty years.

ⓘ Rubicon (Cab S / M / Cab F) 🍇 PN, Chard, Cab S, M, Cab F, PV 🕐 Mon–Fri 09:00–16:00, Sat 10:00–14:00 (Apr–Aug). Mon–Fri 09:00–17:00, Sat 10:00–14:00 (Sept–Mar) Tour groups by appt only 📞 +27 (0)21 843 3587 ✉ info@meerlust.co.za, www.meerlust.co.za 🍷 Red 10 y+, white 5 y 📷 86, 91, 95, 98, 01 🏛 Cape Dutch architecture

Bottelary Pocket

Gentle undulating hills – The Bottelary Hill creates gentle flowing aspects for precision viticulture

The Bottelary Pocket is situated on the northern slopes of the Bottelary range of granite hills, located about 12 kilometres to the northwest of Stellenbosch.

The mesoclimate varies within the L-shaped Pocket as vineyards on higher elevations and plateau positions benefit from air movement which cools and dries the vines, while lower-lying vineyards experience warmer conditions. Although granite is the main soil parent material, significant portions of shale also occur, resulting in soil variation between sites. At higher altitudes, the soils are typically yellow to reddish-brown, well drained and favourably structured. Often in association with some stony or gravelly soils, these structured soils allow for extensive vine root development (horizontally and vertically) and a far greater water-retention capacity throughout the vine's growing season.

Towards the valley bottom, the soils become more duplex and sandy. These soils tend to

Red & yellow – Two different grape varieties show different autumn colours

retain more water during spring and dry out in late summer, requiring more managerial skills in terms of viticultural practices and soil water regulation. Situated in this Pocket is the north – south running valley of Koelenhof, a wide, open basin with soft, undulating hills at 120 to 200 metres above sea level. It is a relatively cool area due to air from the sea funnelling inland during summer, creating favourable ripening conditions. The soils are almost exclusively derived from shale, with structured medium-vigour soils on the lower slopes changing to more gravelly soils on a clay base on the convex hillside positions. On the flat valley bottom, the clay base is covered with sand. These sites are prone to excessive wetness, particularly in winter.

The Bottelary Pocket is characterised by vineyards on northern slopes as well as on the valley floor. In the shallow, layered soils, vines are planted on ridges to increase soil volume with scions grafted on specific rootstocks which are adapted to shallow soils. On the hills, a selection of red and white vines is cultivated on warmer and cooler slopes, depending on the aspect. The north- and west-facing slopes favour Shiraz and Pinotage, producing excellent red wines with firm tannins and dark fruit. Most Pinotage, as well as many Chenin Blanc vineyards, are cultivated as bush vines as this reduces water requirements. These plants have shorter shoots which are less prone to wind damage. The bush vines in particular give highly concentrated fruit with Pinotage showing more of its pinot-like character. Bush vines are generally not irrigated, while new plantings of high-trellised vines receive supplementary irrigation to assist in the root development.

Rustic welcome – The old fermentation cellar, circa 1800s, now hosts Bellevue's tasting room

Bottelary can be described as Pinotage headquarters, with excellent examples from Bellevue, Kaapzicht, Mooiplaas and Beyerskloof. Bellevue produced the first commercial Pinotage in the country. The farm's unique *terroir* shines through in the unmistakeable cassis and blueberry flavours on the nose, as is also evident in its Malbec. Shiraz in Bottelary tends to have less pronounced white pepper and spicy notes, showing more sour-cherry and plum fruit, backed by savoury and beef notes. Frequently oaked with a percentage of American oak, the wines show definite vanilla sweetness and dark chocolate aromas. Cabernet Sauvignon also fares well with structured single varietal examples from Goede Hoop and Hartenberg, and Cabernet blends from Mulderbosch and Hazendal. A good example of a red blend containing Pinotage is Kaapzicht's Steytler Vision. This wine has up to 40 per cent Pinotage, depending on the vintage.

Mooiplaas produces delicate Sauvignon Blanc from a cool hilltop vineyard, while the aromatic

Red Leaf shop – Quirky mementos from your visit to Beyerskloof

Sauvignon Blancs from lower-lying vineyards on Mulderbosch and Villiera are more structured. The first *Cap Classique* (sparkling wine fermented and sold in the same bottle) in South Africa was produced by Simonsig, with Villiera's Chardonnay-Pinot Noir MCC joining the ranks with bone-dry richness, good mid-palate weight and fine acidity.

DRIVING ROUTE: BOTTELARY

From Stellenbosch, drive towards the N1 freeway, in a northerly direction. About five kilometres out of town, the first two wineries' white-walled entrances lie side-by-side to the left. Take the first entrance left and drive along a gravel road to Beyerskloof. The image of a red Pinotage vine leaf, which has become synonymous with Beyerskloof, is featured on the walled entrance. The new tasting facility boasts a delightful restarunt and gift shop featuring the red leaf on clothing, gadgets and sundry gifts.

From Beyerskloof, take the next left entrance from the R304 to visit Mulderbosch. Mulderbosch's white wines in particular are recognised for their ability to age well. From Mulderbosch, drive about three kilometres north to the Bottelary Road (M23) turn-off. At this intersection, visit the Bottelary Hills Wine Centre for some vinous retail therapy.

Along the M23, notice the range of granite hills to the left. About six kilometres from the turn-off, a cluster of pine trees and a white-walled entrance with a variety of flags announces the entrance to Bellevue. Turn right and follow the gravel road around the winery to the tasting room, in the historical cellar. Bellevue proudly cultivates one of the oldest blocks of Pinotage (planted 1953) still in production. It was planted only one year ahead of the Pinotage blocks on Kanonkop, the vineyards which made the Paul

Sauer wine famous. Further along Bottelary Road, turn left to Fischer Road to visit Goede Hoop (Eng. Good Hope), another family-owned winery. Follow the gravel road along the hillside to the entrance on the left. The old farmhouse, circa 1880, is now home to the third-generation Bestbier winemaker and his family. The route continues west to a cluster of gum trees on the left. Follow the gravel road to Kaapzicht Estate. Not only does this property have a lovely view on Table Moutain, but it is also a true family-owned business: brothers Danie and George are winemaker and viticulturist respectively, while their wives manage the venue and accommodation.

GPS WAYPOINTS

Bellevue S33° 52.788 E18° 45.821
Beyerskloof S33° 53.418 E18° 49.526
Goede Hoop S33° 54.552 E18° 45.227
Kaapzicht S33° 54.750 E18° 44.209
Mulderbosch S33° 53.326 E18° 49.441
Villiera S33° 50.247 E18° 47.573

TRAVELLING TIPS

Accommodation:
Kaapzicht Vineyard Cottage +27 (0)82 737 8329, steyrena@mweb.co.za

Restaurants:
Red Leaf (Beyerskloof) +27 (0)21 865 2135

Interests:
Bottelary Hills Wine Centre +27 (0)21 865 2955
Devonvale Golf Estate +27 (0)21 865 2080
Picnic (Villiera) BYO

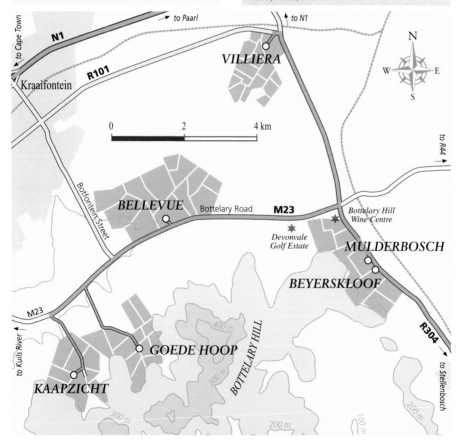

BELLEVUE

Bellevue's Morkel Family has been in residence since 1861. They crushed their maiden vintage under their own label on the historical Cape Dutch farm in 1999. One-hundred-and-ninety hectares of vines are cultivated along a valley floor and hills, with various slopes and a wide variety of soil types. Pinotage is predominantly cultivated as bush vines, mostly on high-lying areas, with some blocks expressing more Pinot Noir characters. Heat-sensitive varieties like Sauvignon Blanc and Merlot are planted on south-facing hillslopes to maximise cool afternoon breezes. Mature vines, together with the slightly denser planting, lead to more concentrated flavours while controlling growth vigour as well as crop level on the higher potential valley floor soils. The PK Morkel Pinotage is a fruit-driven wine with strong wood flavours. This wine ferments below 30°C, with extended skin contact to extract colour and flavour and give complexity to the wine. It is matured in 100 per cent new French oak barrels for 24 months, which contribute to the intensity and filling mid-palate of the wine.

ℹ️ PK Morkel Pinotage, Tumara (Cab S / F/ M / Mal / PV) 🍇 P, Cab S/F, M, Malbec, PV, Shz, S.bl. 🕐 Mon –Fri 10:00–16:00, Sat, non-religious hols 10:00–15:00 📞 +27 (0) 21 865 2055 📧 info@bellevue.co.za, www.bellevue.co.za 🍷 8 y 🍾 03, 04 ℹ️ Oldest commercial Pinotage block planted 1953

GOEDE HOOP

Three generations of the Bestbier family have farmed Goede Hoop since 1928. Ninety hectares of vines are planted on slopes facing north and northwest. Elevations range from 100 to 350 metres above sea level where the higher sites benefit from greater air movement and subsequent cooling. These are planted to white varieties. Red varieties are cultivated in warmer ripening conditions, which benefit colour and tannin development. The high moisture retention of decomposed granite soils allows for dry-land cultivation and, row directions (east – west) combined with slightly wider plant spacing take full advantage of the wind's cooling effect. Hand-harvested grapes are sorted and crushed in open vats. Natural fermentation with regular pump-overs and extended maturation (18 months) in older barrels add to the complexity and savoury notes of red varieties. Overnight skin contact and post-fermentation lees contact adds complexity to Sauvignon Blanc, while wood-fermented and matured Chardonnay yields a powerful and aromatic yet fresh wine.

ℹ️ Cab S, Shz, M, P, Car, Chard, Sauv Bl 🕐 Mon – Thurs 10:00 – 16:00, Fri 10:00 – 15:00, Sat 10:00 – 13:00. Open publ hols 📞 +27 (0)21 903 6286 📧 goede@adept.co.za, www.goedehoop.co.za 🍷 White 3 y+, red 8 y+ 🍾 82, 86, 99, 00 ℹ️ Tours, meals, refreshments by appt, BYO picnic, conference venue, conservation fynbos

BEYERSKLOOF

An historic circle, broken over a hundred years ago, was finally closed when Beyers Truter bought this farm near Stellenbosch which had belonged to the Beyers family for five generations.

Beyers has planted a combination of 5 000 Cabernet Sauvignon and Merlot vines per hectare on shallow, gravelly soil, almost twice the norm, to optimise a small 8,5 hectare pocket of land within this farm. The vines are aligned east–west as row direction is considered an important factor for heat management. With this axis, Beyers can maximise long sunlight hours for great colour development while allowing the prevailing winds to dry and cool the vines. All the vines are vertically trellised to spread and thin out the canopy. As a result, more leaf surface is exposed to direct sunlight and bunches are protected from burn damage. An additional 77 hectares are planted to Pinotage, Cabernet Sauvignon, Merlot and Pinot Noir on slopes facing in various directions at elevations between 50 to100 metres above sea level.

The Field Blend's Cabernet Sauvignon and Merlot grapes are harvested, vinified and matured together to achieve the best possible integration of their fruit structures. This blend is matured totally in new oak for two years before bottling. This results in a highly structured and powerful wine, which requires decanting while young. New additions to the stable are the flagship FAITH (a Cape Blend) and the ultra-premium Diesel Pinotage, named in honour of Beyer's dog that passed away in 2008. Pinotage is fermented at a high temperature (29°C) to produce a scented wine with deep, dark cherry fruit. Beyers' pure passion for Pinotage is reflected in a range of Pinotage products from Pinotage salami to Pinotage frozen yoghurt, Pinotage Sparkling Brut and even a Pinotage dessert wine. A true Pinotage lover's paradise.

Beyerskloof – Amongst the Cabernet Sauvignon and Merlot vineyards

ℹ️ FAITH (Cab S / M / P / S), Field Blend (Cab S / M), Pinotage Reserve 🍇 P, Cab S, M, Cin 🕐 Mon–Fri 08:30–16:30, Sat 10:00–14:00. Closed Sun, Easter, Dec 25, 26; Jan 1 📞 +27 (0)21 865 2135 📧 wine@beyerskloof.co.za, www.beyerskloof.co.za 🍷 10 y+ 🍾 91, 95, 97, 98, 99, 03, 05, 07 ℹ️ Cellar tours, harvest experience (in season, booking req.), Red Leaf Restaurant (open Tue–Sat 10:00–16:00)

Pinotage

In 1924 Professor Abraham I Perold experimented by crossing Hermitage (Cinsaut) and Pinot Noir. It created a new variety, Pinotage, South Africa's national grape. Intending to create an offspring which combined the classic Burgundy Pinot flavours and the easy-to-grow, disease-resistant quality and taste of Rhône Valley Cinsaut – his experiment yielded seed which he planted, but regrettably it was soon forgotten. The seedlings would have been lost were it not for a young lecturer, Dr Niehaus, who rescued them. The plants were re-established at the Elsenburg Agricultural College nursery by Perold's successor, CJ Theron.

The first recognition came in 1959 when a Bellevue wine (100% Pinotage) was voted champion wine at the Cape Wine Show. The achievement was repeated in 1961 by a Pinotage from Kanonkop Estate. Distell was first to use the name Pinotage on a label in 1961. These successes and the robust and early-ripening character of this variety inspired many farmers to plant Pinotage. The 1970s saw widespread uprooting of the variety, as it was said to have no future.

A few producers, however, convinced of Pinotage's potential, continued to search for ways of improving grape quality and vinification. The 1987 Diner's Club Winemaker of the Year was dedicated to Pinotage. Four years later, Kanonkop's Beyers Truter was the first South African winemaker to win the prestigious International Winemaker of the Year at the 1991 International Wine and Spirit Competition. All the more fitting that he did so with South Africa's own wine variety.

In South Africa, most Pinotage is cultivated as bush vines, as it tends to yield the best result. Bush vines produce an average yield of 32 to 52 hectolitres per hectare (5 – 8 tons/ha). Pinotage can be trellised, however, low trellis systems are used, bringing grapes closer to the surface of the soil to increase radiant heat. Trellised, Pinotage may yield up to 10 tons per hectare of high quality grapes. An early ripener, Pinotage can be harvested a little earlier than most other red varieties.

Optimum flavour development is achieved at higher alcohol levels. Medium-bodied wines are generally produced at between 12,5 and 13,5 per cent alcohol, while a full-bodied wine may reach 14,5 per cent alcohol. Oak maturation takes eight to 12 months (medium-bodied wines), up to 14 to 18 months (full-bodied wines). Modern Pinotage offers dark plum and raspberry fruit, wines with classic balance. Pinotage can produce wines in both the light, dry and fruity style as well as the oaked, powerful and enduring style.

The new concept of a Cape Blend, with a percentage of Pinotage included in the blend, emerged in the late 1990s. Advocates came to a consensus that, for the best expression of a red blend from South Africa, Pinotage – the local variety – had to be included. Opposers question it as an essential ingredient in a Cape Blend. If included, guidelines propose the blend contain 30 to 70 per cent as reasonable. Most producers do not want to be restricted to specific percentages, but prefer the freedom to adjust the blend depending on vintage conditions, vineyard sources and their own goals. Thus few place a Cape Blend designation on their labels. See Cape Blend page 211.

KAAPZICHT ESTATE

Three generations of the Steytler family have been at the helm of this estate, which bottled its first vintage in 1984. The original 174 hectares of northwest facing granite slopes are suited to red varieties. Sixteen hectares on elevated east-facing slopes, along the crest of the Bottelary Hills have been added, for white varieties and reds such as Malbec, Pinot Noir and Cabernet Franc. Red grapes for the Steytler's flagship, Vision, are hand harvested, crushed and cold soaked for 48 hours before fermentation. Interestingly, only pump-overs are used to mix the skins and fermenting wine, as this closed-system is considered a more hygienic method. Then, malolactic fermentation occurs naturally before wines are transferred to barrel. Following up to 24 months in French oak barrels, the blend is made. This wine shows ripe red fruits, Christmas cake spiciness and a vibrant acidity. The red wines all show dense, rich fruit with soft tannins from classic-styled wooding, ensuring great aging potential.

ℹ️ Vision (Cab S / P / M) 🍷 Cab S, Shz, P, M, Sauv Bl, Chenin Bl, Chard, Hanepoot ◑ Mon–Fri 09:00–16:00, Sat 09:00–12:00 ⚡ +27 (0)21 906 1620 ✉ cellarmaster@kaapzicht-wines.co.za, www.kaapzicht.co.za 🍴 6–10 y ⬛ 95, 01, 06, 07 ℹ️ Potstill brandy & grappa, cottage & guest house, venue & caterers: 300 pax, picnic, views, developed crèche & school for farm children

VILLIERA

The Grier family has been producing wine with a 'Villiera signature' since 1983. Grapes ex-Koelenhof farm are used for the flagships while a small portion of additional grapes blend complementary *terroirs*. The lack of significant slopes provides even sun exposure and row directions (east – west) maximise cooling from prevailing southeasterly wind. It also necessitated drainage and drip irrigation to manage soil water content. Clay soils give drought-sensitive Merlot a denser character and are blended with Cabernet Sauvignon from clay soils in Devon Valley. Monro Red is fermented slowly to preserve red fruit flavours and two years maturation in new French oak provides strong tannins for the rich, elegant fruit character. Bush vine Sauvignon Blanc from sandy soils shows fresh herbaceous and grass notes. In the denser Chenin Blanc canopies occasional *Botrytis* develops to ensure sufficient grapes for Noble Late Harvest production. The vintage bubbly (50/50 PN & Chard, own grapes) matures for five years on the lees and Brut Natural is naturally fermented with no SO_2 additions.

ℹ️ Monro Red (M / Cab S), Monro Brut (MCC), sgl vineyard Sauv bl 🍷 MCC, dessert, fortified, red white, Rosé ◑ Mon–Fri 08:30–17:00, Sat 08:30–15:00. Closed Sun ⚡ +27 (0)21 865 2002/3 ✉ wine@villiera.com, www.villiera.com 🍴 Whites 6 y, reds 10 y ⬛ Bush Vine SB 01, 05, 06, 08; Monro red 01, 02, 04; MCC 93, 96, 97, 99, 01 ℹ️ Wine tours, game farm

MULDERBOSCH

Mulderbosch is among the best South African white wine producers and its wines age remarkably well. Twenty-seven hectares are cultivated on east-facing hills in granite and shale soils. The elevation (300 m) and prevailing south-easterly winds moderate daytime temperatures. Vines yield a limited crop (5 ton/ha) of aromatic fruit. Cabernet Sauvignon and Chenin (bush vines) require less water and are less affected by the prevailing winds. The bush vines produce high extracts and great complexity. Chardonnay Barrel Fermented is naturally fermented, lees maturation adding a creamy texture to the crisp acidity and citrus fruit. Lees contact also strengthens the varietal character of Sauvignon Blanc, adding weight to the wine. The Centauri blend (Cab S/F, PV) is made only in exceptional vintages and 18 months wood maturation blends seamlessly with the concentrated fruit structure. Grapes for the flagship red wine, Shiraz, are sourced from Stanford and this spicy wine shows meaty undertones and a dense mouthfeel.

ℹ️ Sauv Bl, Shz, Chard Barrel Fermented (sgl vineyard) 🍷 Cab S/F, M, Malb, PV, Sauv Bl, Chard, Chenin Bl ◑ Sales: Mon–Fri 08:00–17:00. Tasting by appt only ⚡ +27 (0)21 865 2488 ✉ info@mulderbosch.co.za, www.mulderbosch.co.za 🍴 Reds 8 y+, whites 4 y+ ⬛ 07 ℹ️ Visits by appt only

Chardonnay

Chardonnay was first brought to South Africa in 1920, but the first clones were virus infected; growth was weak, production was limited and ripening difficult. Clone choice is critical and both Old World (citrus and peach) and New World (melon and butterscotch) styles are produced. Natural fermentation allows for a more precise expression of the individuality and locality of the variety.

The diverse *terroir* generates three Chardonnay styles: wooded (100%), semi-wooded and unwooded. Cooler climate Chardonnays show a stronger acid structure and are better able to integrate percentages of (new) oak. Chardonnay is generally trellised with good concentration and ripeness. Key producers are Glen Carlou, Durbanville Hills, Hamilton Russell Vineyards, Jordan Estate and Mulderbosch.

Helderberg Blaauwklippen Pocket

View from the top – *Vineyards of the Blaauwklippen Pocket with Helderberg in the background*

The Helderberg Blaauwklippen Pocket, located south of Stellenbosch, is a wide valley runing in an east – west direction. It forms the northern border of what is locally known as 'The Golden Triangle'. This Triangle stretches along the Helderberg and is reknowned for its outstanding quality red wines. An aerial view indicates the three points of reference, namely the Stellenboschberg, Helderberg and the R44 between Stellenbosch and Somerset West (see page 61). In the 2008 *New York Times* tasting, 60 per cent of the Top 10 Wines were from the Golden Triangle (De Trafford, Rust en Vrede, Graceland, Waterford, Bilton, Alto). Vineyards are planted mainly on the west-facing foothills of the Stellenboschberg and the northern foothills of the Helderberg. The soils of these sites are derived from shale and granite respectively, often covered by a mantle of colluvial sandstone material, its calcium carbonate content neutralising the acidity of the granite. The soils become more duplex and sandy in the lower-lying areas (150 – 250 metres).

Down to earth – *The Graceland cellar epitomises functionality*

Although the Helderberg partly restricts the airflow from False Bay, this Pocket still benefits from its cooling effect, especially vineyards at higher, more exposed elevations. These vineyards also benefit from the cooling effect of the harsh synoptic southeasterly winds, prevalent during early summer. These winds contribute to grape quality, as they curtail excessive early season growth on the high-potential soils. By limiting excessive vine growth and balancing it with fruit production, vines tend to produce naturally smaller berries of high concentration. This leads to greater skin to juice ratios and subsequently increases colour and flavour extraction vinification.

Vineyards are planted from the fertile high foothills down to the poorer valley floor and growth vigour varies accordingly. A small percentage of vines on the east-facing slope (Kleine Zalze) receive early morning light and benefit from the drying effect and reduced occurrence of *Botrytis* infections.

Bush vines make an important contribution as many older blocks are still cultivated this way. On very fertile soils, vines are trained on trellises of 1,2 to 1,8 metres, creating a vertically extended canopy which reduces leaf density and increases airflow. The red wines generally have a powerful structure and show velvety tannins and dense fruit aromas. Cabernet Sauvignon shows pencil shavings, mintiness and a mineral finish in the varietal wines (Waterford, Kleine Zalze, De Trafford, Graceland and Blaauwklippen). These Cabernet characteristics are slightly quietened in the blends from Dornier and De Trafford, as Merlot and Cabernet Franc add their respective aromas. Vriesenhof, on the other hand, uses Pinotage as the main blending partner for its Enthopio (Greek 'Indigenous'). Its Pinot Noir shows strong Burgundian earthy savoury and berry notes. Other interesting red wines from this Pocket include the smoky Shiraz from Stellenzicht and the Blaauwklippen Zinfandel with sappy, cranberry fruit.

Warm welcome – *The Blaauwklippen Visitor's Centre offers wine tastings and a restaurant*

Chenin Blanc and Sémillon are favoured white varietals. The unwooded Chenin Blanc from Kleine Zalze (bush vines) produces a fragrant, floral nose with fresh acidity. Sensitive oaking on De Trafford's Chenin Blanc and Stellenzicht's Sémillon give these aromatic white wines a full and complex structure.

DRIVING ROUTE: HELDERBERG BLAAUWKLIPPEN

The Pocket is situated on the foothills of the Stellenboschberg and Helderberg. Take the R44 south towards Somerset West. As the road rises past the Stellenbosch Golf Course, turn left onto Paradyskloof Road. Passing through a quiet residential area, turn left at the T-junction and immediately right as the road rises over the hill. Take the gravel road right to Vriesenhof Vineyards. Rugby legend, Jan Boland Coetzee, is championing Pinotage as a blending partner with other red varieties in a Cape Blend.

Return to the R44 and continue a few hundred metres to the traffic lights on the crest. Turn left onto Blaauwklippen Road. A petrol station and small shopping centre flank the turn-off. Shortly after the road turns to gravel, take the left turn-off to Dornier. The magnificent architecture has earned it international recognition, and its Bodega restaurant serves lunch with a spectacular mountain view.

Less than two kilometres further on the right, lies Waterford. An orchard-lined driveway guides visitors to the Cape Mediterranean buildings, where tastings are presented in the courtyard with a delectable chocolate and wine experience. Further along (3 km), take the left fork through a small gate and drive the last few metres to De Trafford winery. Architect-turned-winemaker David Trafford tends some of the steepest vineyards in South Africa to make powerful, yet balanced, red wines as well as a delicate straw wine. Retrace the route and turn left onto the gravel road.

TRAVELLING TIPS

Accommodation:
Graceland Cottage +27 (0)21 881 3121
Kleine Zalze Guest cottages +27 (0)21 880 0717

Restaurants:
Blaauwklippen Restaurant +27 (0)21 880 0133
Bodega (Dornier) +27 (0)21 880 0557
Terroir Restaurant (Kleine Zalze) +27 (0)21 880 8167

Interests:
Dylan Lewis Studio +27 (0)21 880 0054
Paintings, Rita Trafford (De Trafford)
Stellenbosch Aerodrome +27 (0)21 880 0294

Colluvial / Colluvium: Unconsolidated deposits of soil or rock fragments which accumulate at the foot of slopes.

The next winery, Stellenzicht, is on the left. A pioneer of Shiraz in South Africa, Stellenzicht's dramatic 1994 Shiraz and, more recently, 2002 vintage from a mature vineyard have set a benchmark for this variety.

Drive two kilometres to the next winery, Graceland Vineyards, on the left. Buzz the intercom at the gate for access. Graceland's use of stylish packaging for the flaghip and Strawberry Fields is a visual feast. Continue on the gravel road to the T-junction with the R44 about 300 metres further. Here you can only turn left. The next large intersection with an access road to a local shopping mall provides a place to turn around.

Driving north on the R44 (in the direction of Stellenbosch), the road rises to meet the town. Near the crest, two grand ladies await. Turn left at the Kleine Zalze signs and left again to the security check point. A few hundred metres further is the visitors' area, restaurant (aptly named *Terroir*) a pristine golf course and a luxury guest house. From Kleine Zalze, cross over the R44 to Blaauwklippen's imposing entrance. Signs indicate the visitors' area. Adjacent to the tasting room is a restaurant, deli and gift shop. A stroll around the exquisite gardens provides photographic opportunities as sculpted lawns meet historical Cape Dutch architecture.

GPS WAYPOINTS

Blaauwklippen S33° 58.364 E18° 50.805
De Trafford S34° 00.765 E18° 53.921
Dornier S33° 59.536 E18° 52.283
Graceland S33° 59.608 E18° 50.022
Kleine Zalze S33° 58.219 E18° 50.157
Stellenzicht S33° 59.833 E18° 51.996
Vriesenhof S33° 58.262 E18° 52.031
Waterford S33° 59.875 E18 52.206

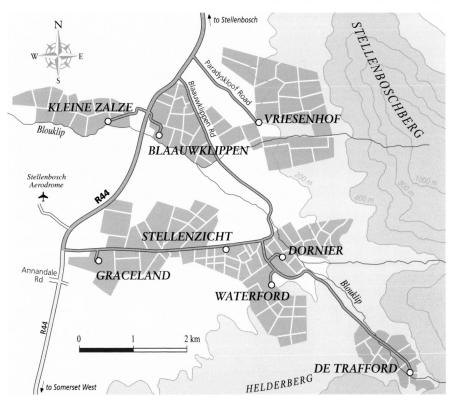

DE TRAFFORD

The Trafford family's winery is set spectacularly in the heights of the Helderberg. A small cultivation of five hectares is established on north-facing slopes, more than 320 meters above sea level. This secluded valley is well protected from prevailing winds, and enjoys mountain airflow from the steep slopes as well as the cooling effect of higher elevations. Merlot is planted closer to the river on clay soils as it requires more water. Shiraz is sited on higher slopes in poor soil to control growth vigour. Grapes are harvested at high sugar levels and undergo spontaneous fermentation, adding to the complexity of the wines. Components for the powerful Elevation 393 red blend (Cabernet Sauvignon/Merlot/Shiraz) are individually oaked and bottled without fining or filtration after 22 months. The *Vin de Paille* is a sweet straw wine made from Chenin Blanc, sourced from a neighbouring farm on the valley floor. The Cabernet Sauvignon is made from vines each carrying only one kilogram of grapes, rendering a luxuriously dense wine.

ℹ️ Elevation 393 (Cab S / M / Shz), Straw Wine 🍷 Cab S, M, Shz, Chenin Bl 🕐 Fri, Sat 10:00–13:00 📞 +27 (0)21 880 1611 📧 info@detrafford.co.za, www.detrafford.co.za 🍾 10 y 🍷 98, 00, 01, 03, 05, 06, 07 ℹ️ Family artwork on labels of each vintage, secluded valley scenery, self-catering cottage

STELLENZICHT

Dating back to 1692, the Stellenzicht farm received its name in 1981, literally 'view of Stellen(bosch)'. Situated in the heart of the Golden Triangle, the wine labels bear testament to this exceptional *terroir*. With a long history of winemaking, the 1994 Syrah set a new benchmark, taking laurels in an international taste-off. One-hundred-and-three hectares of vines are grown on west and northwest-facing slopes on medium fertility soils of decomposed granite and sandstone. Elevation (100 – 400 m above sea level) as well as the close proximity of the ocean provide a cooling effect on the trellised vineyards. Sémillon free-run juice (from a mature, low-yielding vineyard, 4,4 ton/ha) completes alcoholic and malolactic fermentation in new oak, with eight months of *bâttonage* while maturing in barrel. This process results in a waxy wine showing citrus fruits, vanilla and smoky oak. Warm fermentation and extended barrel maturation (20 – 30 months) yields powerful and structured red wines. The mature (16 y) single vineyard still produces a prominent ripe, smoky Shiraz wine .

ℹ️ Syrah 🍷 Cab S / F, M, Mal, Shz, P, PV, Sauv Bl, Chard, Sém 🕐 Mon–Fri 09:00–17:00 Sat, Sun, Publ hols 10:00–16:00 Closed Easter, Dec 25, Jan 1 📞 +27 (0)21 880 1103/4 📧 info@stellenzicht.co.za, www.stellenzicht.co.za 🍾 Syrah 10 y, Sém 7 y+ 🍷 Shz 99, 01, 05; Sém 98, 99, 02, 03 ℹ️ Label features a Golden Triangle (ref to Helderberg area)

GRACELAND VINEYARDS

Graceland, a boutique cellar, is located at the foot of the Helderberg. Elegant packaging in purple tissue presents the flagship blend, known as Three Graces. Similarly exciting is the colourful design for Strawberry Fields, a new Shiraz/Cab blend.

Ten hectares of red varieties are planted on cool south-facing slopes – an interesting change from the norm, as reds are usually planted on north-facing slopes to maximise sun exposure. The structured soils of sandstone on decomposed granite allow for good drainage and adequate air circulation at root level. Vines are slightly water stressed in the dry summer months, reducing berry size and increasing the skin to juice ratio. Vines are planted to a very low planting density of 2 850 vines per hectare on the steep slopes.

Careful canopy management sees the removal of excess leaves and shoots to open the canopy, increasing sunlight and airflow to ensure good colour development and to dry the grapes. This practice reduces disease and promotes fertility in the buds. Vineyards are harvested several times, selecting only fully ripened grapes.

Grapes are fermented in open-top cement tanks and several daily punch-downs ensure sufficient skin to juice contact for colour extraction. Extended barrel maturation of 20 months gives the blend a pronounced wood character, but the slow, controlled oxidation integrates and softens the tannins. The classic styled Three Graces, a seamless blend of Cabernet Sauvignon, Merlot and Shiraz, is structured and dense, needing several years to develop.

Innovative packaging – The eye-catching packaging of the Strawberry Fields wine

ℹ️ Three Graces (Cab S / Shz / M) 🍷 Cab S, Merlot, Shz 🕐 By appt only 📞 +27 (0)21 881 3121 📧 graceland@iafrica.com, www.gracelandvineyards.com 🍾 7 y 🍷 98, 01, 03, 05 ℹ️ B&B cottage

BLAAUWKLIPPEN

Blaauwklippen Vineyards, situated on the slopes of the Stellenboschberg, is one of the oldest wineries in South Africa. Founded in 1682, the farm celebrated its 325th anniversary in 2007. This milestone was highlighted with, among others, the inauguration of an annual Farm Festival and Market and the release of a trio of Zinfandel wines reflecting the unique tradition of Blaauwklippen.

Blaauwklippen's winemaking philosophy is best summarised in this quotation from their managing director and cellar master, Rolf Zeitvogel: 'Winemaking is treated with respect, and handled with discipline. Here winemaking is not a job, it is a passion and we surround ourselves with people who feel the same way. We are a proud farm, proud of our heritage, our products, and our people.'

Traditional architecture – Blaauwklippen's Cape Dutch homestead (circa 1790)

Resting vines – During winter, vines need a period of rest before the next growth phase

Today Blaauwklippen cultivates 100 hectares with most of the vineyards having been replanted during the past seven years. These new vineyards incorporate the latest virus-free material, as well as a selection of clones within each variety which are best suited to the *terroir*. The oldest Zinfandel vines are 20 years old and give great concentration to the resulting wines. The new vines are planted on a higher trellising system, lifting the canopy off the ground to increase airflow under the grape zone. The average planting density has increased to 6 500 vines per hectare.

Red cultivars make up approximately 98 per cent of the vineyards which are planted to Cabernet Sauvignon, Cabernet Franc, Merlot, Petit Verdot, Shiraz, Malbec and Zinfandel. The remaining two per cent is planted to Viognier. Zinfandel is planted, together with Shiraz and Cabernet Sauvignon, on the lower west-facing slopes of the mountain in sandy soils with a granite component. These soils seem to influence the floral and fruit expression in wines. Merlot excels on the south-facing slopes, with sea breezes tempering the hot summer days.

Vineyard road – The tree-lined entrance to the tasting room

The Blaauwklippen Vineyard Selection Zinfandel has been the leading label for this variety over the past decade in the Cape. Natural fermentation is used for both the alcoholic and malolactic stages of the winemaking process. The successful implementation of this high-risk technique is testimony to the quality control in the cellar. Executed correctly, it develops a completely different range of flavours in wine, supporting the development of spicy and dried fruit flavours. The Blaauwklippen Vineyard Selection Zinfandel is matured in French oak, steering away from the sweetness and vanilla characters of American oak. By using old barrels like many neighbouring cellars, maturation is extended to 16 months. The flagship blend, the Cabriolet (Cab S, Cab F, M) is done at the latest possible stage, and each component is matured separately to obtain the most from its own development in wood. The annual Blaauwklippen blending competition, held publicly, is now in its 26th year and is still a great favourite with wine enthusiasts.

Spring wedding – Final preparations for a wedding feast under the giant oak trees at Blaauwklippen

Blaauwklippen offers a wine centre and shop, cellar tours and a restaurant, with lovely outdoor seating (weather permitting) under magnificent trees. Relive a bygone era with horse-drawn rides through the vineyards (seasonal). The Manor House and Werf are magnificent settings for private functions and romantic weddings.

🛈 Blaauwklippen Vineyard Selection, Blaauwklippen Cultivar Selection, Landau range 🍷 Zin, Cab S, F, Shz, Malbec, M, PV, Viog 🕐 Mon–Fri 09:00–17:00, Sat 10:00–17:00, Sun 10:00–16:00. Closed Dec 25, Jan 1 ☎ +27 (0)21 880 0133 ✉ hospitality@ blaauwklippen.com, www.blaauwklippen.com 📧 5–10 y 🍇 04, 07, 09 ℹ Blending competition, cellar tours, restaurant, wine shop, conference centre, functions venue

DORNIER

Located on the foothills of the Stellenboschberg, Dornier is one of the South African Winelands' architectural gems as the simple yet bold lines of the cellar building embody the balance between the opposites of change and stasis, seriousness and pleasure, complexity and simplicity. Dornier is also the proud guardian of an historical Sir Herbert Baker homestead.

The team at Dornier is governed by a philosophy that is (to be) led by the principles of tradition and inspired by perfection; yet they realise the power of innovation'. From a single focus on grape cultivation in the early 1990s, the acquisition of outstanding neighbouring plots ensured that fine winemaking could start. Late owner Christoph Dornier sought to design a facility as 'a visual translation of our wines – elegant, clear yet complex and distinctly unique' and in 2003 the loft-styled building came into

Positive reflections – The towering mountains reflected in the glass panelled office suites

being. With its curved roof, face brick and reflectinve materials, the building resembles two large waves (or together with its reflection in the pond, two fish), blending architecture creatively into the dramatic scenery of Stellenboschberg.

Bodega – A relaxed atmosphere and fine dining at Dornier

Since its maiden vintage in 2003, this cellar has been dedicated to understanding Dornier's *terroir* in order to produce premium wines. The cellar now offers three ranges focusing on elegance and freshness. Located less than 20 kilometres from False Bay, the farm enjoys a maritime climate. Dornier's soil is predominantly made up of decomposed granite with varying degrees of clay, providing good moisture retention through the ripening period. The vines are cultivated on northwest-facing slopes, which provide full sun exposure for optimum ripening, while cool afternoon breezes promote slow ripening conditions.

Currently 60 hectares are cultivated and another 20 hectares are being planned. Planting density for new vineyards is to increase to 5 500 vines per hectare to encourage greater surface to leaf exposure and restrict root growth for greater concentration in the developing fruit. Younger vines are suckered (removal of underdeveloped shoots) and green harvested (removal of underdeveloped and unrequired bunches) to ensure that the plants develop properly before being allowed to carry fruit, as well as ensuring a balance between the vegetative growth and fruit production in established plants. This strategy proves successful as vines get older as most will achieve a consistent production of approximately six to seven tons per hectare. Technologies such as infrared spectrometry, soil water measurements and leaf analysis are done to provide a comprehensive report of vineyard performance and management requirements.

Ahoy me mates – Even pirates of the smallest stature can enjoy the surroundings at Dornier

Fountain – The fountain outside Bodega restaurant sends a happy water song through the lunch hour

Grapes are hand harvested and cleaned from any leaves or damaged or underdeveloped grapes. A careful second sorting is done in the winery before the grapes are crushed and destemmed. The premium red wines receive about five days of cold maceration to extract colour before they are inoculated with selected yeast strains for alcoholic fermentation. Malolactic fermentation is done in a combination of oak barrels and stainless steel tanks. The wine is then racked with intentional air exposure. Not only does the oxygen serve to avoid reductive aromas, but also assists in the chemical stabilisation of the colour molecules.

Attention to detail – *The sculpted shape of the wine cellar is continued in signage throughout the farm*

The flagship range includes a red and a white wine, Donatus Red and Donatus White. Cabernet Sauvignon and Cabernet Franc, the components of the Donatus Red, are matured in 225 litre French oak barrels (40 % new wood), for up for 14 months. After maturation, the final blend is created. In this dense and highly structured wine, the Cabernet Sauvignon gives dark fruit aromas, density and body, the Cabernet Franc provides finesse and a delicate violet perfume. On the palate, tannins are refined and silky, contrasted by a distinctive minerality to an elegant finish.

In the white flagship, Donatus White, the focus is to bring together the opulence and complexity of barrel-aged Chenin Blanc with the freshness and rich mouthfeel of Sémillon. Only free-run Chenin juice is used. While alcoholic fermentation starts in stainless steel tanks, it is transferred to barrels to complete the process. The wine is then aged in a combination of new and older 300 litre French oak barrels for up to eight months, resulting in a weighty yet crisp wine with a gentle oak character. Sémillon is aged on the lees after alcoholic fermentation with regular *bâttonage* (stirring of the lees) to promote the development of a rich mouthfeel. The wood lends an opulent colour to the final blend, with aromas of white pear, peach and honey complemented by roasted coffee and citrus.

The Dornier range offers four single variety red wines, still within the premium quality range. They show the typical varietal character at their best. The Cabernet Sauvignon, Merlot and Pinotage are top examples of Stellenbosch single varietal wines. The Dornier Chenin Blanc is sourced from old bush vines in the Swartland Pocket, adding another excellent *terroir* to the portfolio. The Cocoa Hill range consists of perfectly accessible quality red, Rosé and white wines for everyday consumption.

At Dornier, lifestyle and visual aspects are also of great importance. The golden thread of design flows throughout: Managing Director, Raphael Dornier, equates the pioneering work on architecture with pioneering work on Chenin Blanc and white blends in particular, in an environment where Chenin was historically seen as a poor quality grape.

The wave shape of the building's roof is repeated on the winery's labels and the logo is a symbol of the seduction of Leda by Zeus as he transformed himself into a swan. The Dornier Bodega Restaurant has become one of the most popular in the Winelands. Situated in an historical barn, its large veranda, bright colours and arts joyfully blend to welcome visitors to a relaxed experience with some of the best food, wine and views the Winelands have to offer.

Modern architecture – *Dornier's loft-style winery with its curved roof, face brick and reflective materials*

[i] Donatus Red (Bdx Blend), Donatus White (Chenin Bl, Sém) ▧ Cab S, Cab F, M, P, Chenin Bl, Sém, Sauv Bl ◯ Tasting: daily 10:00–17:00. Restaurant: Lunch 12:00–17:00, dinner 18:00–21:30, booking essential ✆ +27 (0)21 880 0557 ✉ info@dornier.co.za (wine), bodega@dornier.co.za (rest), www.dornier.co.za ▤ Red 10 y+, white 5–6 y ▬ 06 ℹ Nature & wine & food experience, art & crafts for sale, cellar tours on request, no booking for tasting, venue for corporate functions

KLEINE ZALZE

Wine has been produced on this family-owned wine estate since 1695. It is now owned by Kobus Basson, Rolf Schulz and their families.

Eighty hectares of classic grape varieties are cultivated in two distinct planting areas. Twenty-six hectares of Cabernet Sauvignon, Shiraz and Merlot have been planted on the slightly warmer southwest-facing slopes where they produce bold, fruity wines with great structure. Small parcels of Chardonnay and Chenin Blanc, which require a little more heat for even bud break, are also located on these warmer slopes. The cooler south-facing slopes host 48 hectares of vines. Here Cabernet Sauvignon, Merlot and Shiraz produce elegant, spicy wines. Some Sémillon and Sauvignon Blanc are also planted on these slopes with typical cool-climate characteristics.

Luxury getaway – The Kleine Zalze Lodge is the perfect luxurious getaway

Terroir – Aptly named, Terroir restaurant offers seasonal produce from the area

The canopies of vines on the warmer sites are denser to protect grapes from sun damage. The deep red soils of granite and clay are well drained and the vines are spaced further apart to encourage root development and subsequent growth vigour. Canopies are vertically spread on the trellis system in order to create a balance between the vine's growth and grape production and to allow grapes to ripen evenly. The old cellar has been renovated and upgraded to reduce mechanical handling. Natural winemaking methods include whole bunch pressing to reduce harsh tannins in the wine and the use of free-run juice and gentler peristaltic pumping of liquids. A temperature-controlled barrel-fermentation cellar has been installed along with a 1 500-barrel capacity maturation cellar embedded in the cool granite earth as well as berry selection by hand on a conveyer belt to ensure only the best quality fruit is selected.

Quality control – Hand sorting of individual grape berries

The flagship Family Reserve range includes a Shiraz and a Cabernet Sauvignon from single vineyards, and a Sauvignon Blanc. These varietal wines are only produced from exceptional vintages and are award-winning wines. Red grapes receive three days of cold maceration before fermentation commences with regular pump-overs to extract colour and flavour. The wines go through malolactic fermentation in barrel, and are then matured for 18 to 22 months totally in new wood. These labour-intensive practices ensure that wood characteristics are well integrated with fruit flavours. White grapes are pressed and the clear juice is cold fermented to retain its crisp, fruity flavours. Chenin Blanc, from bush vines, is available in both unwooded as well as wooded versions and is produced in an off-dry style (6,5 g/l sugar), producing wines with powerful alcohols of around 14 per cent, neatly hidden within white flower aromas and rich tropical fruit flavours.

Glenrosa soil – Winemaker Johan Joubert showing the highly prized Glenrosa soil in the Cabernet Sauvignon vineyard

Also on the wine estate is the *Terroir* Restaurant, featuring Provencal cuisine with a Cape twist, which has consistently been voted one of the Top 10 restaurants in South Africa since opening in 2004. Kleine Zalze Lodge, a 4-star lodge, 41-bedroom country house, is situated adjacent to the first fairway of the world-class De Zalze Golf Course. The Lodge enjoys panoramic views of the Stellenbosch Mountains, the vineyards of Kleine Zalze or the golf course. Facilities include a relaxed restaurant, swimming pool, sauna and gym. The Kleine Zalze Function Room caters for conferences and weddings in a unique setting overlooking the wine cellar.

ℹ️ Family Reserve Range: Shiraz, Cabernet Sauvignon (sgl vineyard) Sauvignon Blanc ⬛ Cab S, Shz, Sauv Bl, P, Chenin Bl, Chard, Gamay, M, Shz, Cab S blends 🕐 Mon–Sat 09:00–18:00, Sun 11:00–18:00. Closed Easter Fri, Dec 25, Jan 1 ☎ +27 (0)21 880 0717 ✉️ quality@kleinezalze.co.za, www.kleinezalze.co.za 🍷 White 3–4 y, reds 5–7 y ⬛ 98, 03, 04, 05, 06 ℹ️ Tours by appt, restaurant, guest lodge, golf course, play area for children, venue (conferences, weddings)

VRIESENHOF

Jan 'Boland' Coetzee produces three distinct wine ranges under the Vriesenhof, Talana Hill and Paradyskloof labels. His belief that Pinotage creates its finest expression in a blend gave birth to the Enthopio (Greek 'Indigenous') blend. Vines are planted on south-facing slopes in granite and shale soils at varying elevations (200 – 240 m). Coastal breezes from False Bay moderate the climate and vineyard management focuses on protecting heat-sensitive grapes while ensuring sufficient exposure for its red varieties. While most varieties are planted in an east–west row direction to reduce direct sunlight during the day, the Cabernet Sauvignon is planted along a north–south axis on a north-facing slope to capture the maximum sunlight. This ensures proper ripening and colour development.

The Pinot Noir, planted on south-facing slopes, receives fewer hours of direct sun and the tops of its high canopy are bent at an angle to give protective shade during the summer. The Pinot Noir blocks are planted on both granite and shale soils to enhance the complexity of the inherent aromas of this grape variety. Trellised vines are planted at a relatively high density (4 700 vines/ha) to restrict vigorous growth with the exception of a hilltop Pinotage vineyard, where low bush vines and rich shale soil enhance its fruity flavours.

Hi-tech equipment blends seamlessly with traditional methods of punch-downs. Components of the Kallista and Enthopio are blended before maturation and age in French oak barrels. The Pinot Noir is matured exclusively in Burgundian barrels. The use of barrels are to support the aromas of red berries, stewed fruits and forest floor. Talana Hill, a tiny 7,2 hectare southwest-facing vineyard hosts two single-vineyard wines: a Chardonnay and a Merlot/Cabernet Franc blend.

Guardian mountain – Helderberg towering above Vriesenhof manor house

[i] Kallista (Cab S / F) P, PN, Cab S / F, M, Chard Mon–Fri 10:00–15:30, Sat 10:00–14:00, 1st Sat of month (Jun–Aug). Closed Sun, pub hols. +27 (0)21 880 0284 info@vriesenhof.co.za, www.vriesenhof.co.za 10 y+ 91, 92, 95, 03, 05, 07 Tours, meals and refreshments by appt

WATERFORD ESTATE

Established in 1998, Waterford Estate has been a leading Cape winery from the moment it opened its doors. The philosophy to create 'top wines that are unique and can successfully compete with rest of the world' resulted in three flagship wines: Kevin Arnold Shiraz, Waterford Cabernet Sauvignon and, most recently, The Jem.

Unlike Helderberg's generally fertile, rich red soils, Waterford Estate is located on one of two ridges with granite and sandstone soils. Fifty hectares are cultivated and red varieties benefit from this low-potential soil to produce concentrated fruit. The white varieties and the Merlot are planted on more fertile red soil. On higher elevations, an east – west orientation protects grapes from sunburn and accommodates the prevailing wind, while on lower-lying areas rows are directed north – south. The grapes are hand harvested and each parcel is fermented separately. Gravitational advantages are employed in the single-storey cellar, with tanks hanging from the roof, eliminating unnecessary pumping of the wines. Chardonnay is 90 per cent barrel fermented and matures on the lees for up to nine months. Regular *bâttonage* adds a rich toastiness and fleshes out the mid-palate.

Once the components of The Jem have completed malolactic fermentation, the blend is made and aged in a combination of new and older French oak. This dense wine shows pencil shavings, truffles and distinctive Helderberg spice and earthiness. The Shiraz has black cherry with hints of coffee, spice and cured ham while the Cabernet Sauvignon's blackberry and violet nose combines pencil shavings with fennel seed. The red flagships all show minerality, a rich palate while remaining lean and elegant.

The Waterford Way – A philosophy that celebrates prosperity, life, food, wine, family and friends

[i] The Jem (Cab S / Shz / Cab F / Malb / M / Mourv / Sang / Barb), Kevin Arnold Shz, Waterford Cab S Cab S, Shz, Chard, Sauv Bl (sgl vineyard), NLH, Chenin Bl Mon–Fri 08:00–17:00, Sat 10:00–15:00 +27 (0)21 880 0496 info@waterfordestate.co.za, www. waterfordestate.co.za 20 y+ 03, 05, 07 Cape Mediterranean courtyard from local sandstone, chocolate & wine experience, reserve tasting by appt (older vintages)

Helderberg Annandale Pocket

Mountain aspects – The Annadale Pocket enjoys the sun exposure and cooling air movement on the mountain slopes

Bordering the Helderberg Blaauwklippen Pocket to the south is the Helderberg Annandale Pocket, the southern secton of The Golden Triangle (see page 61). Although climatic conditions are very similar to those of its northern neighbour, vineyards in this Pocket are sheltered from False Bay due to their specific location. Situated on the northern slopes of Helderberg at elevations of 150 to 300 metres, the vineyards are exposed to the harsh southeasterly summer winds. Most vines are trellised to protect the developing vine shoots.

History and humour – An historical slave bell becomes a friendly inviation at Annandale (cellar 1700s, farm 1688)

The soils are almost exclusively derived from granite, ranging from structured subsoils covered by sandstone to the coveted yellow to reddish-brown mountain soils. These soils generally have a high potential, but the strong, cold winds during the early summer months generally give a balanced growth and production by restricting vegetative growth in the vines.

As this Pocket stretches up the Helderberg, vines are cultivated on both low- and high-lying sites with vigour varying accordingly. Bush vines form a large percentage of the total hectares under cultivation. Trellised vines are trained between 1,2 and 1,8 metres high, creating a vertically extended canopy which reduces leaf density and increases airflow. The classic noble varieties are well represented in this Pocket, as are other varieties such as Chenin Blanc, Viognier, Petit Verdot and Mourvèdre. This Pocket is one of the oldest established wine-producing areas in Stellenbosch and, with its highly desirable granite soils and northern exposure, it became one of the first premium red wine areas. The generous fruit flavours of wines effortlessly absorb higher alcohol levels to an elegant finish of silky tannins.

Cabernet Sauvignon and Merlot are firm favourites to produce highly structured blends with some Shiraz, Cabernet Franc, Malbec and Petit Verdot softening the blends' muscular edges. Highly recommended wines from these varietals are made at Rust en Vrede, Bilton, Hidden Valley and Ernie Els Wines. As single varietal wines, the reds produce fragrant red berries and savoury notes while retaining the tight tannin structure, with very impressive examples from Hidden Valley (Cab S), Annandale (Shz) and Bilton (M). High-lying Uva Mira specialises in Chardonnay. The cool ripening conditions yield wine with high natural acidity, fragrant white fruits and restrained alcohol levels, and good structure from the sensitive oaking.

GPS WAYPOINTS

Alto S34° 0.173 E18° 50.823
Annandale S33° 59.886 E18° 49.758
Bilton S33° 59.877 E18° 50.951
Haskell Vineyards S34° 00.211 E18° 51.621
Uva Mira S34° 01.411 E18° 51.491

DRIVING ROUTE: HELDERBERG ANNANDALE

Leave Stellenbosch on the R44 driving towards Somerset West. Just outside the town, at the intersection with Annandale Road, turn left (into Annandale Road) at the traffic lights and drive in the direction of the mountain. Annandale is on the immediate left. Annandale's owner, South African rugby legend Hempies du Toit, is a man of the earth. His big frame belies the gentle way in which he cares for his vines. The rustic cellar (circa 1866) is home to a charming tasting room.

Turn left back onto Annandale Road. About two kilometres further, turn right at the signs indicating Uva Mira. Take the right fork and continue on the tarred road up the steep mountain slope. The new tasting room boasts one of the most impressive views over the

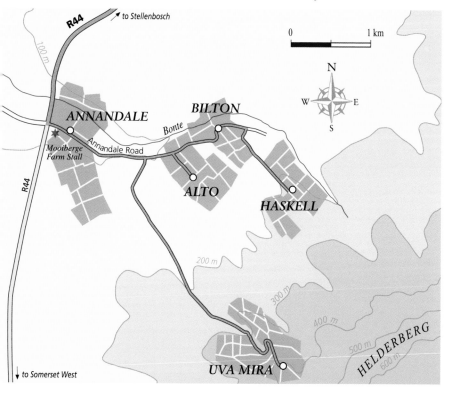

Helderberg towards False Bay. The farm also sells proteas and fynbos. Return to Annandale Road and continue a few metres to the entrance of the Pocket's oldest winery, Alto. Alto produces wines with Old-World class combined with New-World appeal. Continue past the security gate to visit Bilton. A premium Merlot producer, Bilton's tasting facility offers deep leather chairs and a large fireplace for cosy wine tastings in winter. Continue on this road as it passes behind Bilton's cellar to the entrance of Haskell Vineyards on the right. This tranquil setting is the perfect ending to a day in the Winelands.

TRAVELLING TIPS

Restaurants:
Bilton Restaurant +27 (0)21 881 3721

Interests:
Mooiberge farmstall (strawberries) +27 (0)21 881 3222
Picnics, chocolate tasting (Bilton) +27 (0)21 881 3721
Proteas and fynbos on sale (Uva Mira)
Venue (Bilton) +27 (0)21 881 3721

ALTO

Alto dates back to 1693 as a red wine specialist. The Latin name refers to the aspirations of the estate and its elevated location. Since 1972, Alto has been world-renowned for its handcrafted, bold red wines. Today, 93 hectares of the total 191 are cultivated to vines, clinging to the granite slopes at an elevation of 100 to 500 metres above sea level. The north-facing slopes receive ample sun exposure while the late-afternoon sea breezes from False Bay moderate the temperature, thus lengthening the ripening period and producing complex flavours. Vines are trellised against occasional strong winds and are irrigated when required. Grapes are hand-picked and cold fermented with regular pump-overs to extract colour and flavour from the skins. Malolactic fermentation is completed in tanks; thereafter the wines are transferred to oak barrels for maturation. A small percentage of American and East-European oak (5%) complements the savoury notes from French oak with hints of spice and sweet vanilla. Following the Rhône style, the wines are dense with bright fruit and fine tannins.

Cab Sauv, Cab S, Shz, Port Mon–Fri 09:00–17:00, Sat 10:00–16:00. Closed Sun & public hols +27 (0)21 881 3884 info@alto.co.za, www.alto.co.za 10–15 y Stunning views, Port & sweets pairing (booking req)

HASKELL VINEYARDS

Haskell Vineyards is nestled in the folds of the Helderberg. Purchased, and subsequently developed by Preston Haskell in 2002, Haskell Vineyards has focused on creating small volume, super premium wines that reflect the individuality and character of the estate's unique *terroir*.

Approximately 16 hectares of red varieties are cultivated on warm, north-facing slopes of granite rocks. Vineyards have been planted on sites that have been chosen for their suitability to specific varieties. Two elevated, high stone fraction areas are planted to Shiraz while Cabernet Sauvignon and Merlot are situated on lower slopes containing more clay. One Shiraz vineyard is planted on a single south-facing site where conditions are cooler and the vines are protected from the prevailing wind.

Vineyard canopies are opened by removing leaves to ensure sufficient sun exposure and air movement, which in turn discourages diseases. Yields are low and reflect Haskell Vineyards' total commitment to excellence from vineyard to bottle. Red varieties are hand harvested and crushed, destemmed and sorted on a sorting table before fermentation is allowed to occur naturally. By avoiding excessive pressure, the extraction of bitter tannins from the pips is minimised. Following malolactic fermentation, the clear wine is racked to French oak barrels, maturing for a period of 12 to16 months.

The flagship wine, Haskell IV matures for an additional 12 months in bottle and shows spicy, savoury notes and well-integrated tannins. The Haskell team also produce the award-winning Dombeya range of wines which comprises a Shiraz, Cabernet Sauvignon/Merlot blend, Chardonnay and a Sauvignon Blanc.

Be in touch – At the stylish Dombeya tasting room, visitors can see into the cellar and be part of the action

Haskell IV (Bdx blend), Haskell Aeon Syrah, Haskell Pillars Syrah (both sgl vineyard) By appt Mon–Fri +27 (0)021 881 3895 info@dombeyawines.com, www.dombeyawines.com 6 y+ 07 Restaurant, coffee shop

BILTON

Vines were first planted on Bilton's historical property in 1726. The original cellar (circa 1824) has been restored to a tasting room, restaurant and wine bar. Sixty-five hectares of vineyards are cultivated on various exposures of the Helderberg. The highest elevation (680 m) has mainly granite and clay soils with increased sand content found on lower slopes, providing two distinct *terroir* origins as building blocks for its signature red blend. Planting densities are increased and the canopy is vertically extended on a higher trellis to increase the sunlight exposure.
A new gravity flow cellar was built in 2006. Red grapes are cold soaked and then fermented in open-top vessels. Maturation is extended to 22 months using about 90 per cent new barrels and the alcohol goes almost undetected as it fits seamlessly into the fine tannin structure and upfront fruit. The Wine and Chocolate experience matches a style of chocolate to each individual wine for a gastronomic indulgence.

Sir Percy (Cab S, M, PV) M, Cab S, Shz, P, Sauv Bl, Viog, PV Mon–Fri 08:30–17:00, Sat 10:00–15:00. Closed Christian holidays +27 (0)21 881 3714 sales@biltonwines.com, www.biltonwines.co.za 20 y 02, 06 Chocolate & wine tasting, 5 km vineyard walk, restaurant, picnics, weddings, vintage cars and child friendly

UVA MIRA

Uva Mira is a family-owned boutique winery, perched high on the slopes of the Helderberg. The farm is one of the highest vineyard sites, boasting views of Table Mountain, Cape Point, Robben Island, False- and Table Bay. Thirty hectares of vines are located at 420 to 620 metres above sea level, providing grapes a cool climate for ripening. Trellising protect vines against strong prevailing winds. Grapes from the single vineyard Chardonnay (550 m) are whole-bunch pressed, avoiding skin contact and harsh tannins. Naturally fermented in barrels, it produces a rich and elegant wine. Fruit from mature Sauvignon Blanc vines (20 y) are fermented reductively at low temperatures (12°C) and lees aging adds to the concentrated tropical fruit and gooseberry flavours. Merlot-Cabernet Sauvignon and Red Blend are vinified separately with the emphasis on capturing site expressions, complexity and development potential, showing the distinctiveness of these high-altitude vineyard sites.

Vineyard Selection Uva Mira Cab S, Cab F, M, Shz, Sauv Bl, Chard Mon–Fri 08:00–17:00, Sat 10:00–16:00, Sun 10:00–16:00 (Dec–Feb). Closed Easter Fri, Sun; Dec 25, 26; Jan 1 +27 (0)21 880 1683 info@uvamira.co.za, www.uvamira. co.za Whites 6–8 y, reds 8–10 y Winetasting, spectacular 360° views, cheese platters, protea and fynbos conservation

ANNANDALE

The historical Annandale Wine Estate dates back to 1688 and is home to some serious red wines. Springbok rugby legend Hempies du Toit established 45 hectares of vines along the west- and south-facing foothills of the Helderberg. An additional 20 hectares of the property remains in its natural state as a conservation area. This includes a unique two-hectare wild olive forest.

Nine-to-fourteen year old vines are cultivated on high-potential gravelly granite-based soils ensuring balanced growth. Grapes on Annandale ripen to a dark, dense colour expressing the concentrated characteristics of each cultivar as the crop is limited to seven tons/ha by strict canopy management and slightly increased planting densities of 3 750 vines per hectare. Vertical trellising protects the vines from the strong prevailing southeasterly wind and spreads the canopy to optimise sun expsoure and photosynthesis during ripening. Hand-selected grapes are crushed and destemmed before fermentation with selected yeast culture. The extended skin contact creates wines with great extraction and depth. Maturation is between 36 and 66 months, with a combination of new and older French oak barrels delivering an elegant, well-integrated wine. The flagship wine matures for 48 months in 100% new French oak.

Hempies regards walking through the cellar and vineyards as 'food for a person's soul', and in his office he proudly displays the philosophy he shares with the great André C Simon: 'Wine is as old as the thirst of man, not the physical thirst which man can so easily quench with water, as his horse or his dogs do, but the heaven-sent thirst [that] will still our fears – our minds be at peace, our sense and sensibility stirred – that we shall not ignore nor excuse God's good gifts, wine not the least of them.' The Du Toit family of Piet and Hempies recently celebrated 50 years of red wine-making since 1959.

Rustic experience – Wine tastings in the 1800s cellar at Annandale

Shiraz Cab S, F, Shz, M Mon–Sat 09:00–17:00. Closed Christian hols +27 (0)21 881 3560 info@annandale.co.za, www.annandale.co.za 10–5 y 99, 01 17th-century rustic cellar, six generations of wine tradition

Helderberg Foothills Pocket

Viticultural paradise – The foothills of the Helderberg are home to a variety of well-known wines

This Pocket covers the foothills of the towering Helderberg. Vineyards are planted at a relatively high elevation and as the Pocket lies within seven to eight kilometres from False Bay, it enjoys the full benefit of cooling sea breezes.

These foothills are part of a historical glacierated valley. As the Eerste River and ocean retreated, they removed a great proportion of the top soil. What remained was a mixture of sand, gravel and clay from granite parent material. Due to this removal-action, the soils tend to be shallow, (max depth approx. 1,5 m). As with its neighbouring mountain Pockets, soils are yellow to reddish-brown and well drained with a high potential. The induced growth vigour of the vines is halted by cold and often strong early summer winds. This ensures a good balance between the vigour of the vine and its fruit production, a requirement for premium quality wine grapes.

The Pocket's vineyards are spread over the foothills with elevations of 60 metres to over 400

Local 'clos' – The unmistakable white wall around the homestead of Stonewall

metres above sea level. Due to the elevation and subsequent soil variation, vines are cultivated both as bush vines and on vertical trellises. Bush vines are largely concentrated in the lower-lying areas. Large variations in planting density occur due to the steepness of slopes, from as little as 2 500 vines on the steepest slopes to 4 500 vines per hectare in lower-lying areas.

This Pocket is well known for its refined white and red wines. Red wines have very prominent blue and black berry aromas, a fine tannin structure and a moderate alcohol level. All the noble varieties are represented in this Pocket, as well as a significant portion of Chenin Blanc. Cabernet Sauvignon, Merlot and Shiraz are the favourite red varieties and are represented in blends as well as in single varietal wines. Grangehurst's weighty red blends benefit from extended oak maturation while by releasing the wines after substantial maturation (3 y) in their own cellar, they ensure these wines have attained a degree of accessibility. Interestingly, Cordoba has a Cabernet Franc-based blend with some Cabernet Sauvignon and Merlot adding a mineral tone to the wine.

Vineyards lying on the lower slopes tend to produce more rustic wines, with the old bush vines of Stonewall yielding a highly concentrated Cabernet Sauvignon with typical plum and cassis flavours. Wines from Avontuur, Eikendal, Yonder Hill and Somerbosch show more upfront sweet fruit and choc-mintiness. In line with the substantial wines from this Pocket, JP Bredell produces fortified red wines from traditional Portuguese varieties. Seriously styled Chenin Blancs are produced at Post House and Ken Forrester. The Chenin Blancs have a definite Old-World structure and great complexity with aromas of apple, marzipan, a lime acidity and steely finish.

DRIVING ROUTE: HELDERBERG FOOTHILLS

Take the R44 (south) from Stellenbosch. About 10 kilometres from town, pass a large dam on the left and turn left onto Eikendal Road. Less than one kilometre further is the entrance to Longridge. New ownership has developed a Longridge range of varietal *terroir* wines.

Return to the R44, turn left and drive south. Here, the foothills even out to a gentle slope towards the ocean. Two kilometres further turn

GPS WAYPOINTS

Ken Forrester S34° 01.691 E18° 49.122
Longridge S34° 00.974 E18° 49.996
Post House Cellar S34° 01.150 E18° 48.637
Stonewall S34° 01.962 E18° 49.237

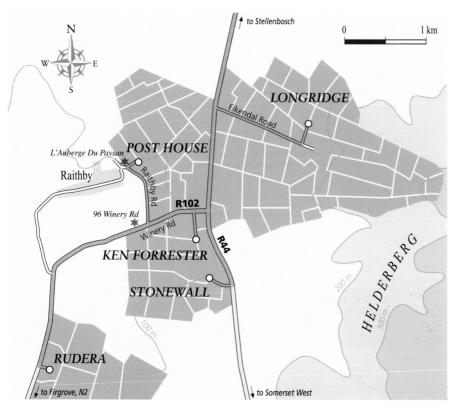

right onto Winery Road (R102) and left again to visit Ken Forrester. Known for his Chenin Blanc, Ken also makes an exciting red blend Gypsy (Shz, Grenache).

From here, go left and turn right after a few metres to Raithby Road. Less than a kilometre further is the entrance to Post House Cellar on the right. Previously the official post office of the settlement of Raithby, this property still boasts a bright red post box at the entrance. Next door to Post House, is the L'Auberge Du Paysan restaurant, serving French cuisine in a brasserie setting. Owner Thermann makes his own wines from a tiny two-hectare vineyard.

Further along this road, is a section of the vineyards which supply Rudera. Located on this driving route, this innovative producer highlights various *terroirs* by making wine from various selected areas: Cabernet Sauvignon is sourced from the Stellenbosch West Pocket, Rudera

Chenin from the Helderberg Foothills and Rubusto Chenin from the Bottelary Pocket. For tasting and purchases, please contact the Rudera office. Return to the R44, turn right and a drive to the last winery on the route. Stonewall takes its name from the low, white-washed wall that encloses the farmyard like a typical French *clos*.

TRAVELLING TIPS

Information:
www.helderbergwineroute.co.za

Accommodation:
Ken Forrester cottage +27 (0)21 855 2374
Post House cottage +27 (0)21 842 2409

Restaurants:
96 Winery Road (Ken Forrester) +27 (0)21 842 2020
L'Auberge Du Paysan +27 (0)21 842 2008

Interests:
Helderberg Food & Wine Festival, annually in November, see local website
Sunset concerts on balcony (Longridge)
Venue (conference) (Stonewall) +27 (0)21 855 3675

LONGRIDGE WINES

Longridge Wines, recently taken over by the Van der Laan family, has added an additional 46 hectares of neighbouring farmland to the property. Now its mature Cabernet Sauvignon vines can produce dense, flavourful wines and the range can be extended with exciting new varieties such as Verdelho and Viognier.

Soils consist of decomposed shale, with the higher slopes having a greater clay content. Whites are placed at 160 – 200 metres above sea level, maximising the cooling effect of high altitude. Red varieties, however, benefit from sun exposure on lower-lying slopes (100 m). The north – south row direction offers midday sun protection and allows the southeasterly wind to blow through the rows and cool the vines. This orientation is incidentally exactly along the contours and minimises soil erosion.

A brand-new barrel cellar has boosted maturation to a capacity of 1 200 barrels since 2007. Chardonnay is naturally fermented in barrel, 70 per cent in new oak with lees contact adding rich buttery notes. Sauvignon Blanc benefits from cold fermentation with dry ice to preserve its delicate floral and white fruit aromas. The MCC, made from Chardonnay exclusively, is bottle aged for 18 months before being disgorged.

Red varieties are cold macerated and start natural fermentation before being inoculated with selected yeast strains. Following three weeks of skin contact, wines are matured for 16 to 18 months in new French oak; a small proportion of American and European oak adds dimension. The red wines all show a dense fruit character with powerful tannins and a great aging potential.

Sundowners – Relax on the terrace with live music and watch the sunset over the Winelands

ℹ️ Longridge Wines range 🍇 Sauv Bl, Chard, MCC, M, P, Cab S, Shz 🕐 Mon–Fri 09:00–17:00, Sat 09:00–13:00, pub hols. Closed Sun ☎ +27 (0)21 855 2004 📧 info@longridgewines.co.za, www.longridge.co.za 🍷 White 3–6 y, red 8–10 y 🍾 MCC 07; Sauv 08; Chard 07, M 07, P 07, Cab S 07 🎵 Sunset tastings (summer), wheelchair friendly, every 2nd Friday music events, venue (conference)

KEN FORRESTER

Originally named Zandberg(h) (circa 1689), 1 200 vines were first planted on Ken Forrester's farm in 1692. The Atlantic Ocean's close proximity (5 km), when combined with the farm's bowl-like shape, tempers the climate (approx 3 – 4°C compared to Stellenbosch). Precision viticulture ensures that each shoot offers no less than 16 leaves per bunch, ensuring even ripening. Green harvesting removes underdeveloped bunches to ensure phenolic ripeness. The flagship FMC(100 % Chenin Bl) is made from 36-year-old bush vines. Clear juice is barrel fermented using natural yeast to add complexity. The wine's complex stone fruit and honeyed character is underpinned by fresh ripe grapefruit acidity. Grapes for The Gypsy, (Grenache / Syrah) are cooled before maceration which extracts soft tannins and colour. The flamboyant wine is matured mainly in new French oak for 12 months, then blended and barrel aged for a further 12 months. The fynbos and savoury notes are supported by fine, dense tannins.

The FMC (Chenin Bl), Gypsy (Gren / Shz), "T" NLH (all sgl vineyards) Chenin Bl, Sauv Bl, Shz, Gren, M, Cab F Mon–Fri 08:00–17:00, Sat 10:00–14:00. Closed Sun +27 (0)21 855 2374 info@kenforresterwines.com, www.kenforresterwines.com 8–10 y 00, 02, 05 Restaurant (96 Winery Road), cottages

POST HOUSE

Post House cultivates 38 hectares of vines on the foothills of the Helderberg. Red varieties are located on the gentle west-facing aspects while Chenin Blanc is planted on cooler terroir. The gravel and clay soil have good water retention, giving balanced vine growth. Cool breezes moderate the summer temperatures and the east – west row direction provides afternoon shade. Trellising spreads the canopy vertically allowing filtered sunlight to aid colour development. Red grapes are naturally fermented in open steel tanks and punch-downs ensure colour development. Following malolactic fermentation, wines are matured for 18 months and bottled without filtration. The inky Penny Black flagship blend is made with Shiraz and Merlot with some Cabernet Sauvignon and Petit Verdot. White grapes receive two hours of skin contact before pressing and cleared juice is naturally fermented in barrel. Lees contact softens the acids and gives weight to the mid-palate of this steely dry wine.

Penny Black (Shz / M / PV / Cab S), M (sgl vineyard) Cab S, M, Shz, PV, P, Chenin Bl, Viog Mon–Fri 08:30–17:00, Sat 09:00–13:00 +27 (0)21 842 2409 info@posthousewines. co.za, www.posthousewines.co.za Chenin 5 y, reds 8–10 y 99, 00, 01, 03 Bonsai garden, cellar tours, B&B cottage

RUDERA

Rudera Wines has grown to be a Chenin Blanc specialist with a terroir-driven philosophy. The name Rudera is Latin for 'broken fragments of stone'. Chenin Blanc is harvested from old bush vines (30 y+) in the Koelenhof-Bottelary Hills area and grown on decomposed granite, shale and sandstone soils. Grapes are hand harvested in the early morning to preserve the white and yellow fruit. Only the free-run juice is used. After overnight clearing, the juice is transferred to barrel and fermented with natural occurring yeast. No enzymes, fining agents or filtration are used. Flagship Chenin shows citrus and yellow fruit with a mineral finish and refined tannins, while easy-drinking Chenin (ex-Koelenhof) is smokier with a hint of sweetness. Noble Late Harvest from Botrytised grapes is naturally fermented (without any yeast) in wood, the toasted oak adding sweet wood notes to the preserved fruit and racy acidity. Cabernet Sauvignon and Shiraz receive extended maturation in oak (up to 22 months), yielding intense wines with super-fine tannins and rich varietal fruit.

Chenin Blanc, Cabernet Sauvignon Chenin Bl, Cab S, Shz, Chenin Bl (NLH) By appt only +27 (0)76 752 5270, 021 852 1380 info@rudera.co.za, www.rudera.co.za Cab 20 y, Chenin 5–10 y Cab 2003; Chenin 06, 09

STONEWALL

In true French clos style, Stonewall's farmyard is separated from its vineyards by an historical wall. Of the 75 hectares of vineyards, Stonewall selects only 10 per cent of the yield for its own label. Planted on north-facing foothills of the Helderberg, the vineyards are situated in shallow, sandy loam soils. Vines receive supplementary irrigation on the poor sandy soil and naturally produce a low grape yield; green harvesting is not required. The small berries have a higher skin to juice ratio, improving colour and flavour extraction. The close proximity of the ocean and frequent breezes create cool, even ripening conditions. Grapes are hand harvested and fermented with regular punch-downs for colour extraction. Once fermentation is completed and the required level of extraction is achieved, the skins are pressed. Malolactic fermentation is completed before wines are transferred to barrels. Fifty per cent new wood and 18 months of maturation yield a concentrated Cabernet Sauvignon from the low-yielding bush vines.

Cabernet Sauvignon Cab S, Cab F, M, Chard, Sauv Bl By appt Mon–Fri 09:00–17:00, Sat 09:00–13:00. Closed Easter Fri, Sun, Dec 25, 26, Jan 1 +27 (0)21 855 3675 stonewall@mweb.co.za 6–10 y 03 Historical stone wall dating to 19th century, wine cellar circa 1828

Schapenberg Pocket

Schapenberg vista – The vantage point at Waterkloof offers spectacular views over False Bay at sunset

The Schapenberg Pocket is situated 100 to 200 metres above sea level around the northern, western and southern slopes of the Schapenberg. The very close proximity to False Bay (5–7 km) renders relatively cool ripening conditions and both red and white grape varieties achieve excellent flavour concentration here.

Geologically, Schapenberg is a granitic summit surrounded by shale foothills. Most of the vineyards are situated on the latter, which range from moderate potential, very stony residual soils to high potential and highly weathered yellow to reddish-brown soils which are well drained and favourably structured. Excessive vigour on the latter is curtailed by the strong southeasterly wind during the early summer months. This wind not only reduces growth vigour but also causes damage to plants and thereby creates great difficulty in canopy management.

Open-top fermenters – Newly harvested grapes are fermented in open tanks at Waterkloof

Star-light – The impressive Vergelegen barrel cellar, as seen from its octagonal roof structure

Detailed attention is given to windbreaks around vineyards and the spacing of trellis wires to protect the young shoots. Alongside the classic noble varieties, some Nebbiolo, Sangiovese, Petit Verdot and Viognier are also cultivated. The Schapenberg Pocket is known for its equally good red and white wines, showing cool climate characters. Lourensford's delicate Viognier has sweet floral aromas, while the white wines from Vergelegen are more powerful. Vergelegen's trademark Sémillon, with incipient waxiness, gives structure and weight to the white blend as well as producing a rich reserve wine for aging. Sauvignon Blanc and Chardonnay vineyards on the Schapenberg show distinct minerality and wet slate characters. The red wines of the Schapenberg Pocket are dominated by Cabernet Sauvignon, with hugely powerful and dense blends bearing the mark of Old-World elegance and restraint.

However, some fynbos and herb characters show their South African origin. The red wines from Morgenster and Lourensford are more restrained, while Vergelegen's blends are complex and single varietal reds have graceful elegance.

DRIVING ROUTE: SCHAPENBERG

Schapenberg is the southernmost Pocket of the Stellenbosch region. Facing the ocean, this Pocket's vineyards are never far from the cooling ocean breezes. Drive south on the R44. About 16 kilometres from Stellenbosch, turn left at the traffic lights of a large intersection onto Main Road (M9). At the fourth traffic light, turn left onto Lourensford Road.

At the following four traffic circles (3 km),

take the second exit each time. Turn right into Vergelegen Avenue, and at the fork, turn right to visit Morgenster. This historic farm has been restored to its former glory. The farm boasts six perfectly proportioned gables, the front *holbol* gable, with its delicate scrollwork and scallop shell apex framing the morning star, is considered one of the finest existing examples of the baroque style in the Cape. This emblem has been adopted as the Morgenster logo.

GPS WAYPOINTS

Morgenster S34° 05.035 E18° 53.090
Onderkloof S34° 06.610 E18° 53.811
Vergelegen S34° 04.816 E18° 53.170
Waterkloof S34° 06.191 E18° 52.786
Wedderwill S34° 06.153 E18° 56.307

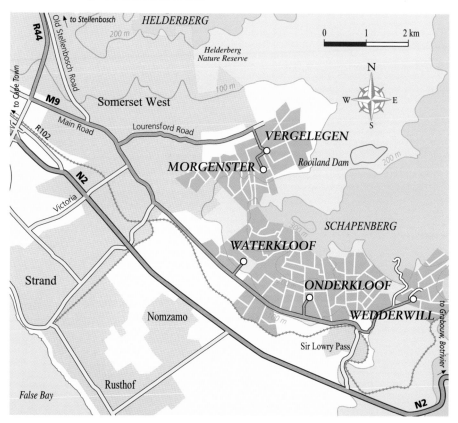

Emblazoned on the dark glass of the olive oil bottle and on the label, it also appears on the Morgenster wine bottles. The steep slopes, inaccessible to tractors, are planted to vines and olive groves which are lovingly hand-managed.

The impressive gates of Vergelegen (Eng. Far placed) on the right welcome visitors to this internationally renowned winery. Steeped in history from the Simon van der Stel era, Vergelegen's cellar is anything but old fashioned. High-tech equipment and precision measurements provide detailed information on every aspect, from the soils and vineyards to the grapes, juice and wines in the cellar. Vergelegen also offers a variety of culinary experiences, namely: the Camphor Forest Picnic, the Rose Terrace for alfresco meals and the Lady Philips Restaurant for a fine dining experience.

Retrace the route back to Main Road and turn left. About 1,5 kilometres further the name of the road changes to Sir Lorwry's Pass Road. About two kilometres further is the turn-off to visit the new winery of Waterkloof, on the left. This ultra-modern winery also incorporates traditional winemaking techniques such as basket-pressing to produce its outstanding wines. The restaurant has a spectacular view over the False Bay area. When visiting the highest placed vineyards, one observes the valley shaped location of the farm, while the residential areas

Music room – The John Broadwood & Sons piano in the Music Room at Vergelegen's manor house

disappear below the horizon.

Less than a kilometre further along the M9, turn left to visit Onderkloof. This winery is one of a few producers to focus on single vineyard wines. Onderkloof prodces no less than four varietal, single vineyard wines, Chardonnay, Chenin Blanc, Sauvignon Blanc and Shiraz.

Driving through the tiny hamlet of Sir Lowry's Pass Village, turn left at the signs to Wedderwill. At the fork, continue to the right, past the security gate. Drive with care along the gravel road to visit the cellar, set high on the mountainside. Wedderwill is not only developing its vines for premium *terroir* wine production, but has also launched an exclusive real-estate development and luxury guesthouse. Plans are in place to reintroduce indigenous wildlife in an area of rehabilitated natural fynbos on the extensive property.

TRAVELLING TIPS

Accomodation:
Cape Country Living (Wedderwill) +27 (0)21 858 1607
Lalapanzi Lodge (Wedderwill) +27 (0)21 858 1982

Restaurants:
Camphor Forest picnic, Rose Terrace, Lady Philips
(Vergelegen) +27 (0)21 847 1334
Waterkloof +27 (0)21 873 2418

Interests:
Helderberg Nature Reserve +27 (0)21 851 4060

MORGENSTER

Three-hundred-year-old Morgenster estate's resurrection started in 1992 when Italian owner Giulio Bertrand set about reuniting and restoring the various parts of the farm. The original manor house (circa 1786) has been beautifully preserved. Today, a selected 35 hectares are cultivated to vines. All the plots face north, northeast or northwest and red Bordeaux varieties were planted with small plots of Sangiovese and Nebbiolo. Strong prevailing winds necessitate trellising with olive groves acting as wind breaks. A lower planting density (2 700 vines/ha) afford each vine sufficient space in the lean soil. Merlot grapes are cold soaked using dry ice and fermented reductively to preserve the fruit quality. Gravitational flow ensures sensitive handling of grapes. Malolactic fermentation occurs partly in barrel, softening and integrating the acidity, fruit and savoury oak flavours. Extended maturation (15 months) in larger barrels (300 l) prevents excessive wood tannins. The fruit-driven wines are elegant and structured, retaining a crisp acidity and tannic grip for great aging potential.

ℹ Morgenster (Bdx Blend) 🔲 Cab S, Cab F, M, PV, Neb, Sang blend ⏱ Mon–Fri 09:00–17:00, Sat, Sun & publ hols 10:00–14:00. Closed on Good Friday, Dec 25 ☎ +27 (0)21 852 1738 ✉ info@morgenster.co.za, www.morgenster.co.za 🖷 12 y ▣ 00, 03, 04, 05 ⓘ Olives (Italian varieties), oil tasting, balsamic vinegar, sales of older vintages

ONDERKLOOF

Onderkloof cultivates twenty-five hectares on the slopes of the Schapenberg, facing the Atlantic Ocean. White varieties maximise the cooling effect of False Bay breezes, reducing the average temperature by as much as 4°C. Rows of trellised vines are directed against the wind so that the first few rows can act as a buffer. Onderkloof's wines all reflect their cool *terroir* and are treated carefully in the cellar. The Cabernet Sauvignon is macerated as whole berries, yielding a richly spiced wine with long maturation potential. Bush-vine Pinotage produces concentrated fruit with 80 per cent new barrels adding firm, dry tannins. The white wines show typical cool-climate fresh acidity. The single vineyard Chardonnay is harvested ripe so that the higher alcohol content and gentle oaking can round off an intense citrus palate. Chenin Blanc, from a high-lying single block is also harvested late showing a dense body while retaining fresh lime and pineapple aromas. The unique Floreal Blanc de Blanc blend (Chenin, Sauv, Muscat A) shows an elegant off-dry palate.

Cab S Sgl vineyard: (Chard, Chenin Bl, Sauv Bl, Shz, P, Cab S) Muscat d'Alexandrie Mon–Fri 09:00–17:00. Sat by appt. Closed Sun, pub hols +27 (0)21 858 1538 wine@onderkloofwines.co.za, www.onderkloofwines.co.za Red 6–8 y, white 3 y 99, 02, 05 Schapenberg conservancy wine walks

WEDDERWILL

Wedderwill offers a rare combination of boutique wines and conservation: vineyards are adjacent to a wildlife reserve focused on rehabilitating the Cape Floral Kingdom. The best nine hectares of 42 are selected for own vinification. While the white varieties are planted on south-facing slopes of the Schapenberg, red varieties are planted on warmer north-facing slopes with fertile granite and sandstone soils. Strong prevailing winds restrict yields (5 tons/ha) offering concentration. Fermentation includes longer skin contact and lasts up to 30 days. During maturation, American oak (10%) adds a hint of vanilla to the meaty and violet notes of cool-climate Shiraz. The Bordeaux Blend is matured in French oak, supporting the plum and earthiness of Cabernet Sauvignon. After 20 months, the wines are bottled and aged for a further two years before release. Sauvignon Blanc balances tropical notes of gooseberries with nettles and mineral richness. It is bottle matured for two years before release.

Shiraz Bordeaux Blend, Shz, Sauv Bl By appt only, Mon–Fri 09:00–16:00, Sat min 10 pax by appt +27 (0)21 858 1558 contact@wedderwill.co.za, www.wedderwill.co.za Red 10 y, white 5 y Red 04, white 05 BWI champion, hiking trail, B&B, BYO picnic, game reserve

VERGELEGEN

Vergelegen was originally granted to Governor Willem Adriaan van der Stel in 1700 by the Dutch East India Company. A knowledgeable and practical farmer, he proved his skills by cultivating 500 000 vines, camphor trees, fruit trees and vegetables.

Today, Vergelegen is planted to 140 hectares of vines on the slopes of the Hottentots-Holland Mountains in fertile gravel and clay soils. Planting densities have been increased to between 6 000 and 8 000 vines per hectare to control vegetative growth. Heat-sensitive white varieties are planted on elevated (220 –300 m), south-facing slopes to maximise cool ocean breezes from False Bay while a vertical trellis system protects young shoots from the prevailing southeasterly wind. Since the eradication of all virus-infected vineyards and the implementation of annual virus testing, major replanting has taken place and today Vergelegen can boast 100 per cent virus-free vineyards.

White grapes are whole-bunch pressed with press and free-run juice fermented collectively, providing structure to the wine. Barrel fermented and matured for 10 months, the Sémillon's waxy mouthfeel and the Sauvignon Blanc's melon and citrus tones combine with the spicy, subtle oaking to give a rich, dense blended white wine. Schapenberg Sauvignon Blanc Reserve receives skin and yeast lees contact to soften piercing acidity and the wine shows rare blackcurrant and fynbos notes on a mineral palate. Red grapes are macerated for three weeks to achieve maximum tannin and colour extraction. Skins are pressed and the young wine completes malolactic fermentation in barrels to soften the acid and to add mid-palate weight. The powerful red flagship matures for 24 months totally in new oak. Its dense fruit balances the strong oaking. Components are blended after 14 months when they have developed their own distinct characters.

Impressive facade – Vergelegen's homestead with its towering camphor trees

Vergelegen Red (Bdx blend, Cab S / F / M), Vergelegen White (Sém / Sauv bl), Schapenberg Reserve Sauvignon Blanc (sgl vineyard) Cab S / F, Sauv Bl, M, Chard, Sém, Shz Daily 09:30–16:30 +27 (0)21 847 1334 info@vergelegen.co.za, www.vergelegen.co.za Red 10 y+, white 5–10 y 98, 01, 03, 04, 05 "Interpretive centre" depicting the farm's history and self-guided tour of homestead, gifts, tour groups, winery tour, restaurants

WATERKLOOF

Waterkloof (Eng: Water valley), encircled by the Hottentots-Holland mountain range, has recently been established on either side of the Schapenberg Mountain along the Schapenberg Ridge and the False Bay slope.

The property was acquired in 2003 and, after detailed *terroir* analysis, most of the vineyards were re-established. Of the 120 hectare property, 53 hectares have been selected for vine cultivation. Waterkloof lies in an amphitheatre opening south, directly to False Bay, and as such it receives the full benefit of cool ocean breezes. Vines are planted at an altitude of approximately 280 metres, adding to the cooler conditions during ripening. The amphitheatre presents a further benefit in the variation of aspects and subsequent sun exposure for a variety of grape cultivars.

Ocean proximity – The vineyards are regularly exposed to cooling ocean breezes

Soils on the eastern side of the valley are mainly derived from shale, with a high percentage of rocks, which reduces the soil temperature and improves water-holding capacity. Vineyards are planted here, with the red varieties on lower areas and the whites on the higher, south-facing slopes for maximum cooling effects. The western side has more granite, creating an intermediate section of soils along the contact zone with sandy-loam topsoil and clay subsoil. Here Mourvèdre, Shiraz and Grenache are best suited to the area. Both these sections produce wines with steely, mineral and restrained fruit characteristics. Most of the vines are trellised due to strong prevailing winds; however, the wind gives the added benefit of reducing the crop yield significantly and concentrating the flavours. Exceptions are Mourvèdre and Grenache, which are cultivated as bush vines.

Lady G – A Percheron horse is employed as biodynamic 'tractor' to apply soil preparations, particularly on the very steep aspects.

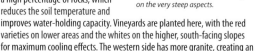

Ascending the slope – Neat vineyard rows on the high slopes of Schapenberg

The first few vintages were vinified in rented cellar space, but in 2009 Waterkloof crushed its maiden vintage in its ultra-modern cellar on the property. The building boasts a wholly gravitational-fed production facility, luxury maturation space, tasting centre and restaurant. The extensive application of technology works alongside the use of traditional methods as Waterkloof still follows a minimalist approach in the winery. With this approach the winery gets more elegance, with a longer finish, from our wines, so as to be most suited to go with food'.

White varieties are whole-bunch pressed to ensure only the highest quality, clear juice is extracted. Natural fermentation is done in stainless steel tanks at temperatures of between 18° to 20°C to allow the natural floral and white fruit flavours of the grapes to express themselves. Partial maturation in large barrels (600 l) adds toasty, buttery notes to the Chenin Blanc, Chardonnay and Viognier while restricting harsh tannins. About 30 per cent of the Waterkloof Sauvignon Blanc is fermented in 600 litre oak barrels as the added lees contact adds complexity to the wine's mineral structure.

Red varieties are naturally fermented in open-top wooden fermenters with manual punch-downs. This ensures integrated, elegant wines. Following a gentle pressing in a basket press, the wines are matured in French oak barrels for 18 to 24 months. Typical of traditionally made wines and a cool climate, the wines all show restrained and elegant flavours, classic in expression, often with a certain degree of minerality. Natural acidity is well balanced, promising a long and successful maturation.

Ultramodern restaurant – Waterkloof's eatery has floor-to-ceiling glass to showcase their views

ℹ️ Waterkloof Sauvignon Blanc 🍷 Sauv Bl, Chard, Chenin Bl, M, Mourv 🕐 Mon–Fri 09:00–16:30, Sat & Sun 10:00–15:00
📞 +27 (0)21 858 1292 ✉️ sales@waterkloofwines.co.za, admin@waterkloofwines.co.za, www.waterkloofwines.co.za
🌡️ Whites 2–4 y, reds 5–8 y ℹ️ Biodiversity walk, restaurant

Stellenbosch-Simonsberg Pocket

Majestic Simonsberg – The towering peaks of the Simonberg with the Rustenberg winery in the forefround

The Stellenbosch-Simonsberg Pocket is situated along the southwestern slopes of the Simons-, Skurweberg and Klapmutskop. Characterised by high-lying sites (200–500 m) and soils with a high potential, this Pocket runs over folding slopes creating variations in exposure and cultivation techniques. Although it is located 25 to 30 kilometres from the ocean, the relatively high elevations and southwestern aspects ensure that the vineyards benefit from cooling airflow. However, the average summer daytime temperature in this Pocket is slightly higher than for areas to the south of Stellenbosch.

Simonsberg hideaway – The guest cottages at Knorhoek offer tranquil luxury

The diverse topography of the foothills and mountainside valleys allows a wide variety of options concerning the choice and placement of grape varieties. Soils here are almost exclusively derived from granite, yielding high potential. These soils are yellow to reddish-brown and acidic but favourably structured with good water and nutrient-retention properties.

Excessive growth due to the high potential of the soil is curtailed by strong southeasterly winds which blow during early summer as well as high planting densities (4 000 vines/ha+) to create inter-plant competition and restrain growth. As the very strong easterly winds can cause extensive damage to the developing shoots and bunches, vines are trained on a vertical trellis system with the wires offering protection to the young shoots.

Most vineyards are trellised between 1,4 and 1,8 metres with spur pruning vertical positioning shoots. Several plantings of Sangiovese, Mourvèdre, Petit Verdot, Pinot Noir, Viognier, Chenin Blanc and Sémillon are found alongside the classic noble varieties. In most cases, vine row direction is dictated by the slope, but where possible rows are orientated southwest – northeast in order to utilise the cool summer breezes to moderate the warm days.Windbreaks are used on sites which are exposed to the strong southeasterly winds early in the growing season.

The Stellenbosch-Simonsberg Pocket is primarily suited for red wines and Bordeaux-styled red blends, although exuberantly fruity Chardonnay wines are produced at Rustenberg, Morgenhof and Warwick. Simonsberg *terroir* characteristics include earthy and abundant fruit aromas on red wines and tropical fruit and flinty flavours on white wines. The reds are generally well structured and mature well, usually requiring some time to reach their best form.

Rustenberg labyrinth – The Chantres-style labyrinth was completed in 2003

Pinotage from this Pocket has more earthy tones than the wines from Bottelary. L'Avenir, Morgenhof and Kanonkop produce their Pinotage from old bush vines, yielding highly concentrated wines with a dense strawberry fruit structure, spicy earthy notes and dry tannins.

The Cabernet Sauvignon-based blends from Muratie, Knorhoek, L'Avenir and Delheim are less overtly powerful, but show dark fruit, cassis and cedar notes. The single varietal wines (Rustenberg, Uitkyk) show a boldly ripe structure, cassis notes and fine tannins. Interestingly Marklew, Knorhoek and Remhoogte include a small portion of Pinotage in their red blends, which have a rich, velvety palate and fine tannins. Muratie's Pinot Noir is made from the first vines of this variety to be planted in South Africa, more than 75 years ago. The wines show hints of forest floor and delicate red currant flavours with a silky, soft finish.

DRIVING ROUTE: STELLENBOSCH-SIMONSBERG

Drive north on the R44 (towards the N1 freeway). Leaving Stellenbosch, the Simonsberg rises from the East. On the periphery of the town lies the Nietvoorbij Research Centre, where research is done into wine-related issues such as trellising systems, soil analysis and winemaking. The first winery on the route is Morgenhof,

owned by Anne Cointreau-Huchon. Arriving at the gate, you can see the vineyard rows following the contours of the hills. Morgenhof caters for larger groups and offers a restaurant.

Continue on the R44 to the boutique winery of Remhoogte situated on the right. World-famous consultant Michel Rolland has teamed up with the Boustred family to produce their wines. A game camp on the property is home to zebra, springbok, eland, black wildebeest and the shy black swan.

Over the next hill lies the small, secluded valley of Knorhoek. At the Knorhoek Road sign, turn right into the valley and follow the road. The left fork leads to Muratie. A wall of remembrance outside the homestead reflects the centuries of owners of this property. Exercise care when driving through Muratie, as the road leads straight through the farmyard which ducks, dogs and wine tasters cross.

Retrace the route back to the fork. The right fork leads further up the valley to Knorhoek Winery. Knorhoek has taken its name from 'the place where lions roar'. During the pioneering days, feline predators scaled the high kraal walls at night to prey on domestic livestock. The Cape mountain lion became extinct by the late 1700s. However, caracal are occasionally seen on the farm and leopard sightings still occur in the higher reaches of the surrounding mountains, hence the use of the leopard on the Knorhoek estate flagship wine labels.

From the R44, the road rises to reknowned wine producer, Kanonkop, on the northwestern side of Simonsberg. A pioneer in many regards, Kanonkop is today regarded as one of South Africa's top estates. The winery features an art gallery adjacent to the tasting room and visitors are invited to take the self-guided tour through the cellar. Continue along this road to historical Uitkyk (circa 1712). Restoration work in 1995 uncovered cultural history treasures,

GPS WAYPOINTS

Kanonkop S33° 51.285 E18° 51.634
Knorhoek S33° 52.751 E18° 52.315
Le Bonheur S33° 50.016 E18° 52.356
Morgenhof S33° 53.675 E18° 51.559
Muratie S33° 52.225 E18° 52.666
Remhoogte S33° 53.181 E18° 50.972
Rustenberg S33° 53.747 E18° 53.565
Uitkyk S33° 51.413 E18° 51.845

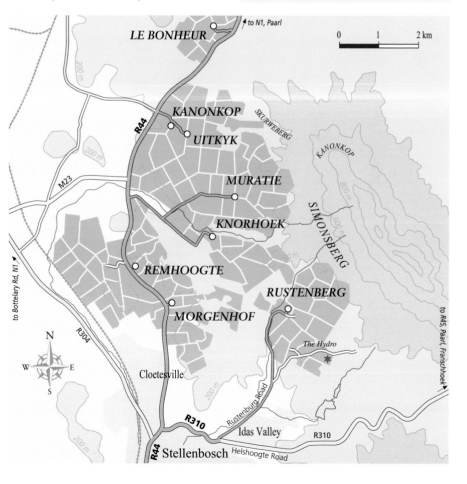

two murals, featuring spring and summer scenes of birds feeding their young and a still life of fruit. These frescoes were probably executed just after the homestead was built and testify to the owner's exceptional sensitivity towards the Cape European heritage. The two murals have been painstakingly restored.

Further along the R44, descend a small hill and turn left to visit Le Bonheur. While a new maturation cellar ensures wines are released at their optimum, the farm retains an air of timelessness. Retrace the route and turn left onto Helshoogte Road (R310) at the periphery of the town. At the first traffic light, turn left onto Rustenberg Road, and follow the road to the southern foothills of Simonsberg. At the fork, keep left to visit Rustenberg. Magnificent oak trees line the road to the winery and modern tasting facility. A stone labyrinth in the garden offers a moment of quiet introspection, while the lush gardens make for wonderful walks.

KNORHOEK

Knorhoek's Van Niekerk family has been in residence for five generations, but only crushed their maiden vintage in 1997. The guest house, originally a clay-and-stone structure housing stables, offers Old-World charm. One hundred hectares of vineyards are cultivated on the north- and west-facing foothills of the Simonsberg. The high altitude (200 – 380 m) provides some cooling effect and canopies of east – west-directed rows shade grape bunches during the hottest hours of the day. A low planting density is used on the steep slopes and vines are trellised to protect the grapes from the strong summer winds. In the recently upgraded cellar, winemaking stays traditional, using open-top fermenters and warm temperatures (close to 30°C to prevent the paint-like character in Pinotage) for red wines. The Pantere Red Blend receives extended maturation (24 months) before bottling, resulting in a dense wine showing rich, sweet berry fruit with a high alcohol content.

ℹ️ Pantere (Red Blend: Cab S, Shz, M, Cab F) 🍷 Cab S / F, Shz, M, P, Chenin Bl, Sauv Bl 🕐 Mon–Fri 10:00–17:00, Sat–Sun 10:00–15:00. Closed Easter Fri, Sun, Dec 25, Jan 1 ☎ +27 (0)21 865 2114 ✉ office@knorhoek.co.za, www.knorhoek.co.za 🍾 5–7 y 🏆 97, 01, 03 ℹ️ Cellar tours by appt., guest house, venue (conferences, functions), entertainment, children's facilities, tour groups, walks

KANONKOP

Johann Krige, co-owner of Kanonkop, opines: 'Wine must be unique, but soil alone does not make it unique.' This philosophy has held over the past 40 years as the estate's three successive winemakers have kept true to producing elegantly styled, *terroir*-driven wines. Since its inception under politician and businessman, JW Sauer, the estate's approach saw *terroir* supported by technology, research and development. Cabernet Sauvignon and Merlot are planted on lower-lying areas of sand with underlying clay structured into ridges to increase soil volume. Blocks planted on south-facing mountain slopes (200–250 m) add a slightly different flavour profile, highlighting Pinotage's Pinot Noir aspects.

One hundred hectares are cultivated, divided evenly between Cabernet Sauvignon and Pinotage, with small parcels of Cabernet Franc and Merlot. While Cabernet is trellised against the wind, the old Pinotage vines (50 y+) are cultivated as bush vines to deliver more fruit concentration. Bunches are destemmed, hand sorted , crushed and then moved into open concrete fermenters where fermentation is controlled at 28°C with manual punch-downs taking place every two hours. Approximately 20 per cent of all wine undergo malolactic fermentation in oak, with the balance completing it in tank. Seventy per cent of the blends are made up before barrel maturation.

Pinotage is matured in oak for up to 16 months (75% new oak) whilst the straight Cabernet Sauvignon and the flagship Paul Sauer for up to 26 months in new oak – all French 225 litre barrels. The results is concentrated wines with a very clasical feel, complex flavours and a lingering, though dry, aftertaste. According to Johann Krige, these wines are food wines and are akin to Sophia Loren – elegant yet structured.

Signaling an icon – The instantly recognisable canon of Kanonkop, which used to signal boats arriving in Cape Town

ℹ️ Paul Sauer (Cab S, M, Cab F) 🍷 Red Blend, Cab, P 🕐 Mon–Fri 09:00–17:00, Sat 09:00–14:00. Pub hols 10:00–16:00 ☎ +27 (0)21 884 4656 ✉ wine@kanonkop.co.za, www.kanonkop.co.za 🍾 8–15 y 🏆 95, 98, 03 ℹ️ Cellar tours by appt, art gallery & art sales, wheelchair facilities and picnic (cheese boards)

LE BONHEUR

Le Bonheur (meaning Happiness) is situated on the slopes of the Klapmuts Hill. Originally a resting place for travellers between Cape Town and Paarl, the H-shaped Cape Dutch homestead is a classic architectural gem. The estate has definitely preserved its timeless atmosphere. Seventy hectares are cultivated on mountain slopes where higher elevations (200–350 m above sea level) moderate the summer temperatures. Red varieties are planted on high-lying, north-facing slopes in granite and loam soils. A few cooler sites facing east and southeast are dedicated to white varieties, with Sauvignon Blanc flourishing in clay soil. Hand-harvested grapes are hand sorted to select the best fruit. Red wines are warm fermented in rotating tanks, mixing skins and juice for optimum colour extraction. Following pressing, the wines are matured in French oak, with a small percentage of American oak (15%) adding sweet vanilla notes to the classily austere palate. For white wines, free-run juice is fermented, producing a medium-bodied, fresh, dry Chardonnay and a flinty, tropical Sauvignon Blanc.

Cab S, Red blend, Cab S, Chard, Sauv Bl Mon–Fri 09:00–17:00, Sat 10:00–16:00. Closed Sun, religious hols +27 (0)21 875 5478 info@lebonheur.co.za, www.lebonheur.co.za 10–15 y Venue (functions, conference)

MURATIE ESTATE

Established in 1685, Muratie was the first estate to plant Pinot Noir (1927). The winery is set in the historical cellar dating back to the 1800s. Forty-five hectares are cultivated on gentle northwest-facing slopes in granite soils. The high elevation (185 – 300 m) and afternoon breezes assist in cooling the vineyards. This cooling effect is increased by a higher cordon trellis (1 m), permitting air movement under the vines as well as reducing radiant heat to slow and extend the ripening period. The flagship red wine, Ansela van De Caab is named after an emancipated slave who married the first owner, Lourens Campher in 1699. Red grapes for the blend are fermented slightly cooler (26°C) to restrict tannin extraction from the skins. The wine is matured for 16 months with 35 per cent new French oak, giving an elegant tannin backbone to the sultry, dark wine. The hedonistic Shiraz is any Shiraz lover's dream. The ever-popular vintage Port, produced from vines planted in 1976 is a field blend consisting of Tinta Barocca, Tinta Roritz, Souzao and Francesca.

Ansela (Cab S / Merlot) Cab S, F, M, Shz, P N, Chard, Port varieties Mon–Fri 09:00–17:00, Sat & Sun 10:00–16:00. Closed Easter Fri, Dec 25, Jan 1 +27 (0)21 865 2330 info@muratie.co.za, www.muratie.co.za 8–12 y 04, 05, 06 Classic Cape Dutch architecture, charming wine tasting room , Sunday lunch (booking req.)

UITKYK

Historical Uitkyk (circa 1712) is one of only three existing double-storey flat-roof 18th-century townhouses in the Cape. The manor house is a Georgian-styled masterpiece. The first vineyards date back to the early 1890s and today, 200 hectares are cultivated. Granite soil dominates, with the lower slopes (200 m) planted to red varieties, while white varieties flourish on higher slopes with cooler mesoclimate (500 m). The flagship wine Carlonet dates back to 1957. In the state-of-the-art cellar, each block is vinified separately to preserve its characteristics. Moderate fermentation temperatures (27°C) and pump-overs ensure colour and flavour extraction for the red wines. Following malolactic fermentation, the Carlonet is aged in 300 litre barrels for 17 to 19 months in a combination of new (61%) and older (39%) oak. The dense fruit palate is underpinned by a fine tannin structure and a hint of sweet spice from American oak. Sauvignon Blanc shows a luscious white fruit and crisp acidity, while oak-matured Chardonnay combines hints of vanilla, butterscotch and citrus palate.

Carlonet (Cab S) Cab S, M, Shz, Sang, Mourv, PV, Sauv Bl, Char, Sém, Viog, Chenin Mon–Fri 09:00–17:00, Sat & Sun 10:00–16:00 +27 (0)21 884 4710 info@uitkyk.co.za, www.uitkyk.co.za 10, 15, 20 y 01, 05, 07 Summer picnics

REMHOOGTE

Remhoogte's boutique cellar produces French-styled red blends under the guidance of world-renowned viticulturalist Michel Rolland. Thirty-three hectares of vines have been established on the mountain slopes in heavy clay soils. A high planting density (2 800 vines/ha) restricts vigour and the vines are trellised with a vertically extended canopy to increase sunlight exposure and airflow. The summer southeasterly winds cool and dry, and lightly stress the vines resulting in greater fruit concentration. To express its dark fruit characters (plum and blackberries), Pinotage is cultivated as bush vines. Merlot is planted on cooler south-facing slopes to avoid water stress. Shiraz is planted on warmer northern slopes giving ripe fruit. Grapes are hand sorted on a vibrating table before vinification in French oak tanks. Malolactic fermentation in barrel softens the acid and rounds off the mid-palate. The wine is matured for 20 months, resulting in an intensely rich wine with a fine tannin structure. Chris Boustred is now the winemaker. He has added a Chenin Blanc and a Merlot to the Remhoogte portfolio.

Bonne Nouvelle (Cape Blend: M / Cab S / P) M, Cab S, P, Shz, Chenin Bl (sgl vineyard) Mon–Fri 09:00–17:00 +27 (0)21 889 5005 remhoogte@adept.co.za, www.remhoogte. co.za 8–10 y 03, 04 Game, olives, collection of hunting trophies, Remhoogte Zebra Cottage

MORGENHOF

Morgenhof holds a sense of history (est. 1692) in the French/Old Cape-toned yard with tree-shaded lawns and beautiful Tastevin. Only 75 hectares of this large farm are planted to vines, in deep granite and shale-based soils. The clay component provides good water retention and dry-land cultivation is practised. Vines are trellised to spread the canopy vertically and increase sun exposure. Wider spacing (2 800 vines/ha) on steep slopes encourages extensive root development. The Sauvignon Blanc is planted on elevated (400 m) south-facing slopes that benefit from a cooling effect for expression of varietal flavours. Reds are placed on warm northern slopes to fulfil their heat and sun-exposure requirements for ripening. Drought-sensitive Merlot is sited on lower slopes (150 m) in clay soils with ground cover to prevent water loss.

White grapes are pressed and the cleared juice cold fermented (12°C) to preserve delicate flavours. Mature Chenin Blanc vines (40 years old) provide quince and honey flavours with gentle oaking softening the crisp acidity. The dry MCC is Chardonnay dominated, with a fine mousse after two years' lees maturation in bottle.

Reds are fermented warm (28°C) with pump-overs for better colour extraction. Complete malolactic fermentation adds complexity. The blend is matured for 20 months in a combination of old and new wood barrels to ensure elegant oaking. Once bottled, the wine is matured further for three years before being released into the market. Fantail Wines targets the younger wine drinker, distinctive as the eye-catching fantail which graces the label. There are seven wines under this popular label, including the award-winning Pinotage.

Formal garden – Morgenhof's barrel cellar rests underground, with a pristine formal garden and its signature tower above

ℹ️ The Morgenhof Estate (Bdx blend Cab S / M / Cab F / Malb) 🍇 Sauv Bl, Chard, Chenin Bl, Cab S / F, M, Malb, PV, PN 🕐 Mon–Fri 09:00–17:30, Sat & Sun 10:00–17:00 (Nov–Apr); Mon–Fri 09:00–16:30, Sat & Sun 10:00–15:00 (May–Oct). Closed Good Friday, Dec 25, Jan 1 📞 +27 (0)21 889 5510 📧 info@morgenhof.com, www.morgenhof.com 🍷 8–12 y 🍷 93, 94, 97, 98, 01, 04, 05 🍴 Restaurant, tour groups, children welcome, helipad, venue (functions), formal rose garden, Morgenhof guesthouse

RUSTENBERG

Rustenberg is located in the southern Simonsberg amphitheatre. Winemaking started on the farm in the late 1600s, but it was only in 1892 that the first Rustenberg wine was bottled by John X Merriman. Only five winemakers have overseen the crush in the last 100 years, testimony to the commitment and long-term vision of the proprietors. The range of wine includes two site-specific wines, a regional *terroir* range (incl. John X Merriman blend) and a lifestyle range called Brampton.

One-hundred-and-fifty hectares are now cultivated on decomposed granite with the alluvial component increasing near the Kromme River. Cabernet Sauvignon is cultivated in the bowl of the amphitheatre, where warmer air accumulates. On elevated slopes (180 – 480 m), white and red varieties are planted to a slightly lower density, where the vines also benefit from cooler ripening conditions. Mature vines dominate (80% of the vines are 10 – 20 y) resulting in consistent, bold, strong wines. In the single block Cabernet Sauvignon, selected bunches are individually tagged at the onset of the growing season and berries are selected at harvest to create an intense and highly structured wine.

Natural fermentation on specific batches adds complexity to the wines with the reds fermented at 23 to 28°C with regular pump-overs and one-and-a-half to three weeks of extended maceration to extract soft tannins and stabilise colour. The Merriman blend includes fruit from 28 to 40 parcels and is only blended towards the end of 20 months' oak maturation. Use of 300 l and 500 l barrels for natural fermentation, with maturation for 14 months gives the Chardonnay a rich and dry mid-palate with subtle wood flavours.

Grand design – Classic Cape Dutch architecture set in autumn colours at Rustenberg Estate

ℹ️ John X Merriman (Bdx blend), Peter Barlow (Cab S, Site-specific vineyard), Five Soldiers (Chardonnay, Site-specific vineyard) 🍇 Cab S/F, Chard, M, Malb, Mourv, PV, Shz, Viog, Rouss, Sauv Bl 🕐 Mon–Fri 09:00–16:30, Sat 10:00–13:30, publ hols 09:00–15:30. Closed on Sun & religious hols 📞 +27 (0)21 809 1200 📧 wine@rustenberg.co.za, www.rustenberg.co.za 🍷 P Barlow 15 y+, John X 10 y+; Soldiers 8 y+ 🍷 P Barlow 99, 01, 03, 05; Five Soldiers 01, 02, 03, 06; John X 97, 99, 01, 02, 03, 05 🍴 Labyrinth, exquisite garden, dairy viewing

Banghoek Valley Pocket

Idyllic Banghoek Valley *– The peaceful Banghoek Valley stretches northeast from Stellenbosch (seen from Bartinney)*

The Banghoek Valley Pocket is nestled in the southwestern extremities of the Simons- and Drakensteinberg. Characterised by high-lying sites (200–500 m) and soils with a high potential, this relatively small Pocket produces wines with very distinct cool-climate characteristics of mintiness and berry flavours.

The location, together with pronounced southern aspects, creates markedly cooler conditions during ripening compared to those of the immediate surrounds of Stellenbosch. The valley is more continental than maritime in character with cold winters, but fortunately no frost. The secluded nature of the valley results in shelter from wind except for the higher altitudes, which benefit from moderate mountain breezes.

Hands-on viticulture *– Anton Malan tending the season's new growth at Rainbow's End*

The soils are almost exclusively derived from granite, with some mixing of sandstone material at higher altitudes. These highly weathered soils are acid and have high growth potential. However, due to its favourable structure, good drainage as well as water-retention properties make it desirable for vine cultivation. The cold winds which blow during the early summer months restrict growth and ensure that plants have a balanced yield of fruit. Rain clouds brought on by the southerly winds provide a high annual rainfall of about 1 000 millimetres and run-off water from the mountain slopes increases soil moisture. Frequent mist and constant airflow along the slopes create slow, even ripening conditions for an array of grape varieties. Due to the intense folding of the slopes, great variation is found in exposure and cultivation. Most vineyards are vertically trellised between 1,4 and 1,8 metres. Row direction is mostly dictated by the slope but, where possible, rows are orientated southwest – northeast to make use of the cool summer breezes. Windbreaks are used on sites which are exposed to strong southeasterly winds early in the growing season. White wines are extremely fruity with good palate weight and the reds are less overtly powerful with understated elegance. Whereas most producers in Banghoek blend Cabernet Sauvignon and Merlot, the single varietal wines (Thelema, Zorgvliet) show cassis and blackcurrant (Cab S), and leafy and fennel notes (Merlot) respectively. Cabernet Franc is a rising star, joining the red blends (Camberley, Rainbow's End, Delaire). Shiraz also displays mintiness and savoury notes. The Chardonnay and Sauvignon Blanc wines (Bartinney, Thelema) show citrus and white fruit and a high natural acidity due to the cool cultivation conditions.

GPS WAYPOINTS

Bartinney S33° 55.590 E18° 55.957

Rainbow's End S33° 56.424 E18° 56.691

Turn-off to Rainbow's End S33° 55.011 E18° 55.951

DRIVING ROUTE: BANGHOEK

From the R44 / R310 intersection in downtown Stellenbosch, drive towards the N1 in a northerly direction, with signs indicating Paarl. At the third traffic light, turn right onto the R310 east out of Stellenbosch towards the Helshoogte Pass. This road traces the perimeter of the town before ascending the spectacular Helshoogte mountain pass. Vineyards cling to the steep slopes on the left and right as you reach the crest. Notice how the very steep slopes necessitate vines to be planted in small patches.

Row directions change from following the contours to following the incline to allow each patch of vines maximum sun and heat exposure. Start the descent into the Banghoek Valley. About two kilometres further is the turn-off to

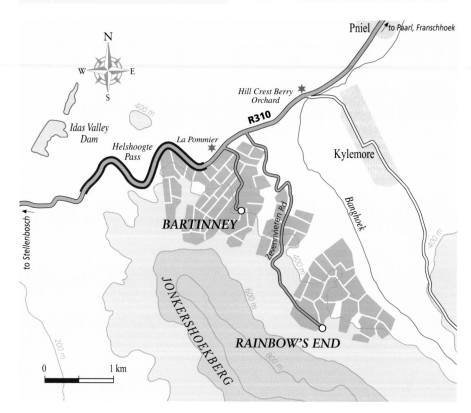

the first winery. At the Bartinney road sign, turn right and follow a narrow gravel road. Bartinney is a family-owned boutique winery overlooking the Banghoek Valley with spectacular vineyards.

The next winery on the route is Rainbow's End, where retired consulting civil engineer Jacques Malan and his sons are making some impressive red wines. You may phone the owners to fetch you or attempt the narrow, winding road yourself. From Bartinney, turn right onto the R310. Six-hundred metres further, turn right onto Zevenrivieren Road (Eng. Seven rivers). Turn right just before the bridge over the small river. Follow the gravel road and turn right again at the first turn-off ascending a steep incline. Keep left at the fork and turn left to the farm gate of Rainbow's End. Pass the office, dam and a small dwelling to the homestead where wine tasting is hosted. The elevated slopes, up to 530 metres above sea level, and varying rock component of the soil allow powerful Shiraz, Cabernet Sauvignon and Merlot wines to be made. Back on the R310, the road winds down into the Banghoek Valley.

At the lowest point of the Bankhoek Valley, a small road turns off to the left to Hillcrest Berry Orchard. Sample seasonal fresh berries cultivated in the orchards set high on the mountain at the restaurant. Their self-catering cottages offer cosy fireplaces for winter and mountain walks in summer. This area is also home to many stables and local riders are frequently seen on their equestrian outings.

TRAVELLING TIPS

Accommodation:
Hillcrest Cottages +27 (0)21 885 1629

Restaurant:
Hillcrest Berry Orchard +27 (0)21 885 1629
La Pommier Restaurant +27 (0)21 885 1269

RAINBOW'S END WINE ESTATE

The Malan family boutique winery of Rainbow's End only produces red estate wines. Twenty-two hectares of mountain slopes are cultivated to vines in deep, homogenous granite soils. A variation in stone fraction (in places up to 70%) moderates soil temperature and restricts growth with vines naturally producing smaller berries with greater fruit concentration.

Merlot is planted on high north-facing slopes (540 m above sea level), giving a fantastic cooling effect. This is one of South Africa's highest Merlot blocks. Cabernet is planted on lower-lying, northwestern slopes where increased sun exposure ensures proper ripening. Shiraz is planted on cooler east- and south-facing slopes, which receive early morning sun, yet are well protected from late afternoon heat by the mountain's shadow. A low planting density (2 600 vines/ha) allows sufficient space for each vine's development on the steep slopes. Occasional late afternoon mists during summer help to cool the vines during the growing season.

Hand-harvested grapes are cold soaked prior to fermentation in self-made, insulated open fermenters. Dry ice (frozen CO_2) is used for the initial cooling of the must during cold maceration and thereafter natural fountain water is circulated through cooling plates in order to control must temperature during fermentation. Frequent manual punch-downs ensure optimum extraction. Malolactic fermentation is done in French oak barrels. The barrel cellar is situated under the main homestead next to the perennial fountain.

Wines are matured for at least 12 months in French oak. The vines produce elegant fruit-driven wines showcasing Rainbow's End's unique mountain *terroir*.

Finding gold – Explores interesting red varieties at Rainbow's End, nestled high in the mountain

Cab Franc | Shz, Cab S / F, M, PV, Malb | By appt | +27 (0)83 411 0170 / 082 404 1085 | info@rainbowsend.co.za, www.rainbowsend.co.za | 7 y | 07, 08 | Spectacular scenery, cellar tour, fynbos servitude

BARTINNEY PRIVATE CELLAR

Bartinney was first established in 1920 high on the Helshoogte Pass above Stellenbosch, although its winemaking history only commenced in 1992 when the Jordaan family built the first cellar. Today Michael and Rose Jordaan continue the family's winemaking tradition in their boutique cellar.

Bartinney's manor house (circa 1923) is an attractive mixture of English Tudor and Cape Dutch design. Recent renovations have been done with great sensitivity to preserve these historical buildings while adding new structures as the winery has been extensively upgraded with a new barrel maturation facility and tasting room. The 2007 vintage was the first to be crushed in the new cellar. Bartinney's philosophy – Wine made on the Mountain – also includes the natural surroundings, where indigenous fynbos has been meticulously re-established.

Standing proud – An old bell marks the entrance to the new barrel cellar and entertainment area

Sun exposure – The winter landscape illustrates the varying sun exposure on the north-facing (front) and south-facing (back) blocks of vineyards

Half of this 40 hectare property is planted to grapes on north and northeasterly slopes. A wide range of elevations is used, with vineyards ranging from 300 to 600 metres above sea level. This results in significant temperature differences as well as varying sun exposure. Cabernet Sauvignon is planted in deep red soils on the lower foothills. This location is shadowed in the early afternoon, relieving the heat of the day. White varieties, on the other hand, enjoy cooler conditions on the higher slopes. Here soils contain more clay and loam, which assist in the development of delicate fruit and floral aromas. All the vines are trellised to protect them against wind damage and drip irrigation adds to the natural soil moisture during the growing period.

Barrel tasting – Tasting the barrels to assess the wine's development

Row directions generally follow the mountain contours to counteract the difficulties of farming on a steep incline, but high-density planting on the fertile soils compels the vines to compete with each other, reducing both growth and grape production. This results in a more balanced vine with high fruit concentration. Both the white and red varietals carry less than six tons per hectare, but as the varying altitudes produce a differing ripening consistency, discipline when harvesting is paramount and every block is picked several times.

Chardonnay is hand harvested and cooled overnight, before being sorted and crushed. Selected yeast cultures are added and the wine is fermented in French oak barrels. Malolactic fermentation is also done in barrel, ensuring integrated yet subtle tannins. Another 12 months of maturation follows, with lees contact adding elegant toasty and butter notes. The Chardonnay has a typical cool-climate expression of minerality and fresh acidity, alongside New World fruitiness. Cabernet Sauvignon is also hand harvested and once crushed, a small volume of juice is removed to increase the juice to skin ratio to aid

concentration. Fermentation is done with selected yeast, and the wine is matured in French oak barrels for up to 20 months. Due to the extended maturation period, only a small percentage of new wood, about 20 per cent, is used to ensure that the wood component is not overpowering. The wine is aged in bottle for an additional three years before release, yielding a delightfully intense Cabernet with rich red fruit and restrained velvety tannins.

Bird's eye view – A view from the highest vineyard site over Bartinney's property

Bartinney (Chard) 🍷 Chard, Sauv Bl, Cab S (to be released) 🕐 Mon–Fri 10:00–16:00. Closed publ hols 📞 +27 (0)21 885 1013
info@bartinney.co.za, www.bartinney.co.za 🍴 3 y ℹ️ Farm cottages, view over valley from tasting facility, restoring indigenous fynbos

Devon Valley Pocket

Magnificent scenery – The fertile and cool Devon Valley

Located to the southwest of Stellenbosch, the Devon Valley Pocket is accessible by a single narrow, winding lane. The valley lies on an axis from northwest to southeast. It is surrounded by the prominent, rounded Papegaaiberg and Bottelary Hills, forming a horseshoe of slopes.

These hills (240–470 m) provide a barrier to the prevailing southeasterly winds, as the valley opens to the south,. it benefits from the cooling sea breezes from the nearby Atlantic Ocean, only 17 kilometres away.

Tranquil drive – Devon Valley's narrow winding road

The Pocket has deep, yellow to reddish-brown soils with good water-retention properties, even through the dry summer months. Derived almost exclusively from granite material, these soils induce high growth vigour in the vines.

The challenge in the Devon Valley Pocket is to curtail this potentially excessive vigour in order to achieve a balance between vegetative growth and the production of grapes in the plant. This balance is vital to the production of high quality grapes. To ensure sufficient water reserves in the soil during the critical ripening phase, especially on sites where no irrigation water is available, low vigour, drought-resistant rootstocks are used. In the shallow soils near the low end of the valley, vines are either planted on ridges, which increases soil volume or they are cultivated untrellised. The smaller untrellised plants require less soil volume.

Although a predominantly red wine Pocket, some excellent white localities do exist, mainly planted to Chardonnay. Popular noble varieties such as Cabernet Sauvignon and Merlot share the Pocket with lesser known varieties such as Petit Verdot, Malbec and Mourvèdre. Cabernet Sauvignon, however, features most strongly in the Devon Valley vineyards. Structured Cabernet Sauvignon-Merlot blends are very popular, with wines from Clos Malvern, Devon Hill, Meinert Wines and Louisvale showing polished tannins and structure on the palate as well as opulent fruit on the nose.

Jonkershoek Valley Pocket

Jonkershoek Valley – Nestled at the foot of the imposing Hottentots-Holland Mountain range

The Jonkershoek Valley Pocket is set in a relatively narrow valley running in a southeasterly direction between the Jonkershoek and Stellenbosch mountain ranges (1 000 m). Although most of the vineyards are mainly situated on elevations of between 200 and 300 metres above sea level on the steep southwest-facing foothills, this area is also home to some of Stellenbosch's

Eerste River – The Eerste River offers many photo opportunities along the Jonkershoek Valley

highest vines at around 600 metres above sea level. This particular topography creates shorter daylight hours as the sun rises late over the Jonkershoekberg and sets early behind the Stellenboschberg. The lower sun exposure, together with the synoptic southeasterly winds that funnel down this valley, result in relatively cooler ripening conditions than the mesoclimate would indicate.

Annual rainfall in this secluded valley is relatively high at about 1 000 millimetres,

Secluded valley – Driving along the Jonkershoek Valley, shaded by indigenous trees and lush undergrowth

compared with 713 millimetres at the Nietvoorbij Research Station, just north of Stellenbosch. The largest portion of rain occurs during the winter and is brought on by winds from the south.

A small proportion of summer rain is induced by infrequent northern winds. Fortunately, rain rarely occurs during the harvesting season.

The parentage of the soils is diverse, with a band of shale running along the lower eastern slopes, topped by granite at the higher elevations. Due to the generally steep slopes, the soils are usually a mix of parent materials with some material from still higher sandstone mountain caps. This results in highly weathered, acid, often stony soils with good drainage properties and moderate to high growth vigour potential. However, the sites containing shale remain mostly uncultivated, with the majority of vineyards planted on the stony, decomposed granite soil. Only a few blocks located on the valley floor are planted in alluvial soil near the river. Here high growth vigour is induced due to the rich soil and strict vineyard management aims to create balanced vines by pruning and green harvesting.

In the Jonkershoek Pocket, the combination of complex topography and strong winds requires the adaptation of viticulture practices. Vineyards are planted to manage wind effectively and row directions are orientated to allow the wind force to flow down the rows instead of directly into vines, potentially causing damage. Because soils are relatively shallow (less than 1 m) on the valley floor, ridges are used to increase soil volume and afford each plant sufficient space to grow. This practice also improves drainage on these potentially problematic sites.

Most of the vineyards in this Pocket are trellised, but on the slopes the deep fertile soils allow vines to be trained on extended vertical trellising. The Pocket is host to all the noble cultivars and planting density varies from relatively low (2 000 vines/ ha) to moderate density (4 000 vines/ha) on the differing altitudes. This small valley produces very finely textured reds and delicate, floral white wines. Neil Ellis's barrel-fermented Sauvignon Blanc has a definite mineral quality, giving a sleek edge to the gooseberry fruit, while the Chardonnay from Le Riche shows creamy, citrus notes, supported by toasty notes from new oak.

Catching a rainbow – Fishing for rainbow trout is a leisurely way to spend a weekend

Cape Leopard – This magnificent animal roams the mountain ranges, but is rarely seen due to its extremely shy nature

As in many of the Stellenbosch Pockets, Cabernet Sauvignon and Merlot are firm favourites, however, in Jonkershoek these varieties show their greatest expression as single varietal wines. Cabernets from Neil Ellis and Stark-Condé are powerful with elegance and cassis, blackberry and mineral notes, while their Shiraz wines have spicy warmth and smoky characters. These wines tend to show softer tannic structures and good natural acidity and therefore require long cellaring. Merlots in this Pocket have a more fruity style, with moderate alcohol levels. Le Riche produces several Cabernet-Merlot blends with juicy fruit while Lanzerac produces a single varietal Merlot.

The Jonkershoek Nature Reserve (9 800 ha) functions as a rain catchment area, providing water for the town of Stellenbosch and its surrounding areas. The natural mountain fynbos includes more than 1 100 plant species, of which quite a few are rare and/or endemic. Distinctive species are *Protea repens, P. neriifolia*, mountain cypress, as well as various ericas and restios. Several old forest communities occur in narrow kloofs where they are relatively sheltered from fire.

The reserve's mammal population includes leopard, honey badger, baboon, klipspringer, mongoose, and numerous smaller animals such as mice, shrews and rats, but most are shy and seldom seen. Raptors such as black eagle, fish eagle, spotted eagle owl, as well as kingfishers and typical fynbos birds – the sugarbird, orange-breasted sunbird and protea seed-eater – are abundant. On warm winter days, agama lizards are seen basking in the sunlight on rocks. Snakes (Berg adder, puff adder, boomslang and Cape cobra) are fairly common and hikers should be alert.

TRAVELLING TIPS
Catch rainbow trout, Jonkershoek flyfishing, Trout Café +27 (0)21 866 1011
Hiking, Jonkershoek Nature Reseve, picnic and wildflower garden +27 (0)21 866 1560

Elgin Pocket

The mist effect – Combined with the surrounding mountains, mist from the Palmiet River is one of the other great geographical influences in Elgin, as seen at Shannon Vineyards

Elgin is unique in that it is geographically and geologically a very clearly defined mountain basin (Hottentots Holland range) at a high elevation (200–300 m), surrounded by sandstone rims and peaks (500– 1 000 m). One of the coolest Pockets, Elgin is traditionally a fruit (especially apples) growing region. Its viticultural potential is being realised with the country's foremost winemakers buying grapes from established vineyards and developing more viticultural land.

Although Elgin receives more sunlight hours during summer than Constantia, the high elevation and prevailing southerly winds greatly influence the temperature. The average February temperature is a mere 19,7°C, indicating cool conditions and subsequent late ripening of all grape varieties. It can be as much as seven weeks later than most other areas and the season can last until the end of April. There are, however, some warmer locations and, with the varying soil potential,

Preventative measures – Vine growers spray the young growth against diseases

site selection is emphasised. There is a marked difference between locations. Higher-lying Iona (420 m) is close to the ocean (3 km), which results in significantly cooler conditions and the harvest commences two to four weeks later than for other Elgin producers.

Annual rainfall is more than 1 000 millimetres, with summer precipitation from southeasterly blown-in clouds. The prevailing wind during the summer is the famous 'Black Southeaster', which brings with it a mantle of cloud that covers the Elgin Valley, keeping it cool. The close proximity of the ocean and the Palmiet River further moderates temperatures, the latter causing frequent mist during summer. Temperature fluctuates as much as 15 to 20 degrees between day and night during summer. Tthe cooling of bunches at night slows down the ripening process and provides development of flavours, while preserving the natural acidity. Most vineyards are trellised, firstly to vertically elongate the canopy for optimum sun exposure and photosynthesis, and secondly to protect the shoots from the strong prevailing winds. Interestingly, the height of the cordon is varied depending on the mesoclimate, bringing the canopy closer to the soil surface to benefit from radiant heat for improved ripening or distancing the canopy to ensure cooler ripening conditions where required.

The geology of the Elgin basin is predominantly shale with small areas of sandstone. The shale soils are characterised by gravelly topsoil on structured clay. The acidic soils require the addition of lime, as well as deep soil preparation to eliminate the chemical and structural limitations. Given the high annual rainfall, irrigation is generally not necessary, even when developing new vineyards. Although a young viticultural area, Elgin seems particularly well-suited to the more delicate varieties like Sauvignon Blanc, Pinot Noir and Merlot.

Rocky soils – Vines grow in the structured clay with gravelly topsoil at Iona

Elgin wines have typical cool-climate characteristics, modest alcohol levels and high natural acidity creating freshness. Pinot Noir is delicate with fine tannins, berry and earthy notes reminiscent of the Burgundy style. Ross Gower's MCC, (100% Pinot Noir), shows delightful fruit acids. Chardonnay offers green lime and toasty flavours, while Sauvignon Blanc wines have great complexity and pronounced gooseberry, green fig and nettle aromas (Oak Valley, Iona, Shannon Vineyards, Almenkerk). A local highlight is the Noble Late Harvest from Paul Cluver. This wine's rich sweetness is balanced with the Riesling's racy acidity. The red wines show poise and elegance, with modest alcohol levels. Iona's Cab-Merlot blend and a single varietal Cabernet Sauvignon (Paul Cluver) have less pronounced capsicum (green pepper) and eucalyptus aromas, tending more to dark cherry and savoury notes.

TERROIR

Soil: Sandstone with granite and shale, gravelly

Climate: Cool, high rainfall, windy, sunlight

White varieties: Sauvignon Blanc, Chardonnay, Chenin Blanc, Sémillon

Red varieties: Pinot Noir, Cabernet Sauvignon, Merlot

Wine styles: Red, white, dessert

DRIVING ROUTE: ELGIN

Follow the N2 south from Cape Town, through Somerset West and over Sir Lowry's Pass. About 65 kilometres from Cape Town (45 km from Stellenbosch), shortly before the town of Grabouw, turn right at the Rockview Dam turn-off. Take the left fork, and continue for about three kilometres. Turn left at the entrance to Shannon Vineyards. Its Merlot label depicts a rugged, weathered Mount Bullet (Kogelberg), towering at 1 289 metres above sea level. Their other labels show the frequent mists from Palmiet River.

Pass the town of Grabouw, the centre of the apple farming community. A few kilometres further, turn left onto the R321 Elgin / Villiersdorp. A little further, shortly before entering the town of Elgin, turn right at the T-junction to Elgin Station and Oak Valley. A short drive brings you to Oak Valley's entrance.

TRAVELLING TIPS

Accommodation:
Iona Guest cottage +27 (0)28 284 9678 / 9953
Ross Gower Guest house +27 (0)21 844 0197

Restaurants:
Orchard Restaurant & farm stall +27 (0)21 859 2880
Peregrine Farmstall +27 (0)21 848 9011

Interests:
BYO picnic (Elgin Vintners)
Mountain bike trails (Iona)
Mountain bike trails (Oak Valley)
Oak Valley Flowers +27 (0)21 859 3245
Water ski school +27 (0)21 846 8345

This 1 780 hectare property is a major supplier of apples, pears, cut flowers and naturally reared beef cattle. It also boasts 30 hectares of protected-in-perpetuity English oaks and 500 hectares of mountain fynbos reserve.

Return to the N2, turn left and 100 metres further past the Peregrine Farm Stall on the right, turn right to Viljoenshoop Road. Almost immediately, turn right to visit Elgin Vintners. Elgin Vintners is a partnership of six grape growers, combining their resources to cultivate, produce and market their range of fine quality wines. Their signature bright orange makes a bold statement on wine labels and branded clothing.

Nature in harmony – A young deer visits Shannon Vineyards

Continue on the Viljoenshoop Road (5 km), to the sign: R44 via Highlands. Here Viljoenshoop Road splits into Arumdale Road and Highlands Road. Follow the former as it heads down to the Palmiet River and Aurmdale's entrance on the left. Arumdale's vineyards are run on a minimum carbon-footprint principle, including minimal soil disturbance and irrigation. Arumdale's signboard reflects: 'Our concern is to protect our Natural Environment'. The diversity of plant and insect life is evident and wildlife is frequently spotted on the farm.

Return to the R44 intersection and turn right. Continue for about eight kilometres, passing over a small bridge in a low-lying area. The road rises

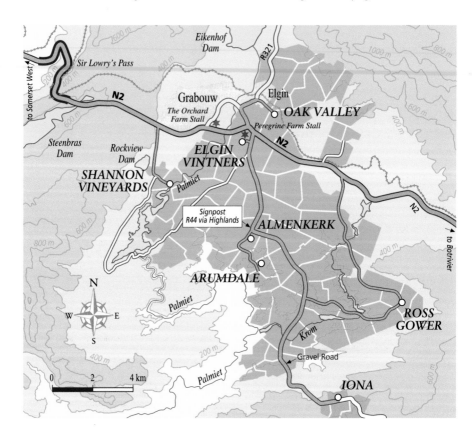

and turns to gravel. Continue on this road for another four kilometres. The turn-off to Iona is indicated on the right. Iona was previously a fruit farm, but has been cultivating vineyards with great success.

Follow the road back to the Valley Road turn-off and continue along the gravel road (6 km). Take turn-off to the right to visit Ross Gower. Alternatively, use the Valley Road turn-off from the N2 (indicated on the map). The farm offers accommodation, meals, picnics and tours.

GPS WAYPOINTS

Almenkerk S34° 12.727 E19° 01.950
Arumdale S34° 13.188 E19°02.522
Elgin Vintners S34° 10.107 E19° 02.164
Iona S34° 16.724 E 19° 04.941
Oak Valley S34° 09.411 E19° 02.905
Turn-off to R44 S34° 12.437 E19° 02.144
Ross Gower S34° 14.287 E 19° 07.038
Shannon Vineyards S34° 11.185 E 18° 59.495

ALMENKERK

Almenkerk's 100 hectare farm spreads over south-facing slopes surrounded by pristine fynbos and fairy-tale ravines. The high gravel and clay content eliminates the need for irrigation on the 15 hectares of vines. Sauvignon Blanc's eastwest row direction allows precision management of flavour components. Red varieties are planted with north – south row directions to maximise radiation.White grapes are pressed using a nitrogen press (eliminating all oxygen). Both free- run and press juice are used, the latter's higher phenol content giving richer wines. Sauvignon Blanc is aged on lees for 3 months, adding mid-palate weight to the fresh cool-climate acidity. Barrel-fermented Chardonnay is aged on lees (3 months), rending a rich, luscious wine. Red wines are fermented naturally while skin contact ensures colour and flavour development. Each vineyard section has its own tank in the cellar to track its development over vintages. Wines are blended after 18 months, mainly in French oak, offering elegant, smooth wines with fine tannins.

Sauv Bl, Family Reserve (Bdx Blend), Chard Sauv Bl, Chard, Bdx Blend, M, Rhône blend Teus–Fri 09:00–17:00, Sat 10:00–16:00, Sun & Mon by appt +27 (0)21 848 9844 info@almenkerk.co.za, www.almenkerk.co.za Red 6–10 y, white 2–5 y Tasting with owners, walking tours by appt (vineyards & fynbos), cellar tours by appt

ARUMDALE

Arumdale was acquired by the Simpson family in 1962. Today this micro-cellar focuses on Châteaux-styled 'house blends' in favour of varietal vines. A selected 10 hectares of a total of 56 are planted to vines.Red varieties are planted on north-facing slopes, maximising sun exposure in the cooler conditions, while southern slopes are ideal for white varieties. Vine rows are orientated north – south to ensure sunlight penetration into the canopy. High ambient humidity necessitates leaf removal in the bunch zone to increase air flow and the drying of grapes. Recognising the 'green side' of life, organic practices encourage fauna activity in the vineyard and owls are frequently spotted. The young vines (8 y) are restricted to eight tons per hectare, balancing growth with fruit production. The flagship St. Andrews blend shows fresh, upfront fruit. Grapes are destemmed and fermented in open-top tanks with selected yeasts. Fifteen to 20 months in French (80%) and American (20%) oak adds sweet wood flavours to the fresh acidity. Sauvignon Blanc is fermented and aged on lees (sur lees) for three months before bottling.

Arumdale St. Andrews (Cab S 60%, M 30%, Shz 10%) Cab S, Shz, M, Sauv Bl (sur lees) By appointment only +27 (0)21 848 9880 royalwine@arumdale.co.za, www.arumdale. co.za 7 y+ 05, 06 First Shiraz vineyard in Elgin, pick own fruit (apples, pears, plums), bird-watching

ELGIN VINTNERS

Paul Wallace, viticulturist for nearly three decades, set out with five partners to explore Elgin's *terroir*. Together, they cultivate 100 hectares of vines within a 10 kilometre radius in the Elgin Pocket, on a variety of altitudes, soil types and slopes. The six families see themselves as 'publishers of fine wines' and use fruit selected from the various vineyards to tell their wine story. Vines are trellised with rows orientated in a northwest – southeast direction to optimise sun exposure, protect vines against the prevailing winds and minimise diseases by allowing air movement. Each wine is vinified by a winemaker proficient in the particular wine style. Cabernet Sauvignon and Merlot for the Agama blend (Blue-headed lizard) are warm fermented (25°–27°C) with regular punch-downs ensuring good colour development. Malolactic fermentation is done in barrel and wines are matured totally in new French oak for 11 months. Then the best barrels are blended. The red wines are medium bodied and accessible earlier due to the focus on fruit flavours and sensitive oaking, whereas the white wines show cool climate freshness and minerality.

Agama (Cab S, M) Various Mon–Fri 09:00–17:00. Closed Sat, open by appt +27 (0)83 255 1884 (tastings), +27 (0)21 848 9587 (office) elginvintner@mweb.co.za, www. elginvintners.co.za 5 y Red 06, white 08 Lunch by appt, venue (conference), bird-watching, BYO picnic

IONA VINEYARDS

Iona Vineyards, situated high on the Hottentots-Holland Mountain Range, records some of the lowest average summer daytime temperatures of all South African vineyards. Twenty-five hectares were established on a flat plain where post-glacial activity deposited gravelly, alluvial soils. The soils are deep and well drained. Low planting density (3 000 vines/ha) discourages extensive root formation and excessive growth vigour. The low temperatures (17,2 °C) and frequent mists require open canopies with air movement to combat fungal diseases. Sauvignon Blanc is planted in sandstone soils, two components are based on row direction and sun exposure: east – west rows give green fig and white fruit flavours while fruit from north – south rows show riper tropical fruit. Clear juice is cold fermented, resulting in a typical steely, mineral character. Reds are cultivated on gravelly sites and grapes are fermented with pump-overs to extract colour. Malolactic fermentation followed by 14 months maturation in French oak resulting in elegant, fruit-driven wines with fine tannins.

ⓘ Sauvignon Blanc 🍷 Sauv Bl, Sém, Chard, Shz/Mouv, Bdx blend (Cab S, M, PV) 🕐 Mon–Fri 08:00–17:30. Closed Easter Fri, Sat, Sun; Dec 25, 26; Jan 1 📞 +27 (0)28 284 9678 📧 gunn@iona.co.za, www.iona.co.za 🍾 Sauv 5–10 y, M 5–10 y 🍷 06, 07, 09 🚶 Walks, mountain bike, BYO picnics

OAK VALLEY

Oak Valley, family-owned since being purchased by Sir Antonie Viljoen in 1898, made its maiden vintage Sauvignon Blanc in 2003 after supplying many celebrated producers such as Bouchard Finlayson and Rupert and Rothschild. This 1 780 hectare property boasts 30 hectares of protected-in-perpetuity English oaks and 500 hectares of mountain fynbos reserve. With the original cellar decommissioned in the 1940s, Oak Valley is planning a new winery. Forty nine hectares of vines are cultivated on steep slopes at 600 metres above sea level. South-facing slopes support low-vigour soils of shale and sandstone where planting density is decreased to 2 900 vines/ha. The canopies are vertically extended on trellising to maximise sun exposure and to ensure full ripeness. Cloud cover, mist and rain create cool, even ripening conditions, but the prevailing southeasterly ensures that grapes are dried to prevent *Botrytis*. Oak Valley uses a reductive winemaking process to preserve its herbaceous Sauvignon Blanc aromas. The wine is left on the lees for two months to soften its naturally high acidity. The practice also adds a mid-palate weight, resulting in a full-bodied, dry minerally white wine .

ⓘ Sauvignon Blanc 🍷 Sauv Bl, Sém, Chard, Viog, M,Cab F, PV 🕐 Mon–Fri 09:00–17:00, Sat 10:00–14:00 or by appt 📞 +27 (0)21 859 2510 📧 wines@oak-valley.co.za, www.oakvalleywines.com 🍾 3 y+ 🍷 03, 04, 05, 06, 07, 08 🚲 Mountain biking trails, tours of cut flowers production

ROSS GOWER WINES

Ross Gower (ex-Klein Constantia) pinpointed Elgin as the ideal *terroir* for his own venture. Wines are produced on the principles of sustainability and minimal intervention. The winery is constructed of rammed earth. As yet only six hectares of the 83 hectare property are planted to vines. Delicate Sauvignon Blanc enjoys the cool southwestern sandstone slopes, while the shale on north-facing slopes are ideal for Shiraz, with Cabernet Sauvignon and Muscadel in the pipeline. Most of the grapes are bought from very carefully selected vineyards in the area. The flagship MCC, Ross Gower Pinot Noir Brut, is a 100 per cent varietal, and boasts a zero dosage. After crushing, the grapes are macerated for a few hours on the skins to achieve the trademark *l'oeil de perdrix* (eye of the partridge) colour. The superb natural fruit acids achieved in Elgin make it an ideal region for *Cap Classique* production. The wine is aged for two years on the lees before disgorgement. The Sauvignon Blanc shows strong pyrazine characters (grass, green pepper) and crisp acidity, while the reds are fruit-driven with fine, dry tannins.

ⓘ Pinot Brut (MCC) 🍷 Sauv Bl, MCC (PN, Blanc de Blanc), Riesl, Shz, M, Cab S 🕐 Mon–Fri 09:00-17:30. Weekends & pub hols by appt 📞 +27 (0)21 844 0197 📧 info@rossgowerwines.co.za, www.rossgowerwines.co.za 🍾 6–10 y 🍷 05 🏠 Self-catering cottages, olives, tours by appt.

SHANNON VINEYARDS

Shannon Vineyards is nestled along the banks of the Palmiet River. The high elevation, misty mornings and close proximity of the river accentuates the already cool climate. Five clones of Sauvignon Blanc are blended to give asparagus and capsicum flavours with minerally flintiness, while a component of barrel-fermented Sémillon adds mid-palate weight. Grapes are cooled (3°C) before processing. Only Sauvignon Blanc is inoculated while the rest undergoes natural ferments. Red wines complete alcoholic and malolactic fermentation, then they are aged for 12 and 20 months respectively in a combination of old and new French oak. A multi-clonal approach to the Pinot Noir develops berry fruits and density (from heavy clay soils), while Italian clones add savoury flavours to the Merlot's dark red fruits. The Merlot is planted on warmer northeast-facing slopes, using a low trellis to maximise reflective light. Soil types vary greatly and a high planting density (3 800–4 500/ha) ensures balanced growth. Row direction, leaf removal and a higher trellis for the other varieties capitalises on air movement to keep grapes dry and disease free.

ⓘ Sauv Bl, PN, Mount Bullet (Merlot) 🍷 Sauv Bl, PN, M 🕐 By appt 📞 +27 (0)21 859 2491 📧 info@shannonwines.com, www.shannonwines.com 🍾 Sauv 10 y, PN 15 y, M 15 y 🍷 PN 07; Bullet 07; Sauv Bl 08

Walker Bay Area

Heading up the road – A relaxed drive takes you past the wineries of the Hemel-en-Aarde Valley

The Walker Bay Area stretches from the small village of Botrivier in a southerly direction through the Hemel-en-Aarde Valley and encompasses Stanford, the Kleinrivier Basin and Hermanus. All these vineyard areas are markedly affected by the maritime influence of the ocean at Walker Bay and surrounded by the Klein Babylonstorenberg.

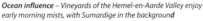

Ocean influence – Vineyards of the Hemel-en-Aarde Valley enjoy early morning mists, with Sumardige in the background

Central to this area is the seaside town of Hermanus – a popular holiday destination with locals and overseas visitors alike. The relaxed atmosphere, moderate climate and spectacular views make this a prime real-estate area. In the early 1800s, Hermanus Pieters was a school teacher to farm children in the Walker Bay area. It was this dearly loved educator who gave his name to the seaside town of Hermanus first in 1855 as Hermanuspietersfontein (Eng. Hermanus Pieters fountain). It was later shortened to

Measuring sugar – Peter Finlayson uses a refractometer to determine sugar levels in the grape juice

Hermanus. The town is perhaps most well-known for its whale watching, as the whales socialise in the shallow water near the coastline during the spring months of August to November. The best viewing point for whale watching is near the old harbour. Even more than in the Elgin Pocket, the summer rain originating from clouds against the surrounding sandstone mountain ridges by the synoptic southeasterly winds, is a prominent feature of Walker Bay. These summer rains contribute towards the relatively high annual rainfall (up to 1 000 mm). Structured soils in certain sites rarely dry completely and deep soil preparation is required. The mean February temperature at Hermanus is 20,3°C, which is fairly warm. However, the cool, moisture-laden flow from the ocean creates cool ripening conditions. Strong southeasterly and southwesterly winds are common and vineyards are trellised to protect the shoots from damage.

Geologically the area is diverse, with gravelly or stony soils derived from highly weathered granite and shale as well as calcareous, solidified quaternary sand dunes. These marginal soils are a unique feature of this coastal area and, together with the persistent winds, serve to curtail excessive vigour and restrict crop yields for improved grape quality. The vineyards enjoy various aspects. White varieties are planted along southeast-facing slopes on the lower-lying sites and reds on the slightly warmer higher slopes.

The topography with north- and south-facing aspects modifies the macroclimate considerably over short distances, allowing a wide range of wine grape varieties to be cultivated.

After the harvest – Hemel-en-Aarde Valley vines in autumn colours

> ### TERROIR
>
> **Soil:** Granite with shale, some solidified sand
> **Climate:** Maritime influence, cool, high rainfall, windy
> **White varieties:** Sauvignon Blanc, Chardonnay
> **Red varieties:** Pinot Noir, Cabernet Sauvignon, Shiraz
> **Wine styles:** Red, white

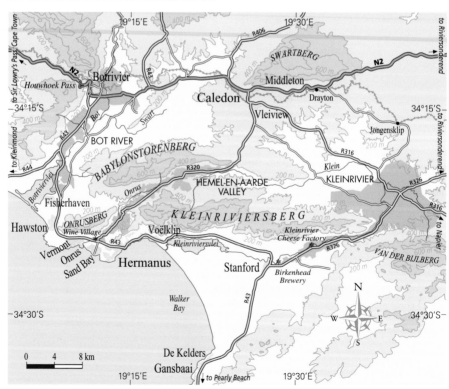

Botrivier Pocket

Open landscape – A view over the vineyards of Gabriëlskloof

The Botrivier Pocket encompasses the Botrivier village and valley, stretching from the Botrivier lagoon up into the foothills of the Groenland- and Babylonstorenberg ranges, and bordering the Kogelberg Biosphere. The area is renowned for its cool maritime microclimate, which is mainly influenced by its proximity to the lagoon and Walker Bay – cooling afternoon winds blow up the valley off the sea. The undulating hills provide winemakers with various aspects for the cultivation of both red and white grape varieties.

Soils in this area are mainly homogenous shale and sandstone. Due to the location at the foot of the mountain range, soils tend to be deeper as greater volumes have been deposited by erosion from the mountain slopes. Vines are trellised against the strong prevailing winds and planting densities tend to follow a standard practice of around 300 plants per hectare. Chenin Blanc, Sauvignon Blanc, Pinotage, Shiraz and other Rhône varietals fare

Rainbow for good luck – Benguela Cove's vines enjoy a refreshing summer rain shower

particularly well here. Botrivier is home to an eclectic mix of wineries which handcraft their wines. The town's quirky character lies in its rustic and tranquil charm.

Sauvignon Blanc wines are powerful with green fig, capsicum and a mineral edge, with examples from Beaumont, Barton and Bengueala Cove. A few Shiraz wines are also produced, with elegant, spicy examples from Luddite and Beaumont. The latter also produced South Africa's first single varietal Mourvèdre. Gabriëlskloof has an interesting selection of red varieties coming into production with Shiraz, Mourvèdre, Petit Verdot, Malbec and Cabernet Sauvignon showing great promise. Benguela Cove, a wine and residential estate, boldy planted vines in former sheep paddocks, on a shale hill. The adjacent estuary is a bird-watcher's delight and illustrates the conscious way in which the property is cultivated. Wines show cool herbaceous tones and a slight savouriness.

DRIVING ROUTE: BOTRIVIER

Leave Cape Town on the N2 freeway, past Somerset West and over the Hottentots Holland Mountain range via Sir Lowry's Pass. Descending the mountain on the southern side, take Exit 92 to Botrivier. At the intersection, turn left into the main road. Pass through the small village, and exit on the northern side. Turn right onto a gravel road, indicating Villiersdorp.

Continue for about two kilometres, until you reach the entrance to Luddite on the left. This boutique cellar specializes in Shiraz, making wines in a restrained, traditional style. Winemaker Niels Verbrug says: 'Luddism reflects our belief in winemaking where we choose to practise our craft conscientiously and thereby retain our individuality. Technology and mechanisation will

Family affair – Everyone pitches in to help with pressing of the Shiraz at Luddite

never be a substitute for passion'. Do try their cured meat products.

Drive back along the R43, through Botrivier and join the N2. Continue in a southeasterly direction. About five kilometres further, turn right onto Swartrivier Road. Five hundred metres further, turn right to Gabriëlskloof. Their new state-of-the-art cellar specialises in red wines with a small percentage of white varieties. In addition, the farm cultivates olive trees and lavender for oil production. Retrace the route back to the Botrivier turn-off and continue for about four kilometres. Shortly after the stone quarry, turn right to Barton Vineyards. Complementing the wines, this property also produces olives and lavender and boasts five luxury villas. Drive along the R43 and pass the turn-off to the R44 and Kleinmond. About 3,5

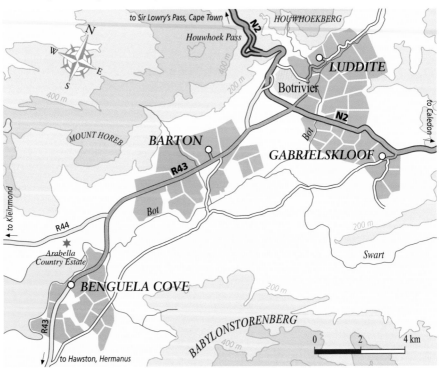

kilometres after the turn-off, Benguela Cove lies on the right. Its ocean vistas are unbeatable and some vines are only a few hundred metres from the Botrivier estuary.

GPS WAYPOINTS

Barton Vineyards S34° 15.730 E19° 10.487

Benguela Cove S34° 19.819 E19° 08.314

Exit 92 to Botrivier S34° 14.110 E19° 11.899

Gabriëlskloof S34° 15.385 E19° 15.642

Luddite S34° 12.842 E19° 12.377

TRAVELLING TIPS

Information:
www.botriverwines.co.za

Accommodation:
Arabella Country Estate & spa +27 (0)28 284 0000,
Barton Villas +27 (0)28 284 9283

Interests:
Bot River barrel race, annually in October
Green Mountain Eco Route +27 (0)21 844 0975,
   www.greenmountain.co.za

BARTON VINEYARDS

Barton Vineyards (est. 2003) aims for sustainable agriculture in an eco-friendly way. The 198 hectare farm lies on the cool south-facing slopes of the Kogelberg. Thirty-eight hectares of vines are planted on low-potential soil composed of sand, gravel and sandstone with underlying clay. Judicious irrigation prevents water stress and the iron content imparts a strong mineral character to the wines. Vines are trellised due to strong winds, which curb fungal diseases. Afternoon mountain shadows over vineyards amplify the ocean cooling effect. Dry ice is added to white varieties at crushing to inhibit juice oxidation. The must is pressed and only the free-run juice is fermented. The Sauvignon shows rich granadilla and passionfruit with hints of green pepper and a strong minerality. Red varieties are subjected to cold maceration for two days and fermented cool at 26°C. Following natural malolactic fermentation, the wines are matured in French oak (95%) for 18 months. The wines' berry fruit is supported by herbaceousness, lead pencil (Cab), spice and white pepper (Shz).

ℹ️ Sauvignon Bl, Shz / Cab S 🍇 Shz / Cab S, Chenin Bl, Sauv Bl, white blend 🕐 Mon–Fri 09:00–17:00, Sat 09:00–13:00 📞 +27 (0)28 284 9283 ✉️ info@bartonvineyards.co.za, www.bartonvineyards.co.za 🍷 Sauv bl 3 y, Red 8 y 🍷 Sauv 09, Red 06 ℹ️ Self-catering villas, fly fishing, natural products (honey, olive oil, organic lavender products), horse riding, hiking

GABRIËLSKLOOF

Gabriëlskloof, Bot Rivier's latest addition, crushed its first vintage in its brand-new wine cellar in 2009. Seventy hectares of vineyards are cultivated on diverse slopes, taking advantage of extended sunshine to ripen grapes in the cool climate created by the aspect, prevailing wind and frequent mists from the nearby ocean. While predominantly shale, inclusions of clay and sandstone allow cultivation of both red (70%) and white (30%) varieties. The lean soils ensure naturally low yields and concentrated fruit. A selection of clones planted on different soils provides building blocks for the varietal and blended wines. To ensure colour and flavour development, the cellar combines hand-sorting of berries, gravitational flow and traditional methods of punch-down and open-tank fermenting for red wines. Red wines are then matured in French, European and American oak barrels (min 12 mnth), imparting dense texture to support the rich fruit structure. White grapes are gently pressed and the free-run juice is cold fermented, preserving delicate white fruit and floral aromas.

ℹ️ Magdalena Sémillon/ Sauvignon Blanc 🍇 Shz, Mouv, Malb, PV, Cab S/F, M, Sauv Bl, Sém, Viog 🕐 09:00–17:00 📞 +27 (0)28 284 9865 ✉️ info@gabrielskloof.co.za, www.gabrielskloof.co.za 🍷 5–8 y 🍷 09 ℹ️ Restaurant, deli, bird-watching, olive oil

LUDDITE

Luddite represents the philosophy of keeping mechanical intervention to a minimum. This boutique cellar nestles on the east-facing slopes of the Houwhoekberg, facing Walker Bay. Shiraz is the sole focus and the six hectares of vines are largely dedicated to this variety. Emphasising natural farming, seven hectares of natural fynbos remain under conservation. The decomposed shale with underlying clay is suited to red varieties and a high planting density, in addition to strong prevailing winds channelling through the valley, limits excessive growth. As eastern slopes are considered slighter cooler, the Shiraz here tends to develop more towards spice and meat characters than red fruit. In 2009 the first vintage was crushed in a new cellar. Fermentation is kept as natural as possible. Extended maceration ensures a balanced tannin structure. The wine is matured in French oak (95%) together with a small percentage of Hungarian oak to add complexity. In taking care not to overwhelm the wine, only 25 per cent of new wood is used, resulting in an intense, complex wine, opening richly with age.

ℹ️ Luddite Shiraz 🍇 Sh, Mourv, Cab S 🕐 Mon–Fri 09:30–16:30, Sat, Sun & pub hols by appt 📞 +27 (0)28 284 9308, +27 (0)83 444 3537 ✉️ luddite@telkomsa.net, www.luddite.co.za 🍷 4–12 y 🍷 00 – 06 ℹ️ Pork products, Green Mountain Eco Route, fynbos surrounds the tasting room

BENGUELA COVE

Benguela Cove is one of South Africa's latest lifestyle property developments, on the coast of the Atlantic Ocean in Walker Bay. This 200 hectare wine farm is situated on two small hills, consisting mainly of clay and calcium-rich decomposed shale soils. Sixty-five hectares are planted to vines.

Located on the banks of the Botrivier estuary, the close proximity of the cold Benguela current together with frequent wind movement creates cool ripening conditions. Extensive soil preparation and mulching allows for supplementary irrigation, even with an annual rainfall of only 570 millimetres. The hills provide northern aspects to fully ripen red varieties, whereas white varieties are planted on cooler south/east-facing slopes. The strong prevailing wind restrains vegetative growth as the resulting shorter internodes produce smaller bunches with concentrated flavour and better colour intensity in the wines.

The vineyard is almost equally divided between red and white varieties and a new 150-ton cellar is expected to be in full production by 2011. Sauvignon Blanc is harvested during the early morning and the grapes undergo cold maceration on the skins for a few hours, strengthening the varietal flavour. Cold fermentation is done at 10°–12°C and the young wine is aged on the lees for four to five months. A small percentage is aged in older barrels for two to three months as the slight oakiness rounds off crisp acidity. During red wine fermentation, a few pump overs daily are sufficient to extract colour and tannins, and the wine is macerated on the skins for up to 10 to 16 days. The red wines are aged for 12 to 15 months in French oak barrels of medium to light toasting, adding structure to these elegant, fruity wines.

Closest to water – Benguela Cove's vines overlook the Botrivier estuary and the ocean, which ensures cool ripening conditions

🛈 Sauvignon Blanc, Shiraz 🍇 Sauv bl, Chard, Shz, Mouv, Viog, Malbec, CS, CF, M, PV, PN (MCC in future) 🕐 Mon–Fri, Sat & Sun by appt 📞 +27 (0)21 671 5417 ✉ info@benguelacove.co.za, www.benguelacove.co.za 🍷 Red 3–5 y 📅 07, 09 ℹ Cellar, restaurant, chapel, hotel, venue and weddings, new cellar ready for 2011, estuary & birdlife, olives and lavender

Pinot Noir

Pinot Noir has been quoted as an exasperating variety for growers, winemakers and consumers alike. It is sometimes said to be feminine, alluring or capricious, but mostly it is the pursuit of richness and elegance which makes it ultimately satisfy the Holy Grail of winemaking. The first Pinot plantings were based on the Swiss BK5 clone. These vines were prone to leaf roll, which causes the vines to degenerate.

In addition, this clone did not offer the classic red wine characteristics of Burgundy, but rather presented wines that were weak-coloured and austere, with low extract. In the 1980s, newer, virus-free clones were introduced and vines were pruned to the French double guyot method. This marked a change in vine cultivation

which proved more productive. The new clones display moderate growth vigour, are fairly shy bearers and the fruit ripened early. Disease resistance is increased, although *Botrytis* rot does occur. Pinot Noir now produces better colour (which was previously insufficient) and higher tannin levels, yet these are still refined. The fruit flavours tend to be highly complex in the best examples, including the characteristic sweet cherry flavours. Key producers are Bouchard Finalyson, Blaauwklippen, Hamilton Russell Vineyards, Meerlust, Rustenburg and Vriesenhof.

Hemel-en-Aarde Valley Pocket

Creation tasting room – Glass panelling of the exquisite tasting room creates the feeling of enjoying wines within the surrounding fynbos

The Hemel-en-Aarde Valley Pocket can be divided into three sections, due to a north – south ridge running through the valley. The first section comprises the valley, which opens in a southerly direction towards the ocean. Its boundry is the northern side of Bouchard Finlayson. From here, the second section spans the ridge, up to and including Sumaridge Wines.

Over the ridge, the valley slopes away, in an easterly direction. Here, soils lose much of their water due to run-off and drainage, making water management vital. The first and third sections are more exposed to the prevailing winds and thus recorded temperatures, both in summer and winter, are slightly lower. Soils are mainly composed of shale, clay and sandstone; the good water-holding capacity results in vines rarely being irrigated. The middle section, however, has more decomposed granite.

The prevailing winds are northwest (winter) and southeast (summer), cooling the vines and reducing the humidity in the canopy. While this

Hermanuspietersfontein 1855 – The roadside wine cellar maximises natural light with extensive glass panelling

necessitates trellising to protect vines, it has the benefit of reducing humidity-related diseases. The changing landscape offers various sites that receive more sunlight exposure and others that are protected against wind and sun. It is therefore not surprising that a range of cultivars achieve success in the Hemel-en-Aarde Valley.

Wines have pronounced varietal flavours and are complex yet elegant. The generally cool conditions benefit the temperature-sensitive varieties. Sauvignon Blanc wines are powerful with green fig, capsicum and a mineral edge (Creation, HPF1855). Chardonnay is complex and flavoursome with a mineral finish. Good examples include both barrel-fermented and unwooded wines (Ataraxia, Bouchard Finlayson, Hamilton Russell Vineyards, Sumaridge).

Leading Cape examples of Pinot Noir show a luxurious, creamy texture and cherry fruit with very fine tannins (Bouchard Finlayson, HRV). Other examples show more forest floor and earthy notes. Red varieties are placed on northern-facing slopes to fulfil their heat requirements, producing interesting blends, such as the succulent and exotic Hannibal blend from Bouchard Finlayson (Sang, PN, Mourv, Neb, Barb). Bordeaux varities find a mineral core with deep fruit expression and velvety tannins (Spookfontein, HPF1855).

DRIVING ROUTE: HEMEL-EN-AARDE

Leave Cape Town on the N2 freeway, past Somerset West and over the Hottentots Holland Mountain Range via Sir Lowry's Pass, descend along the mountain pass on the southern side. Take the exit to the R43 Hermanus on the left. The road winds in a southerly direction. Drive carefully as the road runs through several costal villages and the speed limit changes accordingly. Turn left onto the R320 (27 km from N2). Just past the small shopping centre, turn left to visit Hermanuspietersfontein. This innovative producer not only presents all wine names

and labels in Afrikaans, but has also reached champion status for their conservation efforts. A great place to purchase South African wine is the Wine Village at the shopping centre, right at the entrance to the valley. Wine Village boasts a comprehensive collections of South African wines, representing more than 380 wineries.

Drive along the R320 as it makes its way into this beautiful, secluded valley. When you reach the entrance to Bouchard Finlayson, on the right, follow the road to the thatched tasting room and offices. Here Peter Finlayson's focus remains on Pinot Noir, while he continues to experiment with his beloved Italian varieties, Sangiovese and Nebbiolo.

A little further, just over a crest, lies

GPS WAYPOINTS

Bouchard Finlayson S34° 22.931 E19° 14.225
Creation S34° 19.861 E19° 19.584
Hermanuspietersfontein S34° 24.648 E19° 11.969
Spookfontein S34° 21.221 E19° 16.986
Sumaridge S34° 21.667 E19° 16.193

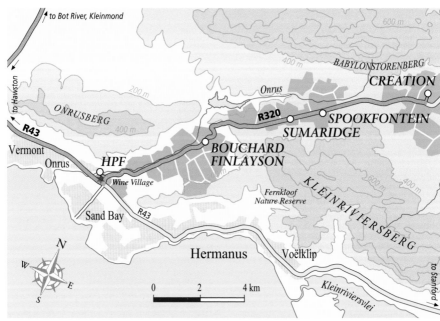

Sumaridge on the left. Enjoy the view of the valley and notice the string of water bodies which cool the wind as it flows up the valley. Sumaridge's social awareness has a special project: partnering with a criminal rehabilitation centre, it provides a year of employment as part of a reintegration program into the work place.

About 1,7 km on, take the turn-off on the right to Spookfontein (Eng. Ghost fountain). The name Spookfontein is derived from the natural spring found on the farm. Rain water collects high in the mountains seeps through various rock layers ending the journey passing through iron-rich slate rock. Spookfontein is the only Bordeaux-style blend specialist in the valley.

Continue along the road to the turn-off to Creation Wines. Take care on the gravel road to the winery. Their slogan explains the new development on virgin land, matching specific clones to each site: 'From wilderness to paradise'.

TERROIR

Soil: Sandstone with granite and shale, gravelly

Climate: Cool, windy, high rainfall, sunlight

White varieties: Sauvignon Blanc, Chardonnay, Chenin Blanc, Sémillon

Red varieties: Pinot Noir, Cabernet Sauvignon, Merlot

Wine styles: Red, white, dessert

TRAVELLING TIPS

Accommodation:
Spookfontein +27 (0)28 313 0668
Sumaridge +27 (0)28 312 1097

Restaurants:
Mediterea +27 (0)28 313 1685

Interests:
Green Mountain Eco Route +27 (0)21 844 0975,
    www.greenmountain.co.za
Overberg birding routes, Dr Anton Odendaal
    www.westerncapebirding.co.za
Wine Village +27 (0)28 316 3988

SPOOKFONTEIN

Spookfontein's winemaking journey commenced with the new millennium. Their vision is to understand the whole farm as one organism and thus create 'single vineyard, organic' wines. Vines are cultivated (12ha) on steep slopes facing north-west and north-east with high altitudes (350 m above sea level) moderating the greater sun exposure. Soils consist of sandstone topsoil with underlying clay, giving physiological ripe grapes with fine tannins, a good natural acidity with moderate alcohols. One block of Cabernet Sauvignon, however, is planted on iron-rich slate, offering greater palate weight. Organic viticulture aims to improve the soil's overall health. Vines are trellised against strong prevailing winds. The Merlot-dominated flagship blend, Phantom, is the only non-single vineyard wine. Following natural fermentation, a wooden basket press separates the young wine from the skins. The wines are bottled after 20 months of maturation with light filtering and without fining. The small percentage of new French oak (30%) gives wines with great fruit expression, a fresh mineral core and a medium body.

📱 Phantom (Bdx blend) 🍷 MCC, PN, Bdx varieties ⭕ By appt only 📞 +27 (0)21 461 6252, (0)82 265 1071 ✉ miked@dragons.co.za, cjswine@hotmail.com 🗓 10–12 y 🍾 08, 09 ℹ Self-catering cottage & farmhouse, walking, hiking, mountain biking, horse rides by appt only

HERMANUSPIETERSFONTEIN 1855

Named after the original 1855 name of Hermanus, the HPF team differentiates their brand to get to the forefront of markets. A combination of elevated (200–300 m) south- and east-facing aspects and the nearby ocean create exceptionally cool ripening conditions for the 62 hectares of vines. Sauvignon Blanc flourishes on higher-lying sandstone-granite soils while reds are planted on mid-slope weathered shale. Vines are given greater space due to the low soil potential (2 900–3 700 vines/ha) and rows are directed east – west as protection against excessive sun exposure during summer. White grapes for Die Bartho are cooled overnight and fermented cold (13°C) to preserve the capsicum and nettle aromas. Sémillon is fermented in French oak, adding rich oaky notes to the citrus and grassiness of Sauvignon Blanc and Nouvelle. The red wines show typical cool-climate acidity and intensity. The Shiraz blend offers fynbos and white pepper, and the Bordeaux-style Blend sweet red fruit and velvet tannins.

📱 Die Bartho (Sauv Bl / Sém / Nouv), Die Martha (Shz / Mouv / Viog), Die Arnoldus (Cab S / M / Cab F / Malb / PV) 🍷 Various ⭕ Mon–Fri 09:00–17:00, Sat 09:00–13:00. Closed Easter Sun, Mon; Dec 25, 26; Jan 1 📞 +27 (0)28 316 1875 ✉ kelder@hpf1855.co.za, www.hpf1855.co.za 🗓 8 y 🍾 07 ℹ Food & Wine Market Sat 09:00–13:00, quarterly regional Wine Festivals, accommodation, picnic, conservation area

BOUCHARD FINLAYSON

Peter Finlayson is aptly described as the pioneer of Pinot Noir in the Hemel-en-Aarde Valley and, for that matter, South Africa as a whole. After extensive experience with this variety on a neighbouring farm, Finlayson joined Burgundian Paul Bouchard to set up the boutique winery of Bouchard Finlayson. Today, the winery is owned by the Tollman family, under the leadership of Victoria Tollman and winemaker Peter Finlayson.

With its thatched roof and predominant white walls, the luxurious winery – which is elegantly featured on its label – maintains a Cape feel with clean lines and low-slung walls. A pitched roof supports vast thatch overhangs, which form a wraparound veranda that protects the building and cellar from the heat of the midday sun. Since its maiden vintage of 1991, the cellar has been dedicated to Pinot Noir, Chardonnay and Sauvignon Blanc. Sangiovese, however, and a handful of Tuscan and French varieties are also vinified – Sangiovese, Nebbiolo, Barbera and Mourvèdre.

Unusual trellising – Nebbiolo vines are trellised high to ensure sufficient sun exposure on the leaves

Homestead – The Bouchard Finlayson homestead against the magnificent backdrop of the Hemel-en-Aarde Valley

Located only six kilometres from the Atlantic Ocean, the farm enjoys a maritime climate. The sheltering Galpin Peak (810 m) and the Tower of Babel (1 200 m) trap cloud cover and moisture from the prevailing cool Atlantic sea breezes which in turn promote slow-ripening, flavour-rich grapes from even the most sensitive varieties. Bouchard Finlayson's soil is predominantly shale and its duplex structure, consisting of stony gravel and fine clay shale, ensures good moisture retention, while gentle slopes drain excess water to aerate the vine roots.

Only 19 hectares are planted to vines with 50 per cent devoted to Pinot Noir – the variety for which the valley is most acclaimed. The additional farm land (100 ha) is dedicated to the conservation of indigenous fynbos. Viticultural practices are based on the Burgundian philosophy of high-density planting, with 9 000 vines planted per hectare. This encourages greater surface to leaf exposure and restricts root growth, improving fruit concentration, while expanding sunlight exposure to the vines, which are planted on gentle west-facing slopes in a north-south direction. Vineyards are trellised at a lower level on a Guyot system so that the reflected heat from the soil will aid phenolic ripeness. Green harvesting is practised annually to remove underdeveloped or damaged grapes and to restrict the quantity of bunches per shoot so that grapes may ripen fully. Due to high-density planting, the vines protect each other from strong prevailing winds and suckering (removal of underdeveloped shoots) may be delayed in case of excessive wind.

Barrel cellar – The double doors lead to the new barrel cellar, where each wine is gently 'elevaged' or given time to grow up

Winemaker in the vineyard – Early morning tending of the vines allows the winemaker to understand the terroir influence

Grapes are harvested by hand with commonly more than one pass through the same vineyard to select only the fully ripe grapes.

Grapes for the Burgundian-styled benchmark, Galpin Peak Pinot Noir, are crushed and destemmed before fermentation in closed tanks. Fermentation temperatures are kept well below 30°C to preserve the truffle and forest floor aromas of the Pinot Noir in particular. Regular pump-overs and slight aeration of the fermenting wine ensures a deep colour and rich mouthfeel. The wine is matured in small Burgundian barrels for 10 months. About 30 per cent new wood is used to prevent the subtle varietal flavours from being overpowered by the wood. In the best vintages, however, a Tête du Cuvée Galpin Peak Pinot Noir is made from selected barrels and matured for 14 months in 80 per cent new wood, resulting in a dense, structured wine with fine-laced tannins.

Wine sales – Older vintages of Bouchard Finlayson's wines are cellared at optimum conditions to provide drinking pleasure

The Cape's first Sangiovese blend, Hannibal, was born from experimental varieties and incorporates Sangiovese, Pinot Noir and small amounts of Nebbiolo, Barbera, Shiraz and Mourvèdre. The blending of Sangiovese and Pinot Noir is unique. Fermentation temperatures are slightly increased (28°C) to bring out the varietal character of the Tuscan varieties and the components are individually oaked for 16 months before blending. Although an elegant blend, the wine shows deceptively substantial power. Red wines are bottle matured for 12 months before release onto the market.

Once harvested, white grapes are destemmed and lightly pressed to remove juice from the skins. The cleared juice is fermented at low temperatures (13°–16°C) to preserve the varietal flavours. The classically styled white flagship, Missionvale Chardonnay, takes its name from the historical site where a Moravian missionary, Peter Leitner, established a hospice in the region. One hundred per cent barrel fermented, it also undergoes malolactic fermentation in the barrels. The wine is kept on the primary lees for five to nine months with regular *bâttonage* softening the wine's acids and giving weight to the mid-palate. The unwooded Chardonnay and Sauvignon Blanc are made in a riper, more tropical fruit style and are bottled without malolactic fermentation.

For certain wines, grapes are selected from within the region – one such contracted vineyard is Kaaimansgat (Crocodile's Lair). Situated in a blind valley high in the Cape Coastal Mountains, the Chardonnay grapes are grown in the cool region of Villiersdorp on non-irrigated slopes at an elevation of 700 metres above sea level. This wine has typical gravelly tones and lemon fruit. Partially oaked, it carries a slightly higher alcohol (Alc.14% by Vol.) with grace.

Since 2006, Bouchard Finlayson has been an active member of the Biodiversity and Wine Initiative. Ninety per cent of the estate is classified free of alien vegetation. Two hectares of alien vegetation have been retained as a research site for the UCT Biological Control Operations. This research assists with calculating the benefits of indigenous vegetation versus alien vegetation. Bouchard Finlayson is proud to be contributing to the preservation and conservation of the rich Cape Floral Kingdom.

Trademark cellar – The widely recognisable Bouchard Finlayson cellar, with its protective thatched roof

Tête du Cuvée Galpin Peak Pinot Noir, Galpin Peak Pinot Noir PN, Sauv Bl, Chard, Sang, Nebb, Mourv, Barbera, Shz Mon–Fri 09:00–17:00, Sat 09:30–12:30 +27 (0)28 312 3515 info@bouchardfinlayson.co.za, www.bouchardfinlayson.co.za 5–20 y PN 95, 97, 01, 05; Chard 00, 03 Spectacular views, groups by appt

CREATION WINES

In 2002, Swiss winemaker Jean-Claude Martin and his wife, Carolyn, purchased an undiscovered 'piece of wine paradise' high in the Hemel-en-Aarde Valley, establishing the first vineyard there. In 2005 the Martin's friends, Swiss winemaker Christoph Kaser and his wife, Heidi, co-invested. The farm boasts 22 hectares of vines alongside 13 hectares of fynbos. The proximity of the ocean and an elevation of 350 metres above sea level create cool ripening conditions while the near-constant airflow reduces humidity-related diseases. A few warmer north-facing slopes are planted to red varieties; however grapes ripen physiologically with moderate sugar content and thus moderate alcohol levels.

Deep shale soils laced with clay and organic material allow for deep root development (3,5 m) and good water retention, which acts as a buffer during the summer months. In the red varieties, leaves are removed to maximise sunlight interception while a denser canopy is retained to enhance the delicate flavours of white varieties. A custom-designed winery was completed for the 2007 vintage. Grapes are destemmed without crushing and fermented whole. White grapes receive a short maceration (6 h), developing mineral characters and ripe tropical fruit flavours. Red grapes are fermented cool (25°C) and gently pressed. The wines are aged in French oak with 30 per cent new wood.

The Pinot Noir shows succulent red berries and spicy vanilla with supple tannins. Syrah, combined with Grenache, gives sumptuous flavours of ripe plum, black pepper and subtle smokiness. The Bordeaux-style Blend, with blackberry and blackcurrant notes, eases seamlessly with harmoniously smoky oak.

Climatic blessing – The moisture-laden, cool air from the nearby ocean ensures slow ripening of the grapes at Creation

NA Sauv Bl, Viog, Chard, PN, Rhône blend (Shz / Gren), Bdx Blend (Cab S, M, PV) Daily 10:00–16:00 (15 Nov–15 Jan). Mon–Sat 10:00–16:00 (16 Jan–14 Nov). Closed Dec 25, 26, Jan 1 +27 (0)28 212 1107 info@creationwines.com, www.creationwines.com 6 y 08 Food pairing & antipastos platters by appt, venue (conference, retreats, product launches, team-building), vineyard and cellar tours

SUMARIDGE WINES

Sumaridge Wines, owned by the Bellingham Turner family, lies on the slopes of the Klein Babylonstorenberg, in the Hemel-en-Aarde valley. A number of large lakes and dams create 'stepping stones of water bodies', which amplify the maritime climate created by the nearby Atlantic Ocean. Forty hectares are cultivated to vines on northwest-facing slopes, and the cool maritime climate is further modified by these high slopes which lie from 180 to 260 meters above sea level. The cool growing and ripening conditions allow for the development of wines with distinctive cool-climate elegance, natural high acidity and ample body to support the complex flavours.

The six cultivars are distributed over the two main soil types: sandstone and a granitic inclusion. The top soil is fairly shallow (30–50 cm) but gravelly and well aerated. The clay subsoil is free-draining, but it maintains sufficient soil moisture. Vineyard management focuses on sustainability and greater awareness to include natural methods. Indigenous grasses are used as a cover crop year-round to encourage fauna development in the vineyards – guinea fowl are regular visitors. Attention to detail sees each variety harvested in small batches according to vine age, soil type, aspect, elevation, varietal clone and even row direction. Chardonnay receives 100 per cent malolactic fermentation adding roundness and toasted notes while retaining lively acidity. Nine months of barrel maturation presents gentle oak, supporting the rich citrus and floral flavours. Pinot Noir completes alcoholic and malolactic fermentation before being matured totally in Burgundian oak (40% new oak) and the moderate aging period of 10 months allows for good integration of oak character. This lends a smoky spiciness to the well-integrated palate of dark berry and forest fruits.

Natural cooling – The airflow off the cold ocean is accentuated by stepping stones of waterbodies cooling the air flowing towards Sumaridge

Pinot Noir, Chardonnay Chard, PN, Sauv Bl, M (rosé), M, White Blend, Red blend, P Daily 10:00–15:00. Closed Easter Fri, Sun; Dec 25, Jan 1 +27 (0)28 312 1097 info@sumaridge.co.za, www.sumaridge.co.za PN 5–7 y, Chard 4–5 y 06 Light luncheons (12:00–15:00), self-catering guesthouse, venue (wedding, conference, events), walks, horseback trails (appt only)

Kleinrivier Pocket

A hidden valley treasure – The view from Raka's entrance shows the fynbos-rich Kleinrivier Valley

The Kleinrivier Pocket is situated at the foot of the Kleinriviersberg range near the picturesque Akkedisberg Valley on the R326, between the villages of Stanford (17 km) and Caledon (35 km).

The average annual rainfall is high at around 700 millimetres. Ambient temperature is moderate due to the close proximity of

Straight ahead Captain – A nautically inspired winerack at Raka

the Atlantic Ocean and the average daytime temperature in summer is a reasonable 23° to 25°C. Cold winters ensure a proper dormant phase for the vines. Fortunately, the area is frost free, while hail and thunderstorms take place very occasionally. Waterflow from the mountain catchment is sustained throughout the year, although it becomes less during the warm summer months. Southeasterly winds dominate the area and summer rain potentially poses problems for

Sunrise – Sun expsoure management is of vital importance for optimum ripeness at Boschrivier

the ripening grapes. Due to the valley location, southeast- and northwest-facing aspects are found. However, due to the cool claimte, it is mostly the warmer northwest-facing slopes that are cultivated. The underlying soils consist of ganite and shale with a clay component which increases water-holding capacity. On the higher slopes, the soils tend to be more gravelly. Red varities do particularly well in these soils, with richly perfumed Bordeaux varities and Shiraz examples from Raka and Boschrivier. Sauvignon Blanc also shows great cool climate characters, with a lean acidity and gooseberry and herbal notes (Raka).

The Kleinrivier Pocket offers some of the most unique land-based whale watching spots in the world. The best season for whale watching is in early spring to summer, from September to late November. From the spectacular cliffs of De Kelders, past the white sandy beaches of Pearly Beach and onwards to Dyer Island, the mysterious and graceful Great White Sharks have drawn visitors from across the globe. Consequently Gansbaai has become known as the Great White Shark capital of the world. From the small coastal town, various operators take

Majestic hunter – A Great White shark (Carcharodon carcharias) breaches as he captures his prey

visitors out to sea to observe and even dive (using a protectative cage) with these animals. Also in the vicinity, are various seal colonies and the penguin colony of Dyer Island. Various trails on the mountain slopes offer fynbos discoveries, including some 1500 species. Ancient milkwood forests grace the surroundings and their dense canopies are home to a host of insect, rodents and plant species.

African penguins – In the vicinity of Dyer Island, there are several African Penguin (Spheniscus demersus) colonies

The laid-back coastal town of De Kelders (Eng. The Caves) has numerous caves, penetrating deep into the rock formations. A well-known cave, Freshwater, is a very deep grotto leading to what seems to be an underground swimming pool. However, due to conservation measures, it is not open to the public.

DRIVING ROUTE: KLEINRIVIER

From Cape Town, take the N2 freeway past Somerset West and over the Hottentots Holland Mountain range via Sir Lowry's Pass. Take the exit to the R43 Hermanus and continue past the coastal town of Hermanus. Drive carefully in this area as the road runs through several coastal villages and the speed limit changes

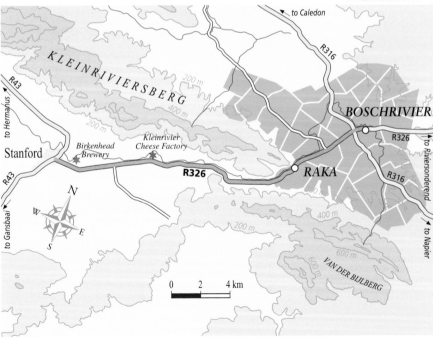

accordingly. About 30 kilometres southeast of Hermanus, pass through the coastal town of Stanford. This picturesque and tranquil village is buzzing with artists from all realms and is a great weekend getaway.

In the centre of town, take the R326 turn-off to the left. Continue along this road for about 18 kilometres until you reach Raka on the right. The Raka brand was named after owner Piet Dreyer's black fishing vessel. Dreyer's first love has always been the sea and for some 36 years he braved the challenges of the coast, ever in search of the best catch. As their motto states, these wines are 'born of the seas, guided by the stars and blessed by the earth', and made in a modern gravity flow cellar.

About nine kilometres further along the R326, visit the winery of Boschrivier.

The name 'Boschrivier' (Eng. Bush River) has a two-fold history: The Bosch River runs through the farm, feeding into the Klein River. This name was thus given to the land by generations gone by. Previously a sheep, wheat and wine farm, owner Dr De Villiers' dictum: *'La main à l'oeuvre'* (hand at work), shows the dedication to top-quality red wines.

TRAVELLING TIPS

Information:
www.gansbaaiinfo.co.za

Accommdoation:
In Stanford village +27 (0)28 341 0900

Restaurants:
Mariana's +27 (0)28 341 0272
Paprika +27 (0)28 341 0662

Interests:
Birkenhead Brewery +27 (0)28 341 0183
Crayfish festival, annually over Easter weekend
Kleinrivier Cheese Factory +27 (0)28 341 0693
Shark cage diving +27 (0)21 461 6583

GPS WAYPOINTS

Boschrivier S34° 23.250 E19° 37.900
Raka S34° 23.871 E19° 37.445

BOSCHRIVIER

Boutique cellar Boschrivier lies at the foot of the Kleinriviersberg. In 1998, the first seven hectares were planted in virgin shale soils to Shiraz (50/50 trellis and bush vine) and Cabernet Sauvignon. A combination of warm north- and cooler south-facing slopes offer greater complexity in the wines as the grapes ripen with different flavour profiles. Strong prevailing winds necessitate trellising and rows are directed northwest – southeast in order to minimise wind damage and conversely to regulate humidity and subsequent diseases. Shiraz (sgl vineyard) produces a naturally low yield (7 ton/ha). Grapes are hand picked and inoculated with a selected yeast culture. Once fermentation is complete, grapes are pressed, avoiding tannin extraction through extended maceration. Wine is matured in French oak (60/40 new to second-fill barrels) giving polished tannins to this savoury, elegant wine. Following 18 months in barrel, the wine is bottle aged for a further three-and-a-half years, offering generous rich berry fruits, cool-climate floral scents and spice.

[i] Boschrivier Shiraz (sgl vineyard) Shz, Cab S Mon–Fri 08:00–17:00, Sat 09:00–17:00, Sun 10:00–13:00 +27 (0)23 347 3313 / 082 821 4799 drnjtdevilliers@mweb.co.za, www.boschrivier.co.za 10–20 y 03, 05, 07 Coffee shop, fresh products, tractor rides, picnics, blue cranes, steam kettle in tasting room

RAKA

Established in 2002, Raka has become synonymous with quality and good value wines. Seventy hectares (of 740) are cultivated to vines. Situated in a narrow valley in the Kleinriviersberg, both north- and south-facing slopes are used. White varieties enjoy the cooler, high slopes (120 m) of decomposed sandstone, with Viognier and Sauvignon Blanc planted on moist sandy river banks. Reds are planted on lower-lying shale. The mountain offers some protection from summer rains, and vines are trellised against the wind that funnels through the valley. Preserving quality, the cellar uses gravity-feed and small stainless steel tanks to ferment each vineyard block separately. Grapes are hand harvested, sorted and crushed directly into tanks for cold maceration. Manual punch-downs and extended skin contact develop a generous berry character with herbaceousness and fresh acidity. Malolactic fermentation is completed in barrel before the 12-month maturation period in French and American oak. Wines are aged for a further 12 months before release. The elegant yet rich flagship Quinary reveals aromas of blackberries, spice and liquorice with cigar box notes.

[i] Raka Quinary (Bdx Blend) Sauv Bl, Chenin Bl, white blend, red blend, Shz, Cape Blend, M, PV, Malb, Cab F Mon–Fri 09:00–17:00, Sat 10:00–15:00. Closed Sun +27 (0)28 341 0676 info@rakawine.co.za, www.rakawine.co.za 10 y 03, 04, 07 BYO picnic, conservation

Franschhoek Pocket

Gourmet capital – The picturesque Franschhoek Valley is as highly regarded for its wine as for its cuisine

The narrow Franschhoek Valley is enclosed on three sides by towering mountains: on the southwest the Groot Drakenstein, on the southeast the Franschhoek and on the northeast the Wemmershoekberg. The mountain peaks rise as high as 1 700 metres above sea level, with the valley floor far below, at an elevation of less than 300 metres. These mountains create shaded periods which directly influence viticultural practices and winemaking in the valley.

This prominent valley (about 5 km wide) stretches in a northwesterly to southeasterly direction and is mainly drained by the upper reaches of the Berg River, flowing to Paarl, the Swartland and eventually into the Atlantic. The climate is typically Mediterranean, with an annual rainfall in excess of 800 millimetres. The enclosed nature of the valley combined with the average February temperature of 23,5°C indicates that it is a warmer region, comparable to the greater Stellenbosch area.

French flair – Franschhoek has many French-inspired features, even its lamposts

The geology is predominantly sandstone (ca. 500–400 Ma) with some shale around the southern extremes of the valley and small outcrops of granite towards the north. The soils are sandy and alluvial along the riverbanks, changing to yellowish-brown, well-drained and light-textured soils on the higher lying mountain foothills. The sandy nature of the soil necessitates irrigation on all but some of the heavier-textured, dark soils close to the river course.

The changing aspects provide various sites for cultivation and vines are planted from the valley floor to elevations as high as 600 metres above sea level. Due to these variations, the soil depths and soil types vary. Vine spacing ranges from a relatively low density of 2 500 vines per hectare on the steep slopes, and almost doubles on the flat soils of the valley floor. Some small plots of bush vines still exist, although new plantings are trellised to spread the canopy vertically ensuring that a greater leaf surface will be exposed to the sun.

The two mountain ranges in the northern part of the valley decrease the daylight hours with the early onset of mountain shadows in the southeast end of the valley. Viticultural practices are adapted to accommodate this loss of sunlight by high trellising. The range of soils and relatively high rainfall permit production of a wide variety of wines, with particular attention to Chardonnay and Cabernet Sauvignon. Shiraz and Merlot are also well represented while Chenin Blanc is becoming more popular for vinification in a more serious wooded style.

Franschhoek's white wines are very fruity, particularly Chardonnay and Sauvignon Blanc. On the south-facing slopes these white varieties are very popular with La Petite Ferme and Cape Chamonix producing Chardonnay wines with chalky and mineral tones. Towards the centre of the valley, Chardonnay shows tangy citrus and tropical fruit with structured examples from Glenwood, Mont Rochelle and Rickety Bridge. A fine example of single varietal Sauvignon Blanc from this area comes from the Boschendal cellar that, together with Akkerdal and L'Ormarins, has proved the extremely versatile character of Sauvignon Blanc in white blends. These blends tend to show more earthy lime and citrus flavours with a smooth finish.

The red wines from the Franschhoek area are medium textured with concentrated fruit (dark berries, plums), generally soft and ripe tannins and gentle minty undertones. Merlot produces ripe fruit with savoury notes and a herbaceous finish with examples from Dieu Donné and Akkerdal. Franschhoek seems favourable for Shiraz with the wines showing attractive violet and smoky beef characteristics with a lengthy finish. Single varietal wines are produced by La Motte, Vrede en Lust, Stony Brook and Boekenhoutskloof. In the western area of the Franschhoek Pocket, towards the entrance of valley, the soil and differences in aspect are reflected in the wines. The red wines can be characterised as medium bodied with silky tannins and expressive fruit while the white wines are generally pleasantly perfumed and very accessible. Cabernet Sauvignon is especially popular, showing dense dark berry fruit and firm tannins, with powerful single varietal wines coming from Graham Beck Wines, Plaisir de Merle and Boschendal. Interestingly, L'Ormarins produces a Cabernet Franc with dense richness and firm tannins.

Classic flagships in the form of red blended wines from Boschendal, Graham Beck, Plaisir de Merle, Vrede en Lust and Akkerdal show velvet fruit supported by sensitive oaking with a firm tannin backbone. Classic noble varieties are blended with newcomers such as Mourvèdre, Malbec and Pinotage.

Herb garden – La Motte gardeners lovingly tend the lavender fields, Cape snow bush and rose geraniums

Remembering our past – The Hugenot Monument is dedicated to the French Hugenots who arrived from 1688

TERROIR

Soil: Sandstone with shale, granite sites, sandy and alluvial near river, yellow-brown in foothills

Climate: Warm, abundant rainfall, mountain shadow

White varieties: Chenin Blanc, Sauvignon Blanc, Chardonnay

Red varieties: Cabernet Sauvignon, Merlot, Shiraz, Pinotage

Wine styles: Red, white, sparkling, dessert, fortified

DRIVING ROUTE: FRANSCHHOEK

Follow the N1 northbound in the direction of Paarl. About 60 kilometres from Cape Town, take Exit 55 to Paarl / Franschhoek. At the intersection, turn right onto the R101 and drive southwest for two kilometres. About 1,2 kilometres further, turn off left onto the R45 towards Franschhoek.

Le Quartier Français – One of South Africa's top-rated restaurants offers fine dining and luxury accommodation

The first winery to visit is Plaisir de Merle. Its newly renovated tasting centre, once an old barn (circa 1823), has a relaxed lounge atmosphere, where visitors can sample wines at their leisure. Take time to stroll through the grounds and request to view the line house (Afr.

Lynhuis), one of only two remaining examples in South Africa. The cellar is surrounded by a koi-filled moat, complete with a working water mill. Follow the R45 in a westerly direction. Take the R310 turn-off to Stellenbosch via the scenic Helshoogte Pass. Boschendal's grand property is only a few hundred metres down the R301. This winery boasts an impressive list of wine styles to suit almost every palate. Enjoy a leisurely wine tasting and a light lunch in dappled sunlight under the oak trees.

Continue eastwards on the R45. Only a few kilometres further is the cellar of historical L'Ormarins (circa 1698). This renowned wine icon boasts a remarkable feat: both the

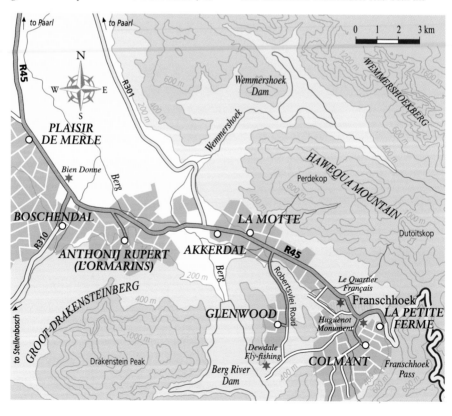

homestead (1811) and cellar (1799) are national monuments and fully restored to their former glory. It is also home to South Africa's only car museum. A wild rose bush and a black sign in the shape of a horse on the right announce the entrance to Akkerdal Wines. Winemaker Pieter Hanekom has created a fantastic mix of French, Spanish and Italian varieties.

Blushing bride – The flower of the delicate fynbos plant at Glenwood

Further towards Franschhoek, the entrance to La Motte on the left is adorned by bougainvillea – a stunning sight in full bloom. La Motte's grand tasting hall is also the venue for classical concerts in the summer months under the auspices of South African vocalist, Hanneli Koeglenberg née Rupert. A large sign indicates the right-hand turn-off to Robertsvlei Road. Continue along this road to the breathtakingly beautiful Glenwood. The tasting room provides a serene venue to observe the secluded valley over a glass of fine Sémillon.

Restaurants and cafés line the streets of Franschhoek and are best explored on foot. The French Huguenot Monument, situated to the east of the town, is well worth a visit. It is here that the annual Champagne and MCC festival is held – a feast of delicate wines, oysters and fine food.

Dedicated to gentle handling – The cellar at Colmant

Heading left at the intersection (northeast) up the Franschhoek Pass on the R45, the entrance to the last winery on this route, La Petite Ferme, lies slightly disguised on the right. Drive very carefully and be aware of traffic descending the pass. La Petite Ferme's small winery is adjacent to its celebrated restaurant, where magical dishes are paired with its wines. The terrace offers magnificent views of the valley and the rolling lawns make for a perfect summer picnic. Book well in advance for weekend dining. Follow the road back to the monument and continue for about one kilometre to the turn-off to Colmant on the left. This *Cap Classique* producer not only makes it own fine bubblies, but also imports French Champagne, with most offered for tasting.

GPS WAYPOINTS

Akkerdal S33° 52.707 E19° 02.843
Boschendal Wines S33° 52.646 E18° 58.356
Colmant S33° 55.373 E19° 07.621
Glenwood S33° 54.945 E19° 04.950
La Motte S33° 52.908 E19° 04.043
La Petite Ferme S33° 55.040 E19° 08.181
L'Ormarins S33° 52.975 E19° 00.253
Plaisir de Merle S33° 50.518 E18° 57.500

TRAVELLING TIPS

Information:
www.franschhoekwines.co.za

Accommodation:
Akkerdal cottages +27 (0)21 876 3481
La Petite Ferme guest cottages +27 (0)21 876 3016
Le Quartier Français +27 (0)21 876 2151

Restaurants:
French Connection +27 (0)21 876 4056
La Petite Ferme restaurant +27 (0)21 876 3016
Le Quartier Français restaurant +27 (0)21 876 2151
Reuben's +27 (0)21 876 3772

Events:
Bastille Day, annually 12 July
Bubbly festival, annually in December
Cheese Festival (Bien Donne), annually in March
Literary festival (various venues), annually in May
Monthly classical concerts (La Motte)
Seasonal food and wine experiences (La Motte)

Interests:
Dewdale Fly-fishing +27 (0)21 876 2755
Huguenot Fine Chocolates +27 (0)21 876 4096
Motor museum (L'Ormarins) +27 (0)21 874 9000
Museum (Boschendal) +27 (0)21 870 4200

AKKERDAL

The small family winery of Akkerdal cultivates an unusual blend of French, Spanish, Italian and South African varieties. Vines are cultivated on the banks of the Berg River in sandy and alluvial soils, which change to yellowish-brown, light textured soils further away from the river. Good drainage allows slight water stress in the dry summer months, reducing berry size, achieving a better skin to juice ratio and improving colour and flavour concentration. Summer cover crops are planted between vine rows to reduce possible damage caused by excessive light and heat reflected from the sandy surface. The flagship, Wild Boar, is aptly named after the wild boars which created severe vineyard problems for the early French Huguenots. Grapes are fermented in open-top fermenters at a lower 24°– 28°C, resulting in a natural reduction of excessive alcohol. Each of the components is fermented and matured separately and, once completed, barrels are selected for the blend. This New World-styled wine shows concentrated fruit with soft tannins.

ℹ️ Wild Boar 🍷 Mal, Tannat, PV, M, Mouv, Cab F, P
🕐 Mon–Fri 08:00–17:00, Sat 09:00–13:00 by appt 📞 +27 (0)21 876 348 📧 wine@akkerdal.co.za, www.akkerdal.co.za
🍴 5–9 y 🍷 04, 05 ℹ️ Self-catering guest house; wild boars spotted on occasion

GLENWOOD

Hidden in the glorious Robertsvlei Valley is Glenwood boutique cellar. The first vines were planted in 1989 and produced its maiden vintage in 2002. Only 30 hectares are cultivated with the remaining mountain and wetland areas dedicated to conservation. Sémillon is planted in alluvial river soil, whereas red varieties are placed on higher ground with greater sun exposure ensuring full ripening. Drainage reduces humidity and subsequent diseases, and the canopy is opened by removing surplus leaves and shoots, thus creating greater air movement and sun penetration. Chardonnay is whole berry pressed and naturally fermented in French oak barrels, preserving its natural peach and citrus fruit. Natural malolactic fermentation is followed by lees maturation, with regular bâttonage adding gentle vanilla and nutty flavours. Red grapes are inoculated with selected yeast without maceration and fermented warm (up to 30°C) with regular punch-downs by hand. The Syrah is pressed traditionally – by foot stomping. Fifteen months of oak maturation presents a full-bodied red wine with spicy red fruit with a distinct minerality.

ℹ️ Vigneron's Selection Chardonnay 🍷 Shz, M, Chard, Sauv Bl, Sém 🕐 Mon–Fri 11:00–16:00, Sat–Sun 15:00–15:00 Sept–Apr 📞 +27 (0)21 876 2044 📧 info@glenwoodvineyards.co.za, www.glenwoodvineyards.co.za 🍷 Red 8 y, white 5 y 🍷 03, 05, 07 ℹ️ Nature walks, cellar & vineyard tour daily @ 11:00

COLMANT CAP CLASSIQUE & CHAMPAGNE

Colmant is dedicated exclusively to producing bottle-fermented sparkling wines. Deciding to fulfil their passion, Jean-Philippe and Isabelle Colmant started production of MCC in 2006. Three hectares were developed with Chardonnay vines. Similarly to Champagne, Colmant selects from various areas to perfect its blend. Chardonnay from its own vineyards (60%) is complemented by fruit from Robertson. Pinot Noir is selected from six different vineyards located in Robertson, Elgin and Stellenbosch.The state-of-the-art cellar was erected in 2005. Overnight cooling to 0°C results in extraction of juice from only the inner section of the grape berry during pressing. This results in only the purest juice with the least amount of polyphenols. Batches are fermented separately in small stainless steel tanks and in barrels to aid the blending process. Following the second fermentation, the wines mature for two to four years at a steady 14°C temperature, developing fine, smooth bubbles, complexity, secondary flavours and yeastiness.

ℹ️ Colmant Brut Reserve 🍷 Brut Reserve, Brut Rosé, Brut Chardonnay 🕐 Wed–Sat 10:30–13:00 or by appt 072 368 4942 📞 +27 (0)21 876 4348 📧 info@colmant.co.za, www.colmant. co.za 🍷 3–4 y 🍷 Non-vintage only

LA MOTTE

Although La Motte was initially established in 1695, French Huguenots only planted the first vineyards at La Motte in 1752. The beautifully preserved manor house (circa 1751), historical cellar (circa 1782), Jonkershhuis (circa 1751) and water mill (circa 1741) have all been declared national monuments. Eighty hectares of irrigated vines are cultivated on varying altitudes, from the valley floor to the slopes of the Drakensteinberg (206 m). The different soil profiles all hold a high sand percentage which ensures good drainage. Vines are trellised and canopies protect developing bunches from harsh sunlight. Grapes are also bought from Darling, Paarl, Wellington and Walker Bay. Red grapes are partially natural fermented with extended maceration, ensuring wines with ample body and structure. Malolactic fermentation and maturation in French and American barrels give smoky and spicy notes. Shiraz is also blended with Grenache and with Viognier. Chardonnay is partially barrel fermented and 12-month maturation in French oak yields a spiced, citrus wine with silky consistency.

ℹ️ Shiraz 🍷 Cab S, M, Shz, Gren, Sauv Bl, Chard, Viog 🕐 Mon–Sat 09:00–17:00 Closed Sunday, Christian religious hols 📞 +27 (0)21 876 3119 📧 cellar@la-motte.co.za, www.la-motte.com 🍷 5–10 y 🍷 88, 91, 95, 96, 98, 04 ℹ️ Classic music concerts, restaurant & museum (May 2010)

Road sign – All the road signs in Franschhoek have a French inspired design

Rocky mountain soil – The soils on the mountain slopes of Franschhoek have a high gravel and rock content

Weather station – Satellite weather stations are placed through the Winelands to gather data on rainfall, sunlight hours and intensity as well as to record wind speeds

Rustic centemporary cuisine – La Petite Restaurant perched high in the Franschhoek Pass

LA PETITE FERME

The small boutique winery of La Petite Ferme cultivates only 14 hectares of densely planted vines (5 000 vines/ha) on steep north-facing mountain slopes, in shallow shale and gravel soils. The elevation (220 m) and mountain shade during morning hours creates cool growth conditions. White varieties are planted on the highest sites and canopies are kept closed on the west side to protect fruit from sun damage. Red varieties are sited on lower slopes and canopies are opened to maximise the long, warm afternoons to ensure proper ripening and colour development. White wines are made from a very reductive process and fermented at a low 9° – 12°C to protect delicate floral aromas. Partially natural fermented Chardonnay completes malolactic fermentation in barrel, softening the acid to a full, rich wine. The flagship Sauvignon Blanc is flinty and mineral with granadilla fruit and lively acid. The wine is matured on yeast lees adding mid-palate weight. Shiraz, Chardonnay and Merlot are all from single vineyards.

ℹ Sauvignon Blanc 🍇 Sauv B, M, Cab, Chard, Shz ⭕ Tasting by appt 📞 +27 (0)21 876 3016 ✉ info@lapetiteferme.co.za, www.lapetiteferme.co.za 🍷 Sauv 2–4 y, reds 5 y 🍾 M 06, Chard 05, Sauv Bl 05 ℹ Restaurant, cookbook, luxury guest suites, gift shop

ANTHONIJ RUPERT WINES (L'ORMARINS)

The historic L'Ormarins (circa 1698) is a renowned wine producer, its philosophy 'the source of supreme wine quality lies in the land'. This estate boasts 70 hectares planted on mountain slopes, where granite soils produce expressive wines. Higher density planting offers concentrated fruit. Focusing on matching site and soil to cultivar, the estate developed two more sites to vines. A Kasteelberg farm, with deep slate soils, was planted with Rhône varietals (Shz, Mars, Rous, Gren, Mourv, Carig). Bordeaux varieties and Sangiovese are cultivated on granite soils, producing dense wines, while Burgundian grapes are cultivated on clay soils. Sauvignon Blanc excels on granite and sandstone soils. Red varieties are naturally fermented with extended maceration. Fourteen-month aging in French oak renders dense, rich red wines with fine tannins. White varieties are fermented in oak and aged for 14 months. The Nemesia blends Swatland, Darling and Franschhoek *terroirs* to a spicy, smoky wine with rich fruit aromas and perfume.

ℹ Cabernet Franc, Nemesia (Chenin Bl, Chard, Viog) 🍇 Cab S, F, M, Sauv Bl, Chard, Sang, PG ⭕ Mon–Fri 09:00–17:30, Sat 10:00–15:00. Closed Sundays, Good Fri, Sun, Dec 25 📞 +27 (0)21 874 9000 ✉ info@rupertwines.com, www.rupertwines.com 🍷 White 10 y, red 30 y 🍾 05, 06 ℹ Franschhoek Motor Museum: Tues–Sun 09:00–16:30

BOSCHENDAL WINES

Boschendal was established in 1685 when French Huguenot Jean le Long prepared the soil to plant his first vines. A sense of history lives on at the five historic Cape Dutch houses on the farm. The old manor house, converted into a museum, is open to the public who frequent the Boschendal wine tasting facility and restaurants.

Situated on the lower foothills of the Groot-Drakenstein and Simonsberg Mountains and dissected by the Dwars River, Boschendal has east- and southeast-facing slopes angling towards the valley floor. Two-hundred-and-twelve hectares of vines are cultivated on a range of soil types, from the elevated valley floor at 160 metres above sea level (avoiding sandy alluvial river banks) to the foothills towards the mountain where rich, deep, red soils, with a high clay content, deliver an excellent growth potential, good drainage and optimum sun expsoure.

Pavilion – The grand centrepiece of the picnic garden

African curios – *Traditional African accessories are on sale in the gift shop*

Sauvignon Blanc and Shiraz are Boschendal's flagship grape varieties. Sauvignon Blanc is planted on the most elevated sites (200–390 m), benefiting from the cooling effect. The Shiraz is planted on sites with a higher percentage of rocks in order to restrict vigour and to achieve a more concentrated fruit. Cabernet Sauvignon and Merlot are planted on east- and northeast-facing sites, which provide more sunlight to ripen the red grapes properly. These vineyards supply fruit for the flagship wines.

The Sauvignon Blanc grapes are crushed and destemmed after harvest and pressed gently to avoid extraction of any harsh tannins. The latest technology is used to ensure minimal air contact with the crushed grapes. Only free-run juice is used for the reserve wine, which is made in a reductive process using sulphur and ascorbic acid to protect the juice from oxidation. Cleared juice is fermented cold (14°–16°C) to preserve subtle floral and fruit aromas and

Boschendal Manor House – *Lovingly maintained, the Cape Dutch Manor House dates back to 1812*

the fermented wine matures on its lees for six months, adding some weight to the palate. The unwooded Sauvignon Blanc shows pungent tropical fruit with granadilla, grass and gooseberry characters – a fresh wine and rather full compared to other Sauvignon Blancs in the region.

The Shiraz grapes for the premium wine are fermented in open-top vessels at a relatively low (for red wines) fermentation temperature of 25°C with regular pump-overs and two week's maceration to extract maximum colour. The young wine is drained off and skins are pressed. Only a portion of the press wine, which is rich in tannins and highly structured, is blended back with the free-run wine in order to give structure and longevity to the wine. Malolactic fermentation occurs spontaneously and the wine is gently oaked in French barrels (with only 10 per cent new wood) for up to 18 months. All premium red wines are bottled and stored for a further two to three years

to ensure correct aging before release onto the market. A Rosé *Méthode Cap Classique* was introduced in 2008, adding a further sparkle to the Boschendal portfolio. This wine, made from a selection of premium red grape varieties, underwent secondary fermentation in the bottle and spent 12 months on its lees for a classical flavour profile and vibrant bubble.

The Boschendal experience includes a cellar door offering tasting and sales, cellar tours, restaurants, picnics on the lawn and the manor house museum, which is open daily.

Vinoteque – *A collection of the older vintages is put aside for future tastings to evaluate the maturation over time*

Cecil John Rhodes Shiraz Reserve ⬛ Sauv Bl, Shz, Chenin Bl, Chard, Sém, Viog, Cab S/F, Merlot, PN ⬤ Daily 08:30–16:30. Closed Easter Fri, May 1, Dec 25 ✆ +27 (0)21 870 4200 ✉ cellardoor@dgb.co.za, www.boschendal.com ⬛ Sauv Blanc 3 y, Shz 8 y ⬛ 98, 01, 03, 05 ℹ Tours 10:30, 11:30 by appt, restaurant and picnics, tour groups, gifts, conservation area, museum (09:30–17:00)

PLAISIR DE MERLE

Plaisir de Merle dates back more than 300 years to the time of Cape Governor Simon van der Stel. The Marais family, descended from the Huguenots, settled in Drakenstein and land was granted to them in 1693. In a tribute to their roots, they called the farm Le Plessis Marly, but the name evolved over the years to Plaisir de Merle.

The Marais family carried on their winemaking tradition for centuries and large parts of the original manor house building (circa 1764) are still intact. Today, Plaisir de Merle is one of the largest single continuous wine farms in the Cape, spreading across 974 hectares, and approximately 400 hectares are planted to a variety of noble grape cultivars.

Feng shui – A khoi-filled moat surrounds the barrel cellar at Plaisir de Merle

Historical splendour – The beautiful flower garden en route to the manor house, circa 1764

Eighty hectares of prime vineyards are set aside for the Plaisir de Merle cellar. The farm has a variety of soils derived from decomposed granite which are cultivated dry-land – soil moisture is fed by mountain springs as well as a river on the farm's borders. Additionally, a myriad of slopes and elevations, ranging form 140 to 500 metres above sea level, offer different aspects and varying wind conditions. Thus each grape variety has been placed for optimal sunlight exposure. Vineyards are trellised on an extended system, mostly planted in a north – south direction. Sauvignon Blanc and Chardonnay vineyards are planted at higher altitudes to benefit from cooler average temperatures as well as early afternoon shade. Red varieties are situated on the intermediate slopes where an abundance of sunlight ripens the grapes to optimum conditions before harvesting.

Long house – Dating to 1821, one of Plaisir de Merle's historical treasures

In 1993 a new cellar building was opened. The philosophy here calls for wines with juicy tannins from the fruit rather than harsh tannins from excessive oaking, and while wines show aging potential, they are ready to drink while still relatively young. The Plaisir de Merle range consists of a Chardonnay, a Sauvignon Blanc (unwooded), a Cabernet Sauvignon and a Merlot and other special release wines such as a Shiraz and Grand Plaisir are available on a limited basis only from the cellar. Strict vineyard management sees ripening, flavour and tannin development monitored to the point of harvest. Grapes are destemmed and crushed grapes are pumped into stainless steel tanks where the juice ferments on the skins. Daily pump-overs, differing in time and frequency, take place until the wines are dry. Malolactic fermentation occurs naturally, with a combination of barrels and tanks rendering different flavour profiles. For the red wines, barrel maturation extends from 12 to 16 months in 50 per cent new barrels, second- and third-fill barrels. Then the different wines are blended and prepared for bottling.

Winemaker, Niel Bester, maintains that successful wine blending is an artform – the challenge of winemaking is having the right components to choose from as well as the ability to create the correct balance between them. The Cabernet Sauvignon is blended from wines from a selection of five to seven different vineyards, all stylistically different due to their situation on the farm, age and clone. A further 10 to 15 per cent of the blend is made up from small quantities of Merlot, Petit Verdot, Cabernet Franc, Shiraz and Malbec adding that extra touch. While Cabernet Sauvignon provides the wine's structure, the blending partners add different dimensions of supple fruit, berry notes as well as spicy and toasted notes.

Watermill – A historical mill deepens the connection to the farm's history

ℹ Cab Sauv 🏅 Cab S / F, Shz, M, PV, Malb, Sauv Bl, Chard ⊙ Mon–Fri 09:00–17:00, Sat 10:00–16:00 (Nov–Mar); 10:00–14:00 (Apr–Oct). Closed Good Friday, Dec 25, Jan 1 ☎ +27 (0)21 874 1071 ✉ plaisirdemerle@capelengends.co.za, www.plaisirdemerle. co.za 🍷 5–8 y 🏆 94, 95, 98, 01, 03, 05 ℹ Cellar tours by appt, tour groups by appt, tasting room (circa 1823)

Paarl Area

Delightful Paarl – Oak trees provide welcome shelter from the afternoon sun in Main Street, Paarl

The town of Paarl is situated beneath a large granite outcrop, formed by three rounded domes. The most prominent of the three is called Paarlberg, (Eng. Pearl rock) as its smooth surface glistens in the early morning light, especially after it has rained. The landlocked Paarl area is large and diverse, situated between the Simonsberg (south), Paardeberg (northwest) and the Hawequa Mountain (east). The Paarl area hosts a mixture of agricultural produce and is known for its highly sought-after table grapes and olives. In addition, cheese, cut flowers and garden plants are very popular produce. Three Pockets have been indentified: Paarl Central, surrounding the Paarlberg; Klapmuts-Simondium lying south towards Simonsberg and Voor-Paardeberg to the north.

A king's treasure – Merlot maturing in the Royal Barrel Room at Veenwouden

Paarl Central Pocket

The area around the mountain contains a complex terrain of valley floors, mountain slopes and plains.

Although Paarlberg is an exposed granite pluton, the soils around can be classified into three main groups. Sandstone-derived soils are found along the Berg River to the east, granite soils on either side of the west and east-facing Paarlberg and weathered shale to the northwestern side. These soils have varying degrees of wetness, medium to high potential on the yellow to reddish-brown soils. In addition, there are small pockets with medium-textured, well-drained and acidic granite soils. The summer daytime temperatures for the western and eastern slopes (24°C) indicate warm conditions, especially in the valley basin around the town. The summers are long and hot. Even with a high annual rainfall (900 ml), irrigation is beneficial in reducing the temperature of the plant.

Resultingly, some of the very best wines come from vineyards on high-lying sites which benefit from increased airflow and resultingly offer cooler ripening conditions. This variation in ripening temperature allows for the cultivation of a wide variety of wine grapes, strongly favouring Chardonnay and Shiraz. As soil types and topography vary, planting density and trellising (bush vine and vertical trellises) are adjusted according to the vineyard's location. The favourable *terroir* of this area makes for an array of wine styles, including white, sparkling, red and Port-styled wines.

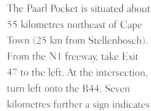

The Polo Club House – *Oversized leather couches welcome visitors to Val de Vie's Sabrage Bar*

Sémillon, Chardonnay, as well as blends of these, produce a bouquet of fruit flavours with occasional citrus and mineral characteristics, with examples from Nederburg and Seidelberg. The rich sweetness buffed with *Botrytis* and a hint of citrus of Weisser Riesling and Sémillon Noble Late Harvest from Nederburg, have proved the area's suitability for this style of sweet wine.

Red varieties produce a medley of fruit with serious structure and richness in single varietal wines but also in blended wines. Cabernet Sauvignon (Vendôme, Seidelberg, Landskroon) and Shiraz features strongly (Coleraine, Domaine Brahams, Ridgeback, Rhebokskloof, Val de Vie). Robust and rustic styled blends are typical of Black Pearl, Nederburg, Fairview and Veenwouden. The latter also produces a richly textured Merlot, with exceptional aging potential. Port varieties give elegant, creamy and ripe fruit textures in the Port-styled wine of this area (Landskroon).

Paarl Valley – *A view over the fertile valley from Veenwouden*

TERROIR

Soil: Sandstone, granite, weathered shale

Climate: Warm, abundant rainfall

White varieties: Chenin Blanc, Sauvignon Blanc, Chardonnay

Red varieties: Cabernet Sauvignon, Merlot, Shiraz, Port-varieties

Wine styles: Red, white, sparkling, dessert, fortified

DRIVING ROUTE: PAARL CENTRAL

The Paarl Pocket is situated about 55 kilometres northeast of Cape Town (25 km from Stellenbosch). From the N1 freeway, take Exit 47 to the left. At the intersection, turn left onto the R44. Seven kilometres further a sign indicates Black Pearl Wines on the right. This boutique winery's vineyards grow right next to its mountain fynbos conservation area. Their innovative label employs dramatic grahic art to spell part of the flagship, Oro's, name.

Continue along the R44 as it makes its way around the northern side of Paarlberg. About eight kilometres further, take the R45 (Noord-Agter Paarl) turn-off to the right to visit Rhebokskloof. The dynamic team at this winey has taken a bold step to replant most of its vineyards in order to be more *terroir*-driven. Its MCC bubbly is particularly enjoyable with a rich, rounded mouthfeel and the restaurant is a great lunchtime stop.

Continue further along this road to the T-junction and turn left towards the town of Malmesbury (R45) to visit Veenwouden. The Veenwouden winery is located a mere 1,3 kilometres along this route, on the righthand side. This producer is renowned for its Bordeaux-style Blend and Shiraz, but its Chardonnay also makes a fine dinner companion. From the barrel room entrance, you have a lovely view over the town, Paarl Valley and surrounding areas.

Retrace the route back to the turn-off and turn left onto the Noord-Agter Paarl Road (R45). Continue through the picturesque town of Paarl in a southerly direction. All along the spectacular 11 kilometre long main road (the longest in the Western Cape), there are historical buildings, sightseeing opportunities and a myriad of eateries. Accommodation ranges from romantic vineyard cottages and family-oriented self-catering suites to luxury hotels and well-appointed B&Bs. Take either Optenhorst, Lady Grey or Langenhoven Avenue to the R301. Continue on this road in a southerly direction, leaving the town behind. Pass under the N1 highway, and continue for about four kilometres to the pristine wine and polo estate of Val de Vie. Turn right to the security gate, where you will be directed to the tasting facility. Sabrage Bar, a wine and cigar bar, is open Teusdays to Saturdays (10:30 – late) while the restaurant offers indulgent Sunday lunches and high teas. Their annual polo day is a highlight on the social calender.

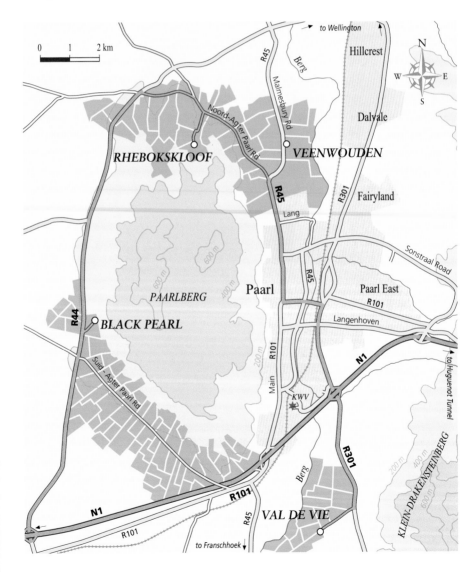

TRAVELLING TIPS

Information:
www.paarlonline.com

Accommodation:
De Oude Paarl Hotel +27 (0)21 872 1002
Grande Roche Hotel +27 (0)21 863 2727

Restaurants:
De Oude Paarl +27 (0)21 872 1002
Marc's +27 (0)21 863 3980

Interests:
Afrikaans Language Monument +27 (0)21 872 3441
Drakenstein Olives +27 (0)21 868 3185
Historical walks +27 (0)21 863 4937
KWV Emporium Wine Tours +27 (0)21 807 3008
Paarl Mountain Nature reserve +27 (0)21 872 3658
Wynland Ballooning +27 (0)21 863 3192

GPS WAYPOINTS

Black Pearl Wines S33° 44.166 E18° 53.683
Rhebokskloof S33°41.100 E18° 55.885
Val de Vie S33° 47.800 E18° 58.600
Veenwouden S33°41.120 E18° 57.860

BLACK PEARL WINES

Black Pearl has grown from a true garagiste to a recognised wine producer. This small vineyard of eight hectares is cultivated on the western slopes of Paarlberg in shale soils. Right next to the vineyards is an area of mountain fynbos, now a conservation area. The mountain provides essential early morning shade, with the afternoon sun creating good ripening conditions. Prevailing southeasterly winds relieve the intense summer heat and the cordon wire is positioned at one metre above ground to reduce radiance from the soil surface. The deep, fertile soil enjoys good water retention, allowing dry-land cultivation. Low planting densities are designed to give balance to the vines. A 4,5 hectare single vineyard is planted to Shiraz. Black Pearl's red blend is named Oro after the God Oro, King of the Firmament, who gave a black pearl as a gift to the ocean. Once fermented, the grape skins are gently pressed in a traditional wooden basket press. The wine is matured in oak and remains unfined. The Shiraz is fruit driven with hints of fynbos and eucalyptus.

Oro (Shiraz/ Cab) Shiraz, Cab S By appt +27 (0)21 863 9200, +27 (0)83 395 6999 info@blackpearlwines.com, www.blackpearlwines.com 3–5 y 07 Indigenous conservation area

VAL DE VIE

The recently renovated Val de Vie cellar (1825) crushed its first harvest in 2006. Their philosophy of minimal intervention is supported by a traditional cellar. The farm lies in a basin with prevailing southeasterly winds that dry and cool the vineyards. Twelve hectares of river valley are cultivated to vines, with a pebble bed four metres deep, reminiscent of the Châteauneuf-du-Pape. The sandy topsoil also increases fruit concentration. The low to medium potential soils necessitate a planting density of 2 600 vines per hectare to ensure optimal growing conditions. Red grapes are cold macerated. Vigorous pump-overs, combined with punch-downs during fermentation, maximise extraction. Wines are matured for 18 months before the components are blended. The Shiraz shows a burst of violets, red berries, cassis and rich, aromatic oak. White wines are partially fermented in large oak barrels, adding a rich dimension to the vibrant citrus and floral nuances.

Val de Vie (Mouv/ Shz/Car/ Cins/ Gren) Shz, Viog, GVC (Gren Bl, Viog, Clairette Bl), Polo Club Red (Shz, Gren, Carg, Cin, Mourv), Polo Club White (Viog, Clairette Bl) By appt only +27 (0)21 863 6162 wine@valdevie.co.za, www.valdevie. co.za 15 y Polo estate, hikes & mountain bike trails, conservation area, wedding, functions & events venue

VEENWOUDEN WINE ESTATE

Situated on the northern side of Paarl, Veenwouden's boutique cellar is wholly contained within a valley, facing northeast towards the Berg River. Merlot is planted on clay soils, requiring more soil moisture, while Cabernet Sauvignon is cultivated on granite soils. On nearby Thornhill farm, Rhône varieties are cultivated on rocky soils with high planting density (6 000 vines/ha) providing natural shading. Leaves are removed only on the morning-sun side, the increased air movement regulates humidity and prevents related diseases. Grapes are hand harvested and fermented using a combination of natural and dried yeasts. The red wine is macerated on the skins for 12 to 18 days before pressing, developing a deep colour and concentrated flavours. The free-run and pressed wine is aged separately for up to two years in French oak barrels. Wines are racked every six months to remove sediments and the moderate aeration assists in maturation. The dense, austere red wines are aged for two years before release, allowing the juicy fruit and fine tannins to integrate.

Merlot, Classic (Bdx Blend) Chard, M, Cab S, Cab F, Malb, Shz, Mourv, Viog, Gren, Temp Mon–Fri 10:00–16:00 by appt only +27 (0)21 872 6806 sales@veenwouden.com, www. veenwouden.com M 6 y+; Classic 9 y+ 95, 97, 98, 01, 03, 04 Tasting room, restaurant in planning

RHEBOKSKLOOF

Rhebokskloof is transforming into a premium wine producer, focused on *Methode Cap Classique* and red wines (Rhône-styled Shiraz and Pinotage). The dynamic management team is raising the bar as the majority of the vineyards have been replanted to better-suited varietals and clones.

The 183 hectare farm is nestled into one of the folds of Paarlberg, in a secluded valley with predominantly northeast- and northwest-facing slopes. These aspects receive greater sunlight exposure or longer sunlight hours due to the absence of afternoon mountain shadow. This would suggest higher temperatures during the ripening season. However, the farm spreads over altitudes ranging between 180 and 460 metres above sea level and this offers significant cooling during summer.

Rhebokskloof restaurant – A lovely spot for a relaxed lunch, a team-building event or even a conference

Manicured garden – The gardens of Rhebokskloof receive the same detailed attention as the wines

Vine cultivation is limited to the slopes below the 340 metre contour, as above this boundary, the terrain becomes too steep for agriculture. The farm has extensive soils from granite rock, which is found in different stages of weathering. In these high-potential soils, vines are rigorously managed: suckering of underdeveloped shoots, leaf removal and green harvesting in order to restrict excessive growth. This program ensures that yields are naturally restricted to approximately seven to eight tons per hectare. While Rhebokskloof's own vineyards are being replanted, the production is supplemented from farms in the surrounding Paarl Pockets as well as selected vineyards in the Stellenbosch and Darling Pockets.

The old cellar lends itself to traditional-style handcrafted winemaking, preserving the romantic mystique of wine. However, the latest technology such as a sorting table for both bunches and individual grape berries, has been added to maintain the highest quality.

Shiraz grapes, for the flagship wine, are cold macerated for up to three days as the low temperature (10°–15°C) prevents naturally occurring yeasts from starting alcoholic fermentation. Once the colour extraction has reached the desired level, the must is allowed to warm to about 22°C and then it is inoculated with selected yeast strains.

Winelands wedding – The perfect setting for a romantic Winelands wedding

An oxidative policy encourages as much oxygen-contact to the fermenting wine as possible to aid the stabilisation of colour. Regular pump-overs are supplemented with delestage (rack and return) where the wine is racked from the skins and returned, incorporating oxygen as it is transferred. Warm fermentation temperatures (30°C) further aid the development of colour and flavour before the wine is pressed. The young wine is transferred to barrel, where it completes malolactic fermentation. Maturation is done in mostly French oak barrels and takes 14 to 16 months. About ten per cent American oak adds a hint of sweet tannins to the backbone of French oak. Fining and filtration is kept to a minimum and the bottled wine is aged for a further 12 months before release.

The sparkling wine is made exclusively from Chardonnay grapes. The non-vintage sparkling shows lively mousse, fresh acidity and smooth, buttery aromas, and a vintage sparkling is produced only in exceptional years. Following second fermentation in bottle, the wine is matured for a minimum of 24 months before being disgorged.

Wine sales – The wine-tasting room offers great wine-and-food pairing advice

ℹ️ Black Marble Hill Syrah 🍇 Shz, M, Cab S, Chard, Viog, MCC 🕐 Mon–Fri 09:00–17:00, Sat & Sun 10:00–15:00. Gourmet tasting and tours by appt ☎ +27 (0)21 869 8386 ✉ info@rhebokskloof.co.za, www.rhebokskloof.co.za 🏠 5–6 y 🍷 07, 08 ℹ️ Venue (wedding 30-300 pax, conference, team-building), restaurant, play area for children, horse riding, quad bikes

Klapmuts-Simondium Pocket

Wine tourism experience – The tasting room at Backsberg offers a variety of their wines, as well as novel wine gifts, gadgets and books

The Klapmuts-Simondium Pocket includes the northern and eastern foothills of Simonsberg and the Klein-Drakensteinberg. The majority of vineyards are situated on reddish-brown, medium-textured, well-drained soils derived from the granite base of the mountain, grading into sandier soils with an alluvial nature on lower slopes. Soils are deep, allowing for extensive root development and excessive growth is a potential problem. The summer daytime temperature (22,6°C) indicates that this Pocket is warm, but receives abundant rain (annual rainfall 800 mm). Cooler sites on the mountain slopes are used for heat-sensitive white varieties.

This area is quite diverse in style, making very juicy whites and very interesting, layered red wines. Glen Carlou is recognised for its intense, rich Chardonnay and seriously styled reds.

Shiraz from Klapmuts-Simondium has deep, complex layers of fruit, with some savoury and peppery characteristics. Drakensig, Lindhorst, Glen Carlou and Mont Destin are the main Shiraz producers in the area. Cabernet Sauvignon and Merlot and blends thereof show cedar, herbal and minty hints with firm acids and ripe tannins. The blends incorporate Petit Verdot, Cabernet Franc and Mourvèdre. Wineries which produce Cabernet, Merlot and blends are Backsberg, Rupert & Rothschild and Vrede ed Lust.

DRIVING ROUTE: KLAPMUTS-SIMONDIUM

The Klapmuts-Simondium Pocket lies between the towns of Stellenbosch and Paarl on the Klapmuts Road. Take the N1 freeway towards Paarl. About 40 kilometres from Cape Town, take Exit 47 to the left. At the intersection, turn right onto the R44 and drive in the direction of Stellenbosch. Cross the intersection with the R101. Take the following turn-off to the left onto Klapmuts Road. Look out for Silver Kestrels, which are seen hunting for potential prey in vineyards and shrubbery. A little further, turn right to Backsberg winery where a lane of trees leads up the mountain slopes.

At the entrance to the property, very sandy soils are noticeable. The sand component is particularly important for the steely white wines produced here. Backsberg's airy tasting room is complemented by the restaurant, appropriately named Tables.

A lane of oak trees leads up to Drakensig, a winery set high on the foothills of Simonsberg. Drakensig's boutique cellar produces excellent red wines and uses a small percentage of selected fruit from Durbanville and Paarl to complement certain wines.

The next winery on this route is Vrede en Lust. Translated as 'Peace and Eagerness', the name is also the ethos of this farm. With its Cape Dutch architecture, breathtaking mountain scenery and *terroir* wines, Vrede en Lust is an ideal wine-tourism location and a magical setting for unforgettable wedding celebrations.

Follow the route back to the R44 and turn left. About 2,5 kilometres further, turn left to visit Mont Destin. The cellar was designed by world-renowned architect, Luis Barragan. Try the outdoor Pinotage Bath for a romantic outing.

GPS WAYPOINTS

Backsberg S33° 49.717 E18° 54.919
Drakensig S33° 50.113 E18° 56.274
Mont Destin S 33° 49 58.9 E018° 53 27.8
Vrede en Lust S33° 50.237 E18° 57.170

TRAVELLING TIPS

Restaurants:
Backsberg Tables restaurant +27 (0)21 875 5141
Cotage Fromage (Vrede en Lust) +27 (0)21 874 3991

Interests:
Animal Zone +27 (0)21 875 5063
Butterfly World +27 (0)21 875 5628
Cheese platters & chocolates (Backsberg)

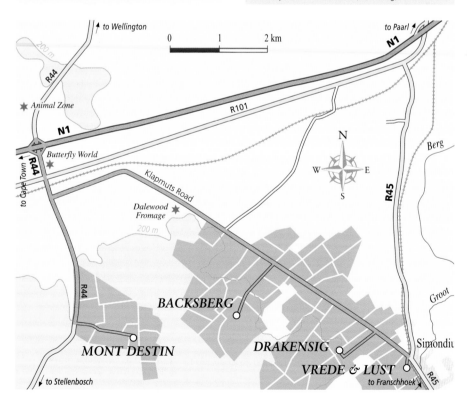

BACKSBERG ESTATE CELLARS

Backsberg Estate Cellars (circa 1916) became the first carbon-neutral winery in South Africa (2006), one of only three worldwide. The winery aims to become self-sufficient for energy. One hundred and thirty hectares of vines are cultivated on the Simonsberg, in the Durbanville Hills and near Houwhoek. Red varieties are planted in lighter soils on lower slopes (below 190 m) to ensure balanced growth, while heat-sensitive white varieties are cultivated on cooler higher-lying sites. Prevailing southeasterly winds further moderate the temperatures. Vines are trellised to protect young shoots, while the canopy shades bunches from the harsh sunlight. White varieties are cold fermented. The aromatic Viognier shows a rich mouthfeel, while Chardonnay's rich fruit flavours combine with oak maturation. The reds are fermented in open-top vessels and macerate for up to eight weeks. This ensures dark-coloured wines with rich fruit and soft tannins. The flagship red wine, Babylons Toren Red, matures in French oak for up to 36 months.

Babylons Toren Red (Cab S / M / Shz) Various Mon–Fri 08:00–17:00, Sat 09:30–16:30, Sun 10:30–16:30. Open all year round +27 (0) 21 875 5141 info@backsberg.co.za, www.backsberg.co.za 10 y 03, 04, 05, 07 Self-guided tours, restaurant, venue (functions & weddings), gift shop

DRAKENSIG

Drakensig means 'view of the Dragons' and aptly names this small boutique cellar perched on the northern side of the Simonsberg. The farm comprises only 13 hectares of red varieties planted on east- and west-facing slopes in deep, weathered granite soils with little clay and good natural drainage. Vineyard blocks are sited in the mountain's afternoon shadow. Its cooling effect allows even ripening of grapes, while retaining high acid levels. Grapes are fermented in closed fermenters without cold maceration to prevent over-extraction and excessive tannins. After 12 months of barrel maturation, the wine is bottled and rested for a further three months prior to release. The reserve Cabernet Sauvignon, complemented by a small percentage of fruit from the Durbanville Pocket (less than 10%), has a smoky, chocolate character. The use of cooler climate grapes adds a touch of elegance to the fruit-driven wine and reduces alcohol levels. Shiraz, sourced from the Swartland Pocket, shows a structured palate, with typical flavours of leather, pepper and spice. An olive grove produces fruit for eating as well as oil production.

Cab S, Shz Cab S, Shz, P Mon–Fri 09:00–17:00, Sat 09:00–13:00, low season by appt +27 (0)21 874 3881 drakensig@mweb.co.za 8 y Cab S 01; Shz 02 Olive oil, conference venue for small groups

MONT DESTIN

Mont Destin cultivates seven hectares of vines on the convex-shaped northern and western slopes of the Simonsberg. The decomposed granite soils with clay offer sufficient water retention during the dry summer and drain excess water during winter. The strong prevailing southeasterly winds necessitate trellising and blocks are purposefully small (0,2 per ha) to facilitate detailed canopy management. Due to the high soil potential, vines are planted wider to offer each plant adequate growth space and rows are directed east – west to maximise sun exposure. Following harvest, bunches are sorted on vibrating tables, crushed and cold soaked for three days. The focus is placed on fruit concentration and avoids harsh tannins. Cold fermentation (28°C) and punch-downs extract colour and flavour, while pressing is gentle to avoid any extraction of green, hard tannins. Malolactic fermentation is completed in barrel then wines are matured for 18 to 24 months. The moderate use of new wood (30%) supports the dense fruit structure of the reds. Chenin Banc is sourced from selected vineyards in Stellenbosch and shows rich tropical fruit and minerality.

Destiny Shiraz Shz, red blend (Cab S / Shz), Chenin Bl By appt +27 (0)21 875 5870 info@montdestin.co.za, www.montdestin.co.za 8 y 06 Pinotage bath

VREDE EN LUST

Vrede en Lust was founded in 1688 by Jacques de Savoye, who planted the first vineyards in 1691. In 1996, the Buys family initiated a new era at Vrede en Lust and their commitment to quality shines through the careful renovation of this historical estate. Today they celebrate three centuries of winemaking passion. The Franschhoek property is dedicated to red varieties. Granite and clay soils offer good water retention and afternoon mountain shadows relieve the summer heat. By contrast, white varieties are cultivated on a cooler Elgin property. Red grapes are fermented warm (28°C) to aid colour and flavour extraction. Peppery Shiraz benefits from the sweet vanilla character of American oak, while French oak adds palate weight and fine tannins to the other red varieties. The red blends show warm-climate red fruit with underlying tobacco and mocha notes. Sauvignon Blanc is cold fermented to preserve subtle grass and fynbos aromas. Both Chardonnay and Viognier are aged in barrel for a few months, adding toasty and honeycomb aromas to the white fruit and lively acidity.

Reserve (Cab S / M / PV) Sauv Bl, Chard, Viog, Chenin Bl (ex-Elgin), Shz, Malb, Rose Daily 10:00–17:00 +27 (0)21 874 1611 info@vnl.co.za, www.vnl.co.za 10 y+ 03, 04, 05, 07, 08, 09 Restaurant, deli, bakery, accommodation, venue (wedding, conferences, events)

Voor-Paardeberg Pocket

New developments – The slopes of the Paardeberg offer varying aspects to viticulturists

The Voor-Paardeberg (Eng. In front of Paardeberg) Pocket lies to the southeast of Paardeberg. This granite outcrop, similar to that of the Paarlberg, is located a few kilometres northwest of the town of Paarl. Generally a warmer area, southerly winds prevail in this Pocket throughout the year, helping to cool the vineyards. Summer daytime temperatures are approximately five degrees cooler than in the general Paarl region. Higher up on the slopes, soils are close to pure granite and of higher potential. Lower on the slopes, granite formations mix with varying percentages of clay, which results in medium to low potential soils. Vines are trellised to curtail excessive growth and offer protection against the prevailing winds. The vertically extended canopies shelter the developing grape bunches from the harsh midday sun during the summer season.

This Pocket has only recently started to vinify grapes under its own labels, making some interesting wines. The hot, dry climate favours red varieties, although high-lying sites allow for the production of white varieties. White wines, such as Chardonnay, are enlivened by grapefruit aromas, with a fresh, restrained finish. Shiraz is the most prominent red variety, with a complex nose and expressive wild flavours in a balance between fruit and spice. Fruity, well-structured Pinotage is emerging, along with interesting red blends and spicy, savoury Shiraz.

Vines were first planted on certain sites in the early 1700s but subsequent high-volume and low quality resulted in the vineyards being neglected. Today, however, many investors are restoring old cellars and developing vineyards.

Paardeberg – A view on the southern (regarded as the 'front') of the Paardeberg, with vineyards on its foothills

Wellington Pocket

Tasting in the presence of **terroir** *– A soil profile in the underground facility of Nabygelegen*

The small town of Wellington lies about 10 kilometres north of Paarl. A quality wine-producing area, it is also a premier vine nursery area with more that 90 per cent of vines for the South African market being produced here. Vineyards stretch out around the town over alluvial terraces towards the Swartland. A percentage of vines are cultivated on the foothills of the towering Hawequa Mountain and Groenberg, where small valleys create unique mesoclimates with varying sunlight exposure changing viticultural practices.

With a relatively high average summer daytime temperature of 24,3°C, Wellington is generally a warm cultivation area. However, the foothill sites (at elevations above 200 m above sea level) benefit from wind exposure as well as the collection of moist air flowing down the mountain slopes. These factors create cooler conditions for vine cultivation. Annual rainfall for the Wellington area is low (500 ml) and supplementary irrigation is necessary to ensure stable, sustainable growing conditions, as well as to prevent excessive water stress during ripening.

In winter, snow covers the mountain peaks and night-time temperatures are lower than at the coast some 60 kilometres away, which makes for good resting periods for the winter-dormant vines.

The geology changes from shale-based soils on lower elevations, to sandstone and granite on the foothills to the east. The latter renders gritty, light-coloured, medium-textured soils with good water and nutrient-retention properties. To the west, fertile alluvial soils are found closer to the Berg River. These soils are mainly used for the vine nurseries.

Chenin Blanc, which constitutes the majority of vineyard plantings, is now making way for classic red varieties such as Shiraz, Cabernet Sauvignon and Merlot. The growing conditions also allow the cultivation of less common varieties such as Mourvèdre, Grenache and Petit Verdot. These render full-bodied, perfumed reds with firm tannins and elegance, both as single varietal and blended wines. White wines are food-friendly with zesty acidity.

The single variety Shiraz wines from Wellington are well structured with a broad spectrum of flavours ranging from pepper and savoury notes to red fruit (Dunstone, Mischa, Hildenbrand, Linton Park). Cabernet Sauvignon and Merlot wines have a velvety, ripe-fruit palate with dry savoury tannins with a firm finish, both in single varietal and blended examples (Welbedacht, Napier and Jacaranda). Nabygelegen's Mediterranean blend incorporates Tempranillo and Malbec, adding exotic sweet berry and spice. Diemersfontein's Pinotage shows dense fruit sweetness and fine tannins.

TERROIR

Soil: Shale on low altitudes, granite and sandstone on foothills, alluvial near river

Climate: Warm, moderate rainfall

White varieties: Chenin Blanc, Sauvignon Blanc, Chardonnay, Sémillon

Red varieties: Cabernet Sauvignon, Merlot, Shiraz, Pinotage

Wine styles: Red, white, sparkling, dessert, fortified

DRIVING ROUTE: WELLINGTON

Wellington is situated 41 kilometres from Stellenbosch. From the N1 freeway, take Exit 47. Turn left onto the R44. When you reach Wellington (23 km), turn left onto Distillery Road. At the train station bridge, turn right to cross the bridge and head up the Main Road. Pass two sets of traffic lights. At the next traffic circle, take the first exit (left) into Bovlei Road. Take the left fork, Berg Road, to visit Hildenbrand. A leader in the Sémillon revival, the estate also offers a guest house, restaurant, olives and olive products. Berg Road makes a horseshoe back into town and joins Church Street. Turn right onto Church Street and drive in the direction of Bainskloof Pass. Turn

GPS WAYPOINTS

Dunstone Wines S33° 38.150 E19° 03.765
Hildenbrand S33° 39.586 E19° 01.754
Nabygelegen S33° 37.896 E19° 03.839

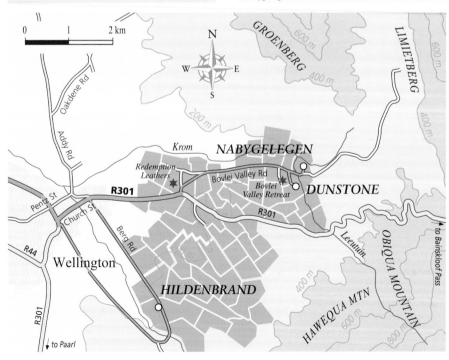

left at Redemption Leathers onto Hill Road. At the T-junction, turn right onto Bovlei Road. Just past the luxury Bovlei Valley Retreat (2 km), turn right to Dunstone Wines, a boutique cellar cultivating a mere 2,7 hectares Shiraz. A kilometre further, turn left to Nabygelegen. Indulge in a game of boules (pétanque) on the boule court or take a picnic to enjoy in the lovely garden, surrounded by evergreen trees.

TRAVELLING TIPS

Information:
www.wellington.co.za

Accommodation:
Bovlei Valley Retreat +27 (0)21 864 1504, www.bvr.co.za
Hildenbrand Guesthouse

Restaurants:
Oude Wellington +27 (0)21 873 1008

Interests:
Leather products (Redemption) +27 (0)21 873 3197
Scenic drive: Bainskloof Pass
Wellington wine festival, anually in March

DUNSTONE

Boutique winery Dunstone produces red wines as well as a Shiraz Rosé. With a hands-on approach, most machinery is avoided and the 2,7 hectares of vines are cultivated without tractors. Shiraz is planted on clay and sandy soils with the resulting two flavour profiles adding complexity to the final wine. Southeasterly winds and drip irrigation relieve the warm summer conditions. The high growth potential of the soil allows for yields of 8–10 ton/ha while retaining quality and concentration. Grapes are hand harvested and cooled overnight before destemming. Berries are then hand sorted and fermented in stainless steel tanks. Following pressing, the free-run and press wines are matured separately. Merlot is aged in French oak with new wood (30 %) adding gentle tobacco and toasty notes to the rich red fruit bouquet. The Shiraz shows dark red fruits and strong spices while the combination of American, French and Hungarian oak adds depth and complexity. High alcohol levels (15% v/v) are balanced with great fruit concentration, resulting in rich and powerful wines.

Dunstone Shiraz Shz, M, Shz Rosé Mon–Fri 10:00–17:00, Sat 11:00–15:00, Sun by appt. Closed Easter Sun; Dec 25, 26; Jan 1 +27 (0)21 873 6770 wine@dunstone. co.za, www.dunstone.co.za 5–7 y Picnic, lunches, dinners & afternoon tea by arrangement, luxury guest house (Bovlei Valley Retreat) & self-catering cottages

HILDENBRAND

In 1853 a wine cellar of remarkable size and architecture was erected on the picture-perfect Rhebokskloof farm. Today the restored estate runs multiple agricultural activities. Eighteen hectares of vineyards are cultivated on the foothills of the Hawequa Mountain in fertile granite soils. Sémillon and mature Chenin Blanc vines (25 y) are cultivated on west and southeast-facing slopes, with less sun hours moderating the summer heat. Red varieties – comprising trellised, bush and experimental vines – are planted on lean soils to reduce growth vigour and increase fruit concentration. Canopies are opened on the eastern side to increase airflow and sun penetration, while the unopened west side provides protection from the hot afternoon sun. Red wines are cold soaked, fermented and then gently pressed to prevent excessive tannins. Skin contact using dry ice, natural fermentation in barrels and *bâttonage* produces dense, buttery white wines. The bush vine Sémillon (4 tons/ha), is hand picked and matured in Hungarian oak to produce a concentrated wine of spice, green fruit and honey with a lingering finish.

Sém, Chenin Bl, Chard, Cab S, Shz, Mal Daily 10:00–16:00. Closed Easter, Dec 24, 25, Dec 31, Jan 1 +27 (0)21 873 4115, +27 (0)82 656 6007 info@wine-estate–hildenbrand. co.za, www.wine-estate–hildenbrand.co.za Sém 2–4 y 05, 07,08 Guest house, olives, olive oil, book on olives

NABYGELEGEN

Established in 1712, Nabygelegen cultivates 17 hectares of vineyards at the foot of the Limietberg. The historical cellar (circa 1748) has been rejuvenated to provide a new expression for the wines of this wonderful old farm. Red varieties enjoy warmer north-facing sites of deep granite soils, while Merlot and the white varieties are planted on cooler south-facing slopes. Due to relatively warm ripening conditions, the white varieties are trellised higher off the ground than the reds, with the cordon at one metre to reduce radiant heat. Denser canopies also protect grapes from the sun. Chenin Blanc rows run north – south as well as east –west; the former giving a richer style of wine which is wooded, and the latter a fruitier style, which is used for the blend. Harvesting at slightly lower sugars gives balanced wines, and cold maceration of red varieties allows gentle colour extraction. Twelve months of maturation in older French oak yields an elegant, spicy and savoury flagship blend.

1712 blend (Merlot / Cab S / PV) Cab S, M, PV, Temp, Sauv B, Chenin Bl, Sém Mon–Fri 10:00–17:00, Sat 10:00–13:00. Closed Easter Fri, Sun; Apr 27; May 1; Dec 25; Jan 1 +27 (0)21 873 7534 sales@nabygelegen.co.za, www. nabygelegen.co.za 10 y 03, 05 Verjuice, boules court, walks, picnic (booking req.)

Swartland Pocket

Home of Shiraz – The Swartland Pocket offers some of the best Rhône varietal wines

Traditionally know for its wheatfields, the Swartland Pocket has developed many fine quality wines, particularly in the last decade. Vineyards are cultivated around the towns of Malmesbury, Riebeek-Kasteel and Riebeek West, stretching north towards Piketberg and Porterville. The main vineyard areas are centred on the lower foothills of the Riebeek-Kasteelberg and Paardeberg.

Long warm summers and water scarcity dictate vine cultivation in this Pocket and play an important role in the variety selection, and siting, for optimum wine quality. The moderate annual rainfall (400–550 mm) and average summer daytime temperature (23,8°C) indicate warm growing conditions, making bush vine cultivation very popular. However, vineyard sites on the higher slopes of the Riebeek-Kasteelberg are sheltered from the afternoon sun by the mountain's prominent peaks at 950 metres above sea level.

Riebeek-Kasteelberg is a sandstone remnant, resting on shale and soils are generally stony, with medium potential. In a northerly direction, towards Piketberg, soils are mainly shale-based. Weathered granite intrusions provide reddish-brown soils in certain sites, with excellent water-retention properties. The soils on the northwest-facing foothills of Paardeberg are light coloured and often sandy in nature, which necessitates irrigation. They have a medium potential, the vineyards benefiting from higher altitude and less sun-exposed eastern and southern aspects.

Impressively for this warm producing area, Chenin Blanc has proved itself in bush vines, showing complexity with ripe honeysuckle and tropical fruit characters balanced with good acidity. These wines benefit greatly from

TERROIR

Soil: Red and brown granite, shale and sandstone from mountain

Climate: Warm, moderate rainfall

White varieties: Chenin Blanc, Sauvignon Blanc, Chardonnay, Sémillon

Red varieties: Cabernet Sauvignon, Merlot, Shiraz, Pinotage

Wine styles: Red, white, sparkling, dessert, fortified

gentle oak maturation, enhancing the seriously styled wines, for example Spice Route. Based on the success of single varietal Chenin Blanc, producers have taken this variety to new heights in blended wines. Viognier, Chardonnay and Grenache Blanc add aromatics and mouth-watering fruit flavours to the already dense wine, for a rich palate and developing complexity. The wines from Sadie Family Wine and Dragon Ridge are good examples.

Flagship red variety, Shiraz, produces a wide array of styles from ripe, New World wines (Meerhof, Pulpit Rock) to the more restrained classical style (Kloovenburg, Allesverloren). Even though styles differ, the definite Swartland character, recognisable in all the wines, gives a natural wild scrub character. Rich, spicy Shiraz blends, with blending partners Grenache, Mourvèdre, Carignan and Viognier, show

savoury, supple tannins, dense fruit and balanced structure. Examples are Sadie Family Wines and Lammershoek. Allesverloren produces a fine Port from the traditional Portuguese varieties, with rich prune and plum flavours with a sweet finish.

DRIVING ROUTE: SWARTLAND

Jan van Riebeeck called this softly undulating land between mighty mountain ranges 'Het Zwarte Land' (the Black Land) because of the endemic Renoster shrubs which turn black after the rains. The wide, fertile plain is the bread basket of Cape Town with its golden wheat fields reaching the foot of the mountains.

The Swartland Pocket starts some 60 kilometres north of Cape Town. Follow the N1 freeway out of the city and take Exit 10 to the N7. Take the right fork as the road runs parallel

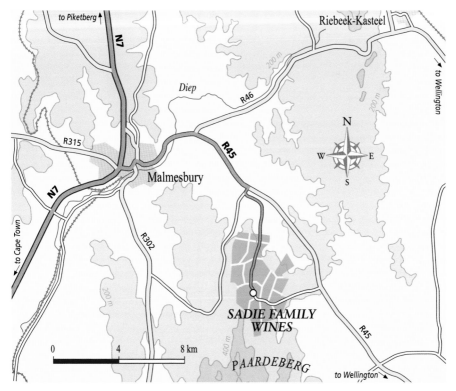

to the N1, past the local shopping centre before turning northwards to join the N7 (at Exit 13), which follows the West Coast. Reaching the town of Malmesbury (63 km from Cape Town), take Exit 65 to the R315 (Malmesbury/Darling). Follow the road as it turns a full 180° and ends in a T-junction. Signage indicates Darling to the right (west) and Riebeek-Kasteel to the left (east). Turn left and follow the signs towards the R45 (Paarl). At the second traffic light, turn left and then the first right turn-off to Piet Retief Road (R45). This leads past the Old Dutch Reformed church with its magnificent spire. Follow the R45 out of the town. About 4,5 kilometres further, turn right at the Aprilskloof Road turn-off. Take the first left and continue along the gravel road. The road makes a long S-bend. One kilometre further is the Sadie

Boutique cellar – Maverick winemaker Eben Sadie hand selects the oak barrles for his cellar

Family Wines cellar on the left. Eben Sadie creates some of the most prestigious wines in the Swartland area. A frequent visitor to Spain, where he makes wine in his bodega in Priorat, Sadie is brimming with passion and mastering the elements to bring concentration and structure to his local wines.

Follow the R46 to the tranquil Riebeek Valley. Artists and arts and crafts people have settled and are bringing creative flair to the timeless country lifestyle in the beautiful twin hamlets of Riebeek West and Riebeek-Kasteel, at the foot of the Kasteelberg. The area includes many olive growers, who produce a wide variety of olives and olive-based products.

GPS WAYPOINT
Sadie Family Wines S33° 31.812 E18° 48.293

SADIE FAMILY

'The most excellent wine is one that gives pleasure through its own qualities; nothing which might obscure its natural taste must be mixed with it.' Columella's *De Re Rustica*, the most comprehensive account of Roman viticulture, made this timeless judgment over two millennia ago. His successor, Palladius, continued to write on this subject and this philosophy has inspired the names for Eben Sadie's two renaissance wines.

Vineyards are cultivated as trellised and bush vines to maximise water efficiency. Vines receive no irrigation and yields are manually reduced in the extremely dry conditions. The three main soil types add distinctive aspects to the wines: in slate soils grapes retain a higher natural acid; in granite they show more "farmyard", berries and spice and in the sandstone/clay mixture the grapes achieve intense toffee and cassis flavours.

White varieties are planted on decomposed granite and alluvial soils with higher draining capacity. Only late-ripening Viognier (8 y) is trellised and its canopy protects the sensitive grapes from the sun. All the other white varieties are cultivated as bush vines (35 – 55 y) and produce intensely aromatic fruit. Hand-picked grapes are cooled, sorted and crushed with about 50 per cent of berries remaining whole. Red varieties are cold macerated and naturally fermented at low temperatures (26°C) with punch-downs to ensure slow extraction. The Columella is oak matured for 24 months and bottled without fining or filtration. The wine shows dense berry fruits and spicy herbal undertones. Free-run juice from white varieties is naturally fermented in barrels, with lees maturation adding a creamy mouthfeel to the aromatic and spicy wine.

Sadie Family Wines – A small cellar inconspicuously guarding some of South Africa's most expensive wines

ℹ Columella (Shz, Mouv), Palladius (Rhône Blend: Chenin, Viog, Grenache Bl, Chard) 🍇 Shz, Mouv, Chenin Bl, Viog, Chard, Grenache Blanc ⏰ By appt 📞 +27 (0)22 482 3138 📧 office@thesadiefamily.com, www.thesadiefamily.com 🍷 Columella 15 – 20 y, Palladius 8 y+ 🍾 06, 08 ℹ Producer also makes own wine in Spain

Darling Pocket

***Blossoming child** – Darling Cellars' vines under the protective view of Table Mountain and the Mother City (Cape Town)*

The Darling Pocket is located around the popular tourist town of Darling, about 65 kilometres north of Cape Town. The Groenekloof range of granitic hills runs parallel to the coastline, a mere 10 kilometres away. Vineyards are mainly developed on the eastern flanks of these hills, which provide protection from the strong synoptic winds. The Benguela current flows north along this coastline, ensuring cooler growing and ripening conditions than the macroclimate would indicate, giving the area an average summer daytime temperature of 22,4°C and annual rainfall of 538 millimetres.

The reddish-brown soils are derived from weathered granite and, mainly found on higher sites towards the west, favour the cultivation of various wine varieties. Their natural acids give a fresh, elegant finish. Darling grapes are highly sought after and other areas source grapes from here to blend with their own, producing much fruitier, naturally acidic wines. Consequently, more producers are establishing their own wineries. Even though the summer daytime temperatures are high with long sunlight hours, the ocean's close proximity creates cooler conditions on exposed slopes and varieties such as Sauvignon Blanc and Merlot perform well.

Protected slopes are warmer and more suited to red varieties. The low annual rainfall necessitates water conservation and drought-resistant rootstocks. Many vineyards are still cultivated as bush vines as these require less water during the growing season. Where vertical trellising is used, it seldom exceeds a height of 1,5 metres to create a denser canopy to reduce water loss through evaporation from the leaves. The denser canopy also protects the grapes from direct sunlight and possible burn damage.

TERROIR

Soil: Granite

Climate: Warm with ocean influence

White varieties: Chenin Blanc, Sauvignon Blanc, Chardonnay

Red varieties: Cabernet Sauvignon, Merlot, Shiraz, Pinotage, Cinsaut

Wine styles: Red, white, dessert

Darling's wines, especially Sauvignon Blanc from the Groenekloof area, have a pronounced and very distinctive character. They show ripe tropical fruit and racy acidity leading to a long finish (Ormonde, Darling Cellars). Chenin Blanc shows ripe fruit concentration with citrus notes and a good, dry finish (Tukulu) and Chardonnay produces rich and fruity wines (Groote Post).

Cabernet Sauvignon is a favourite, showing restrained and firm tannins, both in single varietal and blended wines (Ormonde, Cloof).

Pinotage shows opulent berry fruit, subtle tannins and a hint of smoked beef with its inherent astringency well managed (Tukulu, Darling Cellars).

DRIVING ROUTE: DARLING

Some 60 kilometres north of Cape Town, the Darling Pocket is directly west of the Swartland Pocket. Follow the N1 freeway north out of Cape Town and take Exit 10 to the N7. Take the right fork (parallel to the N1) past a local shopping centre before turning northwards and joining the N7 (Exit 13), which follows the West Coast. At Malmesbury (63 km), take Exit 65 to the R315 (Malmesbury/Darling). Follow the road as it turns a full 180° and ends in a T-junction. The sign indicates Darling to the right (west)

TRAVELLING TIPS

Information:
www.darlingtourism.co.za

Accommodation:
Buffelsfontein Nature Reserve +27 (0)22 492 2405
Darling Hotel + 27 (0)22 492 2263

Restaurants:
Evita se Perron restaurant +27 (0)22 492 2831/51

Interests:
Evita se Perron Cabaret +27 (0)22 492 2831/51
Wild Flower Show in September

GPS WAYPOINTS
Darling Cellars S33° 26.416 E18° 31.416
Ormonde S33° 22.834 E18° 22.399

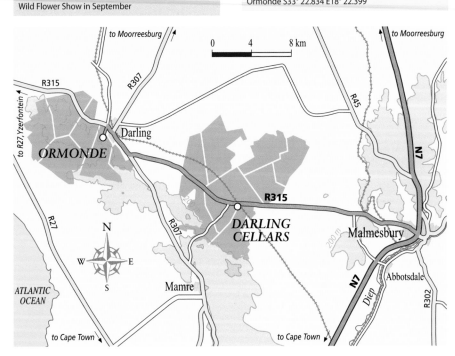

and Riebeek-Kasteel to the left (east). Turn right at the intersection and follow the R315 towards Darling, approximately 30 kilometres away.

Eighteen kilometres further, cross the railway tracks and turn left to Darling Cellars. Established in 1949 by a group of Darling farmers, Darling Cellars today has 22 shareholders and a well-seasoned cellar team. Farming 1 300 hectares of vines, they select only the finest fruit for their wines.

Approaching the town of Darling, the R315 intersects with the R307. The signage may be confusing; turning right, you are still driving on the R315. Continue through the centre of Darling to the far side. Signs indicate the turn-off to Ormonde winery.

Tukulu does not have a visitor centre in the Darling Pocket, however, their prized vineyards producing the 'gift from the red soil' are located here. Refer to the Tukulu Profile for tasting and appointments.

TUKULU

Tukulu is part of Darling, the first wine-producing district to be awarded membership status Biodiversity Wine Initiative (BWI). It is a Black Economic Empowerment project involving Distell, black businessmen and the local community. Its 250 hectares of vines are cultivated on deep (10 m), fertile granite soils on the south facing slopes of Dassenberg and a high planting density is used to reduce vigorous growth. Cool breezes and frequent mists from the Atlantic Ocean moderate the hot, dry conditions. Chenin Blanc is trellised to provide sun protection and thirty-year-old vine Pinotage gives concentrated flavours. The harvested grapes are transported to a Stellenbosch facility for vinification. Red wine fermentation is traditional with pump-overs to extract colour. Wines are matured in French, American and Hungarian oak for complexity. Only free-run Chenin Blanc juice is used, giving rich tropical fruit and citrus notes. The white wine matures for two months on lees and three months in barrel, filling out the mid-palate.

ℹ️ Pinotage, Chenin Bl 🏷️ P, Chenin Bl, Shz, Viog, Sang (organic), Chard (organic) 🅞 Bergkelder, Stellenbosch. Trinity Lodge in Darling, by appt 📞 +27 (0) 21 809 8492 / 8305 ✉️ tukulu@capelegends.co.za, www.tukulu.co.za 🍷 white 2 y, red 4 y + ⬛ P 01, 03, 04, 05 ⓘ BEE project, Organic Range

DARLING CELLARS

Established in 1949 by a group of Darling farmers, Darling Cellars today has 22 shareholders and a well-seasoned cellar team. Of the total farm area of 2 800 hectares, 1 300 hectares are planted to vines. Interestingly enough, all the vines are cultivated as dry-land (no irrigation) bush vines. A lower planting density (2 200–2 400 vines/ha) is used to provide sufficient space for each plant to capture sunlight, as well as access adequate soil moisture. This cultivation style generally gives low yields and concentrated fruit.

Vineyards face northeast and southwest on low-lying hills along the cool Atlantic Ocean. Soils vary and include sandy flatlands as well as deep granite-based soils on the foothills. A deep clay level at three metres below the surface helps retain water for dry-land farming. The single vineyard range, Onyx, includes a Sauvignon Blanc cultivated on granite soils with a southern aspect cooling the vines. The grapes are destemmed, crushed and cool fermented to preserve delicate floral aromas. Lees contact and a small percentage oak maturation adds body to the typical herbaceousness with asparagus, green figs, nettles, grass and green pepper.

Grapes for the flagship Kroon are cooled before any processing occurs. All varieties for the blend are harvested within two days of each other and fermented together giving greater integration. Fermentation is cool at 22° – 24°C and once completed, wines are transferred to barrel for malolactic fermentation. French, American and Hungarian oak adds rich tobacco notes to the dark berry fruit and savoury flavours. With all the wines processed reductively (excluding oxygen), they are understated and benefit from aeration.

Bread and wine – Golden wheatfields glitter in between the emerald-green vineyards

ℹ️ Onyx Kroon (Shz / P) 🏷️ Cab S, P, Shz, NLH, Sauv Bl, M, Chard (All sgl vineyard wines) 🅞 Mon–Thu 08:00–17:00, Fri 08:00–16:00, Sat 10:00–14:00 📞 +27 (0)22 492 2276 ✉️ info@darlingcellars.co.za, www.darlingcellars.co.za 🍷 10–13 y ⬛ 03, 05 ⓘ Picnics – 24 hour notice, cellar tours by appt

ORMONDE

The dynamic winery of Ormonde has grown rapidly. The town of Darling was originally laid out on the farm and the winery's gates are literally in Darling with vineyards fanning out on the hills behind the town. Three-hundred hectares of vines have been developed on this 3 000 hectare property and, where vines do not grow, olives have been planted. The Ormonde Reserve wine range uses grapes from older vines to reflect the *terroir*, while the Alexanderfontein lifestyle range is made from younger, developing vines.

The soil consists of decomposed granite with a high percentage of clay (40%) and excessive growth on this fertile soil is a potential problem. The clay provides good water retention as the annual rainfall is only about 500 millimetres. The vineyards are located on the slopes of the surrounding hills,

Family tradition – The gracious homestead of Ormonde, overlooking the town of Darling

and the vines are planted to a low planting density of 2 500 to 3 000 vines per hectare. The low density encourages deep vine root development. Cover crops are planted between the rows to prevent both further water loss through evaporation and soil surfaces from becoming compacted. These factors allow dry-land cultivation of the vines in a fairly dry climate. With less vegetative growth and a higher concentration of varietal flavours, these Darling wines have a distinctive character.

Close proximity to the Atlantic Ocean, only five kilometres away, with frequent mists and sea breezes, ensures much cooler than expected ripening conditions. Temperatures are further moderated by an elevation of 150 to 350 metres.

The barrel room – Eighteen months of barrel aging gives rich, elegant red wines

Exploring new terroir – New plantings in the sought-after red Tukulu soils

The vines are trellised to protect them against the prevailing winds and the rows are directed along an east – west axis so that the canopies can protect bunches from direct sunlight. Due to the relatively cool ripening period, vines are not stressed during summer and give a good acid balance with lower alcohol wines. The vineyards are suckered (removal of excessive young shoots) and leaves are removed to open the canopies to airflow with the exception of the Sauvignon Blanc canopy which is kept slightly denser to protect these heat-sensitive grapes from direct sunlight. At *veraison* (colour change of grapes) the canopy of the Cabernet Sauvignon (which has a later *veraison*) is opened to allow sufficient sun penetration for colour development. Green harvesting is also done at this stage to reduce the crop of Merlot and Chardonnay in particular.

Grapes are hand picked into small lug boxes to prevent damage. The white varieties are picked only in the cool morning hours to retain their crisp varietal flavours. White grape juice is cold macerated for three days at 6°C to aid glycerol formation and to achieve a more concentrated palete. A small percentage is barrel fermented. Chardonnay offers vibrant lime and mineral notes, stitched together with a dense, yet polished tannin structure. The mineral core and linear acidity follows through on the Sauvignon Blanc, where asparagus and herbaceous flavours fill the palate.

The flagship Vernon Basson blend is matured totally in new wood for 18 months and undergoes a light filtration to remove excess precipitants (proteins and tannins) before bottling. The red wines are fermented warm in open-top vessels, using regular punch-downs to mix the skins and juice and to achieve maximum colour extraction.

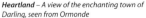

Heartland – A view of the enchanting town of Darling, seen from Ormonde

Ormonde Vernon Basson Sauv Bl, Chard, Chenin Bl, Sém, Viog, R Ries, Cab S / F, M, Shz, Mouv, PV, Malb, PN, Gren Mon–Fri 09:00–16:00, Sat, pub hols 09:00–15:00. Closed Easter Fri, Dec 25, 26, Jan 1 +27 (0)22 492 3540 info@ormonde.co.za, www. ormonde.info.co.za White 3 y, red 10 y+, 2nd label 5 y Cab S 07, Sauv BL 05, 06, 07, 08, M 03; Char 06, 07 Vineyard / day tour with barrel tastings by appt, picnic baskets and BYO picnics, children's facilities, farm produce, walks

Tulbagh Pocket

The Tulbagh basin – Home to art, architecture and fine wines, as seen from the Saronsberg

The Tulbagh Pocket lies at the northern end of a north–south running valley, bordered on the west by the Saronsberg and Obiqua Mountain, the north by the Groot Winterhoek and the east by the Witsenberg. Here, vines grow alongside wheatfields, orchards and olive groves. The deep boulder beds along the upper tributaries of the Kleinberg River on the foothills of the amphitheatre are prized vine sites. This amphitheatre is formed by the south-, southwest- and west-facing flanks of the Witsenberg.

The relatively warm, dry climate is continental due to the isolation of the area. Vineyards are established from the warmer valley floor, up the foothills where the mesoclimate is tempered by the southern aspects, high elevation (over 250 m above sea level) and afternoon mountain shadows. An unique feature of the Tulbagh Pocket is the encapsulating mountains which trap cool night air, reducing daytime temperatures along with the southeasterly wind. The annual rainfall (550 mm) necessitates supplementary irrigation, particularly for newly established vineyards. The average summer daytime temperature (24,3°C) signifies warm conditions during ripening. Cultivation practices such as row direction and cordon height are used to moderate ripening conditions.

Tulbagh's boulder bed soils resemble those of the Rhône Valley in France, whereas the soils on the higher foothills are derived from shale, sandstone colluvium (deposits of soil at the foot of slopes, which accumulate due to gravity) and scree. These are usually stony, with a medium growth potential and good water-retention properties. Poor sandy soils typify the valley floor and are rarely used for vine cultivation.

Strong flavours of cut grass and fresh hay with a citrus dimension give the Sauvignon Blanc

TERROIR

Soil: Boulder beds with large stones

Climate: Warm and dry

White varieties: Chenin Blanc, Colombar, Muscat d'Alexandrie, Chardonnay

Red varieties: Cinsaut, Shiraz, Cabernet Sauvignon, Merlot, Pinotage

Wine styles: Red, white, sparkling, dessert

wines individuality (Saronsberg, Rijks). Chenin Blanc tends to be more honeyed with rich, nutty flavours and a minerality threading the fruit structure (Tulbagh Mountain Vineyards, Rijks, Blue Crane Wines). Shiraz is the firm red favourite, with many single as well as blended wines (Manley, Rijks, De Heuvel). Pervasive blackberry fruit spiced with smoked and black pepper notes, the Shiraz wines have good complexity and approachability. Saronsberg produces Shiraz blends, using Mourvèdre and Viognier as blending partners.

DRIVING ROUTE: TULBAGH

Tulbagh lies 120 kilometres from Cape Town (90 km from Stellenbosch). From the N1 freeway, take Exit 47 to the left. At the junction turn left onto the R44. Continue on the R44 past Wellington. Turn right onto the R46 (63 km from the N1 turn-off). Seven kilometres further, turn left to reach the town. Pass through the town to the northern periphery. Take the road signposted to Saronsberg. Cross over a small bridge and continue to the entrance on the right (6,5 km). The innovative winery is tastefully decorated with glass and steel and an art studio.

Return along the same route back to town. Turn left into Van der Stel Street. A few metres further is the entrance to Manley Private Cellar. Boasting luxurious accommodation, Manley also offers a small chapel as an intimate wedding venue. Drive south, through Tulbagh. Van der Stel Street joins the R46 just outside of town. About 6,8 kilometres further, a gravel road turns

GPS WAYPOINTS

De Heuvel S33° 20.900 E19° 10.300
Manley Private Cellar S33° 16.274 E19° 08.765
Saronsberg S33° 14.693 E19° 06.901

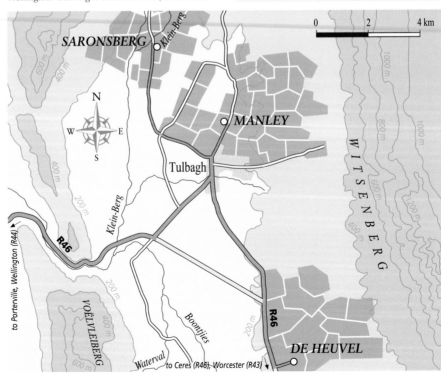

off to the left to De Heuvel. This cellar not only produces structured red wines, but also various olive products. Tulbagh has a rich history of Dutch architecture. Church Street, in the centre of town, is home to the largest concentration of national monuments (32 in total) in a single street in South Africa. Wonderful examples of 18th- and 19th-century architecture exist, many faithfully restored after the devastating earthquake in 1969.

TRAVELLING TIPS

Information:
www.tulbaghwineroute.com

Accommodation:
Manley Wine Lodge +27 (0)23 230 0582

Restaurants:
Readers Restaurant +27 (0)23 230 0087

Events:
Dutch Festival, annually in April
Snow, occasionally in winter
　Matroosberg Reserve +27 (0)22 312 3759

DE HEUVEL

De Heuvel (est. 1714) is one of the oldest farms in the Tulbagh area. From a grazing farm, it was transformed to wine production in 1806 when 27 000 vines were planted on the farm. A previous Italian owner started olive harvesting and today the farm revels in its olive tradition. Situated on the slopes of the Witzenberg, the farm has shale and alluvium soils, planted mainly to red varieties. Vineyard management focuses on creating balanced vines on the high-potential soils and vine canopies are grown a little fuller to protect the bunches from the midday sun. The red grapes are crushed and fermentation starts immediately. A moderate temperature (24°–27°C) ensures full-bodied, rich wines with fine tannins. Following malolactic fermentation, the wines are matured totally in French oak for 18 months and show exceptional aging potential. The wines are cleared by the natural process of racking only. The cleared juice of white varieties is settled overnight. Cold fermentation preserves the citrus and white fruit aromas of Chenin Blanc and Sauvignon Blanc and the wines are filtered clear before bottling.

Range of wines Muscat, P (Rosé), Cab S, P, Shz, Sauv Bl, Chenin Bl Mon–Fri 08:30–17:00, Sat 09:00–14:00. Closed Easter Fri, Sun; Dec 25, Jan 1 +27 (0)23 231 0350 info@deheuvelestate.co.za, www.deheuvelestate.co.za 8+ y 99, 01, 02 Olives, oil/olive products, restaurant, tours Mon–Fri 09:00–16:30

MANLEY PRIVATE CELLAR

The boutique winery of the Manley Private Cellar lies in the heart of Tulbagh. Seven hectares of exclusively red varieties were established on gentle north- and west-facing slopes on shale and clay soils. In the warm, dry climate, water efficiency is vital: irrigation is applied and cover crops improve water infiltration. Canopy density is increased and the rows are directed east – west, offering grapes protection against the sun. The historical cellar (150 years old) houses the small boutique winery where fermentation yields massive wines from high sugar grapes due to the warm climate. Gentle gravity feed and basket pressing sees young wines to the barrel, and 18 months maturation with some American oak adds a touch of vanilla and spice to the robust berry and mineral characters. Manley Wine Lodge, luxury accommodation, fine dining, wedding and conference facilities, and its non-denominational chapel round out this charming boutique winery.

Range of wines Shz, Pinotage, Cab S, Merlot Mon–Fri 09:00–17:00, Sat 10:00–14:00. Closed Dec 25 +27 (0)23 230 0582 bookings@manleywinelodge.co.za, www.manleywinelodge.co.za 8 y+ 04, 05 Cellar tours by appt, luxury B&B, restaurant, conference venue, weddings, gifts, farm produce, walks

SARONSBERG

Saronsberg is a true phoenix. The state-of-the-art-winery was reborn after a devastating fire in 2002. Today 40 hectares of vines are cultivated at the foot of Saronsberg. The marginal shale soils are well drained and yield a naturally low crop. The warm, dry climate, together with medium-growth potential soils, allow for early ripening of most varietals, smaller berries with increased skin to juice ratios, a concentrated fruit structure and naturally high acidity levels. A philosophy of fruit-driven elegance has motivated every step in the winemaking process. In the Saronsberg range, this approach finds expression in bold wines with powerful fruit components integrated with well-structured tannins, epitomised by the Rhône-style Full Circle blend in which Viognier, Mourvèdre and Grenache add dimension and a softening touch to the powerful Shiraz. Contrasting styles, the recently-released Provenance range uses grapes grown in the farm's cooler regions to produce accessible wines with expressive fruit, refined balance and soft tannins that reflect the true versatility of Saronsberg's *terroir*.

Full Circle (Shz / Mourv / Viog), Seismic (Cab S / PV / M / Malb), Shz Shz, Mourv, Viog, Cab S, Malb, Gren, M, PV, Chard, Sauv Bl Mon–Fri 09:00–17:00, Sat 10:00–14:00. Closed Easter, Dec 25, 26; Jan 1 +27 (0)23 230 0707 info@saronsberg.com, www.saronsberg.com 8 y+ 04, 05, 06 Avant-garde tasting room, contemporary art gallery

Robertson Pocket

Springtime – Early spring clothes the Robertson Valley in an array of bright colours

Bordered by the Riversonderendberg in the south and the Langeberg range in the north, Robertson is located about 160 kilometres to the northeast of Cape Town. The Breede River is the lifeblood of this low rainfall area (400 mm). With an average summer daytime temperature of 23°C, the area is relatively warm. However, as the valley is less than 100 kilometres from Agulhas – the southernmost point of Africa – frequent southeasterly winds often channel moisture-laden air into the valley, cooling the vineyards significantly. A majestic contrast exsists in the 'Valley of wine and roses' between the near-barren upper mountain slopes and the lushness of green vineyards and fruit orchards, with brightly coloured roses, bougainvillea and cannas along farm boundary fences.

Open hand – The icon of Fraai Uitzicht makes a fine door knocker

Viticulture is mainly practised along the course of the Breede River and on the mountain foothills. The geology and topography, consequently also the soils, are diverse and quite different to the soils of the coastal belt. Three main soil types are found: sandy soils with boulder beds in the low ravine, dark-coloured lightly textured alluvial soils (promoting high growth vigour) on lower terraces and heavy textured reddish-brown soils on higher foothills. Some outcrops of limestone (calcium rich) soils occur from place to place, which explains the area's dominance as a horse stud centre, the pastures being considered ideal for strong bone structure development. These soils dictate rootstock selection and induce moderate growth vigour. Supplementary irrigation is

TERROIR

Soil: Sandy, alluvial, limestone

Climate: Warm, low rainfall, drastic differences in day/night temperatures

White varieties: Chenin Blanc, Colombar, Muscat d'Alexandrie, Chardonnay, Sauvignon Blanc

Red varieties: Cabernet Sauvignon, Shiraz, Merlot, Pinotage, Cinsaut

Wine styles: Red, white, sparkling, dessert, fortified

applied in warm summer months. Mainly used for cultivation of Chardonnay, the limestone soils induce typical mineral characters in the area's single varietal and sparkling wines.

Planting densities are generally towards the lower or less dense end of the spectrum and vary from 2 500 to about 3 200 vines per hectare depending on the soil potential.

Vineyard perfection – Trellising exposes grapes to dappled sunlight

Most vineyards are trellised with systems ranging from a 1,2 metre vertical trellis to a double-slanting trellis, which gives a greater leaf surface to protect the grapes from direct sunlight.

Chardonnay is the dominant white variety, with many wineries producing great wines from this variety. The wines show ripe yellow fruit and citrus aromas with an elegant textured structure, enriched by oak maturation. Chalky and mineral characteristics clearly indicate the limestone soil cultivation (Bon Courage, Graham Beck, De Wetshof, Weltevrede). The more delicate Sauvignon Blanc is also cultivated in the valley, with the wines depicting passion fruit-dominated flavours with asparagus undertones such as wines from Springfield and Quando.

Shiraz is the most prolific

New life – Fruit trees blossom in early spring

red variety and the wine styles range from fragrant allspice aromas to dark berry fruit. These wines generally have elegant tannin structures and long finishes, such as those from Bon Cap, Bon Courage, Graham Beck, Zandvliet and Viljoensdrift.) A unique Pocket feature is the distinctive fortified dessert wines produced here.

These include red Muskadel from Graham Beck as well as white Muskadel from Rietvlei and Van Loveren.

DRIVING ROUTE: ROBERTSON

The Robertson Pocket lies about 160 kilometres (two hours' drive) from Cape Town in a northeasterly direction. Take the N1 freeway northbound. Pass the town of Paarl to the Huguenot Tunnel through the Drakenstein Mountain range. Have cash available for the toll road as credit cards are not accepted. Driving through the Breede River Valley is a visual feast with hectares of vines spreading out over the river plain. About 37 kilometres further, you reach the town of Worcester. At the first traffic light, turn right onto Rabie Avenue. This road

TRAVELLING TIPS

Information:
www.robertsonwinevalley.com

Accommodation:
Bon Cap guest cottages +27 (0)23 626 1628
Fraai Uitzicht 1798 +27 (0)23 626 6156
Jan Harmsgat country house +27 (0)23 616 3407,
Temenos Retreat Centre +27 (0)23 625 1871,

Restaurants:
Bon Cap restaurant +27 (0)23 626 1628
Bon Courage restaurant +27 (0)23 626 4178
Fraai Uitzicht 1798 +27 (0)23 626 6156
Jan Harmsgat restaurant +27 (0)23 616 3407,
    www.jhghouse.com

Events:
Food and Wine Festival annually in October
Robertson Slow Festival, August
Wacky Wine Weekend annually in June

Interest:
Dassieshoek Nature Reserve +27 (0)23 626 3866
Karoo National Botanical Garden (cactus & succulents)
    +27 (0)23 626 4133
Klaas Voogds Game Reserve +27 (0)23 626 2033,
    www.patbusch.co.za
Soekershof Hedge Maize +27 (0)23 626 4134,
    www.soekershof.com
Temenos Retreat Centre +27 (0)23 625 1871,
    www.temenos.org.za

crosses over a small bridge for a railway track. At the T-junction, turn left into Durban Street. Drive through the centre of the town.

At the next T-junction (traffic light), turn right onto the Robertson road. The Karoo National Botanical Garden has 144 hectares of natural semidesert vegetation and its greenhouse boasts a world-famous collections of stone plants. About 30 kilometres from Worcester, a sign indicates the turn-off to Eilandia on the right.

The gravel road (6,5 km) to organic producer Bon Cap is easily accessible. With outstanding quality wines and visibility in the market, Bon Cap is a driving force in the production of and education on organic wines. Return to the

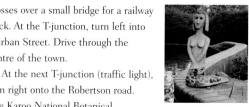

Mermaid – A welcome companion at the pool side, at Fraai Uitzicht

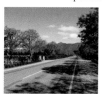

Valley of wine and roses – Robertson Valley is famed for its floral beauty

R60, turn right and continue east. Pass through the town of Robertson. On the outskirts, at the circle, take the second exit to Bonnievale on the R317. About seven kilometres further, Bon Courage is on the right. Bon Courage, producing a wide range of wines, is perhaps most well-known for its Chardonnay, Syrah and sparkling wines. The restaurant offers lunch and children's facilities. Be sure to visit the 'Cultivar Experience' where you can learn first-hand about the different grape varieties.

Continue along the road to De Wetshof (6,4 km). The impressive façade is based on a design by reknowned Cape architect, Jibuit Louis Michal from the 1700s. Father and son team, Danie and Pieter de Wet, are assisted in the cellar

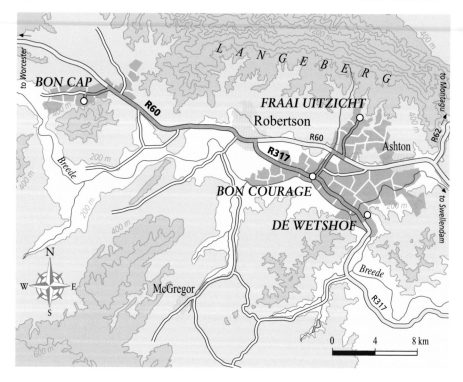

by Mervin Williams. Although Williams only has six years of official schooling, he is a chief winemaker, proving that passion weighs as much as book knowledge!

From here, travel back along the same route, and take the turn-off to the right, directly opposite Bon Courage's entrance. This unnamed road makes a T-junction with the R60. Turn right here and continue for about one kilometre to the Klaas Voogds East turn-off. At the Klaas Voogds East sign, turn left towards the mountain and continue for about four kilometres to Fraai Uitzicht. Their luxury accommodation is the perfect getaway in this valley.

GPS WAYPOINTS

Bon Cap Organic Wines S33° 47.016 E19° 43.577
Bon Courage Estate S33° 50.750 E19° 57.630
De Wetshof S33° 52.650 E 20° 0.580
Fraai Uitzicht 1798 S33° 47.730 E 20° 0.258

Organic Wines

Political isolation pre-1994 left South African wine growers mostly unaware of organic viticulture, but recently many have turned to organic, and biodynamic, practices. The hot, dry summers are beneficial for the non-pesticide approach. Yet, only a few hundred hectares are farmed this way and few producers have embraced it completely. However, this trend has spurred on many local producers to make use of natural vineyard pest control, plant indigenous flora to deter insects from breeding and reduce the amount of chemicals used. The title 'Organic' is also slowly finding its way to the labels as consumer awareness is raised. Key producers are Bon Cap, Tulbagh Mountain Vineyards, Topaz Wines, Tukulu, Reyneke. See *Organic and Biodynamic Agriculture*, Chapter 1, page 19 – 20.

BON COURAGE ESTATE

Three generations of the Bruwer family have produced wines on the Bon Courage Estate. Situated at the confluence of three rivers, the farm is blessed with soils from alluvial as well as the surrounding mountain origins. These diverse soil types provide a range of vine cultivation sites. Red varieties are planted on calcareous red soils, where the fruit flavours are concentrated by difficult growing conditions. Heat-sensitive white varieties are planted in gravelly and alluvial soils with more soil moisture. Canopies are opened to maximise airflow from cooling southeasterly winds. The Syrah, fermented with whole berries to restrain harsh grape tannins, shows complex berry fruit and spice, while the Cabernet Sauvignon has herbal and cassis notes. The red wines mature in a combination of French and American oak, which adds spicy and sweet oak flavours. The MCC matures for 36 months in bottle on its lees, yielding creamy notes, fresh citrus and a lively mousse.

ℹ️ Syrah Inkará, Cab S Inkará (both sgl vineyard), Jacques Bruére MCC Brut Reserve, Jacques Bruére MCC Brut Reserve Blanc de Blancs 🍇 Cab S, Shz, PN, Chard, Riesl, Sauv Bl, Sém 🕐 Mon–Fri 08:00–17:00, Sat 09:00–15:00. Closed Easter Fri, Sun, Dec 25, Jan 1 ☎ +27 (0)23 626 4178 ✉ wine@boncourage.co.za, www.boncourage.co.za 🍷 MCC 5 y, white 3 y, reds 8 y 🍾 MCC 00, Shz & Cab 03 ℹ️ Tasting room in Cape Dutch homestead (circa 1818), restaurant, children's facilities

BON CAP ORGANIC WINERY

Seven generations of the Du Preez family have farmed this property. Bon Cap Organic Winery was created in 2002. Sixty hectares of vines (of a total 300 ha) are cultivated in a river valley on poor sandy soils with a shallow clay layer. Wider plantings compensate for the relatively low soil depth. On the more elevated sites, the soil is composed of fertile red lime, pebbly soils, which have good water retention and drainage. They are planted to the more heat-sensitive varieties like Viognier and Sauvignon Blanc. Due to the relatively warmer climate, canopies are spread (on a vertical trellis) and opened with aggressive leaf removal and suckering to maximise air movement through the vines. Cover crops reduce water loss and vines are irrigated throughout the year. Red wines are cold macerated to extract colour and flavour and fermented at moderate temperatures to preserve their delicate flavour. Three-hundred litre and older barrels are used for maturation to ensure a restrained wood character. White wines are aged for three months on the lees after fermentation to add mid-palate weight.

ℹ️ Organic range of varietals 🍇 Cab S, P, Shz, PV, Viog, Chard, Sauv Bl 🕐 Mon–Fri 08:00–17:00. Sun, public hols @ Bistro 10:00–16:00. Sat closed. ☎ +27 (0)23 626 1628 ✉ info@boncap.co.za, www.boncaporganic.co.za 🍷 3–5 y 🍾 03, 04 ℹ️ Organically certified wines, cottages, venue (wedding, conference), bistro

FRAAI UITZICHT 1798

Fraai Uitzicht 1798 winery (Eng. Beautiful View) was established in 1798, hence the flagship Merlot's name. Their philosophy states: 'Hand-picked and hand-prepared wine with personal attention.' The open hand symbolises the handmade production style of the wine cellar and the award-winning restaurant. The strong life and destiny lines represent the gentle lifestyle of this farming retreat. The luxury accommodation serves as a base from which to explore the surrounding wine areas and the dedicated service at the restaurant is only surpassed by the quality of the dining experience.

Luxurious accommodation offers superb views of the Robertson Valley and surrounding mountains. Of the total 175 hectare farm, 12 hectares of prime land were selected for grape cultivation. Located on a ridge, the south-facing slopes and high altitudes (300–350 m above sea level) provide significantly cooler conditions, complemented by southeasterly winds during summer. Furthermore, early morning clouds are frequent and thus the grape ripening period is extended by two weeks. Large areas of the vineyard lie on soil with a high quartzite stone content with clay subsoil, giving minerality to the wines. Vines are trellised and rows are directed east – west to shade bunches from the midday sun. Only spring water from the Langeberg is used to gently water the vines. Grapes for the flagship Merlot are hand sorted before destemming in an historical destalker (70 years old).

Following cold maceration to extract colour, fermentation is done in open cement tanks, and pressed using a manual basket press. Malolactic fermentation occurs naturally in barrel and the wine is aged for three to six months on its lees. Twelve months of maturation follows, 50/50 French and American oak adding rich toasty and savoury notes to dense berry fruit.

Rustic farm welcome – The open hand symbol welcomes visitors to the relaxed farm lifestyle at Fraai Uitzicht 1798

Fraai Uitzicht 1798 Merlot 🍇 M, Mouv, Shz, Viog 🕙 Mon–Sun 10:00–18:00 ☎ +27 (0)23 626 6156 ✉ info@fraaiuitzicht.com, www.fraaiuitzicht.com 📶 8–10 y 🍷 03, 06 ℹ Restaurant, luxury accommodation, gift shop, walking, bird-watching

DE WETSHOF

The De Wet family arrived at the Cape in 1693 and have been actively involved in the South African wine industry ever since. Their first vineyards in the Robertson area were established by the early 1800s. In 1972, De Wetshof became the first registered estate in the Robertson Pocket and the path to becoming a premier Chardonnay producer was set.

Today, 180 hectares of vines are cultivated on the ancient riverbed. Areas with high clay content give rich, dense red wines and a fruit-driven Chardonnay. The undulating limestone hills are dedicated to Chardonnay, ensuring a strong minerality and fresh acidity. The riverbed also provides sandy areas, where Sauvignon Blanc ripens with delicate floral and white fruit aromas. Vines are trellised with a slightly higher cordon, to protect them against potential damage from hail and frost. An east–west row orientation optimises the onshore airflow from the Indian Ocean, cooling the vines during summer when daytime temperatures may reach 35°C.

Danie de Wet's German education reflects strongly in the elegant, balanced wines and the variety of styles the cellar produces. Two styles of unwooded Chardonnay are made: the first, a lightly structured, steely dry wine with strong citrus and white fruit flavours; the second is matured on the lees producing a fresh, lemony flavoured wine with a citrus, yeasty and nutty finish.

The flagship, Bateleur Chardonnay, is barrel fermented, then matured on the lees in new French oak for 12 months. This gives the wine a golden colour, restrained stone fruit aromas and oaky richness.

Impressive façade – The tasting room and offices of De Wetshof offer visitors a royal welcome

Bateleur Chardonnay 🍇 Chard, Sauv Bl, Merlot, Cab Sauv & F, Ries, PN 🕙 Mon–Fri 08:30–17:00, Sat 09:30–13:30. Closed Easter Fri, Mon; Dec 25, 26; Jan 1 ☎ +27 (0)23 615 1853 ✉ info@dewetshof.co.za, www.dewetshof.co.za 📶 8–10 y 🍷 98, 03, 06, 08, 09 ℹ Tours by appt

Klein Karoo Pocket

Ring of rocks at Boplaas – *This stone circle, erected to honour the ancient people who created stone circles to determine the shortest and longest day, is also a symbol to celebrate the cycle of life.*

The Karoo is a semidesert region of South Africa. It contains two subregions – the Great Karoo in the north and the Little Karoo in the south. Geologically speaking, the Karoo was a vast inland basin, which was glaciated and at various times contained great inland deltas, seas, lakes or swamps. Volcanic activity was severe and despite a baptism of fire, ancient reptiles and amphibians prospered – their remains have made the Karoo famous amongst palaeontologists. Currently sheep and ostrich farming forms the economic backbone, with other forms of agriculture established where irrigation is possible.

The Klein (Eng. Little) Karoo is a long, narrow semiarid area stretching from the rural town of Montagu in the west, through the higher-lying, cooler Barrydale, towards Ladismith, Calitzdorp, Oudtshoorn and De Rust in the east. It is an area of magnificent landscapes and

Vineyard walk – *A DIY vineyard tour at De Krans offers a unique hands-on experience*

Diverse agriculture – *Sun-dried apricots colour the roadside of the Klein Karoo*

towering cliffs, crystal clear streams and an abundance of trees and indigenous flora. The succulent plants are famous for their beauty in the flowering season. The rich diversity neccesitated a conservation effort and the Rooiberg Conserve has been set up on an area of 100 000 hectares. The area consequently supports a diverse *terroir*; however, for the purpose of this Pocket, it is taken as the production area surrounding the town of Calitzdorp, as well as the valley of the Langkloof.

Traditionally, vine plantings were done in low-lying alluvial soils of the valley derived from sandstone or shale. However, with improving viticulture and wine styles, higher-lying cooler sites, in particular soils with clay over gravel, are sought after for cultivation in the finger-like valleys and ravines of this beautiful mountainous landscape.

With relative extremes in both climate and soil composition, the larger part of the area is warm with an average summer daytime temperature of 23,6°C. The Klein Karoo is marked by a general shortage of water due to low, unreliable rainfall which only averages about 200 millimetres per year.

Infamous and adventurous – The long and winding Swartberg Pass

The Tradouw and Barrydale areas are situated at altitudes of 400 to 700 metres in the lee of the Langeberg. Wind-driven clouds from a southeasterly direction often spill over the mountain crest to cool down the daytime temperatures during the growing and ripening season. Weather data interestingly shows an average February temperature of 21°C. By extending harvesting dates, red varieties can be even and fully ripened. Due to the high altitudes, extreme winter

'Port Capital' – Klein Karoo is the self-proclaimed capital of fortified red wine production

frost can occur. The soils, mainly consisting of shale, are stony and well-drained. Due to low annual rainfall, these medium potential soils require supplementary irrigation to satisfy the vine's needs during the growing season. Joubert-Tradauw produces Chardonnay and Shiraz wines with rich fruit flavours supported by a good acid balance.

Calitzdorp has long been associated with fortified wines and its reputation is centred on Port. The hot, dry climate is similar to that of the Duoro region in Portugal. The soils of this area are drained by the upper tributaries of the Gamka River and vines are planted mainly on poor clay soils, avoiding the dark, fertile soils on the riverbanks. These clay soils are well suited to the production of fortified wines made from

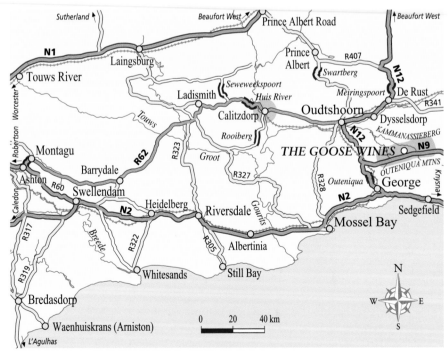

Muscat and Port varieties (Tinta Barocca, Tinta Roriz, Touriga Naçional and Souzão), excellent wines as well as full-bodied red wines.

Port producers from Calitzdorp have proved, over many years, to be the best this country has to offer. Planting density of vines varies from as little as 1 800 vines to 4 000 vines per hectare, mainly due to varying soil potential.

Guinea Fowl walking trail – See vineyards up close at Boplaas

Row directions and trellis systems are adapted from small, untrained bush vines to large vertically trellised vines according to the topography and prevailing wind direction, maximising the available airflow to assist in cooling the vines. As water is scarce, drought-resistant rootstocks are used and irrigation is applied to regulate growth vigour, mainly using drip systems to prevent water loss through evaporation. Fortified and red wines are the focus here, with De Krans, Boplaas and Axe Hill being some of South Africa's most well-known Port producers.

DRIVING ROUTE: KLEIN KAROO

The Klein Karoo Pocket lies about 400 kilometres or three hours' drive from Cape Town (about 360 km from Stellenbosch) in a northeasterly direction. Take the N1 freeway from Cape Town. Have cash available for the toll road (Huguenot Tunnel) as credit cards are not accepted. Reaching Worcester, turn right at the first traffic light onto Rabie Avenue. Cross a small bridge and a railway track to the T-junction with Durban Street. Turn left and drive through the centre of the town. At the next T-junction (at the traffic light), turn right onto the Robertson road (R60), and continue through Robertson.

At the T-junction in Ashton, turn left to join the renowned Route 62 (R62) to Montagu, Barrydale and Ladismith before reaching Calitzdorp – the unofficial capital of Port-styled wines in South Africa.

In Calitzdorp, take the second street to the left and pass the stone church building. Turn right at the stop street. Follow the road to De Krans, one of South Africa's premier Port producers. De Krans also offers a large range of wines. Do not miss the vineyard walk for an up

---

TRAVELLING TIPS

Information:
www.calitzdorp.co.za
www.oudtshoorninfo.com

Accommodation:
Port Wine Guest House +27 (0)44 213 3131
RedSstone Cottages +27 (0)44 213 3783
Rose of the Karoo +27 (0)44 213 3133
Warmwaterberg Spa +27 (0)28 572 1382

Restaurants:
Port Wine Restaurant +27 (0)44 213 3131
Rose of the Karoo +27 (0)44 213 3133

Events:
Port Festival, annually in May

Interests:
Bushmen paintings: Red Stone Hills,
    +27 (0)44 213 3783
Calitzdorp town: Historic walking route, art galleries,
    antique shops
Cango caves, Oudtshoorn, www.cango-caves.co.za
Cango Wildlife Ranch, Oudtshoorn, www.cango.co.za
Hennie Cloete veldtuin (garden): various local plant
    species, sales for home gardens
Ring of rocks (1st stone circle in SA), Boplaas
Rooiberg Conservancy Leopard Trust,
    www.capeleopard.org.za
Scenic drives: Seweweekspoort Pass, Rooiberg Pass,
    Swartberg Pass, Outeniqua Pass

TERROIR

Soil: Alluvial, shale, sandstone

Climate: Warm, low rainfall, dry

White varieties: Colombar, Chenin Blanc, Muscat d'Alexandrie, Chardonnay

Red varieties: Ruby Cabernet, Shiraz, Pinotage, Merlot, Red Muscadel

Wines: Red, white, sparkling, dessert, fortified

close-and-personal look at the grape varieties used to make this wine style.

Then follow the road for a few hundred meters to the right-hand side turn-off to Boplaas. Boplaas celebrated 350 years of South African winemaking in 2009 by making a 2008 Boplaas Dry Rosé and Chardonnay, with the grapes treaded by an elephant. Part of the proceeds will go towards elephant conservation, focused on the Knysna Elephant Park. Boplass is also carbon negative, with 2 200 hectares of natural veld under conservation.

A Karoo speciality is its lambs' meat. Prepared in various ways, this meat offers truly exceptional quality and is certainly a must-try.

To visit The Goose Wines, drive from Calitzdorp to the town of Oudthoorn, along

Colourful Calitzdorp – Bougainvilla blooms in an array of delightful colours in the town

the R62 for about 56 kilometres. Oudtshoorn is the Ostrich Capital, and home of the world-renowned Cango Caves. Many shops in the town sell ostrich products, from leather purchases, to feather boas, ostrich meat and biltong. From the town's main road, turn right onto Langenhoven Avenue (N12) and continue for about 40 kilometres.

Turn left onto the N9, and continue along this road (14 km). The vineyards of Goose Wines are spread along the mountain slopes.

GPS WAYPOINTS

Boplaas Family Vineyards S33° 32.131 E21° 41.004
De Krans S33° 32.105 E21° 41.151
The Goose Wines S33° 48.988 E22° 34.39

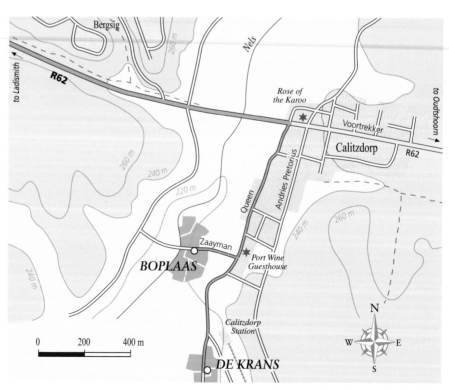

Cape Port Wines

South Africa's 'Port' wines were historically sweet and made from Tinta Barocca, Cinsaut and even Cabernet Sauvignon. Greater market sensitivity introduced drier styles, higher alcohol levels and the best Port varieties, including Touriga Naçional. The word 'Port' has been recognised as the single term to describe a specific product (fortified wine from the Duoro region in Portugal). European legislation requires that the word be phased out of all South African versions, creating distinctly Cape names, such as Cape Vintage, Cape Late Bottled and Cape Vintage Reserve. Quaint Klein Karoo town Calitzdorp is the unofficial 'Port' capital and hosts an annual festival to celebrate this wine style. While Cape 'Port' is comparable to its Portuguese cousin in sugar and alchohol levels, the former tends to be fruitier. Key producers are Axe Hill, De Krans and Boplaas.

DE KRANS

De Krans optimises warm climate cultivation using site selection. Vines are mainly cultivated on hills surrounding the Gamka River. The clay and gravel soils have a low vigour potential and good drainage. Vines are slightly water stressed under these conditions; the effect intensified by increased planting density to optimise the soil depth and water reserves. As a result, the vines naturally reduce canopy growth and produce a smaller berry, translating into concentrated flavours. The Red Stone Reserve is a unique blend (70/30 Touriga N/Cabernet S) that truly depicts Calitzdorp *terroir* with soft tannins and an unexpected average alcohol. The Vintage Reserve Port, that has now received superlative local ratings for four vintages in a row, is slightly lower in sugar than others in the area, but high alcohol and tannin extracts give maturing potential. This Port is aged in old wooden vats, which contribute to the slow, controlled oxygenation and subsequent colour and tannin stabilisation rather than wood flavour extraction.

Red Stone Reserve (Touriga N, Cab S) Touriga N, Tinta B, Temp, Souzão, Cab S, P, M, Chenin Bl, Chard Mon–Fri 08:00–17:00, Sat 09:00–15:00. Closed Sun, Easter Fri, Dec 25 +27 (0)44 213 3314/64 dekrans@mweb.co.za, www.dekrans. co.za Vintage Port 20 y; red 5–10 y 97, 01, 02, 03 Pick your own grapes (Feb, Mar), BYO picnics, vineyard walks

BOPLAAS

Boplaas' distilling heritage dates back to 1880, when owner Carel Nel's great-great-grandfather exported the first Boplaas brandy to England. Alongside the 75 hectares of vineyard, an additional 2 223 hectares of natural veldt is kept under conservation, rendering Boplaas carbon negative. Vines are cultivated on the hills surrounding the Gamka River, where a combination of clay and gravel offer good drainage and balanced growth. Boplaas' crown jewel is a mature vineyard (20–35 y), offering concentrated fruit and extraordinary aging potential. Vines are trellised, spreading the canopy to increase cooling airflow. Components of the flagship Ring of Rocks red blend are fermented separately and, following malolactic fermentation, are matured in French oak for up to 12 months. Individual barrels are then selected for the blend and bottled, offering a powerful, dense wine with elegant fruit flavours. Ports are produced in the traditional, drier Portuguese style, and aged in 500 litre Portuguese oak barrels.

Ring of Rocks (Cab S / M / Tour N), Cape Vintage Reserve Port Port (various), various Mon–Fri 08:00–17:00, Sat 09:00–15:00. Closed Easter Fri, Sun; Dec 25 +27 (0)44 213 3326 info@boplaas.co.za, www.boplaas.co.za Port 20 y+, red 10 y 87, 89, 99, 02, 04, 05 Tasting room, dried fruits & preserves, stone circle, vineyard walk, tours by appt

THE GOOSE WINES

The Goose Wines takes its name from golfing legend Retief Goosen. This extremophile producer established 20 hectares of vineyards in the Langkloof (Eng. Long Valley), at nearly 700 metres above sea level. Combined with the nearby ocean (18 km) and south-facing slopes of the Outeniqua Mountain, the exceptionally cold growing conditions result in grapes ripening very late and being especially concentrated (end April). A stone riverbed was lifted by alluvial soil and creates a unique soil of weathered sandstone with underlying clay, offering good drainage while retaining sufficient water during summer. Strong southeasterly winds necessitate trellising and north – south row direction offers protection, it further concentrates grape flavours. Hand-harvested grapes are fermented, often naturally, with punch-downs to extract colour. Following a gentle pressing, the wine completes malolactic fermentation in oak barrels and maturation may take 12 to 14 months. The combination of older wood and three months on lees ensures the complex yet elegant herbaceous, floral bouquet and rich palate is supported by a fine tannin structure.

The Goose Expression (Cab S / Shz) Red blend, Sauv Bl Visits by appt 27 (0)82 653 6800 info@thegoosewines. com, www.thegoosewines.com 15–20 y 07 Extreme weather, high altitude vineyards

Elim Pocket

Mission station – Elim is one of South Africa's newest wine-producing Pockets

The Elim Pocket is one of the newest coastal wine-producing Pockets in South Africa. The coastal stretch between L'Agulhas and Gansbaai is known to be particularly rugged and has seen many shipwrecks. Here, a handful of winemakers are pioneering vineyards along the solitary road that leads from Bredasdorp to the old Moravian town of Elim. This promising new vine development boasts the southernmost vineyards in South Africa.

Strandveld cellar – The strong lines boldly contrast the gentle landscape

Situated within 10 kilometres of the ocean, Elim is closest to the ocean and its Mediterranean climate has a strong maritime influence. Strong ocean winds are a possible problematic factor. The wind creates favourable conditions for white (and red) varieties by keeping temperatures moderate (20,5°C in February), and curtails vigour. On the other hand, consistent wind causes the internodes of the vine stems to become shorter and thus more wind resistant. The cool climate results in lower yields, but high fruit concentration, and the cool ripening conditions preserve the flavours.

Undulating hills create a variety of aspects for vine cultivation, and soils are mainly derived from sandstone and shale contributing to the minerality and distinct flintiness of white wines from this area. White wines, Sauvignon Blanc and Sémillon in particular, show rich aromas of nettle, capsicum, gooseberry, figs and passion fruit.

The red varieties show dark berries, fine tannins and moderate alcohols and specifically Shiraz, a distinct white pepper and smokey flavour. Sauvignon Blanc is emerging as one of the star performers from this area, while white varities Chardonnay, Sémillon, Chenin Blanc and Colombar as well as reds such as Cabernet Sauvignon, Shiraz Petit Verdot and Merlot are gaining popularity.

GPS WAYPOINTS

Black Oystercatcher S 34° 37.953 E 19° 49.650
Strandveld S 34° 39.588 E 19° 47.248

DRIVING ROUTE: ELIM

From Cape Town, take the N2 towards the town of Caledon (95 km). From the highway, take the turn-off to Hope Street, and drive through the town. This road becomes R316 to Bredasdorp. Pass through the town of Napier. Continue until you reach Bredasdorp. In town, take the turn-off to the R319 towards the coastal town of Struisbaai. About three kilometres further along this road, turn right onto the R 317 (Elim / Die Dam / Gansbaai road). At the T-junction, turn right towards Elim. Approximately 2,5 kilometres further, Black Oystercatcher is on your left. During summer, Black Oystercatcher is open later (weekdays until 18:00, Saturday until 17:00).

Return to the T-junction, and turn right onto the Wolvengat / Die Dam road. About five kilomtetres further is the winery of Strandveld. From Hermanus, take the R43 via Gansbaai to Die Dam. Turn left at the T-junction. At the Y-junction, keep right. At the next T-junction, keep right again. Strandveld is on the right (5 km).

Lomond lies some 30 kilometres away, in the Uilkraals Valley. Opening almost directly south towards the ocean, it enjoys the cooling ocean influence. Currently this location only hosts the vineyards. Wine tasting and sales are done at The Bergkelder (T +27 (0)21 809 8582) in Stellenbosch (see page 61).

TRAVELLING TIPS

Accommodation:
Draaihoek (Zoetendal farm) +27 (0)28 482 1717
Strandveld cottages +27 (0)28 482 1902
Tip of Africa Guest House, Cape Agulhas
　+27 (0)82 774 4448

Restaurants:
Visit the towns of Struisbaai, L'Agulhas and Bredasdorp

Events & interests:
Yellowtail Fish Festival, Struisbaai, end Feb – March,
　www.geelstertfees.co.za
Foot of Africa Marathon, voetafrika@cybertrade.co.za
Visit the southern-most point of Africa in L'Agulhas

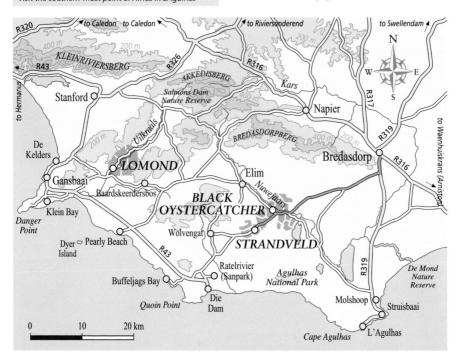

LOMOND

Lomond Vineyards, located near Africa's southernmost point at Cape Agulhas, developed vineyards where none had been before: on the virgin, uncharted territory of the Uylenkraals Rivier Valley. First established in 2000, the 800 hectare farm is a joint venture between drink-giant Distell and private shareholders of Lomond Properties. At this meeting point of two oceans, a concurrence between land and sea produces wines of distinctive cool-climate character. Neighbouring farm, Uylenkraal, is being developed as a black economic empowerment venture. Farm workers receive training in farm management and viticulture, and will eventually own at least 26 per cent of the company. Each of Lomond's vineyards is named after an indigenous plant found on the property, as part of its conservation initiative.

Uylenkraals Rivier Valley – The vineyards of Lomond stretch on both sides of this valley, tunnelling cool air from the nearby ocean

Managing heat – Trellising lowers the canopy of the vines a little to maximise radiant heat from the soil surface

Located a mere eight kilometres from the ocean, the total farm covers 800 hectares, of which 400 hectares will be planted to vineyards. Due to the southerly latitude and maritime climate, the farm sees relatively little variation in day-night as well as seasonal temperatures. In addition, southwesterly and southeasterly winds moderate summer heat, so that the vineyards tend to ripen several weeks later, with harvesting only commencing towards the middle of March. The property's soils are mostly of sandstone and shale origins, with a few sections seeing granite intrusions, creating lean, gravelly soils.

The valley location, providing an array of slopes and marked soil differences, allows for the production of single vineyard wines from individual vineyard blocks. Shiraz is planted on the warmer north-facing slopes, heat-sensitive Merlot and Sauvignon Blanc on the cooler south-facing slopes. Vines are trellised against the strong prevailing winds, as well as to open the canopy to air movement and to reduce humidity-related diseases.

Optimum sun exposure – New Shiraz vines are planted on north-facing slopes to maximise sun exposure in the maritime climate

Sauvignon Blanc grapes for the flagship wines are picked during the early morning and then cooled overnight before being processed. Following destemming and crushing, only the free-run juice is reductively fermented, excluding any oxygen and avoiding skin contact to prevent the extraction of tannins. Cold fermentation preserves the delicate white fruit flavours and three to four months of lees contact adds mid-palate weight. These New World- styled Sauvignons show khaki bush, greenpepper, asparagus and tropical fruit, underpinned by minerality and flintiness. The wines are matured in bottle for a few months before release.

The flagship Shiraz is hand-picked and bunches are destemmed and crushed into stainless steel fermenters. Warm fermentation (26°C) with rack-and-return and pump-over of juice ensures proper colour and flavour extraction. Following pressing, the young wine is matured in new French oak barrels for up to 18 months. Malolactic fermentation occurs naturally in barrel, adding to the integration of the oak and grape flavours.

Meticulous barrel selection ensures that only the very best barrels are blended for the final wine. The cool-climate flavour profile shows a distinctive aroma of white pepper, mixed spice and red berry flavours with a backbone of wood tannins and natural acidity giving the wine an Old World-styling. Bottle maturation of 12 months before release ensures that this wine is consumed at optimum age.

Precision viticulture – Regular visits to the vineyards ensure that management practices (removal of leaves, spraying, green harvest, etc.) are performed timeously

ℹ️ Sugarbush, Pincushion (both Sauv Bl, sgl vineyard), Conebush (Shiraz, sgl vineyard) 🍷 Sauv Bl, Sém, Nouv, Viog, Shz, M, Mourv, PN, Cab S ⭕ Tasting & sales at Bergkelder, Stellenbosch 📞 +27 (0)21 809 8330 ✉️ lomond@capelegends.co.za, www.lomond.co.za 🍷 White 3–5 y, red 5–10 y 🍾 07, 09 ℹ️ BWI member, BEE initiative, Walker Bay Fynbos Conservancy

BLACK OYSTERCATCHER

Black Oystercather's boutique winery epitomises cool-climate winemaking: natural high acidity, low pH and excellent aging potential. The historical farmstead (circa 1930s) serves as the winery. Eighteen hectares are cultivated to vines, where south-facing aspects and the ocean's close proximity ensure moderate ripening conditions. The prevailing southerly winds necessitate trellising; however, a high light intensity enables all varieties to ripen. Shale, sandstone and iron-pherosite soils impart minerality. The canopy of east – west rows shade white grapes, whereas north – south rows maximise exposure for red varieties. Components for flagship, Triton, are processed separately to retain individual cultivar flavours. Older oak adds fine tannins to the rich fruit and mineral mid-palate. Sauvignon Blanc is harvested by three consecutive handpickings and is cold fermented to preserve the complex, rich palate. Extensive lees contact ensures complex and smooth characteristics in the wines.

Triton (Cab S, Shz), Sauv Bl Sém, Sauv Bl, Cab S, M, Shz, Rosé Mon–Fri 09:00–17:00, Sat 10:00–14:00 (by appt); closed Sun, Dec 25, Good Fri. Pub hols by appt +27 (0)28 482 1618 anita@blackoystercatcher.co.za, www.blackoystercatcher.co.za Red 10 y+, white 5 y 07 Venue (weddings, conference, functions)

STRANDVELD WINES

Strandveld Wines was established in 2002 by a group of wine-loving friends. Sensitive restoration transformed the old stable into a tasting room. Today, 69 hectares (of 764 ha) are cultivated on three major soil types. Sauvignon Blanc, grown on red ferricrete soil shows mid-palate weight, citrus and grapefruit flavours. sandstone and quartzite gravel instill a creamy minerality, and koffieklip (coffee stone) produce wines with buchu and fynbos aromas. The cool ripening season ensures slow, even ripening, while trellising protects vines against the strong prevailing winds. Minimum handling preserves the crisp, fresh acidity and bright fruit flavours of Sauvignon Blanc, while the Sémillon component for the Adamastor is barrel fermented and matured for 10 month on the lees. The lanolin vanilla waxiness of the latter underpins the Sauvignon's fig and fynbos notes to a mineral finish. Shiraz is gently pressed to retain rich berry, pepper and chocolate flavours. Eighteen months in French oak (40% new) adds generous cedar and cigarbox notes for a dense yet elegant finish.

Shiraz, Adamastor (Sauv Bl / Sém) Sauv Bl, Shz, PN, white blends Mon–Thurs 08:00–17:00, Fri 08:00–16:00, Sat 10:00–15:00 +27 (0)28 482 1902 info@strandveld.co.za, www.strandveld.co.za White 3–4 y, red 5–8 y+ 06 Self-catering cottages, BYO picnic, scenic walks, birding

Other Pockets

Worcester Pocket

The Worcester area boasts the largest surface area of vineyards (nearly 21 000 hectares) in the country. Brandy production used to be the main production focus of this area with many wines still custom-designed for local *négociants*. Today, there is a large varietal mix with hillsides producing lower yields of more concentrated fruit. Dessert and fortified wines from the Muscat grape have always produced highly aromatic and luxurious wines. The climate is hot with annual rainfall diminishing from high in the Slanghoek Valley and almost adequate immediately east of the mountain chain, to very low further eastward.

The Worcester Pocket is situated along the Breede River, with distinct variations between soils and microclimates in the different river valleys and tributaries. Low to high potential soils occur and virtually all vineyards are irrigated. Soils are mainly derived from sandstone and shale. In Rawsonville, vineyards are planted on a flat landscape of grey to dark sandy alluvial soils and boulder beds. Although most vines are trellised, many vines are cultivated as untrained bush vines. Where trellising is used, the cordons reach only 80 centimetres. Chenin Blanc and Colombar still dominate vine plantings, while Chardonnay, Sauvignon Blanc as well as Cabernet Sauvignon and Shiraz have become popular.

Breede Kloof Pocket

The Breede Kloof Pocket includes the areas of Rawsonville, Slanghoek, Goudini and Breede Kloof. The Breede Kloof valley is formed by the Slanghoek and Du Toits Mountain ranges in the west and southwest and an extension of the Hexrivier Mountains in the northeast. It includes the upper reaches of the Breede River and there are a number of tributaries flowing off the bordering mountain ranges into the river. Soils of the valley are mainly boulder beds with alluvial soils, consisting of bleached to organic rich dark sand.

Sandstone formations form the mountain ranges that border the valley. The foothills are either gravelly colluvial sandstone deposits, or shales and greywackes. On the valley floor alluvial deposits, river terrace gravel (boulder beds), bleached sand to dark, organic rich sand deposits are found. While a few vineyards on the upper foothills are found above 350 metres, the bulk are found on the valley floor below 300 metres, in the alluvial valley.

The Pocket has dry summers and receives winter rainfall associated with frontal weather systems that sweep across the Cape. The rainfall is also influenced by the mountain ranges, with the highest mean annual precipitation (1 029 mm) recorded in the Du Toits Kloof and Slanghoek region. In general the western side (Slanghoek) of the valley has a higher rainfall (>750 mm) than the eastern side towards Worcester. During the ripening period, daily temperatures range between 23° and 24°C, giving the Pocket a moderate climate.

TRAVELLING TIPS

Information:
www.breedekloof.com
Breedekloof Wine and Tourism +27 (0)23 349 1791

Events & interests:
Breedekloof Wine festival, annually in October (Hot-air balloon rides, Anything That Floats)
Mountain to Mountain mountain-bike ride: annual 5 km and 10 km night run through the vineyards
Maps: Inside front and back cover

Wines are generally made in the New World-style, with upfront fruit and complexity. White wines range from dry to semi-sweet and the most popular cultivars found including Chenin Blanc, Sauvignon Blanc, Viognier, Sémillon, Nouvelle and Chardonnay. Red wines offer typical red and black berry characteristics spicy and peppery, with intense colour and soft tannins. They are full and complex, as well as easy drinking. Red cultivars include Cabernet Sauvignon, Merlot, Malbec, Petit Verdot, Pinotage and Shiraz. Furthermore the area produces dessert wines from Hanepoot (Muscat d'Alexandrie) and Muskadel (Muscat de Frontignan), as well as fortified red wines.

West Coast Pocket

Along the west coast of South Africa, large vineyard areas (10 000 ha) span the valley and ultimately the flat terraces along either side of the Olifants River. This large area stretches from Piekenierskloof, through the Citrusdal Valley and the Cedar Berg to Vredendal, Lutzville and Koekenaap in the north, following the Olifants River to the Atlantic Ocean near Bamboes Bay. Various soil types occur ranging from sandy material in the upper reaches of the valley with dark alluvial soils down along river banks, red calcareous soils on the older upper terraces, and some sand deposits on higher positions. Vineyards are limited to deep moisture-retaining soils and available irrigation.

The Cedar Berg has a high elevation reaching more than 1 000 metres above sea level. This elevation is favourable for high quality wine grape production. Annual rainfall is low at 220 to 370 millimetres, and as the soils have low water retention, this necessitates irrigation. Canopy management is strict to keep a balance between growth and grape production. Towards the town of Vredendal, planting density is low (2 200 – 2 800 vines/ha) and large vertical and slanting trellises are used. The area is associated with large volume production of bulk wine, especially for distilling and table wine. Chenin Blanc and Colombar are the dominant varieties, but Muscat d'Alexandrie, Chardonnay and Sauvignon Blanc are also cultivated. Planting of red vines is on the increase with Shiraz and Pinotage as favourites.

KwaZulu-Natal Pocket

Vineyards were first established on the KwaZulu-Natal South Coast in the early 1990s. Varieties include Cabernet Sauvignon, Shiraz, Merlot and Chardonnay. Regrettably, the initial plantings were not very successful due to insufficient cold weather during the winter, which is a mandatory rest period for the vines. This caused delayed bud break and poor grape quality. Consequently, the search began for vines which would be more suited to this climate. KZN has a semi-tropical climate with summer rainfall ranging between 750 and 1 200 millimetres annually. The resultant high humidity levels contribute to higher disease frequency, particularly fungal diseases.

Hail often accompanies high intensity thunderstorms and excessive soil water during summer, when the grapes ripen, impacts significantly on the sugar and acidity levels in the grapes. The soils are mainly derived from granite and are high in organic material and have a naturally high acidity level. Although well drained, excess soil moisture does pose problems for vines, particularly rotting of the roots.

Northern Cape Pocket

This pocket is mainly the Orange River region, which includes the areas from Groblershoop to Augrabies, Douglas and Vaalharts, which lies much further east. The most northerly vine-growing area (for wine production) in South Africa includes the Lower Orange River stretching from Upington to the Augrabies Valley in the west. Annual rainfall

is a mere 120 to 160 millimetres, restricted to the summer months in this semidesert area. Irrigation plays a major part in crop production. The silty alluvial soils, so-called inner soils, are dark, deep and well-drained, from a medium to heavier texture, and are bordered by sandy, reddish, calcareous soils on higher positions, the so-called outer soils.

Several trellising systems are employed to create microclimates within the vines to protect grapes from the extreme heat. Douglas and Vaalharts, well known for their signature fortified wines, also make easy-drinking table wines. A wide selection of varieties are cultivated, including Chenin Blanc, Colombar, Chardonnay, Pinotge, Shiraz, Cabernet Sauvignon, Ruby Cabernet, Merlot and Muskadel (Muscat de Frontignac).

Plettenberg Bay Pocket

The Plettenberg Bay Pocket stretches from the Groot River in Natures Valley to Harkerville in the west and borders on the bay. The organic rich soils consist mainly of sandy loam on an underlying clay layer. Vineyard rows are ridged to improve drainage due to the high rainfall, with vines planted on cooler south- and east-facing slopes.

The cooler climate ensures that the grapes ripen slowly to give phenolic ripeness at potentially lower sugar levels. Furthermore, it ensures a full vine dormancy during winter. The area, due to its climate and soil composition, is particularly suited to the production of white wines.

Currently only Sauvignon Blanc is cultivated for the production of a sparkling wine. With its close proximity to the ocean, the climate is cool Mediterranean. The sparkling wine shows litchi, lime and Granny Smith apple aromas on the nose, and has a rich buttery and limestone palate. The area is also experimenting with red varieties, mainly Shiraz, and focuses on greenpepper and berry fruit flavours.

Garagiste wine

Garagiste – Making wine in the cellar with little equipment but lots of passion

G aragiste (translated as garage owner) is the French term used for a growing number of winemakers who, for want of a farm or cellar, have found an outlet for their passion in their backyards.

In garages, sheds and similar structures dotted around the Western Cape, these self-styled devotees lavish hours of love and attention on one, two or perhaps 12 barrels of wine-in-the-making. With the utmost care and real courage, these garagistes are producing many fine wines. Garagistes traditionally do not own vineyards or wine cellars, and few have any formal training in winemaking.

Many make their wines after hours, as they are employed full-time elsewhere. Grapes are bought from independent growers and the wine is usually made in the cellar space rented from an existing wine producer. By outsourcing, they can select the best grapes (within a budget) and have access to all the required processing equipment and analytical facilities without the vast initial cash investment of developing and equipping a full production and maturation cellar.

IN DEFIANCE OF TRADITION

A group of garagiste emerged in the mid-1990s in reaction to the traditional style of red Bordeaux wine, which is highly tannic and requires long aging in the bottle to become drinkable. The garagistes developed a style which is more consistent with perceived international wine tastes.

Considered a predecessor of the garage wine is Château Le Pin, founded in the late 1970s by Marcel and Gérard Thienpont on less than two hectares. The Merlot-Cabernet Franc blend was produced in a farmhouse basement

Celebrate the harvest – The first wine from the press is tossed into the air as an offering to Bacchus

in Pomerol. In 1992 Jean-Luc Thunevin started Château de Valandraud with grapes bought from the Saint-Emilion area. With meticulous care, he handcrafted what was to become one of the finest red wines ever made. This Merlot-Cabernet Franc blend was rated a perfect 100 by US wine critic Robert Parker, securing its place alongside Châteaux Lafite Rothschild, Latour and Margaux.

Garagiste operations sprang up around France with winemakers working in defiance of centuries' old tradition. It ignited enormous interest in selective production of boutique quantities. Coining the term *Vins de garage*, and the vintners *Garagistes* has been attributed to both French writers Nicholas Baby and Michel Bettane.

This 'new style of winemaking' would, for red wines, relate to the wines being bigger, bolder, fruitier wines, often with a higher alcohol content. For white wines, on the other hand, the new style is a more pronounced oak taste with some residual sugar.

This new style is certainly not without controversy. Purists claim that such wines cannot age well and that they do not reflect the *terroir* of the region or the typicity of the grape varietals used. Characterised by critics as 'a winemaker's wine whose characteristics reflect a disregard for the traditional handling of its particular *terroir*', the term is sometimes used as a backhanded compliment, as these wines come from

Labelling – Hand labelling is reserved for tiny productions

previously unknown producers without a proven track record or pedigree.

The wines produced by garagistes often receive very high ratings from Robert Parker, and are usually sold at prices driven by rarity, hyperbole and fashion. Some garagiste wine commands prices reserved for first growths. In recent years, American wine enthusiasts have awarded cult-like status to some of their own garage wines.

Richard Neill commented on garagiste in *Decanter* magazine: 'The garage phenomenon has given Bordeaux a kick up the collective bum and there is no doubt that we are drinking better wines in a number of appellations because of the ripples that have spread out from the garagistes' activities.' Clive Torr, co-founder of South Africa's garagiste movement, comments: 'We haven't quite got there, but we are making some superb wines which are slowly being recognised locally and internationally.'

SOUTH AFRICAN GARAGISTES

In South Africa, Cathy Marshall pioneered the garagiste phenomenon. She crushed her first grapes on Muizenberg beach in Cape Town with friends and family and started the Barefoot Wine Company in 1995. Since its first harvest, Barefoot has grown significantly and is now an honorary member of the Garagiste Movement.

In 1997, Clive Torr vinified the first grapes for Topaz Wines. 'I began with a winemaking qualification but no farm or cellar,' he says

Picking bins – Fermentation is completed in open top bins to facilitate the manual mixing of grape skins and the juice

simply. 'For me, the greatest honour is to make a wine for my friends and myself. To be creative and receive recognition is very rewarding. In the garage of my house in Paarl, 11 of us got together and made the best Pinot Noir anyone has ever seen. I thought: "If we can do this with Pinot Noir, a fickle and delicate grape, imagine what else we can do." The synergy of people spending hours hand-sorting grapes and lavishing attention on the wine was a huge inspiration.'

With the inspiration and motivation of Cathy Marshall, Clive Torr and Tanja Beutler, many garagistes are now producing their own wines. 'Often these are professionals with a passion for wine. I believe to make it as a garagistes, it takes passion the first year and guts to do it a second year! Every wine created is unique, special and individual. These wines are made with the utmost care and attention to detail,' says Beutler. As the number of operations grew, a desperate need for technical guidance and a structured marketing and sales plan emerged.

Hand sorting – Carefully selecting only the best fruit

Torr and Beutler spearheaded the convergence and a Garagiste Movement was formed in July 2002. The movement provides technical and moral support to aspirant garagiste winemakers. Logistics are a nightmare for small producers in particular and the pooling of resources, equipment and dry goods streamlines operations for members.

Ultimately, the coming together of like-minded producers is about marketing. Members and their products are promoted to the local and international wine trade by gaining access to wine events as a group. While never failing to appreciate the importance of commercial considerations, Beutler adamantly maintains: 'We have to carry the passion forward, extend the love and dedication that defines garage winemaking.' The garagistes pride themselves on the *terroir* of their wines and origin authenticity is a most important aspect.

The Topaz Shiraz 2001 received an outstanding review in Robert Parker's *The Wine Advocate*: 'A Shiraz that was striking for its sensuality and balance came from South African

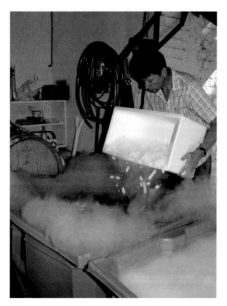

Rustic cooling – *Fermenting grapes are cooled using frozen CO_2 (carbon dioxide). As the substance sublimates, it does not dilute or change the wines*

FACTS ON GARAGISTE WINEMAKING

Total maximum production 9 000 l

Certification and registration by SAWIS (South African Wine Information Systems) and the Wine and Spirit Board

Project must be totally funded by garagistes

The wine must be made by garagistes in South Africa

Wine Master Clive Torr … Garagiste wines [are] less about power and weight than a sensual and almost delicate nuance. Easy to enjoy at a sensual level, they are subtly sophisticated on their expressiveness.'

Chris Williams, chief winemaker at Meerlust, produces his own label named The Foundry. His muscular Shiraz and mineral Viognier wines received acclaim both locally and on the international stage.

Dr Philip Mostert, a country general practitioner, became a garagiste when he joined Clive Torr on a trip to Beaune, wine capital of Burgundy. 'It was one of the best experiences of my life. I returned home determined to make 2002 my first vintage.' The 2002 maiden vintage earned him the Best Garagiste Producer Award at the Michelangelo International Wine Awards in 2003.

The Cheviot Winery was established in 2003 by Elmari Swart and Jaap Scholten over a glass of sparkling wine in the heart of the Mother City, Cape Town. Focusing on Shiraz,

Pressing – Ensuring the newly pressed wine is transferred to barrel for maturation

this garagiste winery produces tiny volumes of about 1 200 bottles per year. Everything is done by hand, from the picking and sorting of the grapes to the bottling and even the labelling and distinctive red wax seal.

Many new garagistes start their winemaking experience each year. For most, the single point of entry into the market is through the Garagiste Movement. Contact the Garagiste Movement at tanja@topazwine.co.za for purchases and more information or winesales@cheviot-wines.com for guided tastings of garagiste wines.

GARAGISTE WINERIES OF SOUTH AFRICA

The following is a list of active members of the Garagiste Movement. Although produced in limited quantities, the wines from these producers are worth finding. as they generally offer exceptional quality at great value-for-money prices. Many of the producers are also well versed in the *terroir* aspects of their favourite sites, and welcome visitors to taste with them. Wines are for sale directly from the producers, via the Garagiste Movement and at selected wine shops and restaurant.

Akkerdal	Dispore Kamma	Oude Denneboom
Anatu	Galleon	SoetKaroo Estate
Anthill	Katbakkies	Topaz
Bergheim	Lady Auret	Matzikama
Black Pearl	Matzikama	Usana
Blyde	Migliarina	William Everson
Cheviot Winery	Milla	

Disclaimer: Not all of the garagistes produce wines from each vintage. It is advisable to check with the Garagiste Movement which wines are available for tasting and sales. For information email tanja@topazwines.co.za or winesales@cheviot-wines.com
Due to the limited quantities, availability at retail outlets and restaurants are subject to change.

Brandy route

Brandy maturation – Barrels of brandy maturing in the Barrydale cellar

B randy is truly unique. It is the only alcoholic beverage made from another.

Brandy production is made possible by a natural process known as distillation, where the liquid vaporises and then condenses. The Chinese discovered the secret of distillation in 3000 B.C. while scientists such as Hypocrites applied alcohol for medicinal purposes. Fascination with this elixir gave rise to the name *aqua vitae*, water of life, as it was widely believed that alcohol could prolong life.

It was only in the 15th century that a truly pure alcohol, known as the soul of the wine was distilled from wine. Towards the end of the 16th century, this alcohol was given the German name *Branntwein* (Dutch:

Traditional potstill – Copper potstills are the traditional method used for brandy distillation

brandewijn), literally meaning burnt wine. During a 17th-century war, French ports were closed for trade and Dutch ships were prevented from loading cargo of newly-distilled Brandy.

These barrels waited patiently on the quayside of La Rochelle in France for the war to end. When the barrels were finally opened, traders were surprised at the miracle – a once colourless liquid, the Brandy was now amber with a rewardingly rich and mellow taste. This discovery led to the development of Cognac.

Today, all Brandy is matured in wood. In 1805 the English fleet under Lord Nelson defeated the French navy at Trafalgar. This was bad news for the French as their merchant ships now came under threat, leading to the decline of French vineyards. It was good news for South Africa as British merchants now looked to South Africa as supplier of Brandy and wine.

South Africa's Brandy industry was born a mere 20 years after Jan van Riebeeck set foot on Cape soil. Historical records show that the first Brandy from Cape wine was distilled on 19 May 1672 by an assistant chef on board a Dutch ship called *De Pijl* lying at anchor in Table Bay.

Today the Brandy industry is an important part of the South African wine industry with more than 70 trademarks in the local market. South African Brandy consumption is approximately 48 million litres per year, contributing over R2 billion to the national economy.

One of the main reasons for its popularity is the diverse styles in which South African Brandy is made. These styles range from firm, upfront Brandies that are suited to being enjoyed with a mixer, to mellow, aged products for neat sipping. South African Brandy producers follow strict regulations to ensure that local Brandies conform to the highest standards. These regulations ensure that the local Brandy industry maintains a reputation of excellence.

BRANDY REGIONS AND PRODUCERS

South Africa has two major Brandy-producing regions. The heartland for vines cultivated for Brandy distillation is found in the Breede River Valley, between the towns of Rawsonville and Robertson. The second region is the Klein Karoo, a beautiful scrubland between Worcester and Oudtshoorn. These hot, irrigated areas are ideal for cultivating Chenin Blanc and Colombar, the primary grape varietals used in the production of wine intended for Brandy distillation.

Yields from these vineyards are higher than those for wine grapes and soils are conducive to producing fruit with the required acid content. Two Brandy routes take the enthusiast through these important regions. One route includes

Volume distillation – A series of stills work side by side at KWV in Paarl

the cellars of the Western Cape, the other runs along the R62 route through the Klein Karoo. Distell and the KWV are South Africa's larger Brandy producers (by volume), while a number of wineries distil their own Brandies, reflecting their unique *terroir*.

ENJOYING BRANDY

Some find the idea of tasting Brandy daunting. It need not be. While it is not the same as tasting wine, using the techniques below, you will soon be able to enjoy all the nuances of fine Brandies. The South African Brandy Foundation aims to inform and educate the consumer on all aspects of Brandy.

When tasting Brandy, there are certain techniques and practices that differ from those employed in the tasting of wine. A good starting point is to taste several, preferably no more than six Brandies in a line-up. This gives you the opportunity to compare different Brandies. The larger producers provide such opportunities with trained tasters to help you.

Appearance

Line up the Brandies, each in a separate glass. You do not have to use a snifter (a special shaped Brandy tasting glass). Pour approximately a tot (25 ml) into your glass. First examine the liquid's colour. The Brandy should be clear, with no sediment. The colour ranges from a pale straw yellow to a golden honey.

Brandy distillation – A set of copper stills at Nederburg

Smell

Smell each Brandy separately before tasting. Unlike a wine tasting, do not give the glass a vigorous swirl before smelling. The air directly above the Brandy develops a complex layer of flavours and aromas. Swirling upsets the balance and will enhance the alcohol evaporation and drown other subtle aromas.

Hold the glass to your face and smell. The first impression is that of wood characters, sweetness and smokiness. Bring the glass to your nose for a closer sniff to notice subtle differences.

One Brandy may smell of wild flowers, dried fruit and coffee, while the next may contain scents of tropical fruit, tobacco and leather. At first you might only detect one or two aspects of the Brandy, but with practice you will discover the subtle aromas and find the layers in the Brandy.

Do not be intimidated by others' comments. Continue to practise more detailed descriptions of the Brandy you are tasting. Also remember that your perception will change and develop over time. Some days you are able to taste more precisely than on other days. Your tasting abilities may even be affected by your eating habits and moods.

Mixing it up – Brandy is particularly well suited to mixing with fruit juices and soft drinks

Development

Brandy also develops in the glass over time. Smell the first Brandy and then the rest. Then go back to the first to see how the initial aromas are developing.

Tasting

Some prefer to add a little water to the tasting glass. Although a slight dilution, the water makes it easier to taste on the palate. Adding water is not the rule – many purists prefer to taste Brandy neat. The sip is small as Brandy is not spat out.

There are many flavours which must be allowed to develop on the whole palate. Swallowing allows a different array of flavours to those on the mid-palate to be appreciated. After swallowing, the warmth of the alcohol component becomes apparent. Between sips, rinse your mouth with water or nibble on a biscuit.

Never heat the glass. There is a fine balance between water-soluble and alcohol-soluble components, which become detectable by evaporation of their respective carriers (water or alcohol). Each aroma develops at its own pace, the combination giving you an overall experience. Heating the glass promotes rapid alcohol evaporation. The resultant increased alcohol content will merely burn your nose and distort the balance of aromas.

Brandy cooper – Skilled hands shape the oak barrel destined for brandy maturation

ROUTE 62 BRANDY ROUTE

Barrydale Cellar +27 (0)28 572 1012
Boplaas +27 (0)44 213 3326
Grundheim +27 (0)44 272 6927
Kango Cellar +27 (0)44 272 6065
Klipdrift Distillery +27 (0)23 626 3027
KWV House of Brandy +27 (0)23 342 0255
Mons Ruber +27 (0)44 251 6550
SA Brandy Foundation + 27 (0)21 809 7618
    Fax +27 (0)21 886 6381
info@sabrandy.co.za www.sabrandy.co.za

Brandy uses

Brandy is a very versatile drink. It can be used in many food dishes and cocktails.

Brandy can be enjoyed neat as an aperitif, a digestive with meals or with mixers. As an aperitif, Brandy is best enjoyed at room temperature, but on hot days it may be slightly chilled. The same applies to when it is enjoyed as a digestive together with the meal.

Brandy with ice and your favourite mixer (cola, ginger ale, soda water or tonic, even fruit juices) makes for a refreshing drink, ideal for South Africa's warm climate. Notice how the characteristic Brandy flavour will remain prominent.

Vintage and potstill Brandies are usually enjoyed neat, perhaps with ice and a little water. They are characterised by their smooth, full flavour and mid-palate weight.

Traditionally used as a preservative, Brandy also adds a special flavour when used in food preparation. As the alcohol evaporates during cooking, the flavour remains and should not overpower the food. The best Brandy-and-food combinations generally are with foods that are rich in texture and weight; made with cream and eggs and those which are highly fragrant on the palate. Brandy is a good companion for chocolate, where a higher percentage of cocoa makes a better match for a higher alcoholic drink. It is also a good companion for soft and creamy cheeses (gorgonzola, mascarpone, ricotta.)

Brandy glass – This specially shaped glass enhances the appreciation of the Brandy

WESTERN CAPE BRANDY ROUTE

Backsberg +27 (0)21 875 5141
Cabriere +27 (0)21 876 2630
De Compagnie +27 (0)21 864 1241
Kaapzicht Estate +27 (0)21 906 1620
Laborie +27 (0)21 807 3196
Louisenhof +27 (0)21 865 2632
Nederburg +27 (0)21 862 3104
Oude Molen Distillery +27 (0)21 859 2517
Oude Wellington +27 (0)21 873 2262
Savingnac de Versailles +27 (0)864 1777
Tokara +27 (0)21 808 5900
Uitkyk +27 (0)21 884 4416
Upland +27 (0)82 731 4774
Van Ryn Brandy Distillery +27 (0)21 881 3875

FACTS ABOUT BRANDY

Brandy is distilled from wine, which is made specifically for this purpose. This is referred to as base wine. The grapes are grown for this purpose and are harvested slightly earlier than grapes for table wine to ensure a higher acid content.

Only healthy, ripe grapes are used for the production of Brandy. Poor or rotten grapes are never used, as the unwanted flavours in the grapes will carry through to the final product.

The base wine is light (lower alcohol, around 11% by Vol.) with a high acidic content to ensure fruit flavours are maintained during distillation.

Brandy must be distilled twice and follows the Cognac production process, this ensures the highest purity.

South African Brandy must be matured for a minimum of three years in French oak casks.

The alcohol content of the final bottled product is between 38% and 43% by volume.

It takes 5 litres of wine to make 1 litre of Brandy.

Every year 3% of the volume maturing in each Brandy barrel is lost through evaporation – this is called the Angel's Share.

From 1999 to 2009 a South African Brandy has won the prestigious title of Worldwide Best Brandy eight times at the International Wine & Spirits Competition.

Brandy is often described as 'the soul of the wine' in its distilled from.

South Africa is unique in the world in that we are allowed to produce three different types of Brandy – blended, vintage and potstill Brandy.

Sparkling wine

Old and new – A fine collection ready for tasting

Sparkling wine is essentially a wine containing significant levels of carbon dioxide, making it fizzy. Wines with bubbles are associated, for many people, with festivities and celebrations. More precious and complicated to produce than still wines, they have traditionally been considered as occasional extravagances. With higher acidity, more delicate flavours, a unique palate tingle with lower alcohol, they are some of the most versatile wines to accompany food. Modern, cost-effective production makes sparkling wines both more affordable and accessible for everyday enjoyment.

Effervescence has been observed in wine throughout history and was noted by Ancient Greek and Roman writers. What caused the mysterious appearance of the bubbles was not known. During the Middle Ages, still wine from the Champagne region had a tendency to sparkle lightly and this was considered a wine fault.

While Benedictine monk Dom Perignon is often credited with inventing Champagne, he actually spent most of his life trying to prevent the bubbles from developing in wine. As cellarmaster of the Abbey of Hautvillers, Dom Perignon was charged to get rid of the bubbles since the pressure in the bottles caused many of them to burst in the cellar. He was not successful in this pursuit, but his most important contribution was in selective harvesting and blending of wines of different vineyards and varieties to achieve a better balance between the individual characteristics.

Later, when deliberate sparkling wine production increased in the early 1700s, cellar workers wore heavy iron masks to prevent injury from spontaneously bursting bottles. The disturbance caused by one bottle's disintegration could cause a chain reaction, with it being routine for cellars to lose 20 to 90 per cent of their bottles to instability.

Today, in deliberate sparkling production, the carbon dioxide may result from either natural fermentation or a carbon dioxide injection. The classic example of a sparkling wine is French Champagne, but many other examples are produced in other countries, such as Cava (Spain), Asti (Italy) and Cap Classique (South Africa). Traditionally sparkling wines are made from one or more of the three Champagne varieties: Pinot Noir, Chardonnay and Pinot Meunier.

Chardonnay provides the fresh, floral and citrus characteristics, and ensures longevity and maturation ability for sparkling wines. Pinot Noir, on the other hand, gives fruit flavours, complexity and depth to the wine. The third partner, Pinot Meunier, has a rich, spicy and fruity character. Maturing earlier than Chardonnay and Pinot Noir, it is especially important in non-vintage sparkling wines as these wines generally need to be ready for consumption earlier.

Dom Perignon – The author, Elmari Swart, visits the birthplace of the father of sparkling wine production in Epernay, France

Sparkling wine is usually white or Rosé, but there are many examples of red sparkling wines such as Italian Brachetto and Australian sparkling Shiraz. It is interesting to note that in Champagne, a wine's total acidity (TA) is measured in sulphuric acid, whereas in South Africa TA is measured tartaric acid. A factor of 1,54 applies and thus a base wine from Champagne with a TA of 5 g/l would have the same acidity as a South African wine with a 7,7 g/l (5 x 1,54) reading.

PRODUCTION

Grapes are harvested early to retain high acidity levels, acting as a natural preservative over the long course of the wine's development. In addition, lower sugar levels ensure that the base wine has a low alcohol volume since secondary fermentation will boost it later. Premium producers harvest by hand as mechanical harvesting may damage the berries. At the cellar grapes are pressed to separate the juice from the skins. While some skin exposure may be

A-frames – Remuage or riddling of bottles in A-frames to move sediment to the bottle neck

desirable in the production of Rosé and some Blanc de Noirs, most producers take precautions to limit skin contact.

The primary fermentation is similar to most other wines and the wines may complete malolactic fermentation, creating a 'base wine'. The base wine then undergoes a secondary fermentation using one of several methods. The most familiar is the **Traditional** or **Champagne** method. Base wine is bottled with a mixture of sugar and live yeast (*liqueur de tirage*), in specially shaped bottles stoppered with a crown cap. Fermentation occurs inside the bottle, and the resultant carbon dioxide produced in the bottle is dissolved building up pressure (on average approximately 6 atmospheres at 12°C).

Once fermentation is completed, the yeast dies and forms a sediment (lees). The wine is kept on the lees for up to three years or more, as it imparts its own unique characters (yeasty, bread, butterscotch, toast). Consolidating the lees for removal is known as *rémuage* or riddling. In 1805, Nicole-Barbe Ponsardin Clicquot became a young widow and head of a Champagne house. Seeking assistance from gravity, she cut holes in her kitchen table to invert the bottles in order to collect the lees in the neck. Traditionally, the bottles are placed at a 45° angle, necks down, in specially built A-frame racks (Fr. *pupitres*). An experienced worker grips the bottom of each bottle, giving it an abrupt back and forth twist and a slight increase in tilt, letting it drop back in the rack. This riddling action recurs every one to three days over a period of several weeks until the necks face straight down and all the sediment is neatly collected in the neck. Computer-automated machines called

Gyropalettes accomplish riddling using bins containing hundreds of bottles, saving time, space and production costs. Hand riddling requires a minimum of eight weeks to complete; gyropalettes finish the task in less than ten days.

Removal of the sediment is called *dégorgement* or disgorging. The bottle necks are dipped in a solution of freezing brine or glycol which freezes a plug of wine and sediment in the top of the neck. Skilled workers then invert each bottle as they uncap it and the internal pressure releases a small amount of wine as the plug of frozen sediment pops out. The bottle is then topped up with a *dosage* of reserve wine, sweetened to fit the particular style (*liqueur d'expedition*). Modern bottling lines accomplish these tasks mechanically with amazing speed and precision. Bottles are corked, secured with wired hoods (*muselet*), labelled and foiled.

Alternative methods include the **Transversage method** – riddling and disgorging are dispensed with, bottles are emptied into a large pressured tank and filtered to remove the lees. A suitable dosage is added and the wine is bottled. The **Charmat method** sees the yeast and sugar mixture added to the wine with fermentation taking place in stainless steel tanks. The wine is then cooled, clarified and bottled using a counter pressure-filler. The process of **carbon injection** (or carbonation) does not involve fermentation. Carbon dioxide gas is injected into the wine as is the case with fizzy cool drinks. This method produces large bubbles that quickly dissipate and is used in the cheapest sparkling wines.

Muselet *recycled – Used muselets become an artwork at Colmant*

SA BUBBLIES

The main varietals used for South African sparkling wine are Chardonnay, Pinot Noir, with Pinot Meunier infrequently used. Blanc de Blanc designates white wine made only from white grapes (Chardonnay); Blanc de Noir is white wine made only from black (red) grapes. The latter is possible since the juice is clear and the red colour only develops through exposure to the skins. Most sparkling wine is non-vintage, which allows the winemaker to blend several grape varieties, vineyards and vintages, to achieve a consistent flavour style, usually the house blend. Vintage-dated sparkling wine can usually benefit from some bottle-aging, providing the consumer with a richer, fatter, less vivacious flavour.

Champagne's ruling body (CIVC) ruled out the name Champagne for Cape sparkling wine long before the European Union trade agreement in 2002. South African producers came up the term *Méthode Cap Classique* (MCC). While *Méthode* and *Classique* refer to the classic Champagne method of bottle fermentation, *Cap* points to the South African geographical origin.

Most MCCs are made with Chardonnay and Pinot Noir, and little Pinot Meunier is used. Some even incorporate a touch of Chenin or Pinotage. Blends are evenly distributed between Blanc de Blanc and the traditional Chardonnay/Pinot Noir styles. South Africa's quality sparkling wines are some of the best value for money in the world.

Sediment – *The dead yeast cells form a lees or sediment, which adds flavour to the wine*

Best Pockets for MCCs are Franschhoek, Robertson, Paarl and the Stellenbosch Pockets, with producers like Bon Courage, Colmant, Constantia Uitsig, High Constantia, Graham Beck, Steenberg. Simonsig, Rhebokskloof and Villiera leading the way.

ENJOYING BUBBLIES

In addition to the normal smell and taste criteria of still wine, the quality of sparkling wine is judged by the size of the bubbles (smaller is better), their persistence (long-lasting is better)and their mouthfeel (how well they are integrated and the relative smoothness of their texture).

When the bottle is opened and wine poured into a glass, the gas is released and the wine becomes sparkling. The average bottle of sparkling wine contains sufficient CO_2 gas to potentially produce 49 million bubbles, while wine expert Tom Stevenson puts the number at 250 million. The bubbles initially form at 20 micrometres in diameter and expand as they gain buoyancy and rise to the surface. When they reach the surface, they are approximately one millimetre in size. The amount of bubbles in the glass is misleading, as 90 per cent of the bubbles or mousse is dependant on the glass itself. If the glass surface has a perfectly smooth texture, almost no bubbles would form. It is the tiny imperfections on the glass surface which create the beautiful strings of bubbles. An old trick to accentuate this is to roll around a diamond ring inside your glasses to create a rougher texture. Rather than a visual judgment, evaluate the mousse in the mouth – it should be crisp and literally bubbling on the palate.

FACTS ABOUT BUBBLIES

- Legend has it that the champagne 'coupe' (a shallow, broad-rimmed goblet) was modeled in the shape of Marie Antoinette's breast, using wax moulds.
- The longest champagne cork flight in the world was 54 metres (177 feet), set by American Heinrich Medicus in New York in 1988.
- A champagne cork leaves the bottle at a velocity of approximately 62 km/h (40 mph), but can pop out as fast as 160 km/h (100 mph).
- The world's largest champagne glass, unveiled at a festival in Spoleto, Italy stands nearly 2,1m (7 feet) tall, and can hold the equivalent of 22 regular bottles, 16 kg (558 ounces) of champagne. That's a lot of bubbly!
- The official champagne of the *Titanic* was Heidsieck & Co Monopole Blue Top Champagne Brut. Rumour has it that a few bottles were brought up with the salvage recently, and still tasted great.
- MCC wines are made from a base wine, which is produced specifically for this purpose.
- Pinot Noir and Chardonnay are the most widely used varieties for SA bubblies.
- Bubblies can be white, Rosé or red (the latter is not very common).
- Grapes are harvested early, to ensure a high natural acidity and a low alcohol base wine.
- The best MCC bubblies are aged on lees for more than two years.
- The pressure inside a bottle of bubbly is approximately 5,5 bar.
- The best serving temperature for bubbly is 6° – 8°C.

STYLES OF SPARKLING WINES

The style is determined by the winemaker and, based on this, an amount of sugar is added after the second fermentation. This, as well as varying aging time will dictate the sweetness level of the sparkling wine.

Brut Natural or Brut Zéro	Less than 3 g/l	Bone dry
Extra Brut	Less than 6 g/l	Dry with no perception of sweetness
Brut	Less than 15 g/l	Slightly sweet
Extra Sec or Extra Dry	12 – 20 g/l	Moderately sweet
Sec	17 – 35 g/l	Translates to 'dry', but is noticeably sweet
Demi-Sec	33 – 50 g/l	Very sweet
Doux	more than 50 g/l	Extremely sweet

*Wines stating 'zero dosage' on the label were filled up with reserved wine but with no additional sugar and are generally dry.

Chapter 3

Tasting and understanding wines and styles

Harvest mosaic – "Ladies picking grapes" at La Petite Ferme

Tasting and understanding wines and styles

Gathering of friends – Share your favourite wines in the tasting room, restaurant or at home

Wine tasting, as opposed to wine drinking, is an art form that teaches us to focus on quality and not quantity. And because wine stimulates all our senses – sound, sight, taste, smell and touch – it is an invitation to hedonism.

TASTING IS NOT SIMPLY DRINKING

Wine gives pleasure associated with the natural desire to eat and drink. Wine used to be like any other drink, consumed at all times of the day, but when it became a strong symbol in the celebration of Catholic Mass, its status rose significantly to that of a special or exclusive beverage. Today wine is consumed as the first-choice lifestyle product of moderation. It has become synonymous with culture and style, playing a major role in the economies of many nations. Wine is also deemed essential to man's survival and is linked to a range of health benefits, as seen in the French paradox. Wine may reduce the risk of heart disease, stress and related diseases. Excessive drinking, however, has detrimental effects, ruining the health, dulling the senses and corroding the social structure.

Were it not for our memory and cultural education, tasting wine (or any food) would remain a strictly sensory pleasure. But one of the attractions of tasting is the identification of an aroma, recognising a certain style of wine or particular vintage. Wine tasting becomes a

THE FRENCH PARADOX

It seems paradoxical that the French, enjoying a diet based on cheese, bread and meat, are generally healthy and have a low risk of heart disease and obesity – diseases associated with protein and fat-based eating habits. Their secret is the moderate consumption of wine on a regular basis.

magical journey in time and space. It does not have to include jargon, pretence or snobbery. Novices often wonder whether wine tasting itself is not a sufficient pleasure, and whether the efforts to describe a wine are wasted. In fact, tasting wine is similar to criticising a painting. Pleasure is always said to be heightened by knowledge. To describe a glass of wine is to prolong enjoyment as each glass of wine tells a unique story, representing a particular technique, recalling a specific time of harvest and reminding us of a specific place of origin.

GREAT WINES

Wine must be produced from healthy, good quality grapes and not have any obvious faults. It should not contain excessive additions or harmful substances. Wine can either be made from one specific grape variety or from a blend of different varieties. These varietal characteristics must be well preserved in the wine, providing an intensity of flavours and aromas and an overall balance. On the highest level, wine represents the specific vintage or year of harvest, the ability to age successfully and is an expression of *terroir* or geographical identity – a specific site from which

Wine additives – Wood chips, sulphur powder, sulphur strip and disk used to disinfect barrels

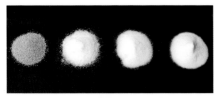

Wine additives – Selected dried yeast, diamonium posphate (yeast food), citric acid and tartaric acid

the grapes were harvested. Competition wines tend to hold the greatest concentration, highest alcohol and most pronounced tannins. One sip may be enough, as they could be overpowering and require food to be best enjoyed. A wine of understated elegance, in the words of Jan 'Boland' Coetzee, will 'drink like water'.

WINE TASTING

Wine tasting, to be fully appreciated, includes a combination of looking at the wine, smelling it

WINE INGREDIENTS

Water: 80 – 90% water, quantity varying with alcohol content.

Alcohol: Ethyl alcohol produced by yeast from sugar, 8 – 20% of volume.

Acids: From grape origin (tartaric, malic) or produced by fermentation (lactic, acetic). Total acidity ranges between 2 – 9 g/l. Main source of acid flavour in wine and stimulates saliva production.

Phenolic compounds
Pigments: Yellow and red pigments give wine its colour (200 – 500 mg/l).
Tannins: Contained in grape skins and pips or extracted from wood barrels. Provide astringency that puckers the mouth and makes wine seem dry. Excessive tannins may cause bitterness.

Sugars: All finished wine has a portion of unfermented sugar called residual sugar. Contributes to the basic flavour of sweetness, creates a balance with acid and gives viscosity. Sugar and alcohol together create richness.

Salts: Wine's major salts are potassium and sodium; however, their tastes are disguised by alcohol and sugar.

Carbon dioxide (CO_2): Wine contains various amounts of CO_2. It becomes detectable at 500 mg/l and creates bubbles at 1 000 mg/l; it adds freshness by accentuating the acidity and diffuses the aroma.

Aromatic substances: These substances give wine its aroma and taste and account for the complexity and richness. Based on their volatility, they contribute to odours ranging from floral and fruity to herbaceous and even spicy. The intensity of odour is influenced by the alcohol and water content.

and then finally tasting the wine. Following these simple steps not only allows us to appreciate the viticulturist and winemaker's dedication but also saves us from consuming spoilt wines. Furthermore, there is a particular joy in the comparison of wines, different grape varieties, different cultivation areas as well as vintages.

Appearances: looking at wine

The first step to enjoying wine is looking at it in the glass. This will reveal something about how the wine was made, how it was stored, its age and alcohol content. Tilt the glass sideways, holding it over a white surface or up to the light. The important elements to notice are clarity, colour, intensity and viscosity.

Clarity – A clean, clear appearance is the first step to ensuring a healthy wine. If the wine seems dull and has little variance from the centre of the glass to the rim, it is probably a very ordinary specimen. Most good wines look interesting, shining brightly. A great wine with depth of colour, though not transparent, should be clear. However, deposits or dullness do not necessarily indicate a spoilt wine.

Colour – The colour depends on the amount of pigment in the wine. The shade can be determined by studying the distinguishable colours visible in the meniscus of a tilted glass. South African red wines age faster than European examples and using shade, a relatively accurate estimate can be made as to its age. If two colours appear in the meniscus, the wine is less than three years of age. Three distinctive colours indicate the wine is aged between four

BLIND TASTING

Tasting wine 'blind' does not mean you cannot see the wine. It refers to the identity of the wine being hidden. The purpose is to identify the origin and winemaking style from its characteristics.

and seven years and if any browning is visible, the wine is older than seven years. Most white wines start out with a greenish tinge. Bottle maturation transforms the colour to pale yellow. Good quality red wines have a similar maturation path to whites: starting with an almost blue or purple colour, changing to cherry red, orange and eventually brown. Differing from white wine, the colour of youthful red wine is influenced by variety, but most age to the same hues.

Intensity – Two wines may have the same colour but one is darker and more difficult to see through when placed on a white background. What do these changing intensities indicate? Good colour intensity denotes it was well-made with fully matured grapes; the wine should age well and benefit from its years in bottle. A pale colour, although occasionally a characteristic of a grape variety, could indicate a fast, poor vinification process, over-cropping of vines or simply an inferior vintage. A low density does not necessarily indicate a poor or spoilt wine. Great colour intensity most often relates to concentrated fruit flavours, complexity and structure, characterising a superior wine.

Viscosity – The threadlike 'tears' or 'legs' formed on the inside surface of a wine glass when the wine is swirled are due to a liquid's

Shades of colour – White wine, Noble Late Harvest, Rosé, red wine

viscosity. Alcohol and sugar content provide viscosity to a wine, modifying the surface tension. This in turn causes liquid running down the glass surface to form tears. The tears are not an indication of wine quality.

Aroma: smelling wine

Assessing the wine's bouquet is based on what is known as the 'nose' of wine. We tend to think that 'smell' is detected by our nose and 'taste' is sensed in our mouth. In fact, the lines between these distinctions are very blurred. When pouring, ensure that the glass is filled no more than a third to allow enough space for the aroma to collect. Smelling while holding the glass still will yield very subtle and fleeting aromas. Agitating the glass to disturb the wine's surface will bring out the least volatile aromas.

As the wine moves from a reductive state (bottle) to an oxygenated state (glass), many aromatic components develop. For example meat and smoky notes disappear when wine is aired, whereas fruit and wood aromas are brought out by aeration.

The aromatics of wine can be divided into six main families: vegetal, floral, fruit, wood, spice and empyreuma (cocoa, toast, gingerbread, etc.), while other, less common, aromatics such as mineral, chemical and animal odours also occur. Wine aroma originates from three major sources: the grape berries themselves (primary or 'grape aroma'); the winemaking process (secondary or 'fermentation aroma') and the maturation process (tertiary or 'maturation aroma').

Grape aromas – All grapes possess their own unique identity and pass this on, in

TABLE OF COLOURS

WHITE WINES

Colourless	Very young, protected from oxidation, possibly tank vinification (less than 1 year).
Pale yellow / green	Grapes from cooler areas, harvested less ripe (less than 2 years).
Yellow / straw	Ultimate colour achievement for most SA white wines, point of consumption (1 – 3 years).
Yellow / gold	Sweeter table wines in youth. Wood matured wines (3 – 4 years).
Copper / gold	Sweet dessert wines. Greatest table wines (5 – 6 years).
Brown / amber	Very old, possibly oxidised, poor storage and excessive light.

ROSÉ

Pink highlights	Good rosé wines.
Onion	Inferior shade, spoiled by oxygen.
Pink / orange	Common for wines from warmer production areas.

RED WINES

Blue / purple	Very young red wines. Good shade for Pinotage or Pinotage blend. Lesser quality wines never leave this infantile stage (less than 1 year).
Ruby / cherry red	Optimum development for most blended red wines (2 years).
Red / garnet	Point of consumption for most as further aging will do little good (2 – 4 years).
Red with orange border	A sign of maturity. Age shows in aromas and flavours (3 – 5 years).
Mahogany	Truly exquisite wines take on this shade without loss of crispness (5 – 7 years).
Amber / brown	Advanced age. Brown tinge is first noticed at the glass edge. Browning may also result from too much exposure to air (5 – 10 years).

varying degrees, to the wine. For instance, aromas of roses and spice are associated with Gewürztraminer and black pepper suggests Shiraz. Aromatics also differ from one region to another. Compare a green, mineral-styled Sauvignon Blanc from Cape Point with a ripe, fruit-driven one from Robertson. The level of ripeness when grapes are harvested also influences aroma – unripe Sauvignon Blanc tends to show vegetal aromas (sage leaves and grass), even an unattractive cat's urine smell. However, when fully ripe, Sauvignon Blanc can give a complex bouquet of white-fleshed fruit and musk.

Fermentation bouquet – Grape juice is not very aromatic, apart from the obvious smell of grapes. Some aromas are present in a latent state in berry skins and they are brought forward by alcoholic fermentation. Yeast, responsible for this conversion, produces alcohol and carbon dioxide along with various secondary products influencing aroma. Fermentation with natural-occurring yeasts, although risky, brings a different spectrum of aromas. During

malolactic fermentation, bacteria soften the acidity of wine by converting malic acid to lactic acid, and produce flavours such as fresh butter, butterscotch and hazelnut.

Maturation bouquet – Following processing, wine (mostly reds and heavier whites) matures for varying lengths of time. During maturation the primary and secondary aromas diminish as the wine loses its youthful character. Oak barrels impart various aromas and flavours such as vanilla, toast, cigar box, coconut and smoky characters due to extraction of wood compounds. In this case, controlled oxidation stabilises the newly introduced compounds. Once bottled, wine enters a reductive state and develops the aromas that come with age: leather, meat, game, mushrooms and smoke.

Wine is a living entity with a life cycle: birth, development and maturity, followed by decline and death. A wine that retains some of its fruit after maturation and aging has every chance of becoming a great, matured wine.

Flavour: tasting wine

Tasting a wine on your palate is above all a question of appreciating the synthesis of flavours. You must appraise the balance of the wine's structure: distinguish the entry, mid-palate and finish and discern the elementary flavours, tannins and alcoholic warmth. This is the essence of wine tasting.

The traditional approach to tasting is aimed at determining the four elementary flavours: sweet, acid, salty and bitter. Also, there are many more 'taste' sensations than the basic four. **Olfactory sensations** are perceived by the retro-nasal passage. When aromas reach the temperature of the mouth, they are perceived as more intense than in a colder wine. **Taste sensations** are chemically based and perceived on the tongue, as a compound dissolves in the saliva and is detected by the mouth's receptors. Taste includes the four basic perceptions of

SMELL: AROMA VS BOUQUET

Aroma is the odours from the grape itself.

Bouquet arises from the processing of the grapes – vinification, wooding and maturation.

TASTING: AROMA VS FLAVOUR

Aroma defines the perception of smell, via our nose or retro-nasal passages.

Flavour is associated with tasting the liquid in our mouth; it is chemically based and supported by smell.

FROM LIGHT TO DARK

Too pale – Causes: poor extraction, wet harvest, unrestricted yields, young vines, unripe grapes, rotten grapes, fermentation at too low temperatures. Deduce: wine of poor vintage, poor aging ability.

Deeply coloured – Causes: good extraction, limited yields, older vines, sufficient vinification. Deduce: good or great wine. Wine with a future.

Flavour developement – Frozen carbon dioxide cools the fermenting must for optimum flavour development

sweet, acid, salt and bitter, as well as various other flavours (fruit, wood, meat, etc.). **Tactile or feeling sensation** is physically based as opposed to chemical. It is illustrated best when tasting a red wine, when tannins create a perception of astringency or chewiness. Excessive tannins make your mouth dry. **Thermal or temperature sensations** depend on the actual temperature of a wine which influences the perception of flavours and aromas. Alcohol content is also important; when excessive, it makes a wine seem warm.

Wine is taken into the mouth and aerated by breathing air over it. The first few seconds are known as the 'entry'. First impressions are of sweetness and subtle aromas. Roll the wine around your mouth for a few seconds. The developing characteristics are called the 'mid-palate' and indicate a wine's complexity (flavours, temperature, viscosity, astringency). Take some time to appreciate the different flavours when you spit out wine and when it is swallowed. The intensity of a wine's 'finish' will reveal its ultimate quality in persistence, balance and structure.

Elementary tastes

Acidity – This is the vital spark. It forms the backbone of a wine, giving crispness, liveliness and an appealing 'zip'. Excess acid makes a wine tart or 'green' while too little makes it bland and lifeless.

Balance – Depends on the relationship between the various chemical components. There is a balance of flavours where tastes (sweet substances, acids, tannins, salts) either strengthen or neutralise another. A wine's harmony is essentially derived from the balance between sweetness, acidity and bitterness.

Bitterness – Caused by tannins, it is often confused with astringency. Bitterness is a taste, while astringency is a physical sensation of puckering.

Body – This describes the intensity of wine flavours and the weight of a wine in which alcohol plays a major role; a higher alcohol level results in a weightier wine.

Flavour and aroma – The balance between flavour and aroma indicates quality as aromas 'carry on' from the nose to the palate, and the expectation created by a wine's aroma is matched by the experience of taste. Great wines are remarkable for the ability of their fruit content to last and evolve.

Persistence / Finish – Referring to the continuation of an aromatic sensation on the palate, lasting after the wine has been swallowed. A richer and denser wine will coat the palate more substantially and prolong stimulation of the senses.

Sweetness – Results from a portion of unfermented sugar, about 1 – 4 g/l in dry wines. This subtle sweetness creates a balance by softening harsher characteristics (acidity, bitterness, astringency). Certain wine styles (e.g. Late Harvest) have high levels of sugar (50 – 150 g/l) resulting in an authentic sweet taste and a more viscous liquid. South African law forbids sugar additions.

Typicity – Typicity relates to two factors: *terroir* and the specific grape variety (or varieties). The variety refers to how strongly specific characters associated with a particular variety have been preserved in the resulting wine. *Terroir* is the area expression.

SERVING WINE

Wine should always be served at room temperature and, as a general rule for South African conditions, all wines should be served slightly chilled. A wine served too cold (from the fridge or cooling system, normally 5°C), can be slightly warmed by cupping the glass in your hands. Even a small rise in temperature can make an acidic, watery white wine seem more interesting, as more flavours and aromas are released at a slightly higher temperature. When tasting, first look at the wine, smell it and then taste it. These steps will give clues about the grape variety or varieties in case of a blend, where it was harvested, how the wine was made and the quality.

Serving wine in the correct order will allow you to enjoy each style at its best. It is not a crime to mix wines, but as your senses become duller through the course of a tasting or meal, the progress should be in order of alcoholic strength. Older wines containing sediment may benefit from decanting. Glass decanters are

Aeration – Oxygen releases the volatile compounds in wine

available from all good wine shops. About six standard wine glasses can be filled to a reasonable level from one 750 ml bottle of wine.

Glasses and bottles – A 'waiter's friend' is by far the most efficient way to remove a cork. Avoid silly cork-pulling gadgets. When opening MCC or sparkling wine, do not allow the cork to shoot out as you will lose some pressure (bubbles) and wine. Let the cork slip out slowly. Choose the right shaped glass: clean, transparent and tulip-shaped with an opening narrow enough to concentrate the aromas. Glasses must be tall enough to allow for swirling. Hand-blown crystal is not necessary, but will enhance the experience. Wash glasses in warm soapy water, rinse thoroughly and dry standing or hung upside down on a glass rack.

GUIDELINES FOR SERVING WINE

White before red, **light before tannic**, simple before complex, **young before old**, dry before sweet

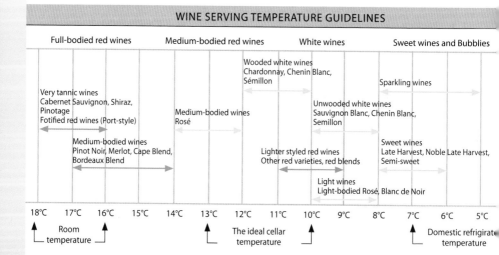

WINE SERVING TEMPERATURE GUIDELINES

Full-bodied red wines	Medium-bodied red wines	White wines	Sweet wines and Bubblies
		Wooded white wines Chardonnay, Chenin Blanc, Sémillon	Sparkling wines
Very tannic wines Cabernet Sauvignon, Shiraz, Pinotage Fotified red wines (Port-style)	Medium-bodied wines Rosé	Unwooded white wines Sauvignon Blanc, Chenin Blanc, Semillon	
Medium-bodied wines Pinot Noir, Merlot, Cape Blend, Bordeaux Blend		Lighter styled red wines Other red varieties, red blends	Sweet wines Late Harvest, Noble Late Harvest, Semi-sweet
		Light wines Light-bodied Rosé, Blanc de Noir	

18°C	17°C	16°C	15°C	14°C	13°C	12°C	11°C	10°C	9°C	8°C	7°C	6°C	5°C
	Room temperature				The ideal cellar temperature						Domestic refrigerator temperature		

FAULTS IN WINE

A faultless wine is not necessarily a quality wine; it may be dull, even if technically sound. Being informed about wine faults will save you drinking a spoilt wine or, even worse, discarding a good producer based on one faulty bottle.

Most particles found in wine are quite harmless, merely a nuisance and can be done away with without discarding the precious liquid. The following guidelines may help you decide on a course of action. Remember, life's too short to drink bad wine!

HARMLESS

These faults are harmless even when ingested. However, in spoiling the appearance of wine, some enjoyment may be lost.

Dull surface	At best it is simply an ordinary wine. At worst, there is a serious fault.
Pieces of cork or deposits from the lip of the bottle	A bottle with a disintegrating cork was opened and served carelessly. Decant the wine into clean glasses, maybe use a sieve.
Crystals	White crystals in white wines and dark deposits in red wines are, in fact, the same substance – harmless solids created through the maturation of wine, usually crystals of tartaric acid. These crystals are dyed dark red by colour pigments in red wines, but in white wines they may look like sugar or glass fragments. To avoid confusion, deposits are removed by cooling wine to very low temperatures and filtering wine clean before bottling. A wine with deposits shows it has not been over-treated.
Excess acid	Due to an under-ripe crop or over-acidification in hot years with over-ripe grapes. Look for another vintage from the producer.
Excess tannin	Under-ripened grapes, over-extraction or over-wooding.
Excess carbon dioxide	Recently bottled (with use of CO_2 gas), should subside after a minute or two.

PROBLEMATIC

These faults are more serious and the wine should not be consumed.

Oxidation	Wine smells of honey, wax or a grain bag. In limited quantities, oxygen may contribute to the aroma profile (barrel aging), but in excess it spoils wine. Incorrect or prolonged storing and extreme temperature changes dry the cork and allow oxygen into the bottle.
Vinegar	Advanced oxidation or bacterial spoilage creates acetic acid or vinegar.
Mouldy	Smells of old, wet shoes due to poor storage.
Corked	Smells of wet cardboard and intensely mouldy. Problems arise when the cork is spoiled by bacterial infection or by sulphur in a wine combining with chlorine in the immediate vicinity.
Mousiness	Smells of rodent urine. Caused by *Brettanomyces* bacteria, a problem mainly in reds when wine is stored in barrels without proper sanitation.
Haziness (cloudiness)	A protein instability found in white wines. Protein is a natural product of grapes and at high concentrations forms a cloud. It is tasteless and harmless but visually unacceptable.
Iridescence or film on surface	Serious micro-organism or enzymatic problems. Wine could be oxidised or vinegary.
Stringiness	Strings are clearly visible holding wine up to a light source, caused by bacterial spoilage.
Rotten eggs or rubber	Smell caused by sulphur-related compounds.

Wine styles

South African wines have certain distinctive characteristics of New World wines in that they show good extract (from the grape skins) and new oak barrels are used extensively. Another hint to South Africa as origin is the acid structure, which is slightly different from that of Old World wines. Because of the warmer climate, addition of acid is permitted and generally gives a distinctive, recognizable flavour profile.

South African wines in general can be categorised into the following quality categories:

Lower-end wines – These wines are generally based on Cinsaut as a red variety and certain Chenin Blanc wines.

Everyday drinking wines – These wines typically have very limited use of new barrels or have been vinified using old barrels, wood staves and chips. The Nederburg range excluding private bins and auction wines typify this class.

Mid-range wines – Wines in the mid range generally have a good fruit concentration, good natural acidity and can age well. Reds have been aged in oak barrels for a significant period.

Upper-echelon wines – Upper-echelon wines are typified by the selection of only exceptional components: outstanding blocks within a vineyard or the best tanks or barrels. Examples are Pinotage from Camberley or Bellevue, Chardonnay from Mulderbosch, Sauvignon Blanc from Neil Ellis and Cabernet Sauvignon from Buitenverwachting.

In the past, South Africa had very few cult or icon wines, but with a better understanding of *terroir*, site selection, complementary variety placements and the use of 'new' varieties, the list is growing. The following wines have become icons

Crystal decanter – Exceptional quality glassware enhances the enjoyment of fine wines

over time, and although the vintage certainly plays a part, one can expect an outstanding product from these producers: Klein Constantia, Vin de Constance; Ernie Els Wines, Ernie Els Signature; De Toren, Fusion V; Boekenhoutskloof, Syrah; Sadie Family Wines, Columella; De Trafford, Cabernet Sauvignon; Kanonkop, Paul Sauer; Vergelegen, Cabernet Sauvignon and Meerlust, Rubicon.

Many winemakers have also turned to blending white wine varietals. The two main varietals are Chardonnay and Chenin Blanc, although more complex tri-varietal blends use Viognier as well as Sauvignon Blanc. No one specific area stands out as optimum, although cooler climate regions do produce the highest quality. For red blends, Cabernet Sauvignon remains a cornerstone, while portions of Shiraz, Italian and Spanish varieties spice up the blends.

Recently, significant changes have been made to the Wine Estate system. Previously, properties farming a piece of land as a single unit could register as an 'estate'. Their wines could be registered as an 'estate wine' provided that it was made only from grapes grown on the property and was made and bottled on the property. However, under the new system, 'wine estates' no longer exist, but 'estate wine' is still recognised. Currently, any producer, in any production area, may register as a 'producer of estate wine' and make an 'estate wine', as long as the wine is made from grapes grown and vinified, and the wine is then bottled, on a single piece of land. The qualifying wine may display 'estate wine' on its label.

Previously, an estate was the smallest registered production unit, however, this has been superseded by the introduction of 'single vineyards'. Each unit must be registered with the Board; it may include one or more blocks of vineyards provided that these are cultivated as a single unit. The total surface area may not exceed six hectares and no boundaries are allowed, unless it is deemed essential such as a road. The wine may only be produced from the specified vineyard and must also be certified as a Wine of Origin. There are many examples of single vineyard wines as the focus on *terroir* increases. Notable wines are single vineyard wines from Boschrivier, Haskell Vineyards, Kleine Zalze, Uva Mira, Zevenwacht, Rustenberg and Onderkloof.

RED WINES

STYLE	CHARACTERISTICS
Fresh, fruity	Light in colour. Raspberries, red apple and cherries; absence of dense tannin. Juicy, plummy wines, unoaked. For early consumption. Merlot, Grenache, Pinotage, Gamay.
Medium body	Firm structure and density. Red berry fruit, spice, chocolate. Gentle oaking. Classic wines for meat dishes.
Powerful, spicy	Intensely mouthfilling, inky black and complex. Higher alcohol (riper picking), powerful tannins (new oak barrels) and ripe fruits. Cabernet Sauvignon, Shiraz, Zinfandel and Mourvèdre. Improves with proper cellaring.

WHITE WINES

STYLE	CHARACTERISTICS
Crisp, light bodied	Pale colour. Fresh-cut grass and wet stones. Low alcohol, crisp acidity, unwooded.
Aromatic	Bone dry to medium sweet. Honey, diesel, straw (Riesling); citrus and peach (Viognier) and florals (rose on Gewürztraminer).
Steely or mineral	Grippy mouthfeel, flinty and firm fruit on palate. Produced in cooler climates. Flint and gunpowder (Sauvignon Blanc); limes (Riesling); hazelnut (Chardonnay) and wax or wet stones (Chenin Blanc, Sémillon). Good food partner.
Full bodied, rich	Honeyed with tropical fruit, creamy, mouthfilling. From warmer climates, increased alcohol levels and wooded. Vanilla (wooded Chardonnay), nectarines and pineapple (Chenin Blanc, Sémillon).

OTHER

STYLE	CHARACTERISTICS
Sparkling	Toast, cookie dough, sweetness. Aggressive mousse, disappearing quickly.
MCC (Sparkling)	Toast, nut, biscuit, buttery. Fine and persistent mousse. Crisp acidity, lingering finish.
Rosé wines	Made from red grapes with minimum skin contact. Lighter alcohol, delicate fruit flavours, rarely tannin or structured. Zinfandel, Pinotage, Cabernet Sauvignon blends.
Sweet wines	Apricots, peaches, spice. High sugar and viscous. Late and Special Late Harvest produced from grapes left on vine, resulting in high sugar content. Noble Late Harvest wines (NLH) produced from grapes attacked by *Botrytis cinerea*. Benevolent form removes water from berries, concentrating sugar, acid and flavour compounds (noble rot). Wines are rich, sweet and perfumed without being simply sugary while concentrated acid provides structure and balance. Aggressive form results in loss of crop. Chenin Blanc, Sémillon, Sauvignon Blanc, Weisser Riesling, Gewürztraminer.
Fortified wines	Berry, tar, chocolate flavours. Port-style wines use Portuguese varieties (Tinta Barocca, Tinta Roriz, Touriga Naçional) or French varieties.

WHITE VARIETAL WINE STYLES

CHARDONNAY

Melon, grapefruit and pineapple
Buttery and nutty

Found in all South Africa's grape cultivation areas, from the cool coastal climate to the extremely warm Orange River region, Chardonnay wines can be classified into cool and warm region styles. The soil in which they grow, however, plays a predominant role. Chardonnays can be wooded or unwooded. Traditionally wines were heavily oaked, but evolved over the past decade to a lighter, more elegantly oaked style. The wines will be exposed to wood either by fermentation or aging in barrels, but are seldom applied to the entire crush. The unwooded component brings a crisp acidity and fresh fruit flavours to the finished product. In higher price brackets, wines are aged in barrels with frequent stirring of the lees (Fr. *bâttonage*). Bâttonage increases the mellowing effect of lees and wines show more buttery and creamy nuances.

Warm Pockets – The Olifants River and Orange River areas are both extremely warm and not favourable for this fairly heat-sensitive variety. To avoid typical baked, jammy characters, grapes are often picked earlier during the ripening period. The resultant wines are lower in alcohol (approx. Alc. 12,0% by Vol.) and show a tropical fruit palate. Often thin, the wines tend to have a short finish and little elegance, a style more for quaffing.

Robertson Pocket – Although this area has a warm climate, predominantly limestone soils impart a distinct lime character. Wine styles are often rich in character with strong tropical fruit characters balanced with a lime and citrus character.

Coastal Pockets – These Pockets produce elegant Chardonnay styles with good finesse. The fruit flavours vary from strong citrus in the coolest areas to more tropical fruits (melon, peach, pineapple) in warmer areas. The wooded examples show vanilla, butter and oily characters.

CHENIN BLANC

Quince, apple and pear drops
Sweet barley and honey

Chenin Blanc is the most prolific in South Africa but the plantings have been reduced based on historically poor quality performance. This variety dominates in warmer Pockets such as the Klein Karoo, Olifants River, Swartland, Paarl, Worcester and Robertson. The variety's naturally high acidity means it can be used to make sparkling wines, crisp dry wines, full dry wines and even well-balanced dessert wines. It can produce very bland, neurtral wines if the vine's natural vigour is not controlled. A good blending partner for other white varieties, the bulk of Chenin Blanc fruit is still used for brandy spirits production. Warmer regions yield light-textured tropical wines with good acidity for a refreshing summer drink. These wines are unwooded and appeal to the broad consumer market. However, in the last decade, some outstanding quality Chenin Blancs have been produced, mainly from the Stellenbosch area (Helderberg and Schapenberg). Old vineyards and bush vines in particular have excelled in producing rich, dense wines. When cold fermented, Chenin Blanc shows pear drops, quince and apple flavours, becoming more peachy and melon-like in fuller dry wines. Wood fermentation and aging produces structured wines in a heavier style. With *Botrytis*, wines acquire barley, sugar and honey characters.

SAUVIGNON BLANC

Cut grass, nettles, asparagus, green pepper
Gooseberry, passion fruit, mango

South Africa's Sauvignon Blanc lies midway between that of Europe and New Zealand. Styles vary from a grassy, herbaceous style to the riper, tropical, gooseberry style and depend heavily on berry ripeness. To add complexity, grapes are picked in three stages: slightly under-ripe grapes give the green grass, green pepper and tinned pea flavours; medium ripeness yields green fig and white asparagus flavours, while fully ripe grapes show fruity nuances such as gooseberries and yellow fruit.

Sauvignon Blanc is very *terroir* sensitive and generally cooler regions are preferred as these give the green pepper or methoxypyrazine notes, as do chalky limestone soils. The best Sauvignon Blancs come from the Cape Point, Stellenbosch, Robertson and Durbanville areas. The aromas and flavours range from freshly cut grass and tropical fruit (Durbanville) to green pepper, flint and fig (Darling), floral, gooseberry and peach (Simonsberg).

OTHER WHITE VARIETIES

Riesling (Rhine Riesling) – Flavours of apple and lime, honey and petroleum. Mostly uprooted in South Africa, but colder coastal Pockets (Constantia, Elgin, Stellenbosch) make wonderful dry Rieslings which can age successfully. However, the variety-typical terpene character becomes evident earlier than in the Old World wines.

Viognier – Typically peach, apricot as well as jasmine. It is rapidly gaining popularity as a single varietal as well as a blending partner for Shiraz to give a Côte Rôtie style. Wines show intense peach blossom aromas while young; however, this floral nose dies rapidly with age.

Concentrated in Stellenbosch, Swartland and Paarl. Some wines are slightly wooded to add complexity and palate weight to balance the intensely powerful nose.

Sémillon – Flavours of lime and citrus, also marmalade and some sweetness. Extensive uprootings due to lack of demand, but currently the Franschhoek Pocket has the largest plantings. In cooler areas wines taste grassy with an oily, lanolin mouthfeel. Often a small amount (5%) of Sauvignon Blanc is blended with Sémillon to enhance its grassy flavours. In warmer regions wines tend to be wooded, giving a fuller mouthfeel and yellow fruit flavours.

RED VARIETAL WINE STYLES

South African red wines can be very alcoholic, up to 16 per cent alcohol, although the average percentage is 13 – 14,5 per cent by volume. In the last decade, grapes were picked riper (later in the season) and more detailed attention was given to sorting of fruit. Gentler processing reduces extraction of excessive tannins, making wines softer and more accessible at a younger age while maintaining a good maturation potential. South African winemakers generally use new oak barrels; however, with a gentler winemaking approach, percentages of new wood have been reduced. This philosophy yields fruity, austere wines balanced with good extraction which expresses a New World fruit character, but maintains some of the Old World undertones.

CAPE BLENDS

The new Cape Blend style is gaining popularity. The first distinct characteristic relates to the origin and indicates a blend made within a particular Cape area. The second indicates use of the South African variety, Pinotage, as a blending partner. Pinotage is a cross between Hermitage or Cinsaut and Pinot Noir and is indigenous to South Africa.

The general understanding among Pinotage advocates is that the Cape Blend should contain a minimum of 30 per cent Pinotage. To date, no legal requirements have been set on this topic and blended examples excluding Pinotage are competing for the same title based on its production area in the Cape. Stunning examples of wineries producing Pinotage Cape Blends are Kaapzicht, Beyerskloof, Remhoogte and Vriesenhof.

CABERNET SAUVIGNON

Capsicum (green pepper)
Blackcurrant and plums
Cedar, eucalyptus, vanilla and coffee

Cabernet Sauvignon is perhaps the world's most widely recognised red wine-grape variety. It is cultivated in nearly every major wine producing country, among a diverse range of climates. Its suitability as a varietal wine or as a blending component is strongly influenced by the climate. However, it maintains a characteristic flavour profile irrespective of the *terroir*. Locally, Cabernet is the flagship wine of many producers and these wines tend to receive high percentages of new oak (as much as 100% or more). The best Cabernet wines require extended aging to reach their peak. Cabernet Sauvignon wine from newer clones is black fruit driven (blackberry and blackcurrant), while older clones show more herbaceousness with green pepper aromas. Since this variety requires some warmth to ripen, flavours tend to evolve from herbaceous to richer dark fruits as you travel inland from the coast. The award-winning Cabernet Sauvignons are concentrated around the Stellenbosch area. Bordeaux-type blends are also very popular, blending Cabernet Sauvignon with Merlot and small amounts of Cabernet Franc.

CABERNET FRANC

Raspberry, pencil shavings and perfumed
Grassy and herbaceous

Cabernet Franc is principally grown for blending with Cabernet Sauvignon and Merlot in the Bordeaux style, but can also be vinified alone. Similar to Cabernet Sauvignon, it buds and ripens at least a week earlier and thrives in slightly cooler climates. Its wines are bright pale red and contribute finesse and a peppery perfume to blends and tend to produce a wine with a smoother mouthfeel. Depending on growing region, additional aromas include tobacco, raspberry, cassis and even violets. Cabernet Franc is often characterised by a green, vegetal aroma, ranging from leaves to green peppers.

PINOTAGE

Plums and raspberries, hints of banana
Smoky, spicy

Pinotage wines fall mainly into two styles, one being very individual and robust, the other leaning towards the elegance of its Pinot Noir parent. A youthful wine has a distinctive jammy, red fruit taste (raspberry and mulberry) mixed with spicy notes. Harvested very ripe, Pinotage may show hints of banana and undesired burnt rubber, nail varnish or acetone characters which are eliminated with improved cultivation and high fermentation temperatures. During aging the aromas evolve towards strawberry, wet pine needles and mushrooms (a Pinot Noir character). Pinotage is generally made in one of three styles: unwooded, a lighter fruity style, or a wooded style. We also find Pinotage in some Cape Blends. The belt from Stellenbosch, through Franschhoek towards Paarl and the Swartland is the main cultivation area.

PINOT NOIR

Raspberry, strawberry, cherry

Incense, game, perfumed

This Burgundian grape commands a small percentage of total plantings in South Africa. Initial plantings yielded a very organic wine due to the character of the Swiss BK5 clone. In the past decade, newer clones have yielded robust and fruit-driven wines. Pinot Noir wines are characterised by a well-structured yet fruity body, soft tannins and pronounced berry, strawberry and raspberry flavours. Some of the best Pinot Noirs hail from Walker Bay and Elgin due to cool growing conditions, and show more earthiness and mushroom characters.

SHIRAZ

Black pepper, spice, smoke

Leather, savoury, chocolate

Shiraz produces inky, aromatic red wines with smoky, floral, minty, peppery and spicy aromas. The occasional medicinal character is undesired and may flow over into a eucalyptus character. In cool climates Shiraz shows mint, pepperiness and spice. Warm climate cultivation gives raspberry and blackberry fruits, evolving to chocolate, tarry and gamey notes with age. Shiraz is very popular in South Africa and cool climate areas are relatively unexplored in favour of warmer climates. Shiraz excels in the Paarl, Wellington and Stellenbosch Pockets. Although not as bold as Australian examples, South African Shiraz wines are typically New World with the style moving

from earthy-oxidative to more upfront fruitiness. A combination of French and American oak for maturation is popular to highlight spiciness, vanilla and coconut flavours.

MERLOT

Capsicum, bell pepper, blackcurrant

Chocolate, spice, soft mint

Merlot plantings are steadily increasing. Merlot has an easy mouthfeel, berry fruit flavour coupled with chocolate and mint. Grown mostly in coastal regions, Stellenbosch, Franschhoek and Paarl are the dominant Pockets. South Africa struggles to make world-class single variety Merlots, but certain examples are very promising. The softer mid-palate and smooth tannins make Merlot an excellent blending partner and it is often combined with Cabernet Sauvignon. Cooler regions with soils that have slightly higher clay content produce minty Merlots while flavours in warmer regions are dominated by violets.

GRENACHE

Roasted nuts, blackberries, spice

Earthiness

Spanish variety Grenache is probably the most widely planted variety of red wine grape in the world. It ripens late and requires hot, dry conditions. It is generally spicy, berry-flavoured, soft on the palate with a relatively high alcohol content, but it needs careful control of yields for best results. It tends to lack acid, tannin and colour, and is usually blended with other varieties such as Shiraz. In South Africa, only 86 hectares are planted and the areas with the best potential seem to be Swartland and Stellenbosch.

Chapter 4

South African wine collection:
Profit and pleasure

*New developments - Young vines being trained
onto the trellising wires at Rainbow's End*

South African wine collection: Profit and pleasure

Solid foundations – The striking entrance to the Sumaridge winery

STARTING A SOUTH AFRICAN WINE COLLECTION

For anyone with more than a passing interest in wine, stocking even a modest wine cellar is as rewarding as building up a collection of fine books or music. As few South Africans are fortunate enough to live in a residence with a functional basement, the term 'cellar' is used very loosely. A cellar can be any space dedicated to the storage of wine, beneath the staircase, an unused fireplace, a cupboard or a Eurocave® (a commercially available, temperature and humidity-controlled cabinet).

The cellar

A cellar should enjoy a constant cool temperature – 11°C is optimal, but consistency is more important than the actual temperature. Fresh air should circulate reasonably freely through the cellar. Sufficient humidity will prevent natural corks from drying out: aim for 75 to 80 per cent humidity. Cellars that are too humid can be improved with a bit of gravel on the floor. Gravel also greatly reduces the risk of breakage should bottles be dropped. Use a sturdy, stable packing system such as racks, shelves or bins in which to pack wine bottles.

WINE STORAGE TEMPERATURE GUIDELINES

Danger, risk of freezing Below -1°C (30°F)	Very slow maturation -1°C (30°F) to 9,5°C (49°F)	Ideal maturation 10°C (50°F) to 15°C (59°F)	Fast maturation 15,5°C (60°F) to 22°C (72°F)	Danger, risk of evaporation above 22°C (72

-1°C (30°F)   10°C (50°F)   22°C

Choose a system that makes for easy adding or removing of bottles, as this can become a cause of frustration if not properly managed. The cellar must be secured against thieves and uninformed persons and it may be wise to insure the contents of your cellar.

Organising wine

In an extensive cellar, it is worth having some kind of system to organise the collection. A very easy option would be to set up a spreadsheet using letters and numbers to identify each row and column. This allows you to put your hand on any bottle of wine, provided you keep the system up to date every time a bottle moves. There are also a variety of cellar management services available online. These range from simple systems which catalog wine to specialised software including barcoding to filter and sort wines, providing optimal aging time and searchable inventory of styles, regions, grape varieties and so forth. To start a cellar, dedicate specific areas to the most important sets of wine. Use the following sets as examples: Current Drinking Wine; Everyday Drinking; Special Occasion Wines; Aging Wines; or arrange the wines by country of origin or style. See also Packing & Storing Wine (Chapter 5, page 229).

The collection

The word 'collection' suggests selecting wines that will develop further complexity and character after a few years' bottle age, not simply stocking up on wines to be enjoyed immediately.

There are many examples of the latter on supermarket and wine shop shelves and it seems a waste to devote cellar space to them. The wine suggestions provided are for special occasions and maturation, but not necessarily for financial investment.

Unlike many of their European counterparts, South African winegrowers are not prohibited by legislation when it comes to matching *terroir* to variety. Consequently, individual farms historically planted a wide range of different grape varieties. This approach is, laudably, changing as winemakers learn which areas best suit which varieties. While there are – and always will be – exceptions, the list of suggested wines on page 219 is based largely on this first tentative research. Obviously, personal taste is paramount; those who prefer red wine to white wine will bias their cellar accordingly. This Pocket-based selection of South African wines is offered as a possible starting point for a 150-bottle cellar. Should you have spatial constraints, you may want to halve the quantities and start with a total of 75 bottles.

WINE BUYING TIPS

Price vs quality – Although price is not a quality guarantee, there is a strong relationship between the two. Grapes which originate from prized areas, with more new barrels, longer aging, packaging and a good marketing strategy have their price which will form part of the shelf price.

Condition – Always check the condition of the bottle on the shelf before you buy. Good

Home cellar – Functional and expandable wine racks for home use

Restaurant cellar – Wine racks adding to the rustic ambience in a restaurant cellar

Elegant design – Wine storage faciltiy in a controlled environment at The Cape Grace Hotel

wines can be ruined by poor storage. Look for dust on the bottle, heat and light sources (sometimes the top wines are displayed on the top shelf; unfortunately this is where most heat-producing lighting is), air conditioning, and the level of the wine in the bottle.

Reputable seller – First prize is, of course, buying directly from the producer, but many specialty wine stores offer prices to match cellar-door prices. Many larger liquor merchants also offer a wide range of wines over a quality

and price spectrum. Wineries often have international agents and this is a great option when travelling abroad.

Never over-buy – Do not be tempted to buy for the sake of it. To buy successfully, you might have to buy certain wines from one retailer and others from another, as each retailer has its preferences, speciality field and pricing strategy. You do not have to buy because the retailer is excited about the wine.

Be bold and experiment – As the industry

VINTAGE REFERENCE

2008 – Unusually cool and rainy season, harvesting late. Favouring elegance with ripeness at lower alcohols.

2007 – Warm vintage, elegant & structured white wines. Red grape berries were smaller, offering intense colour and fruit concentration, particularly Cab S & Shz.

2006 – Perhaps the best white-wine vintage in a decade: Sauvignon Bl & Chenin Bl are particularly expressive. Reds are fresh, gentle tannins and lower alcohols.

2005 – Vintage was early and short, particularly challenging. Concentration in alcoholic reds. Whites mostly average, some brilliant exceptions.

2004 – Healthy grapes due to cooler and dry conditions. Elegant, often age-worthy wines with lower alcohols. Chardonnay, Merlot and Shz are particular promising.

2003 – Outstanding vintage. Reds are especially concentrated and structured, but often slow to show their best. Difficulties with late-ripening varieties.

2002 – Challenging and patchy; track record of individual producers should guide the purchase/cellaring decision rather than variety and *terroir*.

2001 – Warm vintage with heat waves. Excellent reds, fruit-driven and concentrated, good aging potential. Whites delivered flavourful if alcoholic wines.

2000 – Very warm vintage. Predictably potent, concentrated reds, best have excellent aging potential. Whites generally fairly ordinary and not for aging.

1999 – Plump, alcoholic reds with ripe fruit, for earlier consumption. Whites generally ordinary, not for aging.

1998 – Excellent red vintage, concentrated fruit forecasting extended cellaring. Whites not for aging.

1997 – One of the coolest, latest vintages on record. Supple, elegant reds. Exceptionally stylish whites.

1996 – Poor vintage for red & white, not for keeping, except for top NLHs.

1995 – Considered top vintage of the 90s. Concentrated reds are maturing outstandingly.

1994 – Hottest, driest vintage in decades. Early ripening reds fared well.

1993 – Average vintage; some excellent Sauvignon Bl and above-average reds.

1992 – Cool vintage favouring whites, especially Sauvignon Bl. Reds (notably Pinotage) very good.

1991 – Dry and hot vintage favouring early to mid-season ripening varieties. Some enduring reds.

1990 – Uneven year, alternately cool and warm. Both whites and reds are average.

1980s – Even years (82, 84, 86) usually more favourable for reds. Uneven years were slightly cooler, favouring whites. 'White' year 87 and 89 produced remarkable reds.

1970s – Even years generally favoured reds. Best vintage of decade is 1974; however, top wines from other vintages are still delicious.

1960s and earlier – Vintages yielded some astonishingly long-lived wines, prompting a re-evaluation of the winemaking style. Referred to as 'heavy footed', the red wines were high in alcohol with unripe tannins, often made from under-ripe and virus-infected grapes. They tended to be heavy, leathery, pungent, musty and stewed. High sulphur levels, insufficient acidity, excessive skin contact and rough pressings yielded wines with a burned and tarry character, intensified by over-oaking.

SUGGESTED SOUTH AFRICAN WINE COLLECTION

Number	Wine	Geographical Region (Pocket if available)
6	MCC – sparkling wine	Stellenbosch, Robertson
6	Chardonnay – cooler climate, mineral examples	Walker Bay
6	Chardonnay – fruitier, warmer styles	Stellenbosch-Simonsberg, Robertson
12	Chenin Blanc	Stellenbosch-Simonsberg, Devon Valley, Helderberg
12	Riesling	Constantia
6	Sauvignon Blanc	Elgin, Constantia
6	Sémillon	Constantia
6	White blends	Constantia, Elgin, Helderberg
12	Cabernet Sauvignon – restrained styles	Stellenbosch, Helderberg, Blaauwklippen, Annandale
6	Cabernet Sauvignon – bolder styles	Paarl, Wellington
3	Cabernet Franc	Stellenbosch-Simonsberg, Helderberg
12	Red blends (Bordeaux style)	Stellenbosch-Simonsberg, Helderberg, Blaauwklippen, Annandale
6	Merlot	Stellenbosch, Paarl
6	Pinotage	Bottelary, Paarl
12	Shiraz	Paarl, Swartland
6	Pinot Noir	Walker Bay, Elgin
12	Red blends (Cape Blends)	Stellenbosch, Paarl
6	Mediterranean blends	Paarl, Swartland
9	Cape Port style	Helderberg, Klein Karoo

grows, many new areas are starting to produce some unknown but delicious grape varieties for the market. Most restaurants stock a few oddities, because the owner or sommelier enjoys them. Think of these wines as worthy alternatives; they're not stars, but they are certainly not overpriced.

Check the alcohol – That wooded Chardonnay may look perfect for a lunchtime picnic, but a quick glance at the label may warn you that it could be tiresome by the end of the afternoon, or the bottle – if you get that far.

Check the vintage – For simple, aromatic white wines, young is best, while wooded Sémillon or Chardonnay benefits from two to three years of aging. In restaurants, if the vintage isn't specified on the list, ask. See South African Vintage Reference, on the opposite page.

Well-known names – The golden rule when buying local wines is to start with well-known producers. In a difficult vintage, all the skills and resources of the top estates are employed to make a good wine. In dream years, nature is bountiful across the board and experimentation with smaller producers offers great value.

Cork or screw cap? Screw caps are regarded as best for simple wines intended to be consumed young, whereas cork is best for wines destined for some aging (reds, wooded wines). The subject remains contentious though.

White blends – Wine writers the world over have acknowledged the great value for money that South African white blends have to offer. Not only are they good wines, some are truly phenomenal and the price is well below European quality equivalents.

FOOD AND WINE PAIRING

Artichokes: Fresh, dry, high-acid white. Makes most wines taste metallic. Drink water or use lemon juice on artichokes to reduce metallic taste in wine.

Asparagus: Full-flavour dry white, Sauv Bl.

Avocado: Riesling.

Barbecue: See Braai.

Beef, roasted: Any dense, structured red – Cape Blend, Bdx blend, Cab S, Cab F, Merlot, PN. Cold roast beef: Chilled red – PN; Rosé, Blanc de Noir.

Biltong (savoury air-dried meat snack): Shiraz.

Bobotie (baked dish of spicy ground-meat): Dry MCC/bubbly, fresh, young Chenin, Riesling, Pinotage, light red.

Braai (barbecue): Depending on the food being cooked, choose a wine with character to avoid being overwhelmed by the smoke.

Carpaccio: Meat: Elegant red, PN. Fish: Chard, MCC/bubbly.

Cheese:

  Blue cheese: Dessert whites, NLH, Port.

  Cheddar: Red or ruby Port.

  Cream cheese: Full-bodied whites, Sém, Chard.

  Goat's cheese: Full-bodied white or dry red.

Chicken, roasted: Dense red, Cab S or white unwooded Chard. Pie: Medium-bodied Shiraz, Pinotage.

Chinese: MCC/bubbly, dry white with flavour, Riesling.

Chocolate: Off-dry bubbly, fruity red, Merlot, red Muskadel.

Cold meats: Fresh red.

Crudités: Dry, fruity white, Chenin, Sauv Bl.

Curry: Fish curry: Wooded Chard, Chenin. Cape Malay curries

Seared tuna – The rich coastal waters of South Africa offers some of the best seafood for rich white wines

Curry – Cape Malay curries combine flavours and textures for a culinary highlight

Local delicacy – Lean ostrich meat pairs well with both medium and full-bodied red wines

(sweetish): Gewürz, Riesling, Sauv Bl.

Desserts: See Chocolate.

Duck: Fruity young red, MCC/bubbly, Shiraz, Riesling, PN.

Eggs: Omelette: Fruity red blend.

Fruit: MCC, sweet bubbly, Late or Special Late Harvest, Rosé. Strawberries with cream: NLH; without cream: light red.

Game birds: Rosé, PN or Cape Bdx blend. Guinea fowl: PN, Merlot or wooded Chenin.

Ham: Young PN; fresh, juicy red, Merlot.

Hamburgers: Light dry red.

Ice-cream (if not too sweet): Bubbly.

Lamb and mutton, roast: Dense red (Cab S, Merlot, etc.) Chops: Shiraz or young Cab S. Stews: Light red.

Liver: Fruity, forceful young red, Pinotage.

Mushrooms: PN, well-aged red.

Nuts: After a meal: Port. Before a meal: Sherry. Nutty desserts: MCC/bubbly.

Oxtail: Shiraz, Zinfandel.

Pasta: With sauce: See Sauces. With Seafood: Sauv Bl, Chard.

Pastries and cakes: NLH.

Pâté: MCC/bubbly, Gewürz, Riesling, PN, Merlot.

Phutu or mealie meal (equivalent of polenta): Rich red.

Pizza: See Pasta.

Pork: Off-dry white, fruity red, Rosé, Zinfandel. Spare ribs: Pinotage.

Quiche: Full fruity white, Riesling, Gewürz.

Ratatouille: Light, fruity red, Rosé, Blanc de Noir.

Risotto: Fish: Medium-bodied dry white, unwooded Chard. Mushrooms: PN. Vegetable, butternut, etc.: Medium-bodied dry white, unwooded Chard.

Salads (remember, vinegar affects wine):

Green salad: Fresh white, Sauv Bl, Rosé.

Salade niçoise: Fresh white, Rosé.

Shellfish: Chard, Blanc de Noir.

Sauces:

Fish with cream sauce: Chard. **Fish with red-wine sauce:** Red used in recipe, PN.

Mustard sauce: Light red, Pinotage.

Sauces on pasta (cream, cheese, egg, meat, tomato sauces): Rich red.

Shellfish with rich sauce: MCC/bubbly, Chard-Sém blend. **Shellfish with peri-peri** (spicy/hot sauce): Light, off-dry white, wooded Chenin.

Seafood:

Fish:

Cape salmon (geelbek): High-acidity Sauv Bl.

Elf (shad): Chard, dry Chenin, Riesling.

Freshwater: Delicate white, MCC/bubbly.

Grilled: Sauv Bl.

Kingklip: Chard, wooded white.

Salmon: Chard, fruity non-tannic young red, Merlot, Merlot blend.

Saltwater: Dry MCC/bubbly, dry white, Sauv Bl, Chard, Chard blend.

Sardines: Grilled: Crisp white, young red. Smoked: Crisp aromatic white, Sauv Bl, wooded Chard, Gewürz, Riesling.

Smoorvis (braised fish, usually slightly spicy): Dry white, young red, Pinotage.

Snoek: Dry white, young red, Pinotage.

Sole: Grilled: Sauv Bl, Riesling.

Sushi: Chard, dry MCC/bubbly.

Trout: Riesling.

Shellfish:

Sweet endings – Pair sweet wines with desserts for a grand finale to a meal

Crayfish – A highly prized meal for seafood lovers

Classic meal – Grain-fed cattle produce aromatic meat, perfect for pairing with dense, tanninc red wines

Calamari (squid): Sauv Bl, dry white blend, light red.

Crab: Riesling or off-dry Chenin.

Crayfish (Cape rock lobster or *kreef*): Sauv Bl, Chard.

Langoustine (deep-sea, from SA's East Coast): MCC/bubbly, Chard.

Shellfish: Grilled, boiled, steamed or cold (with mayonnaise): Sauv Bl, crisp young Chenin, off-dry Riesling.

Other seafood:

Mussels: Sauv Bl, Chenin. Smoked: wooded Chard.

Oysters: MCC, Sauv Bl, lightly wooded or unwooded Chard.

Perlemoen (abalone): Chard, Sauv Bl.

Prawns: Unwooded Chard, Sauv Bl.

Snacks: Canapé: Aperitif white, fruity, dry to off-dry, MCC/bubbly, Blanc de Noir, dry sherry.

Snails: Chard, PN, Riesling.

Sosaties (local version of satay): Wooded Chard, Chenin.

Soufflés: Cheese: Red; **Fish:** White. **Dessert:** Dessert white.

Steak: Red wine, Cab S, Merlot, Shiraz.

Stews and bredies: Rich red.

Fish casserole: Fresh young white, Sauv, Bl.

Waterblommetjiebredie: Sauv Bl, Chard, Pinotage, Merlot.

Thai: Fresh dry white (cooled). Lemongrass, coconut milk: Wooded Chard, Riesling.

Tomato-based food: Off-dry Chenin, Chenin blend, rich red, blended red.

Tongue: Dry white, fruity red, Merlot.

Tripe: Hearty red, Shiraz, simple dry white or dry Rosé. With tomato: Dry red. With onions or white sauce: Off-dry Chenin or Chenin blend.

Veal: Light red, PN.

Vegetables: Sauv Bl.

Venison: PN, Pinotage, Shiraz, Cape Bdx blend.

WINE AND CHOCOLATE

Wine and chocolate are natural companions. Both have complex flavours and notes; in both instances the texture, weight and intensity are of importance as well as the sugar content. Although wine and chocolate are not the easiest pairing to make, they can produce a delightful culinary experience.

Examine the attributes of the chocolate, noting the aroma, listening for the snap when you break it and checking the shine and glossiness. Just like during a wine tasting, the flavours of chocolate are released in stages. The first notes should be filled with fruity acidity (from the grapes in the wine, and the cacoa beans in the chocolate). More subtle flavours as well as the sweetness unfold during the middle stage. The finish should show tannins, both for the wine and the chocolate. Many of the same flavour notes experienced in a wine tasting will emerge during wine and chocolate pairings. You may observe fruity, nutty, spicy and woody notes, even roasted flavours.

Cacoa heaven – White, milk and dark chocolate pair well with wine

Preferably, the wine should be at least as sweet as, if not slightly sweeter than, the chocolate to be served with it to avoid the wine showing as astringent or even sour. It is recommended to match lighter, more elegant flavoured chocolates with lighter-bodied wines; similarly, more intensely flavoured chocolate matches full-bodied wines. Similar to a formal wine tasting, if you experiment with several varieties of chocolate, start with the lightest (subtle white chocolate, milk chocolate or low percentage cacoa chocolate) and continue towards the darker or bittersweet ones.

The easiest and most inexpensive, do-it-yourself way to experiment with wine and chocolate pairings, is with a few small bars of premium chocolate. The mix-and-match approach will quickly reveal your personal palate preferences and you will gain first-hand knowledge of which wines best complement which type of chocolate. For best results, keep chocolate at room temperature, approximately 18° to 22°C. If it is too warm, the chocolate will be too soft. Too cold, it will affect the ability of the chocolate to melt properly and release flavours in your mouth.

As a general rule, the darker the chocolate, the more likely it will correspond with good red wine. This is in part due to the fact that chocolate with a higher percentage of cacoa has less sugar, which balances with the wine's sugar content. Darker or bitter chocolate, with deep-roasted flavours, pairs well with wines with dark, toasty notes. Fortified (Port-style) reds and sweet Late Harvest wines tend to be the best matches for chocolate desserts. While this does not exclude white wines from pairing with chocolate, it is generally the Late Harvest or wooded examples which pair best.

THE CHOCOLATE

White Chocolate – White chocolate tends to have a more mellow and buttery flavour, making it ideal for paring with Sherry or sweeter bubblies. The Sherry and bubblies will pick up the creaminess. Alternatively, for a contrasting pairing, partner a tannic wine such as a Cabernet Sauvignon with a creamy, buttery white chocolate – the tannins are softened by the chocolate's fat content and make for an astonishingly flavourful pairing.

Milk Chocolate – Pinot Noir or a lighter-bodied Merlot will complement a bar of milk chocolate, a creamy chocolate mousse or chocolate-based cheesecake. Riesling, Muscat, Sauvignon Blanc or dessert wines tend to hold up well to mild milk chocolates. Consider a sparkling wine for pairing with milk chocolate dipped strawberries. Further, a classic milk chocolate pairing to consider is fortified red wine, such as Port.

Dark Chocolate – Dark or bittersweet chocolate requires a wine that offers a robust flavour, with perhaps a hint of its own chocolate notes. Cabernet Sauvignon, Cabernet Franc and Shiraz have a history of perfecting the dark chocolate match, resulting in an unparalleled tasting combination. More feminine wines such as Pinot Noir or Merlot are best for dark chocolate with a cocoa solid mass of approximately 55 per cent. Tawny or Vintage Port offers a very well-balanced pairing approach to a dark chocolate dessert or truffle.

THE WINES

General Wine Suggestions – The flavours of warm chocolate soufflé cake with raspberry sauce come into their own right when paired with a late-harvest Sauvignon Blanc or a late-harvest Chenin Blanc. A sparkling Rosé adds extra sparkle to chocolate fudge cheesecake. A tawny Port or a Muscat is the perfect match for pecan tart with chocolate drizzle. Try chocolate-chip shortcakes with berries and dark chocolate sauce together with a late-harvest wine.

Red Wine Suggestions – Classically styled **Cabernet Sauvignon** often shows black fruit (blueberry, plum, cassis) with the oak maturation imparting notes of toffee, vanilla and cedarwood. Dark or bitter chocolate would suit these wines well, as would a dark chocolate containing the aromatics of Arabica coffee. While the intense flavour of the rich and refined chocolate balances the density of the wine, the Arabica coffee notes add depth to the wine's elegant texture.

A typical South African **Shiraz** shows flavours of black pepper, distinct spiciness as well as savoury and violet notes. This is best paired with an exceptional dark chocolate of 70%+ cocoa solids. This chocolate captures the robust characteristics of the cocoa bean and is therefore a well-balanced option with a full-bodied, aromatic Shiraz.

In a traditionally styled **Cabernet Sauvignon / Merlot blend**, blueberry, plum and cassis would be prominent, with coffee and toffee undertones from the wooding and firm tannins. A luxurious dark chocolate blended with refreshing peppermint creates an intense yet well-balanced sensation.

Rhône blends (Shiraz/Mourvédre/ Viognier) are dominated by red berry flavours with spicy undertones. The varying blend of appetising cultivars results in a combination of elegance and fruit. For these wines, the exotic taste of the Sambirano cocoa, grown in the northwestern part of the island of Madagascar, offers a soft and harmonious character, enriched with a hint of vanilla.

Blended red wines which combine a variety of flavours (e.g. berries from Cabernet Sauvignon, spice and white pepper from Shiraz, and red fruit from Merlot) will suit a mild dark chocolate with citrus such as orange pieces. The combination of cocoa and citrus gives the chocolate a bittersweet and fruity flavour which balances the layered character of the red blend.

Dry Rosé generally offers red berry flavours (strawberry, raspberry) which appeals to many palates, making it the perfect companion for social gatherings. This wine requires a delectable chocolate which melts quickly on the tongue to release its refined and exquisite tastes. Use extra creamy options, preferably set in single portion tablets (5 ml).

Chapter 5

Local knowledge

Peaceful piazza – Savouring the new vintage in charming setting of Waterford's piazza

Local knowledge

Ducks in a row – Local residents not only clean the vines of snails, but offer entertainment to visitors at Steenberg

Local knowledge is one of the most valuable possessions when you are travelling, yet it is not for sale. Experience can only be experienced. The local knowledge and practical tips provided in this section serve as a guide to assist you to get the most out of your stay.

Make sure all medical insurance policies, prescriptions and important travel documents are up to date and that you have copies in a safe place. Although South Africa does not have many of the tropical diseases (yellow fever, etc.), malaria is more prevalent in some northern areas of the country. The Winelands are fortunately a safe area in terms of diseases. Insect repellent comes in handy on warm summer evenings and sunblock is a requirement in the hot African sun, even during the winter months. The following guidelines are provided to help you plan your outings.

Guard dog – Taya welcoming visitors to the Village Wine Centre, Hermanus

Global Positioning System (GPS) is probably the single most useful piece of equipment modern travellers can add to their vehicle or mobile telephone. Most of the major South African cities and their surrounds are digitally mapped for use with a GPS unit. Every driving route described in this guide has been digitally mapped and can be downloaded from the Cheviot Publishing website, http://www.cheviot-publishing.com. Once downloaded onto your computer, the maps can be uploaded onto your GPS unit, providing you with turn-by-turn instructions for the selected driving route. We have also recorded GPS waypoints for the wineries detailed in the text. The waypoints have an accuracy of roughly 10 metres, which is more than sufficient to accurately guide you to your destination.

Should you not have access to the internet, please contact the publishers for a copy of the waypoints and driving routes on CD (contact details on page 4). The digital GPS maps will provide you with additional information that might not be included in this *Guide*.

TOURING THE WINELANDS

South African wineries are surprisingly approachable and many, including the most famous, welcome visitors to sample their products. At larger wineries, visitors are welcomed at the tasting room where wines can be tasted and purchased and where most winery tours start. When visiting smaller wineries, however, you are often hosted by the winemaker or owner. Should you want to meet the winemaker, enquire in advance of the planned visit, as these skilled masters are particularly shy of attention in harvest time (January – April).

When to travel

The timing of a visit to a particular Pocket depends on the requirements and expectations of the visitor. For sightseeing, spring and summer (September to February) are best – the vineyards are lush and the new harvest is maturing, but you will have to share the space and attention with other tourists. Harvest time from January to March is a photographer's dream – no one

Best travel time – Cape Town's stormy winter attracts with magnificent displays

PRACTICALITIES

Enjoy wine responsibly! Do not drink and drive.

Time: Local time is GMT + 2 hours. To check local time, dial 1026.

Flights: Internal flights from Johannesburg to Cape Town take two hours.

Water: Tap water is safe for consumption.

Electricity: South Africa uses 220V.

Climate: Hot, dry summers (Sept – Mar); rainy, cold winter (Apr – Oct). Average daytime temperatures: Jan 25°C, Apr 22°C, July 14°C, Oct 20°C.

Emergencies: Police 10111; Ambulance / Fire 10177.

Money: Local currency is Rand (ZAR). Major banks are open Mon – Fri 09:00 – 15:30, Sat 09:00 – 11:00. ATMs are located at most major banks and shopping malls. Exchange traveller's cheques at major banks with photo ID or passport.

Phones: Dial 1023 for enquiries, international inquiries 0903. Cape Town and surrounds dialling code: 021. International access code: 09. Dialling internationally to South Africa: +27.

Post Office: Open Mon – Fri 08:30 – 16:30, Sat 08:00 – 12:00.

Public Holidays: 1 Jan, 21 March, 27 April, Good Friday, Easter Monday, 1 May, 16 June, 9 Aug, 24 Sept, 16, 25, 26 Dec.

VAT: Value added tax of 14% on most goods, generally included in price stated.

Security: South Africa is generally safe for travellers, especially in the Winelands. As in all countries, the most important rule is to be aware of your surroundings. Lock your vehicle when leaving it and keep any valuables out of plain sight.

Mobile / Cellular phones: Available from the phone rental companies at airports, which should provide you with emergency numbers. Very good mobile signal in most areas.

Tourist information: Usually located in the centre of town; provides information, suggestions and assists with booking of trips, restaurants and accommodation.

Opening time: Generally Mon – Fri 08:00 – 17:00, Sat & Sun 08:00 – 13:00. Certain shopping malls and grocers have extended hours. Shops, wineries and businesses do not close over lunch.

who has watched the pickers in the vineyards or tasted the ripe grapes will ever forget the experience. Keep in mind that farms are a beehive of activity during harvesting and few allow access to the production cellar or winemaker at this time.

Visiting the Winelands after harvest time (end of March to April), you witness vineyards changing colour in an exquisite autumn display. It is true that mostly the red and brown colours of leaves are due to a vine disease, but they pose no threat to grapes or wine and are an eye's delight. Not only is this time of the year cooler, but also generally more affordable. It is also advisable to carry a bottle of fresh water in your vehicle.

Directions – Finding your way made easy at Morgenhof

Family – An unusual road sign that tells a story at Blaauwklippen

South Africa has a wide range of wine cellars – from garagistes making wine in a shed to the ultramodern winery employing hi-tech equipment. Most cellars have a dedicated tasting facility and many incorporate gift shops, local produce such as cheese or olives, and restaurants. Wineries indicate their location along the roads, but legislation restricts the amount of names per indication. Some smaller producers prefer to offer tastings by appointment only, restricting visits to hours that

do not interfere with work. Most wineries are closed on the following days: Easter weekend, Christmas (25 – 26 Dec) and New Year's Day (1 Jan). Certain wineries are open to visitors on weekends and public holidays. Please consult individual winery profiles or phone the cellar.

Decide which Pockets and producers you wish to visit and consult relevant maps. Calculate about one hour for each wine farm visited and try to join at least one cellar tour. It gives an interesting glimpse into the inner workings of winemaking. Preferably arrive for lunch between 12:30 and 13:30 as most restaurants do not serve lunch after 15:00. Arrive at the last cellar at least one hour before closing time to ensure sufficient time to taste its wines. Enjoy wine responsibly! Do not drink and drive; appoint a designated driver.

At the wine farm

A nominal fee is charged for wine tasting to recoup the value of wines used and to keep out unwanted elements. Tasting fees are generally refunded on purchase. Usually the tasting glass is included in the fee and can be taken as a souvenir. Tasting facilities do not allow the use of other wines / liquor on their premises. To prevent misuse of liquor, wineries will limit the amount of wine provided to visitors during a tasting.

Taste dry white wines first, proceed to red wines and sample sweeter wines last. Sparkling wines can be enjoyed in between to clean your palate. The tasting order will allow your palate to progress naturally and allow you to best enjoy each wine style. Use the spittoons provided. Smoking is not allowed in tasting rooms.

Most cellars allow the purchase of mixed cases of wine. Wine can be delivered to your

Autumn colours – Changing seasons brings dazzling colours to the vines at La Motte

door on request at a reasonable fee. Enquire at the winery about international agents or distributors and their shipping arrangements. Most cellars offer secure packaging for your wines, particularly for air cargo. Cash and most international credit cards are accepted at wineries. Due to the high incidence of fraud, cheques are generally not accepted. Remember that wine is a unique gift from the region.

PACKING AND STORING WINE

While travelling

Packing wine bottles when travelling can potentially cause problems. Cardboard boxes make for easy handling and may protect bottles against breakage. However, purpose-made styrofoam wine cartons are preferable, preventing breakage, damage to the label as well as temperature changes. Most standard-sized bottles will fit snugly. These cartons are available from most speciality wine shops.

Due to security reasons only liquor purchased from a duty-free shop may be taken onboard during a flight. All other wine must be checked in with your luggage. Although countries differ, generally a limit of two litres of wine and one litre of spirits is allowed cross-border. Placing wine in a suitcase or keeping it loose in a vehicle is always a risk. A winery agent in your city / country may save you the trouble. Enquire about

international availability when you visit wineries. Alternatively, use a freight company to get your wine home safely. It is worth spending the money to keep your precious wines in a stable environment and the memories of the visit safe.

Safe wine travel – Styrofoam boxes offer temperature and shock control

At home

Open bottles – Bottles half-empty after a meal need not be wasted. Ask the sommelier to keep the cork of the bottle opened at your table. If it breaks or crumbles, ask for a clean cork. Stopper the bottle and store upright in a cool, dark place. The Vac-u-vin® system is by far the best tool – a special rubber stopper is placed in the bottle neck and a hand-held vacuum pump is used to extract the air. It is inexpensive and readily available from wine and speciality gift shops.

Closed bottles – Safely storing wine is easily achieved in most households. Specially designed fridges or 'wine coolers' are best, but should this be out of your price range, follow these simple guidelines:

- Wines are best stored laid down horizontally to keep the cork moist and avoid oxidation and subsequent spoilage.

Wine shop – Selecting your favourite wines at Neethlingshof

TRAVELLING TIPS

Wines travel best laid on their side to keep the cork moist.

Bottles with screw tops can be kept upright.

Keep in a cool, dark place.

Never leave wine bottles loose in a vehicle.

Use a carton or foam box to protect wine bottles from possible damage.

Avoid sudden temperature changes (day and night) and parking areas with exhaust fumes.

- Bottles with screw caps may be stored upright.
- Wines require a cool, dark, quiet place. An underground space is preferable but, failing this, an unused cupboard or space under a staircase will do.
- Ideal storage temperature is 14 – 16°C with humidity at 80%.
- Avoid sudden temperature changes: the specific storage temperature is less crucial than keeping it constant. Extreme temperature variations cause wine to age prematurely or even spoil.
- Do not place wines in an attic, garage where vehicles are parked or against an outside wall of your house. Placing bottles against an inside wall is a better option as wines experience fewer temperature changes.
- Wooden wine racks are a great way to store and have easy access to your wine collection. Use only untreated wood as the chlorine used in treatments may damage wines causing a 'corked' taste.
- Invest in a few larger racks for your MCCs, sparkling wines, as well as magnum bottles.

Travelling – A wire cyclist at Spier reminds of a wonderful holiday

- Keeping an inventory helps to organise your cellar. A selection of cellar management software is available online.
- Use neck tags to identify bottles.
- Dedicate specific areas within the storage space to sets of wines. For example: Everyday drinking, Special Occasion and Maturing Wines.
- Wine is a living thing; it does not last forever and it will 'die' eventually. Read up on your wines to ensure that you enjoy them at their peak.
- Storing wine under favourable conditions will ensure that it matures at the best rate and

WINE ACCESSORIES AND GIFT IDEAS

Decanter Glass decanters allow you to separate sediment from the wine and are attractive on the table.

Drip catcher (1) a thin metal disk rolled up and placed in the bottle neck, or (2) a collar that fits around the bottle neck to catch drops of liquid when pouring. It works and is inexpensive.

Bottle mats Placed under bottles for display on the table and keeps table cloths clean.

Pourer baskets To keep old, fragile wines on their side. Take care when uncorking.

Ice bucket Crucial for keeping both red and white wines at the correct temperature, place wines into an ice bucket only when needed. Many are works of art but remember their job and choose those that are tall enough to immerse even the bottle neck.

Wine thermometer A bit ostentatious, but a must for the serious wine lover.

Bottle holders Can look very handsome next to the table. Could be from wood, wicker or metal, but avoid plastic.

Vac-u-vin® A rubbery, silicone stopper placed in the bottle neck, with a hand-held vacuum pump to secure it. The best possible way to store opened wines.

Carrier bag An insulated bag to carry single or multiple bottles, generally for outdoor use.

Categorise – Neck tags makes for easy identification of wines without disturbing the bottles

that it will reach the best possible maturation.

- If you have a special wine that you want to keep for display purposes, why not enjoy it with good friends and display the empty bottle. It is no use displaying vinegar.

DRIVING IN SOUTH AFRICA

Renting a vehicle – Various agents are available. To rent a car, you will need a valid driver's licence, may not have a criminal record and must make immediate payment, mostly using a credit card and proper insurance. Most rental companies have branches at airports and in cities and may be found on the internet. Smaller companies offer cheaper rates, but terms may not be flexible.

Petrol / Fuel – Fuel or petrol stations are locally referred to as 'garages'. Most are open 24 hours a day, but in small towns they might close at 20:00. Usually includes a shop stocking soft drinks, candy, takeaway meals, newspapers and cigarettes, but no alcohol. Diesel, Lead Replacement and Unleaded fuel are available.

Payment – Petrol stations do not accept credit cards, including international cards. Payment can be made in cash.

Speed limit – Take care as riders frequent vineyard areas

Side of the road – South Africans drive on the left-hand side of the road, similar to the United Kingdom.

Speed – Maximum speed in a residential area is 60 km/h; on the freeway 120 km/h. The speed limit is indicated by a white circular sign with a red outline.

Driver's licence – Local law requires that you have your driver's licence with you at all times when driving. International driver's licenses must be accompanied by the original driver's licence from the country of origin.

Parking – In most urban areas, official parking attendants with hand-held devices record the registration number of the vehicle and parking time. Payment is accepted in cash only and settled upfront with the attendant. Non-payment is fined. In smaller towns, roadside meters are used. Parking near the centre of town can cost as much as R8,00/hour. High-density areas limit the duration of parking, indicated on signs.

Parking attendants – Official attendants wear identification. Unemployed people and even children frequent areas where there are no official parking attendants, asking for money for

WINE GIFTS FOR ENTHUSIASTS

A selection of wine accessories to excite the wine lover

Back row: Crystal decanter (various shapes are available, but generally hold 1 standard bottle of 750 ml), Vac-u-vin™ vacuum pump and silicone stoppers, Bottle bag, Rat calf candleholder, hand-made crystal red wine glass (shapes for particular varieties and styles are available), crystal tasting glass

Front row: Bottle mat for table display, pourer and stopper, "waiter's friend" corkscrew with capsule cutter, cork remover (used for older and fragile corks)

supposedly looking after your car. Giving in to these requests only encourages further begging.

Cellular phones and other electronic devices – The use of a cellular telephone while driving is only permitted when using a car kit or a 'hands-free' kit.

EATING IN SOUTH AFRICA

Restaurants, delis, food shops – The Winelands has abundant eating establishments and many wineries have their own restaurants. Shops charge for plastic carrier bags, but you may supply your own.

Reservations – Booking is advisable at most restaurants and can be made by phone.

Service fee – Ten per cent of the value of the meal is generally accepted and is usually included on the bill for tables of more than six people.

Ordering wine – Most restaurants have a dedicated wine list from which to choose your wines. It is generally divided into four sections: sparkling wine, white wine, red wine and other drinks (including beers, liqueurs, spirits, etc.). Many fine establishments also offer older or rare vintages from top wineries. At luxury establishments, a fully trained sommelier will assist you in your wine selection from the extensive cellar; in most other restaurants, the waitrons are trained to offer a choice from the (generally more limited) wine list. Wine bottles should be brought to the table unopened and the person who ordered the wine should be consulted as to whether it is the correct wine and vintage.

Serving wine – The selected wine should be served in a tasting glass to the person who ordered the wine. Confirm with the waitron that the wine has no faults and is at the correct temperature; they should then serve the guests and lastly the host.

Wine temperature – Remember to asses the wine's temperature at serving; too warm will leave the wine bland and lifeless; too cold will see it diminish to an acidic, watery broth. Keep an ice bucket at hand to pop the bottle into when needed and remember to remove it once it has reached the correct temperature. See also *Wine serving temperature* (Chapter 3, page 206).

Faulty wine – Be sure to check the wine when it is opened. Point out a faulty or suspicious wine to the sommelier and you should not be charged. See also *Faults in wine* (Chapter 3, page 207) for common faults and problems.

Bring your own (BYO) – In South African culture, it is acceptable for people to take their own wine to a restaurant and pay a 'corkage fee'. Between R20 and R40 per bottle is standard. Enquire in advance about the restaurant's policy on BYO, as some may have a very high charge per bottle (R50+), limit the number of bottles or simply not allow it at all. Restaurants will not allow you to bring your own bottle if they have that particular wine on their list.

Beautiful views – Fraai Uitzicht welcomes visitors to a tranquil setting

Klein Karoo hospitality – Quiant architecture at the Port Wine house, Calitzdorp

ACCOMMODATION IN SOUTH AFRICA

Staying in the Western Cape is a pleasurable experience, amidst towering mountains, crystal clear rivers and lush green vineyards. Winelands towns offer a wealth of accommodation, from romantic cottages to luxury boutique hotels, family rooms to rustic getaways.

B&B and Guest Houses – Generally small establishments with only a few rooms. Offer accommodation with breakfast included. These often have the best location and romantic appeal, in blossoming garden settings, between vibrant rows of vines or pitched high on mountain slopes with spectacular views.

Hotels – Generally larger establishments, accommodating larger groups such as families. Breakfast is provided at an additional cost. These are often located conveniently, in or near the town centre or with easy road access thereto.

Reservations – Make a reservation in advance, by telephone, email of fax. Be sure that you receive written confirmation. Most establishments require a deposit which can be paid bye electronic bank transfer or credit card.

Service fee – Required at luxury establishments.

Services – The establishments can inform you about the best local services and products. Ask your host for a reference or visit your local tourist information centre. The information centre is a good place to meet and plan excursions.

Facilities – Numerous establishments have extended facilities. These include spas where luxury treatments made from vine products indulge the senses, sporting facilities such as golf courses or polo fields, or even cooking courses in using local produce together with local wines.

Weddings – A Winelands wedding captures the imagination: a fusion of sensitively restored heritage and contemporary luxury in the magnificent surrounds of natural beauty. While the lush green vineyards in summer speak of the promised harvest, autumn enfolds the Winelands in tranquil shades of red and gold – the perfect backdrop for glorious wedding photography. Many wineries offer venues for both the ceremony and reception. Enquire about using a garden or space next to a vineyard as a lovely, natural background in summer. In winter, the dedicated venues, or even a small maturation cellar with old wine barrels, combine timeless elegance with rustic charm.

Quiet escape – The luxurious hotel at Steenberg

Theraputic stay – Enjoy a relaxing treatment at Constantia Uitsig's spa

Vineyard cottages – Waking up amongst the vines at Manley

Wine dictionary

Accessible, approachable: Flavours are in harmony, wine is ready to drink.

Acid, acetic: Caused by acetic acid bacteria, has a vinegar taste.

Acid, lactic: Produced from malic acid by malolactic bacteria during malolactic fermentation. Gentler tasting acid, also found in milk.

Acid, malic: Naturally occurring in grapes, acidic taste.

Wine Cellar – Gravitational flow transfers the wine from tanks to barrels for maturation

Acid, tartaric: Naturally occurring in grapes, very strong acidic taste. Excess may result in harmless crystals forming in bottled wine, aesthetically undesired.

Acid, volatile: Caused by bacterial spoilage in wine, imparts a vinegar smell.

Acidity: Naturally occurring chemical compound in grapes, forms backbone and gives structure to wine. Wines with good acidity are described as crisp, fresh and alive. Two main acids are malic and tartaric. In South Africa adding certain acids (which occur naturally in grapes) is allowed because of the hot climate.

Aftertaste: The lasting flavours and impressions of a wine; its persistence.

Aging, barrel: Aging wine in barrel causes extraction of flavour compounds from wood – woody, smoky, cigar box, meaty, vanilla, toast. Adds to complexity and quality of wine. Also allows very slow oxidation, resulting in stable colour and flavour.

Aging, bottle: Development of flavours / aromas in bottle. Positive – softening of tannins and greenness, wine becomes more integrated. White wines become less acidic and more syrupy. Negative – over-aging leads to wine going stale.

Alcohol: Produced by yeasts from grape sugar. Gives fullness, richness and sweetness to wine and acts as a preservative. Too much alcohol gives a burning sensation. Measured in volume of total liquid.

Aroma: The fragrance or smell of wine. Aromatics belong to various chemical families classified according to their volatility. Mostly created by a series of closely related chemical substances rather than a single substance being solely responsible for a particular flavour or aroma.

Astringent: A physical characteristic of wine, mouth-puckering sensation caused by tannins. Also closely related to bitterness.

Backbone: A wine with structure, not flabby or insipid. See Acid, Tannin.

Baked: Hot, earthy character associated with overripe grapes.

Balance: The harmony between the major wine components – acid, alcohol, sugar, tannins, wood and fruit. A definite quality indicator.

Balling / brix: Measurements of sugar levels in grapes, expressed as degrees. Used to determine ripeness for harvesting.

Barrel: A wooden wine container made from oak. Various sizes: 225 l, 300 l, 500 l and larger. Most popular is French and American oak. Hungarian oak is gaining popularity because of reduced cost.

Barrel fermentation – An S-shaped cap allows CO$_2$ gas to escape while preventing oxidation during barrel fermentation

Roaming ducks – Ducks serve as a biological pest control of snails in the vineyards (Shannon Vineyards)

Barrel fermentation: Fermentation in oak barrel. Gives greater complexity due to integration of extracts from wood. Mostly used for full-bodied white wines – Chardonnay, Chenin Blanc, Sémillon and Viognier.

Bâttonage: Stirring of yeast lees in the storage container, usually wooden barrels. Intensifies butter and creamy flavours, softens acidity. Very labour intensive, increases price.

Bead, mousse: The bubbles in sparkling wine. A very fine, long-lasting bead is most desirable.

Berg: South African English for mountain or hill, e.g. Simonsberg is Simons Mountain.

Big: Expansive in the mouth, weighty, full-bodied, as a result of high alcohol or fruit concentration.

Biodynamic: See Organic.

Bite / grip: Physical sensation imparted by tannins and acids (and alcohol in fortified wines); important in young wines for aging.

Bitterness: A taste sensed on the finish (back area of mouth). Slight bitterness may be related to cultivar and is acceptable; too much is unpleasant and regarded as a winemaking fault.

Blanc de Blanc: Literally 'white from white'; a white wine made from 100% Chardonnay.

Blanc de Noir: Literally 'white from black'; a white wine made from red-skinned grapes with only the slightest of colour tinge imparted by the grape skins.

Blend: A wine made from two or more different grape varieties, vintages, vineyards or containers. Used to bring out attributes of all components, as well as erasing possible weaknesses in a particular component.

Bloom: (1) Flowering of grape vines; (2) The natural wax covering found on grape skins, protects against diseases.

Blend – Eben Sadie tasting each barrel to select the final blend

White Egret – Many birds species form part of the vineyards' biodiversity

Shale soils – The stony soils of Walker Bay are ideal for vine cultivation (Gabriëlskloof)

Body: Sensation of fullness on the palate. Related to alcohol, tannins and concentration.

Botrytis cinerea: A fungus that attacks ripe grapes, depleting water from berries and concentrating sugar and other compounds. Benevolent form results in 'noble rot' responsible for great sweet wines; aggressive form results in loss of crop.

Bottle age: Positively describes development of aromas/flavours (complexity) as wine moves to maturity, is much valued attribute in fine wines. Negatively, excessive bottle age results in a wine with stale or even off odours.

Bottle shock: A state of 'flavourlessness' noticeable in wine directly after bottling. Most fruit flavours disappear; acid and alcohol stands out. Can last up to a few months. Most wines recover completely with rest.

Bottles: The 750 ml (75 cl) bottle is the most widely used size container for wine; it is by no means the only one. Smaller bottles (375 & 500 ml) are popular with restaurants and airlines, and larger sizes are prized by collectors because of their novelty value and/or their tendency to promote slower wine aging.

Butter: Flavour and aroma associated with barrel-fermented white wines. A rich, creamy smoothness.

Canopy: The leaves and shoots on a vine plant.

Cap: Fermenting (red) wine produces carbon dioxide and pushes grape skins to the surface, forming a cap.

Carbon dioxide (CO_2): Odourless, colourless gas resulting from alcoholic fermentation.

Carbonic maceration or *maceration carbonique*: Fermentation method without crushing the grapes. Whole clusters with stalks are put into closed vat; intracellular fermentation occurs within the grape berries, which then burst.

Chaptalisation: French term for addition of sugar to grape must in order to raise alcohol levels. Not permitted in South Africa.

Charmat: Method of sparkling wine production in sealed tanks under pressure. An easier and cheaper alternative to bottle fermentation.

Traditional closures – Muselet, champagne cork, constituted cork, natural cork, natural cork with wax cover

Clarify: Winemaking operation which removes lees (dead yeast cells, fragments of grape skins and pulp, pips, etc.) from juice or wine. May result in slight loss of flavour.

Classic: Showing characteristics of the classic wine styles of Bordeaux, Burgundy, etc.; usually implying balance, elegance and subtlety.

Clone: A sub-group of genetically identical plants within a particular variety, propagated from a single vine to perpetuate its selected or special characteristics.

Coarse: Rough, unbalanced tannins, acid, alcohol or oak characters.

Cold ferment: Relative term; applied to fermentation of mainly white wines in temperature-controlled tanks, it refers to a temperature between 13 – 16°C. The benefits, especially important in a warm country, include conserving the primary fruit aromas and ensuring fermentation is carried out steadily and thoroughly.

Cold maceration / cold soak: Red winemaking method carried out prior to fermentation. Skins and juice are held, for a few days, at a sufficiently cool temperature to prevent fermentation. This extracts more favourable colour and aromas than after fermentation.

Cold stabilisation: Keeping a wine at -4°C for

Recycled barrels – Barrel heads become an interesting floor inlay at Luddite

Tartaric acid – High natural acidity may lead to crystal formation in the wine if it is not cold stabilised

a week or more to precipitate tartaric acid and 'clean up' the wine, preventing later formation of (harmless) tartrate crystals in bottle. Some winemakers believe this process damages flavour and prefer to avoid it.

Complex: A wine with multiple flavour levels from the vineyards, winemaking techniques and bottle development. A quality indicator.

Concentration: See Intensity.

Cork: Wine bottle stopper made from bark of cork tree. A natural product. Defects may result in tainted wine.

Corked: A faulty wine, smelling mouldy, dusty and of wet cardboard. Caused by yeast, fungal or bacterial infections producing chemical compound TCA (trichloranisole, sulphur and chlorine). TCA diminishes the fruit character of wine, substituting a damp, mouldy smell. Wine must be smelled, not the cork. In a restaurant, a corked wine should be rejected and replaced immediately.

Creamy: A silky, buttery feel and texture, not literally creamy.

Crisp: refers to acidity. Positive: fresh, clean. Negative: too tart, sharp.

Crushing: Breaking open grape berries to facilitate fermentation of juice.

Cultivars: Grape varieties.

Dense: Having intense texture, flavour-packed.

Deposits: (also sediment or crust) Tasteless and harmless tartrates, acid crystals or tannin in older red wines. Evidence that wine has not been harshly fined, filtered or cold stabilised.

Depth: Having many layers, intense.

Destemming: Removing grape berries from their stalks before fermentation to avoid extraction of harsh (green) tannins.

Dosage: Sugar added to *Méthode Champenoise* or *Méthode Cap Classique* wines after second fermentation. Also the sugar added to sparkling wine after the second fermentation.

Dry: In fermented wine, all sugar is converted to alcohol. See Residual sugar.

Dry-land cultivation: Cultivation of vines with rain as main water supply. Supplementary irrigation may be used in extremely hot or dry conditions to prevent damage to vines.

Duplex: Layered soil, generally sand over clay.

Earthy: Wine with soil-derived flavour, mineral, damp, mushroom.

Easy: Undemanding wine, ready to drink.

Elegant: Stylish and refined.

Entry / attack: Sensation as wine enters the mouth. (Sweetness, florals and fruit flavours.)

Esters: Natural chemical compound responsible for floral aromas in wine.

Expressed g/l: An indication of substance and quality: 18 g/l is low; above 23 g/l for white wine is significant; a full-bodied red wine would be above 30 g/l.

Extract: Sum of all solids in wine – tannins, sugar, acids, glycerine, minerals, pigments, etc.

Fat: Big, full in the mouth, but not excessive.

Fermentation, alcoholic: Biochemical conversion of sugar to alcohol and carbon dioxide by yeast. Enhances flavour by (1) releasing flavours from their sugar-linked precursors, and (2) by forming new flavour compounds from chemical building blocks existing in juice.

Fermentation, malolactic: Biochemical

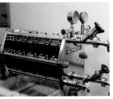

Filter – Clearing of wine to remove suspended solids

A gentleman's sport – The annual polo day at Val de Vie is a highlight on the sporting and social calenders

conversion of malic acid to lactic acid by bacteria. Results in softer / reduced acidity and a more rounded, mellow flavour.

Fermentation, natural / spontaneous: Alcoholic fermentation without addition of yeast. Naturally occurring yeast on equipment populates juice when contact occurs. Potentially risky due to high temperatures. Off-flavours may occur.

Fermentation, stuck: Unfinished fermentation resulting in higher than normal residual sugar, due to yeast death, possibly on sensitivity to excessive alcohol. High potential for spoilage.

Filtration: Method of clearing wine by passing liquid through membranes or cellulose pads to remove suspended solids, yeast or bacteria. Filtration may result in reduction of wine flavour and aroma, therefore the shift to unfiltered wines. Sweet wines must be filtered to remove yeast to prevent refermentation, pressure build-up and possible bottle explosion.

Finesse: Description of polished, balanced wine.

Fining: Traditional method of clearing wine. Insoluble substances bind with wine components and precipitate out so that wine can be filtered clean. Used to reduce tannins or unstable proteins.

Finish / aftertaste: The lingering flavours of wine on the palate after swallowing – its persistence. Should be pleasant. A long finish is a quality indicator.

Firm: Compact, has good backbone.

Flabby: Wine lacking structure, backbone, result of too little acid.

Flat: Characterless, unexciting, lacks acid. Or bubbly which has lost its fizz.

Fleshy: Very positive, meaning a wine is well

Historic road – The main road of Tulbagh is lined with historic treasures

fleshed out with texture and grape flavours.
Floral: Aromas and tastes with floral aspect, as
opposed to fruity. Desirable in fine white wines.
Forward: Opposite of a shy wine.
Pronounced flavours and aromas.
Free-run: Juice obtained from crushed
grapes before pressure is applied. This
juice is purest and most aromatic.
Fresh: Refers to acidity. Lively, young.
A sweet wine without sufficient acid
will cloy; enough acid and taste is
fresh and uncloying.

*Rustic charm – Annadale's wine tasting
room hosts a new season's swallows*

Fruity: Aroma and flavour
characters of various fruits, many associated with
specific grape varieties. Concentration of fruit
characters is an essential quality for fine wines.
Full: High in alcohol and extract.
Gamey: Flavours of game meat,
savoury; in red wines.
Garage wine / garagiste: Generic
term for wine made in minuscule
quantities, sometimes literally in a
garage; producer is called a garagiste.
Glycerol: Product of alcoholic
fermentation. Results in oily, mouth-
filling character, supports sweetness.
Leaves 'legs' in an agitated glass.

*In training – A young vine grows
upright in the rocky soil, before being
tained on the cordon wire*

Gravelly: Minerally, earthy quality; also firm
texture.
Green: Unripe, tannic and hard. Can refer to
wine with excessive acid, unripe
characters.
Grip: Firm on palate and finish.
Acid, tannin and alcohol are
contributors.
Heady: Usually refers to the smell of
a wine. High in alcohol; intense.
Herbaceous: Grassy, hay-like
character. May indicate unripe grapes.

*Springbok – South Africa's national
deer up close at Bon Cap. Children
are welcome to feed the animals*

Honey: Honey and/or beeswax flavours are
typical of sweet-style wines, Noble Late Harvest
or straw wines. Also an indicator of bottle age,
maturity.

Hot: Burning sensation caused by excess
alcohol.
Intensity: Strong character, good expression of
flavours. Not flabby.
Lean: Thin, lacking fruit flavours and
body.
Lees: Sediment that occurs during
winemaking or bottle aging, dead
yeast cells with grape skins and other
solid matter remaining with wine
in tank/barrel (or bottle for *méthode
champenoise* sparkling wines) after
fermentation. May be used to add
flavour and complexity by allowing contact time
with wine (*sur lie* – on its lees).
Length: Enduring, the wine flavour lingers on
palate long after swallowing.
Light: Wines with less than 10% Alc.
by Vol.
Lively: Bouncy, fresh flavours.
Maceration, carbonic: Method
of fermentation using whole
(uncrushed) berries. Grapes are
placed in a closed fermenter with
carbon dioxide gas. Fermentation
occurs within berries, which then
burst. Light-styled wines relating
to Beaujolais Nouveau (low in alcohol and
concentration).
Maceration, cold: Winemaking method used
mainly for red grapes prior to
alcoholic fermentation. Crushed
grapes (skins and juice) are held
at sufficiently cool temperatures
to prevent fermentation for a
few hours to a few days. Used
for extraction of grape varietal
flavours.
Maderised: Oxidised and flat;
colour is often brownish. Over-mature.
Maturation: Aging properties are closely related
to tannin and/or fixed acid content of a wine. A
relatively full red wine with tannin has lasting

power. With age, it may develop complexity, subtlety and smooth mellowness. Lighter wines with lower tannins are drinkable sooner but probably will not reach the same level of complexity. A number of Cape whites, especially Chardonnays and Rieslings, mature well over several years, but most are best drunk young (18 months).

Meaty: Savoury, also aroma of raw meat. Frequent in Shiraz and Merlot.

Aeration – Pump-over of red wine at Jordan

Méthode Cap Classique (MCC): South African term as alternative to the word Champagne. Sparkling wines produced by bottle fermentation.

Méthode Champenoise: Classic method of making sparkling wine by inducing fermentation in bottles.

Micro-oxygenation: Relatively new technique (1990) enabling introduction of precise, controlled doses of oxygen to must/wine. Advocates claim softer tannins, more stable colours and other advantages.

Waiting for maturity – Bottles ageing at Fraai Uitzicht.

Mousse: Fizz in sparkling wines; refers also to quality, size and effervescence of the bubbles.

Mouthfeel: Sensations experienced in the mouth when tasting (body, heat and weight).

Muselet: Wire muzzle keeping a sparkling wine cork secured.

Must: Skins, juice and pulp of crushed berries may contain whole berries or bunches. Red wine is fermented as must including grape skins, white wine as juice only.

Neutral: Wine that has no expressive flavour.

New World: Accessible, bold wines; expressive fruit, wooding and alcohol. Geographically refers to the Americas, South Africa, Australia and New Zealand.

Grape skin – While the flesh contains the flavours, the grape skin contains the colour molecules

Oak: Main source of wood used to make barrels, limited quantities of cherry or other woods are used. Flavours imparted are vanilla, spice, char, wood smoke, etc. Oak balanced by fruit in young wines may lessen with age, but over-oaked young wines will become over-oaked old wines. See Barrel.

Oak chips / staves: Used in either older barrels or stainless steel tanks. Still frowned on by some purists, the 'additives' approximate the flavour effects of a new barrel, far more cheaply, more easily handled.

Oenology: The study of winemaking.

Old World: Subtle wine, less oak and alcohol, more varied and vinous. Geographically refers to Europe.

Organic viticulture / winemaking: Increasingly popular alternative to 'conventional' or 'industrialised' winegrowing, emphasising natural and sustainable farming methods and cellar techniques. A variant is biodynamic viticulture, influenced by anthroposophy, focused on improving wine quality through harmony with nature and its rhythms.

Oxidation: Chemical process requiring oxygen. Changes due to exposure to air: uncontrolled results in spoilt wines, vinegar taste; controlled (in barrels) results in stabilisation of flavour and colour, desirable development of wine.

Palate: Combination of flavour, taste and texture of a wine.

Pebbly: See Gravelly.

pH: Measurement of hydrogen in wine, indicating acidity. Has no unit. Used in determining ripeness of grapes for harvest. Optimum level for juice and wine is between 3,1 and 3,4.

Porty: Heavy, over-ripe, stewed; a negative in unfortified wine.

Pump over: Mixing of fermenting juice and berries by removal and reintroduction of juice.

Punch down: Manual mixing of fermenting juice and berries.

Racking: Drawing or pumping wine from one container to another, to leave behind the deposit or lees.

Reductive: Without exposure to oxygen. Wine in an unevolved, unoxidised state is said to be 'reductive'; usually with a tight, sometimes unyielding character. The absence of air (in a bottled wine) or the presence of substantial sulphur dioxide (anti-oxidant) levels, will inhibit both oxidation and reduction processes, which are linked and complementary.

Residual sugar (RS): Unfermented sugar remaining in wine after alcoholic fermentation.

Rich: Flavourful, intense, generous. Not necessarily sweet.

Robust: Full-bodied, but not aggressive.

Rough: Unbalanced tannins or alcohol, not elegant. Also unripe characters.

Round: Well balanced, smooth, integrated; without jagged edges.

Sales (off-trade): Wine sold to be consumed at a later stage, e.g. supermarkets, shops, wholesalers and wine merchants.

Sales (on-trade): Wine sold where it is consumed on premises, e.g. restaurant.

Sharp / tart: High in acidity, usually unbalanced. But occasionally a sharp, fresh wine is refreshing.

Short: Insubstantial wine, leaving little impression.

Veraison – The grape berries start to change colour as they ripen

Pruning – The final cut to prune the spur requires skill and a trained eye

Sémillon – Grapes drying on straw mats for sweet wine production at La Petite Ferme

Simple: One-dimensional or no flavour excitement.

Skin contact: After crushing and de-stemming, white grapes may be left for a period with the juice, remaining in contact with skins (before being moved into the press, from which the grape juice is squeezed). Some winemakers believe the colours and flavours in and under the grape skins should be maximised in this way; others believe extended (or any) contact can lead to coarseness, even bitterness.

Sommelier: A wine waiter, assisting guests to select a wine to match their food.

Stabilisation: Process in which chemical components achieve a balance, stable or unchanging arrangement.

Stabilisation, cold: Wine-clearing method, prevents crystal formation after bottling. Crystal formation induced by chilling wine and filtering clear liquid off the crystals. See Acid, Tartaric.

Stalky: Unripe, bitter, stemmy.

Stewed: Over-ripe, cooked fruit.

Structure: Refers to wine's composition (acid, tannin, alcohol) in relation to its aging ability; if a wine is deemed to have 'the structure to age', it suggests these principal chemicals are in place.

Sulphur: Chemical compound, preservative. Used in vineyards to prevent spread of disease, as additive in wine to prevent oxidation and browning. Direct exposure to sulphur may cause difficulty in breathing.

Supple: Very desirable (not necessarily subtle), yielding, refined texture and flavours. See Mouthfeel.

Tannins: Astringent and bitter compounds found in grapes and oak, a natural preservative. Oxidises slowly and promotes aging. Excessive tannins create harsh, aggressive wines.

Over time, tannins combine with pigments to stabilise colour. Condensation reduces the astringency.

Terpenes: Natural grape compounds giving strong floral aromas, important in Riesling, Gewürztraminer and Muscats.

Terroir: The interplay of natural elements that make up the environment where vines grow: soil, climate, slope, aspect, altitude. Emphasises the importance and uniqueness of a wine from a specific site, the expression of the wine's origin.

Transport – Whole bunches gently make their way to the cellar

Texture: Tactile sensation in the mouth: hard, acidic, coarse and alcoholic; or: smooth, velvety, 'warm'.

Toasty: Often used for barrel-fermented and aged wines showing a pleasant biscuity, charry character.

Vegetal: Grassy, leafy, herby – in contrast to fruity, flowery, oaky. Overdone, a negative character.

Veraison: Ripening stage indicated by colour change in grape berries.

Selected dry yeast – A yeast variety is chosen for a specific trait, such as increased glycerol production

Vin (de) Paillé: 'Strawed wine'. Generally a sweet wine, made from grapes dried between straw lattices which reduces water content in grapes and concentrates flavour components.

Vines: Bush vine – a vine plant grown in a goblet shape, without the support of a wire or wooden trellis. Trellised vine – a vine trained on a trellis system (wire, wood, etc.) to offer protection against wind, with spreading leaves for greater sun exposure to facilitate easy harvesting of grapes.

Vineyard: A plantation of grape-bearing vine plants, grown mainly for winemaking, but also to produce raisins, table grapes and non-alcoholic grape juice. The science, practice and study of vineyard cultivation are collectively

Wine cellar – Luxury hotels have well-appointed wine cellars and regular guests can even have their own section, stocked with local wines (Cape Grace Hotel)

known as viticulture.

Virus: A collection of vine diseases causing many problems, negatively affecting wine quality and possibly threatening the vine's life.

Volatile acid (VA): An acidity which is volatile, e.g. acetic acid. A high reading indicates a wine is prone to spoilage. Recognised at high levels by a sharp, 'hot', vinegary smell. In SA, most wines must by law be below 1,2 g/l of VA; in practice, the majority are well below 1 g/l.

Watery: Thin, diluted wine resulting from (1) overproducing vines, (2) very young vines, or (3) a winemaking mistake. Not to be confused with a light-bodied wine, which is a particular style that retains elegance and balance.

Whole-bunch pressing: Age-old process of placing whole bunches directly in the press and gently exerting pressure. Seen by advocates to yield fresher, cleaner must, and wine lower in polyphenols which, in excess, tend to age wines faster and render them coarser.

Yeast: Single cell micro-organisms responsible for conversion of sugar to alcohol in winemaking.

Yeast, natural / wild: Yeast populations present in vineyards, grapes and wineries. Frequently participate in early stages of fermentation due to low levels of alcohol and sulphur. May be responsible for entire fermentation under special circumstances.

Yeast, selected / cultured / dry: Yeast produced in mass, sold in freeze-dried format.

Yeasty: Pleasant smell of warm bread or yeast, frequent in barrel-fermented white wines, lees-aged wines and MCC sparkling wines.

Index

Page references in **bold** indicate where you can find a definition or explanation of key terms. Page references in *italics* indicate where you can find maps or illustrations.

Pinot Noir grapes – A mosaic depicting the noble red grape of sparkling wine

Protea – Natural beauty along the roads in the Hemel-en-Aarde Pocket

Expectation – Waiting for the first wine from the press

*Cement fermenter – A 'man-hole' door at
the front of the cement fermenter to ease
removal of grapes (Val de Vie)*

*Eating well – The herb garden of Le
Quartier Français offers seasonal freshness*

*Beauty of nature – An abundance of wild
flowers, bloom in spring in the Darling area*

Crushing – *Grapes off-loaded into the crusher and destemmer at Zevenwacht*

Duck parade – *Indian runner ducks returning to their pens at Vergenoegd, after a day of foraging in the vineyards*

Bush vine – *Old bush vines are prized for their conncentration and make a fine logo for Darling Cellars*

Elegant design – The tasting room of Rustenberg epitomises elegance with strong lines and warm lighting

Retail therapy – Shopping for wine gifts at Constantia Uitsig

Spring – The new growth season brings life to the vineyards and surrounding areas

Author's note

The thirst for knowledge has a very special meaning for wine lovers – we acquire this knowledge directly by tasting and drinking wine. We also deepen and broaden our experience by reading about and travelling to various wine regions of the world. In these experiences, fine wine reveals its two secrets to us: the place of its birth and an artisan's craft.

Although the grape variety is one of the most important factors in the flavour profile of any wine, the *terroir* sets the initial framework for a wine of exceptional quality. Combined with this, is the vital role of the winemaker in the alchemy that transforms a simple fruit into a mystical drink that touches our emotions and lingers for decades in the memory.

This book is a true labour of love – each page vibrates with first-hand experience blended with a passion for fine wines. The aim of the Wine Pockets system is to emphasi the importance of terroir, to create a richer experience by exploring these unique cultivation areas and to understand the processes employed by viticulturists and winemakers.

I hope this Guide will provide you with new paths through the exciting labyrinth of fine South African wines, and that you will enjoy reading it as much as I have enjoyed researching and writing it.

Wishing you joyful wine memories.

Elmari Swart M.Sc. Oenology

Globally recognised as having ideal and distinct conditions for creating wines of particular identity, South African wines are instilled with a unique "sense of place". For the true artist of wine the ultimate reward lies in marrying the place with the grape.

Randall Grahm defined a wine terroir as *"somewhere-ness"*, a concept linked to the beauty of the particular. Just as the beauty in any product or service of distinction, speaks to the individual with so much elegance, so does a particular great *terroir wine*, a label which certainly befits South African Wines.

Grahm went on to say: "Distinctive wines, has a calling card, a quality of expressiveness that provokes a sense of recognition whether or not the consumer

has ever experienced it". This signature trade presents a challenge to the wine enthusiast, to have a richer wine experience by exploring such area and country differences.

The book is a tribute to the local wine makers who acted as ground breakers and visionaries. They realised that the history of a region, the tradition of the farm, the ambition and dedication of hands which laid down the parameters, together with *terroir* elements, must combine to make great wine.

It was Dave De Simone who suggested that wines with distinctive *terroir* are always worth seeking. I trust that the reader will discover this truth too.

Izak Smit

Emptying out – Cellar workers remove grape skins from an open fermenter at Kanonkop

Eagle encounters – Get up close and personal with a variety of birds of prey at Spier's education program

Nature's call – The cool ocean breeze funneling into the Hemel-en-Aarde Valley, as seen from Creation Wines

247

Acknowledgements

Firstly, my heartfelt thanks to the subject experts who acted as contributors to this publication, for their invaluable contribution in sharing their knowledge, experience and passion for South African wine.

Main Contributors
Dawid Saayman, your effort as chief contributor in setting out the Pockets as well as on the subject of South African *terroir* is truly invaluable. Thank you for the authoritative foreword to this book. **Prof. Eben Archer**, thank you for providing information on South African viticulture for this title. I am honoured to have had you and Dawid as my teachers. The masterful ability with which you both convey your endless passion and deep knowledge of the soil and the vines continues to be my inspiration. **Eben Sadie**, thank you for pushing the boundries of winemaking and showing us how to raise the bar, and for your most insightful foreword to this book. **Jaap Scholten**, thank you for your succinct words on Wine and Health, Wine buying tips, Food and Wine pairing and Wine and Chocolate; and for the guidelines on wine storage and serving temperatures.

Additional Contributors
Loftie Ellis, Louis Nel, Charl Theron, Dr Andy Roediger, Cathy van Zyl (MW), Tanja Beutler, Clive Torr (CWM).

Editorial
A great thank you to my editor, **Dr Harry Stephan**, for his fervent enthusiasm for and meticulous editing of this publication.

Cartography
To **John Hall**, thank you for translating my ideas and scribbles into the magnificent maps presented in this book.

Production
A very big thank you to the fantastic production team: proofreader **Rhonda Crouse**, illustrator **Daniel Botha**, designer **Catherine Coetzer** and indexer **Marlene Rose**. A special word of thanks to pre-press manager **Robert Wong** for his dedicated attention to this project.

South African Wine Industry
To **The South African Brandy Foundation** and the participating wineries who sponsored profiles to represent the local industry, thank you for your continued support in our research on *terroir* and the opportunity to photograph your properties.

Photography
All commissioned images © Jaap Scholten. For further information contact www.cheviot-publishing.com or jaap@scholten.co.za.

Additional Photography
The publisher would like to thank the following individuals, companies and image libraries for permission to reproduce their photographs:

Alex Scholten 76t, 76bl. Almenkerk 20bl, 37t. Aquarium V&A Waterfront 137b. Bellevue 80t. Benguela Cove 130m. Bouchard Finlayson 125b, 134m, 134bl, 134br, 135t. Blaauwklippen 86m, 89tr, 89bl. Bon Cap 238m. Boschrivier 138m. Cape Leopard Trust 119m. Chris & Monique Fallows 138t. Carl-Johann Swart 17b, 137t, 137m, 226m. Company of Wine People 22t. Constantia Glen 25b. Constantia Uitsig 233bl. Creation Wines 131t, 136m, 246r. D'Aria 57m. Darling Cellars 38br, 163t, 165b, 243r, 244r. De Morgenzon 71tl. Diemersdal 56mr. Elmari Swart 22b, 37br, 42b, 54m, 57b, 77t, 90bl, 90br, 96b, 100b, 115t, 120m, 140m, 141b, 146b, 153t, 167t, 175t, 175m, 177t, 178t, 171all, 172all, 174b, 187t, 188b, 227b, 232bl, 234t, 234m, 235m, 237b, 238m, 239m, 245l, 246r, 247m, 251m, 251r. Fraai Uitzicht 170m, 174m. Glenwood 143t, 248l. Hermanuspieterfontein 131m. Jacques Smit180t. Jonkershoek fly-fishing 119t. Jordan Estate 69t, 69b, 71ml, 71mr, 72b, 239t, 248r. Kleine Zalze 92all. Knorhoek 107m. L'Ormarins 188t, 249l. Longridge 100b. La Motte 228b. Le Quartier Français 142. Lomond 182all. Luddite 128t, 236m. Manley 233br, 248m. Menanteau Swart 80b, 94m, 112m, 216t, 249m, 249r. Overgaauw 71tr. Paul Scholten 16b, 230m, 246m. Piep Scholten 73m. Prof. Piet Goussard 39tr, 39mr, 65all, 83all, 130bl, 130m, 130br, 210all, 211all, 212 all, 213all. Rainbow's End 115b. Rustenberg 107t, 245l. SA Brandy Route 190all, 191all, 192bl. Sand at the Plettenberg 220m, 221m, 247r. Saxenburg 62b, 67all. Shannon Vineyards 120t, 122t, 234b. Spier 77ml. Steenberg 226t. Stephan Smith 44t. Sumaridge 136b. Strandveld 180b.Val de Vie 149t, 200t, 237m, 243l. Vergelegen 104t, 105b. Vergenoegd 244m. Vriesenhof 93m. Waterford 93b, 224 & 225, 247l. Waterkloof 102t, m, 106all.   (t=top, b=bottom, r=right, l=left, m=middle, tr=top right, tl=top left, mr=middle right, ml=middle left, br=bottom right, bl=bottom left)

Every effort has been made to trace the copyright holders. We apologise in for any unintentional omissions. We would be pleased to insert acknowledgements in any subsequent edition of this publication.

Herbal wellbeing – Harvesting organic lavender at Waterford Estate

Four seasons – The wine farm's four seasonal faces depicted in a magnificent batik at Klein Constantia

Delicate desserts – A mouthwatering collection of desserts at Cellars Hohenort in Constantia

Thank you to the **Cheviot Publishing office** and in particular **Ms Leslé Davids** for her tremendous enthusiasm and invaluable contribution in collecting and collating relevant data for this project.

Special Assistance

Illustrations: Cheviot Publishing would like to thank Dawid Saayman for his kind permission to reproduce his illustration on page 27. Thanks to The Biodiveristy and Wine Initiative for permission to reproduce thier logo on page 21.

Copyright © 2009 Wine Serving Temperature Guidelines, page 206, and Wine Storage Temperature Guidelines, page 216: Jaap Scholten.

Copyright © 2009 Wine and Health (page 36), Wine buying tips (page 217), Food and Wine pairing (page 220) and Wine and Chocolate (page 222): Jaap Scholten.

Statistical data: The data used in Chapter 1 was provided by the South African Wine Industry Information & Systems (SAWIS), unless otherwise indicated. SAWIS, +27 (0)21 807 5703, www.sawis.co.za

Aerial phototography: Birdmen Paragliding facilitated the aerial photography shoot over Meerendal Estate. www.birdmen.co.za.

Food photography: Thank you to La Petite Ferme (Franschhoek) and The Codfather (Cape Town) who allowed our cameras to roam free in their kitchens.

Linguistic advice: Prof Johan Smuts and Dr Ria Smuts.

A special word of thanks to the following individuals and companies for their kind assistance in supplying chemicals, corks, wood products, glassware and food for photography purposes:

Columbit Industries, www.columbit.biz; Protea Chemicals, www.proteachemicals.co.za; FS Smit Coopers, www.fssmitco.co.za; African Cork supplies, www.africancork.co.za; Innovatra (Zork Closure), www.innovatra.com; Michael Schoeman, Aroma Liquors Constantia, T +27 (0)21 794 3143, www.riedel.com, who supplied Riedel decanters and Champagne glasses for the studio shoot; Laura Webb, JMC Inspiring brands, www.jmc.co.za, for information on the pairing of chocolate and wine as well as supplying us with Lindt Chocolate for photography purposes.

MASTER SWISS CHOCOLATIER
SINCE 1845

Cheviot Publishing acknowledges, with deep gratitude, the following individuals and companies for their kind assistance: Melody Botha, Breedekloof Wine & Tourism, T +27 (0)23 349 1791, www.breedekloof.com, for information on the Breedekloof *terroir.* Jean-Pierre Colmant, Colmant Cap Classique, T +27 (0)21 876 4348, www.colmant.co.za, for information on MCC production. Peter Finlayson, Bouchard Finlayson, T +27 (0)28 312 3515, www.bouchardfinlayson.co.za, for reviewing the *terroir* description on the Walker Bay Area and its Pockets. Isabel Habits (Distell) for reviewing and commenting on the copy on the new Pockets. Stephan Smith, Spherical Imagery, T 083 765 3252, www.sphericalimagery.com, for permission to reproduce his image of Cape Point Vineyards. The Cape Leopard Trust for permission to reproduce their image of the Cape Leopard, Tel: +27 (0)27 482 9923, www.capeleopard.org.za

Additional resources

Wine Buying tips section: *Decanter* magazine, August 2007
Resources for Wine and Health section: *South African Medical Journal*, September 2005, vol. 95, no. 9; *Wine Spectator*, 31 May 2009; *Wynboer*, June 2001; *Wynboer*, July 2006

To my family and friends, your love and support carried me through this project. Thank you for helping out in the Cheviot Winery cellar and (unknowingly) posing as models: Alex Scholten; Paul Scholten; Boudewijn and Anneke Scholten; Beverly and Andrew Gericke; Mark, Karin and Mia Johns; Carl-Johann and Madeleine Swart; Menanteau Swart. And thanks for picking up the cameras while I was writing ...

To my husband, **Jaap Scholten**, your dedication to this project was, yet again, limitless in every aspect, from inception to its fulfilment. Thank you for your faith in me which continues to give me the freedom to live my dream. Thank you for sharing in this dream and for being my light.

Elmari Swart,
Cheviot Publishing

Cover front: Vineyard rows following the contours in Franschhoek (main), Barrel cellar at Vergelegen (bl), Hand harvesting of Pinot Noir at Meerlust (bm), Cheetah encounter at Spier (br, Alex Scholten)
Cover back (top to bottom): Ladybird on Shiraz grapes at the Cheviot Winery (main), Gravelly soil at Iona, Hemel-en-Aarde Valley Pocket map, Blind tasting, Icons for winery profile summary

Page 1: **Vitis vinefera** – Vine flowers give birth to a new harvest
Page 2, 3: **Constantia Valley** – Early morning light over South Africa's oldest wine region

Crossing the river – *Observe the towering mountain surrounds while making your way to Glenwood's tasting room*

Buffet – *Eat the healthy way at Manley Wine Lodge*

Chameleon – *The icon of Jordan Wines is frequently spotted in the greenery*

Notes

Meticulous care *– Vineyards are mananged by caring and experienced staff at L'Ormarins*

Olive oil *– Experience the subtle flavours of cold-pressed olive oil at Vrede en Lust*

Wine and chocolate *– The ultimate flavour and texture combination at Waterford*

The Dove

The Griffin

The Frieze

The ornate friezes which crown the cellar entrance tell the picturesque and richly textured story behind the impeccably pedigreed estate of Plaisir de Merle

Grapes aboard – *Grapes are taken from the vineyard directly to the cellar for vinification*

Hillcrest Berry Orchards – *Stock up at the deli after a lovely lunch*

Rainy day – *the beauty of nature after summer rain at Backsberg*

Wine Producing Regions of South Africa

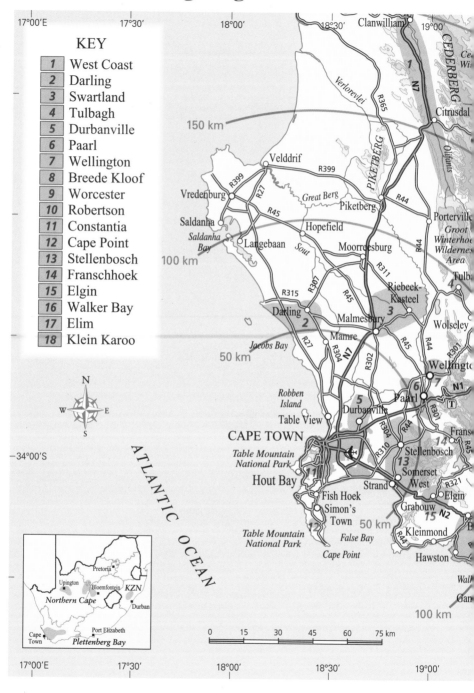

KEY

1. West Coast
2. Darling
3. Swartland
4. Tulbagh
5. Durbanville
6. Paarl
7. Wellington
8. Breede Kloof
9. Worcester
10. Robertson
11. Constantia
12. Cape Point
13. Stellenbosch
14. Franschhoek
15. Elgin
16. Walker Bay
17. Elim
18. Klein Karoo